ALCOHOLISM
AND
HUMAN SEXUALITY

ALCOHOLISM
AND
HUMAN SEXUALITY

By

GARY G. FORREST, Ed.D., P.C.

Licensed Clinical Psychologist and Executive Director
Psychotherapy Associates and
The Institute for Addictive Behavioral Change
Colorado Springs, Colorado

CHARLES C THOMAS • PUBLISHER
Springfield • Illinois • U.S.A.

Book House 1/28/83

Published and Distributed Throughout the World by

CHARLES C THOMAS • PUBLISHER
2600 South First Street
Springfield, Illinois 62717, U.S.A.

© *1983 by* CHARLES C THOMAS • PUBLISHER

ISBN 0-398-04691-3

Library of Congress Catalog Card Number: 82-3213

*With THOMAS BOOKS careful attention is given to all details of
manufacturing and design. It is the Publisher's desire to present books that are
satisfactory as to their physical qualities and artistic possibilities and
appropriate for their particular use. THOMAS BOOKS will be true to those
laws of quality that assure a good name and good will.*

Printed in the United States of America

I-R X-1

Library of Congress Cataloging in Publication Data

Forrest, Gary G.
    Alcoholism and human sexuality.

    Bibliography: p.
    Includes index.
    1. Alcoholism—Complications and sequelae. 2. Sexual
disorders. 3. Sexual deviation. I. Title.
RC565.F57   616.6'9   82-3213
ISBN 0-398-04691-3   AACR2

TO MY PARENTS,
Granville H. Forrest
and
Florence R. Forrest

PREFACE

DURING the past fifteen years researchers and clinicians involved in the treatment of sexual dysfunction and human sexual problems have made tremendous contributions and advances. It is only in recent years that the topic of human sexuality has been perceived as an "appropriate" realm of scientific investigation and study by the behavioral science professions. Many issues associated with human sexuality continue to be controversial. Today, the professional sex therapist remains an enigma in the eyes of many other behavioral scientists. The sexual deviations continue to be poorly understood. While considerable success and progress has been made in the realm of treating the human sexual dysfunctions, relatively little clinical progress has taken place in the field of treating human sexual deviations.

Alcohol addiction and alcohol abuse have always created medical, social, familial, cultural, and personal problems. Approximately 10 million Americans are alcoholic. In every society, throughout the history of mankind, alcoholism and alcohol abuse have been responsible for a plethora of problems and conflicts. However, it is only in recent years that the American collective has recognized alcoholism as a bonafide health problem. The alcoholic denies that he or she is addicted. Likewise, we have collectively denied and avoided the many pathological realities that are associated with alcohol addiction and alcohol abuse.

Quite recently, behavioral scientists have started to realize that alcohol addiction, sexual dysfunction, sexual conflicts, and sexual deviation are consistently interrelated. Counselors and psychotherapists involved in the treatment of alcoholic persons have long recognized that sexual dysfunction, sexual pathology, and sexual deviation are all basic to the alcoholic adjustment style. Yet, behavioral scientists engaged in the treatment of alcoholic and chemically dependent individuals have, for the most part, written very little about these particular clinical cases. Research efforts dealing with alcoholism and human sexuality are limited. Systematic and extensive clinical research in the area of alcoholism and human sexuality is lacking. It is significant that the topic of sex is even generally avoided within the Alcoholics Anonymous community (Alcoholics Anonymous, Al-Anon, and Alateen).

This text is written primarily for behavioral scientists who are involved in the psychotherapy and rehabilitation of alcoholics with sexual problems. Unlike other books dealing with alcoholism and the treatment of addicted persons, this text deals explicitly with the issues of human sexuality and alcohol addiction. Section I of the book provides the reader with an overview of alcoholism and human sexuality. In this section, the basic sexual and identity conflicts of the alcoholic are elucidated. Sexual and identity pathology result in relationship disturbance. Alcoholism is also a relationship disturbance. The first section of the book explores male and female sexual dysfunctions: impotence, premature ejaculation, retarded ejaculation, low sexual desire and arousal problems, frigidity, orgastic dysfunction, and vaginismus. Research and clinical evidence, which pertains to each of these varieties of human sexual dysfunction in combination with alcohol addiction and abuse, is presented. Clinical case studies are also included in each chapter. These case studies demonstrate the roles of alcoholism, personality, and life style in the development of a specific variety of sexual dysfunction. Section II consists of clinical, research, and case study data involving alcoholism and sexual deviation. The "classic" varieties of sexual deviation are discussed in this section: homosexuality, exhibitionism, sadomasochism, pedophilia, voyeurism, and fetishism. Importantly, this section includes chapters on rape, incest, and overdetermined pregenital forms of sexual behavior. Incest occurs in many alcoholic family systems. Rape frequently involves intoxication. The author views these forms of sexual behavior as indicative of sexual deviation.

Strategies of sex therapy and psychotherapy are considered throughout the book. In Section I, specific sex therapy techniques are discussed. These treatment techniques are presented within the context of the alcoholic patient who is experiencing a particular sexual dysfunction. Treatment strategies are also presented in each of the chapters in Section II dealing with alcoholism and sexual deviation. Research data germane to the subject matter in each chapter is clearly and cogently presented. This book has many strengths and assets. The consistent synthesis of research evidence and clinical experience, pertaining to the subject matter of each chapter, is certainly a major asset of this book. Rather than presenting a great deal of theoretical and abstract data specific to the various areas of alcoholism and human sexuality, I have presented this clinical information in a concrete, pragmatic, and concise format.

It is important for the psychotherapist and sex therapist to understand that alcohol addiction and alcohol abuse directly affect patterns of sexual behavior. Alcoholism can cause impotence. Alcohol addiction is frequently associated with the sexual dysfunctions of women. Alcoholism and alcohol abuse result in physiological and psychological changes which, in turn, affect sexual performance and sexual behavior. Alcohol induced psychological and physiological changes are complex and interrelated. Many alcoholic fathers who commit incest only engage in this variety of sexually deviant behavior while intoxicated. Overt homosexual behavior, in the case of the alcoholic, may occur only after heavy drinking. Sexual assault, rape, and child molestation can involve alcoholic and alcohol abusing individuals. Many of the people who commit rape or engage in any other form of sexually deviant behavior do so only while under the influence of alcohol.

Successful treatment for sexual dysfunction or sexual deviation, in the case of the alcoholic, begins with total sobriety. Commonly, psychotherapy and treatment can only be successful after the alcoholic patient has established an extended period of abstinence. When the successfully treated sexually dysfunctional or sexually deviant alcoholic resumes drinking, it is usually only a matter of time until prior patterns of dysfunction or deviation again become floridly manifest. For these reasons, the clinician should reinforce patient behaviors that maintain a long-term commitment to sobriety. It is the author's belief that effective treatment interventions with sexually dysfunctional or sexually deviant alcoholic patients begin with a focus on addiction per se and secondly focus upon sexual pathology.

This book will be an important resource tool for all mental health workers involved in the treatment of alcoholics and problem drinkers. Physicians, medical students, psychologists, nurses, social workers, vocational rehabilitation counselors, family therapists, school counselors and guidance personnel, and virtually all other health service providers who work with alcoholics, problem drinkers, and other substance abusers will find this text extremely useful in their treatment efforts. Hopefully, the clinical material discussed throughout the book will prove heuristic. We are only now beginning to understand and appreciate the role of alcoholism and alcohol abuse in a diversity of our social and health problems. In this respect, the book represents an important first step. Alcoholism, sexual dysfunction, and sexual deviation are most assuredly areas involving social and health problems. We must strive to treat the alcoholic holistically. The sexual conflicts and sexual pathology of the addicted person must be resolved if our treatment efforts are to encompass the whole person.

Many of my colleagues, patients, and friends have contributed greatly to my need and ability to complete this book. Foremost, I must thank my wife, Sandra, and my daughters, Sarah Ellen and Allison, for their loving support, encouragement, and patience. My colleagues and associates at Psychotherapy Associates, P.C. and the Institute for Addictive Behavioral Change, David A. Sena, Ph.D., Larry Wellman, M.S., Joseph Peters, Ph.D., and Barbara Martin, M.S.W., have consistently been helpful and supportive. My ongoing professional associations and work with Father Joseph C. Martin, Arthur P. Knauert, M.D., Albert Ellis, Ph.D., Al Koss, Ph.D., Bill Glasser, M.D., Bob Cate, Ph.D., Ed.D., Tom Bratter, Ed.D., and Ernie Matuschka, Ph.D., have been most facilitative. I must also thank my secretary, Mrs. Eileen Moorhead, for her many typing and secretarial contributions to this book. Finally, my patients are to be thanked. They have provided the clinical experience, knowledge, and understanding essential to completing this book.

G.G.F.

CONTENTS

ALCOHOLISM
AND
HUMAN SEXUALITY

Section I
ALCOHOLISM
AND
HUMAN SEXUALITY

Chapter 1
ALCOHOLISM AND HUMAN SEXUALITY:
An Overview

ALCOHOL is presently the most abused drug in the United States (Forrest, 1978; 1979a; 1982). Chronic alcoholism affects some 10 million individuals in this country. It has been estimated that one of every twelve persons in this country is either addicted to alcohol or a consistent abuser of alcohol (Knauert, 1979). Alcoholism is recognized as a chronic and progressive disorder involving physiological and psychological variables, which render certain individuals incapable of refraining from frequent alcohol ingestion to the point of both continued intoxication and eventual interpersonal and social dysfunction. Alcohol addiction is perhaps the number one health problem in the United States.

The WHO Expert Committee on Mental Health defines alcoholics as "those excessive drinkers whose dependence on alcohol has attained such a degree that it shows in a noticeable mental disturbance or an interference with their bodily and mental health, interpersonal relations, and their smooth social and economic functioning" (Forrest, 1978).

There are numerous definitions of alcoholism. However, extensive review of the literature regarding the definition of alcoholism generally adds very little to the WHO definition. Psychotherapy and rehabilitation experience with alcoholic persons consistently indicates that these individuals manifest four essential characteristics (Forrest, 1978): (1) their drinking is compulsive in nature and as such uncontrollable, (2) their drinking is most typically of long or chronic duration, (3) their drinking results in intoxication, and (4) their patterns of alcohol ingestion

5

are invariably detrimental to their ability to function interpersonally.

While there is no "absolute" or definitive definition of alcoholism, alcoholic persons do manifest these four characteristics with regard to their drinking behavior. The alcoholic is a person who drinks in order to become intoxicated. The alcoholic rarely, if ever, simply drinks because he or she "likes the taste" of a particular alcoholic beverage. Alcoholics do drink in order to get drunk. It is a basic truism that the addicted person is unable to control his or her drinking. Alcoholics do drink compulsively. The alcoholic is unable, within the context of a short-term or long-term basis, to drink only one or two drinks per drinking occasion. Although some alcoholic persons are able to "control" their drinking for a few weeks or even months, eventually they once again become the "slave" of their addiction. The compulsion to drink soon results in drinking one drink after another and thus chronic intoxication. Alcoholism is a progressive disorder. The alcoholic rarely develops alcoholism in a matter of weeks or months. Most typically, alcoholic persons are people who have used and abused alcohol for a number of years. In this regard, one characteristic of the human being is simply that of being biologically susceptible to addiction (Ellis, 1979). Alcoholics do get drunk. In fact, many alcoholics have been intoxicated for as long as twenty or thirty years. While the spouse, employer, and family of the alcoholic may "deny" that the addicted individual is ever drunk, rest assured that anyone who consumes a pint or quart of liquor each day is intoxicated! The addicted person need not be incoherent, staggering, stuperous, or "falling down drunk" in order to be intoxicated. Without exception, alcoholics experience a multitude of interpersonal problems as a direct result of their addiction. Alcoholism is a "people problem." Marital conflicts, child neglect amd abuse (Ackerman, 1978), vocational difficulties, legal problems, and friendship difficulties are but a few of the areas in which the alcoholic creates and experiences "interpersonal conflict."

It is very important to realize that alcoholism is, in fact, a clinically discernable entity. Our society has a long history of denying the reality of alcoholism in its many different guises. Many have been quick to point out that the individual differences among alcoholics are so great that one might question whether alcoholic individuals have much in common, aside from their pathological alcohol consumption. While this last statement is true, it is only partially true! Alcoholism is a very complex, multifaceted, and chameleon-like disorder. These factors have made it all too easy for the family, employer, and loved ones of the alcoholic to avoid and deny the reality of addiction. Likewise, the complexity and abstruse nature of this disorder feed into the process of collective denial. Alcohol addiction involves the complex interaction of psychological, physical, social, interpersonal, and spiritual factors. Personality, body metabolism and physiology, genetic makeup, familial relationships, conditioning and learning experiences, and even religious preference can all play an important role in the process of facilitating the alcoholic symptom choice. Alcoholism, according to the American Medical Association, is a disease. While many behavioral scientists tend to reject this position, it is important to realize that the AMA position with regard to alcoholism as a disease validates the medical significance of this disorder. Obviously, recognizing alcoholism as a disease has resulted in improved medical care for the alcoholic, increased insurance benefits for treatment, a lessening of the social stigma associated with the "alcoholism" label, and increased efforts in the areas of alcoholism education, rehabilitation, and prevention.

Historically, the alcoholic has tended to be perceived as a "skid-row" inhabitant. Alcoholics have also been viewed as social inferiors, those poorly educated, and as tending to be minority group members. The alcoholic is a topic of jokes, and many people have tended to view the addicted person as simply humorous. These factors have impeded treatment and rehabilitation efforts, educational and prevention efforts, and collective concern. Only now are we beginning to accept the many realities of alcoholism. Alcoholism can affect anyone. Educators, physicians, truck drivers, dentists, cooks, lawyers, and people involved in any occupation can and do become addicted to alcohol. Housewives become addicted. All ethnic and racial groups are subject to alcoholism. Education and intelligence are not, unfortunately, deterrents to alcoholism. Socioeconomic class does not determine one's susceptibility to alcohol addiction. Tragically, children and adolescents appear to increasingly become alcoholic. People can become alcohol dependent at virtually any age. Alcoholism is clearly a social dilemma. As touched upon earlier, until quite recently we seem to have denied and avoided the many social issues associated with alcoholism and alcohol abuse. In addition to the data already presented, alcoholism and alcohol abuse result in approximately 25,000 automobile fatalities each year. The alcoholism related yearly cost to industry is over 40 billion dollars. Thousands of deaths each year are due to medical complications specific to alcohol ingestion. Thousands of alcohol related homicides and suicides occur each year, and millions of dollars are spent in the courts each year as a result of alcohol facilitated and related criminal offenses. These figures do not include the emotional pain and tragedy experienced by the alcoholic, the family involving an alcoholic, and those involved in any form of relationship with an addicted person. We are finding in America (Forrest, 1979c) that more and more people are drinking, they are beginning to imbibe earlier in their lives, and the various social and interpersonal problems associated with intoxication and alcoholism are becoming increasingly costly to society.

It is extremely difficult to ferret out the exact reasons which are contributing to the present addiction crisis in this country and throughout many other countries in the world. Worldwide economic instability, the ever-present threat of war and possibly nuclear holocaust, the growing reality of a worldwide energy crisis, political instability, overpopulation, and numerous other monumental social, political, and economic factors may, in part, account for the present addiction crisis. Certainly, modern pharmacology and psychopharmacology have contributed to the problems of substance abuse and addiction in this country. Yet, it must be remembered that alcohol, alcohol abuse, and alcoholism are as old as history! We live in a "stressed" society (Della-Giustina, Brooks, and Forrest, 1978). In response to the "stressors" just mentioned, many people choose to drink alcohol as a method for stress and tension reduction. Perhaps social drinkers and problem drinkers are becoming increasingly vulnerable to alcohol addiction as they rely more and more upon alcohol and drinking in order to cope with the various stresses associated with present social change. The modern media strongly reinforce drinking behavior. Indeed, many television beer advertisements not only reinforce drinking behaviors but also indicate that manhood, sexuality, and social influence are enhanced through the medium of drinking a particular brand of beer. Our society is an addictive society. All of us are continuously bombarded with messages which, in effect, tell us to drink, smoke, eat, and engage in any number of other addictive behaviors. Many of the messages which we receive regarding the matter of the social appropriateness of drinking alcohol are very overt, while others are covert and insidious. In the case of the alcoholic and incipient alcoholic, these "social messages" can and do facilitate the addiction process.

In spite of the realities of alcohol addiction as a social dilemma, a very sizeable segment of our society continues to drink without becoming dependent and addicted. The vast majority of people who choose to imbibe do so without experiencing serious physical, psychological, and interpersonal consequences. Many people simply choose not to drink. It is also encouraging to realize that thousands of people have recovered from alcohol addiction. Alcoholics do quit drinking. The answer for the addicted individual is very simple and yet paradoxically so difficult—stop drinking.

Alcoholism is a disorder of the total person. In this respect, alcohol addiction directly influences and affects the sexuality and sexual behavior repertoire of the alcoholic. For many years, alcoholism researchers as well as clinicians involved in the actual treatment of the alcoholic have recognized that human sexuality plays an important role in the addiction process (Blane, 1968; Blum and Blum, 1969; Paolino and McCrady, 1977; Forrest, 1978; Vraa, 1982). Knauert (1979) has described alcoholism as a "love affair" with alcohol. Within the confines of the Alcoholics Anonymous community (Alcoholics Anonymous, Al-Anon, Al-Ateen, and Al-Atot) the sexual behaviors of the alcoholic are recognized as problematic and related to the addiction process. Alcoholics are people who have never learned how to effectively manage the many issues associated with their sexuality.

The sexual conflicts of the alcoholic are diverse. In this regard, it must be remembered that every alcoholic is an individual and as such uniquely human. Alcoholic persons do not manifest one common set or syndrome of sexual conflicts. This point is poorly understood by many counselors and psychotherapists not clinically experienced in the treatment of the alcoholic. Until rather recently, it was believed by many behavioral scientists that alcoholics, as a group, were "latently" homosexual. Masters and Johnson (1979) and Kaplan (1974) have very accurately demonstrated how nebulous and clinically irrelevant the concept of "latent" homosexuality can be. Some alcoholic persons are homosexual with regard to object choice. Most are not. Likewise, alcoholic males can be premature ejaculators. Alcoholic males can be impotent. Some alcoholic women are frigid or preorgastic. However, not all alcoholic males are premature ejaculators or impotent. As a result of alcoholic addiction the female alcoholic is not ipso facto frigid or preorgastic. In order to both understand and treat the alcoholic person effectively, clinicians and therapists must avoid the irrationality so basic to misconceptions of the variety.

Human sexuality is a matter of emotionality and irrationality. Most parents still find it difficult to discuss the issues of human sexuality with their children. Physicians, as a group, are poorly educated in the realm of human sexuality. Ministers, priests, and the clergy are reluctant to deal with the sexual concerns of their parishioners. When we add alcohol and alcoholism to the realm of human sexuality, we most definitely can expect to encounter emotionality, dogma, and irrational beliefs. Our society is obsessed or overly concerned with both sex and alcohol. Indeed, it is significant that we have collectively related to alcohol addiction and human sexuality with such a high degree of emotionality and irrationality. Our social and emotional beliefs (Ellis, 1979) in the areas of sex and alcohol are generally quite irrational.

The combination of alcohol and sex can be devastating. Each day so-called "social" drinkers engage in any number of socially unacceptable and damaging sexual behaviors simply as a result of being intoxicated. Thousands of unwanted pregnancies occur each year. No doubt alcohol and intoxication play a primary role in many of these unwanted pregnancies. Alcohol, as will be discussed in a later chapter, plays an important role in a high percentage of rape cases. Alcohol often serves as a catalyst in deviant sexual behavior of all types. Alcohol addiction radically affects the sexual adjustment and sexual behavior repertoire of many addicted individuals. While the college student may employ alcohol as a tool for sexual seduction, the alcoholic all too frequently carries out a tragic sexual act as a result of alcohol-impaired judgment and reasoning. Incest is but one example of the reality of the devastating combination of alcoholism and sex. Incest can be a reality within the alcoholic family system (Martin, 1979; Forrest, 1982).

It is apparent that the sexual adjustment and sexual behaviors of the alcohol-addicted person are often significantly affected as a result of the addiction process. However, the sexuality and sexual behaviors of people who are not alcohol dependent are also very often modified simply as a result of drinking or intoxication. The impact of alcohol upon human sexuality is complex and diverse. Early in the addiction process many alcoholics derive a good deal of sexually oriented secondary, if not primary, gain as a result of ingesting ethanol. In the case of some alcoholic individuals, alcoholism is clearly an erotic experience (Forrest, 1978). Rather commonly, alcoholic males are apprehensive and anxious over the matters of dating, courtship, and sexual seduction. A "few" drinks can, in fact, facilitate sexually assertive behaviors upon the part of many male alcoholics. Feelings of strength and power following drinking may help the passive-dependent male alcoholic seek out a sexually willing female companion. Women alcoholics drink in order to feel more feminine (Wilsnack, 1973; 1982), warm, and adequate as women. These issues are clearly associated with sexuality and sexual identity.

Through the medium of alcohol many women and men in our society are able to become sexually intimate. While any form of alcohol-induced sexual intimacy is ultimately "unreal," on a more short-term basis human sexual transactions of this variety can be mutually rewarding encounters. However, this style of sexual relating and intimacy eventually proves tenuous, if not pathological. Many people rely upon alcohol as an agent to facilitate courtship and sexual intimacy and then "discover" that intimacy need not be alcohol based. This general response set, with regard to alcohol and intimacy, may be psychologically quite adaptive. Unfortunately, our society is comprised of many people who never transcend the alcohol as a tool for sexual intimacy paradigm. Such individuals consistently condition and teach themselves to believe that they can only be sexual, in whatever manner, via the medium of alcohol or possibly intoxication.

Society appears to manifest a distorted view of human sexuality. This general statement is accurate in a multiplicity of ways. As society continues to misunderstand and distort many of the issues and realities associated with alcohol and alcoholism, so does society misunderstand and distort many of the issues and realities associated with human sexuality. The American collective appears to be "obsessed" with sex. Sexual literature and magazines, sexual "aids," "porn" shops, pornographic movies, and sex in the media are but a few of the indicators of an American obsession with sexuality. The "best seller" book list over the past decade has included numerous "How to . . . ," "Everything You Always Wanted to Know . . . ," sexual surveys and reports, and humorous as well as novel types of publications. Books and publications of this variety are devoted, in many respects, to the sexual preoccupations, concerns, and obsessions of the reader. Many of our social cognitions and beliefs surrounding the relationships between alcohol and human sexuality are not only irrational and "crazy" but, more importantly, are socially and interpersonally destructive. We are literally bombarded through media exposure with very direct messages that tell us in order to be sensuous, attractive, and sexual, we must drink alcohol. Even more specifically, we are told that we must drink a particular brand of beer, wine, or liquor in order to be seductive, attractive, and sexually appealing! Television, radio, newspaper, and other "media" messages associating alcohol and sexuality are not only overt and direct; frequently, these messages are of a more covert and obsequious variety. Television viewers may not consciously realize or understand that they are being manipulated into believing that their sexual identities are contingent upon drinking a particular brand of wine. In many, many different ways we are told by the media that drinking is acceptable, fun, and socially appropriate. Sexuality somehow seems to be a viable part of these social messages.

When the alcoholic or problem drinker is consistently conditioned to believe that his or her sexual adequacy hinges upon the matter of drinking alcohol, a destructive human dilemma has been created. Obviously, media messages to the effect that one must drink alcohol in order to feel like a "man" or "woman" actively synergize the addiction conflicts of some 10 or 11 million alcoholic Americans. The alcoholic also learns to use these media messages in the service of his or her alcoholism. Alcoholics frequently utilize social communications that support drinking behavior as a means of rationalizing their addiction. Likewise, alcoholics deny their alcohol addiction by this same means. Alcoholic persons, in part, utilize alcohol in order to consolidate a nuclear sense of sexual identity (Forrest, 1979a). Alcoholics are intensely anxious about their sexuality and sexual identities.

Society has conditioned us to believe that we must drink in order to have fun. In response to this set, alcoholics progressively condition themselves to believe that they must drink in order to have fun. For many alcoholics, having fun equates with sex. Alcohol-facilitated sexual acting-out consitues "fun" for a sizeable segment of the alcoholic population. Marital discord, emotional problems, and family conflict are the direct by-products of the sexual acting-out of the alcoholic. This is but another lucid example of the problematic relationships between sexual behavior, alcohol, and alcohol addiction.

The relationship between alcoholism and human sexuality is pervasive and complex. Alcoholism is a disorder of the total person. Alcoholism affects the global sexuality of the alcoholic. Sexual and identity conflicts underlie the addiction process. Alcoholics, in part, drink alcohol in order to neurotically manage sexual and identity problems. Alcoholism creates sexual and identity conflicts. Sexual and identity conflicts can help create alcohol addiction. These clinical issues are paradoxical and poorly understood by professional behavioral scientists, the lay community, and alcoholics as well.

This book represents an attempt to elucidate and clarify some of the more important clinical issues associated with alcoholism and human sexuality. Familial factors, interpersonal factors, internal psychodynamic factors, and social variables all operate to determine the sexual adjustment style of the person who is addicted to alcohol. The sexuality and sexual modus operandi of the alcoholic are always in a state of flux or change. Alcoholism is a static disorder and yet an ever changing disorder. Alcoholism is a disorder of paradoxes (Forrest, 1978). In order to more fully understand the adjustment dynamics and psychopathology of the alcoholic, we must examine the sexuality of the alcoholic and the underlying clinical relationships between human sexuality and alcohol addiction. This task begins with the realization that every alcoholic is uniquely human with regard to both alcohol addiction and sexuality.

BIBLIOGRAPHY

Ackerman, R.J.: *Children of Alcoholics.* Holmes Beach, Florida, Learning Publications, 1978.

Blane, H.T.: *The Personality of the Alcoholic: Guises of Dependency. New York, Harper & Row, 1968.*

Blum, E.M., and Blum, R.H.: *Alcoholism: Modern Psychological Approaches to Treatment.* San Francisco, Jossey-Bass, Inc., 1969.

Della-Giustina, V.E., Brooks, J.D., and Forrest, G.G.: Stress management techniques for the practicing dentist. *Journal of Dentistry,* pp. 18-20, August, 1978.

Ellis, A.: *Rational Emotive Therapy Training.* Lecture, Psychotherapy Associates, P.C. Fifth Annual Advanced Winter Workshop, "Treatment and Rehabilitation of the Alcoholic," Colorado Springs, Colorado, February 1, 1979.

Forrest, G.G.: *The Diagnosis and Treatment of Alcoholism.* Springfield, Charles C Thomas, Rev. 2nd Ed., 1978.

Forrest, G.G.: *Alcoholism, Object Relations and Narcissistic Theory.* Lecture, Psychotherapy Associates, P.C. Fifth Annual Advanced Winter Workshop, "Treatment and Rehabilitation of the Alcoholic," Colorado Springs, Colorado, January 29, 1979a.

Forrest, G.G.: Setting alcoholics up for therapeutic failure. *Family and Community Health, 2(1):59-64, August, 1979c.*

Forrest, G.G.: *Confrontation in Psychotherapy with the Alcoholic.* Holmes Beach, Florida, Learning Publications, 1982.

Kaplan, H.S.: *The New Sex Therapy: Active Treatment of Sexual Dysfunctions.* New York, Brunner/Mazel, 1974.

Knauert, A.P.: *Differential Diagnosis of Alcoholism.* Lecture, Psychotherapy Associates, P.C. Fifth Annual Advanced Winter Workshop, "Treatment and Rehabilitation of the Alcoholic," Colorado Springs, Colorado, January 28, 1979.

Martin, J.C.: *Alcoholism.* Lecture, Psychotherapy Associates, P.C. Fifth Annual Advanced Winter Workshop, "Treatment and Rehabilitation of the Alcoholic," Colorado Springs, Colorado, January 29, 1979.

Masters, W.H., and Johnson, V.E.: *Homosexuality in Perspective*. Boston, Little, Brown, & Co., 1979.

Paolino, T.J., and McCrady, B.S.: *The Alcoholic Marriage: Alternative Perspectives*. New York, Green and Stratton, 1977.

Vraa, C.W.: *Sex Therapy Training*. Lecture, Psychotherapy Associates, P.C. Eighth Annual Advanced Winter Workshop, "Treatment and Rehabilitation of the Alcoholic," Colorado Springs, Colorado, February 2, 1982.

Wilsnack, S.C.: Femininity by the bottle. *Psychology Today*, pp.39-43, April, 1973.

Wilsnack, S.C.: *Recent Research on Women and Alcohol*. Lecture, Psychotherapy Associates, P.C. Eighth Annual Advanced Winter Workshop, "Treatment and Rehabilitation of the Alcoholic," Colorado Springs, Colorado, February 2, 1982.

Chapter 2
ALCOHOLISM, SEXUALITY,
AND IDENTITY

IN Chapter 1, it was indicated that alcoholism creates sexual and identity conflicts. It was also suggested that sexual and identity conflicts can play important roles in the aetiology of the alcoholic symptom choice. Ultimately, the interrelationships between alcoholism, sexuality, and identity appear to take on a "chicken and the egg" characteristic.

Researchers and clinicians in the field of human sexuality (Masters and Johnson, 1970; Kaplan, 1974; Hartman and Fithian, 1972; Leiblum and Pervin, 1980; Vraa, 1980) consistently emphasize the role of emotions and psychological factors in determining and influencing sexual behavior. Identity profoundly influences sexual behavior and sexual adjustment. The alcoholic is rather diffusely conflicted in the realm of identity (Forrest, 1978; 1979; 1982). In a congruous manner, the sexual adjustment style of the alcoholic can be seriously pathological and conflicted (Forrest, 1982). If we begin the difficult task of exploring the relationships between alcohol addiction and human sexuality with the assumption that identity plays a very critical role in sexual adjustment and alcoholism, the "chicken and the egg" dilemma as explained earlier is essentially no longer an insurmountable dilemma.

Many alcoholics continuously and neurotically struggle to establish identity through sexuality. The identity of the alcoholic is fragmented and inadequately consolidated (Forrest, 1982). The many identity conflicts of the alcoholic begin during the earliest epochs of human living. Alcoholics are persons who have experienced profound and consistent narcissistic need and en-

16

titlement deprivation during infancy and childhood, if not throughout the entirety of their lives. Alcoholism in this respect is an interpersonally determined disorder.

Narcissistic needs refer to the life-sustaining needs of the human organism. The need to be fed, held, and cuddled, needs for temperature control and oxygen, the management of excretory functions, and similar basic needs constitute the narcissistic needs of the infant and young child. Most importantly, these narcissistic needs must be met by significant others. When parents or surrogate parents consistently fail to meet the narcissistic needs of the young infant or early child, death may result.

Narcissistic entitlements refer to our generalized entitlement as human beings to be loved, valued, and treated with a sense of dignity, respect, and worth by significant others. While narcissistic needs refer essentially to the more physical needs of the evolving human being, narcissistic entitlements are more psychological and interpersonal in nature. These needs are narcissistic in that they are self-oriented. Physical needs, as well as psychological growth and well-being, are contingent upon adequate narcissistic need and entitlement gratification by significant others during the initial months and years of life. Narcissistic injury occurs when significant others fail to meet the narcissistic needs and entitlements of the infant and child.

Consistent interpersonal encounters with significant others that result in early life narcissistic injury result in (1) a chronic sense of anxiety and feelings of non-well being, and (2) self-system fragmentation. In order to effectively differentiate between self, significant others, and the external world, we must first experience the consistently anxiety-free medium of a self-mother ego fusion (Bowen, 1978; Forrest, 1979). The alcoholic has not experienced an intensely loving, anxiety-free ego fusion with the mother object. The development of an adequately consolidated identity begins with a healthy, anxiety-free symbiotic relationship with the mother object. Most alcoholics have experienced an anxious and highly ambivalent relationship with their mothers or surrogate mothers during infancy and childhood. The anxiety of the adult alcoholic is always interpersonal anxiety. Alcoholics are anxious within the context of their relationships with other people. Prototypically, adult alcoholics have been intensely anxious within the context of the most intimate of human relationships—the mother, infant, significant-others rubric. One primary effect or outcome of this experiential reality in the case of the alcoholic is that of self-system fragmentation. The self-system of the alcoholic is not adequately consolidated. Thus, the alcoholic is pathologically and chronically vulnerable to the experience of intense anxiety. The ego boundaries of the alcoholic remain diffuse and chronically "blurred." Adult alcoholics have never been able to personally resolve the basic question "Who am I?"

Chronic narcissistic injury, occurring within the context of intense and extended human relationships, conditions the alcoholic to feel inadequate, inferior, worthless, and selfless. The alcoholic feels rejected, unloved, and unwanted. The alcoholic believes that he is a failure. Alcoholics are unable to develop a positive self-concept; they have little realistic positive self-esteem.

In order to cope with tremendous feelings of inadequacy and anxiety associated with the matter of not having developed an adequate sense of self, the alcoholic eventually attempts to overcompensate for this deficit through manipulation and acting-out. Quite typically, alcoholics act out their various sexual- and identity-based conflicts. The global adjustment style of the alcoholic centers around the matter of acting-out. Manipulative acting-out upon the part of the alcohol addicted person can very accurately be viewed as a defense against threatening feelings of anxiety. The alcoholic is preconsciously and often consciously aware of feeling chronically anxious over the matters of personal insecurity, inadequacy, and inferiority. Acting-out becomes central to the adjustment style of many alcoholic persons. The acting-out adjustment style of the alcoholic represents a neurotic compromise or solution for internal turmoil and conflicts, which psychologically and interpersonally determine the addiction symptom choice. Within this context, it is important to point out that acting-out serves the purpose of binding or adaptively controlling intense anxiety. It is also germane to note that acting-out congruously effects a neurotic solution to the alcoholic's persistent sense of non-well-being. Once the alcoholic effects a neurotic solution to the intense experience of interpersonal anxiety and feelings of

non-well-being, through the development of an acting-out a
ment style, self-system fragmentation no longer persists as a conscious source of conflict. Self-system fragmentation or ego deficit
intrapersonally determines the chronic anxiety of the alcoholic.
The alcoholic is chronically vulnerable to the experience of intense
anxiety as a result of self-system fragmentation. However, acting-
out extinguishes the alcoholic's conscious awareness of being anxious, thus deterring an awareness of self-system fragmentation.

Alcoholism is acting-out. The addiction process per se represents an acting-out solution to interpersonal and intrapersonal
conflicts. However, the alcoholic most typically acts out sexually
in order to cope with identity conflicts. Alcohol generally facilitates sexual acting-out. It is easier, perhaps more socially acceptable, and less threatening for the alcoholic to act out sexually
while under the influence of alcohol. The behavioral style of the
alcoholic represents, in numerous respects, an overdetermined
flight into heterosexuality (Menninger, 1938; Forrest, 1979a).
Sexual promiscuity may well be the sine qua non of the alcoholic
individual's conflicted sexuality and identity. Commonly, the
alcoholic initiates one affair after another in order to demonstrate
to self and others a sense of identity. Men and women alcoholics
act out sexually in order to reinforce their basic sense of masculinity or femininity. The alcoholic attempts to answer the question.
"Who am I?" via the medium of sexual promiscuity and sexual
exploitation. Seduction and sexual "triumphs" or exploits neurotically tell the alcoholic that he or she is a male or female. While
sexual acting-out serves the purpose of establishing feelings of
adequacy, attractiveness, and power, at a more basic level sexual
acting-out is always in the purpose of identity consolidation.
This clinical issue is paradoxical, as the alcoholic initially in life
has not established an adequate sense of self, which precludes
sexuality and self as a sexual being. Alcoholics neurotically "use"
their sexuality and sexual acting-out as a method for developing
feelings of adequacy as a person. It is only logical and rational
to expect that individuals who have never developed a basic sense
of adequacy as a person will eventually attempt to use their sexuality as a tool or instrument for developing feelings of competence and adequacy. At this psychological level, sexuality is in the

service of identity.

Alcoholism is a disorder of intimacy (Forrest, 1976; 1977; 1979; 1982). The alcoholic is extremely anxious over the matters of interpersonal closeness, involvement, and intimacy. Alcoholics strive to maintain "distance" within the realm of interpersonal relations. Preconsciously and unconsciously, the addicted individual equates interpersonal intimacy and closeness with annihilation, rejection, and potential destruction of the self. The alcoholic morbidly fears psychological and possible physical destruction when confronted with the task of coping with intimate human encounters. By drinking alcohol and through the medium of intoxication the addicted person achieves a distorted or neurotic ability to be intimate. The male alcoholic who exhibits a Don-Juan form of promiscuous sexual adjustment style, upon close examination, depends upon alcohol as an agent of seduction. Alcoholic women who end up in bed with one "lover" after another rely upon alcohol in order to be sexually intimate. Once sober for a few months and actively involved in psychotherapy, an intensive rehabilitation program, or Alcoholics Anonymous, the alcoholic finds it increasingly difficult to "bed-hop." More than nonaddicted people, alcoholics have a very real need to be intimate within the context of meaningful and relevant human relationships. Indeed, most alcoholics have been yearning for intimate, meaningful, noncritical, and loving human relationships throughout the entirety of their lives.

Sexual intercourse and other forms of sexual behavior represent perhaps the ultimate varieties of human intimacy. In theory, at least, this is true. Although intimate on one level, frank sexual encounters may very well exclude relevant human intimacy and relatedness when we get beyond the level of mere sexuality. The alcoholic avoids authentic and meaningful sexual intimacy. Alcohol facilitated sexual conquests and exploits are intimate human encounters, and yet sexual relationships of this variety are the antithesis of authentic and intimate sexual relating. Alcoholics who must rely upon alcohol and intoxication in order to express their sexual needs tragically never get beyond "fucking." Their sexual relationships are always alcoholically determined and distorted. Alcoholic sexuality is often without love, compassion, caring, and giving. The sexuality of the alcoholic tends to be exploitive, manipulative, and self-centered. As the addicted individual becomes progressively more dysfunctional, in a global fashion, sex takes on an ever increasingly exploitive and self-centered form. The sexual adjustment of the alcoholic evolves and changes. Consistently, the sexual adjustment of the alcoholic becomes more pathological as the addiction process unfolds. During the later developmental stages of alcoholism, the alcoholic may begin to act out a plethora of sexually deviant behaviors.

As already indicated, the alcoholic maladaptivity consolidates an identity through the medium of the addiction process. This identity subsequently plays an important role in the evolving sexual adjustment style of the alcoholic. At some point, the addiction process per se radically influences both the identity and sexuality of the addicted individual. In this respect, alcohol addiction both "gives" and "takes away" the identity and sexuality of the alcoholic. The interpersonal experiences of the alcoholic, prior to abusing alcohol and then becoming addicted, shape the identity and sexuality of the addicted person. It is the consistent and ongoing interpersonal experiences of the alcoholic that shape and eventually determine the addiction symptom choice. At some point in the addiction process, many alcoholics simply surrender their already precarious identities and sexuality. Alcoholism destroys identity and sexuality. Alcoholics who drink themselves into a psychosis certainly surrender or lose their identities as a direct result of the addiction process. Feeling shy, inadequate, and socially inept, the male alcoholic often learns that he can approach women while under the influence of "a few" drinks. Such an individual can acquire an alcoholic identity, which includes dating, dancing, sexually assertive and aggressive behaviors, and any number of other extroverted behaviors. This identity and the behaviors that appear to be fundamental to its maintenance are tenuous at best. This identity is not reality oriented. During the middle and later stages of chronic alcoholism, identity begins to crumble or defuse. At this juncture, the male alcoholic may find himself impotent, due to the physical and psychological effects of chronic intoxication. A serious depression or gross decompensation may well follow. Drinking for psychological relief of whatever variety evolves into drinking for the sake of effect or intoxication in the case of the alcoholic. Eventually, the alcoholic must drink in order to deter the trauma of physical withdrawal. At this point, the psychological processes that precipitated or helped facilitate the development of the alcoholism symptom choice may be of little relevance in terms of treatment.

Alcoholism does not simply destroy identity and sexuality. Perhaps more typically and commonly, alcoholism distorts or pathologically alters identity and sexuality. Although identity conflicts initially alter or affect the sexual adjustment style of the alcoholic, chronic alcoholism very often modifies the sexual behavior of the addicted person, which in turn results in basic identity changes. It has been long recognized that chronic alcoholism can even cause physiological changes that alter basic gender identity (Busch, 1882; Arlitt et al., 1917; Gordon et al., 1976). The interactions between identity, sexuality, and alcoholism are obviously quite complex. Aside from biological and physiological bodily changes being induced by alcohol addiction, psychological changes can be facilitated by alcoholism that significantly changes personality, sexuality, and identity. Chronic alcoholism creates role confusion. Personality changes brought about as a result of long-term intoxication may drastically affect the sexual adjustment style of the alcoholic. In many respects, sexual adjustment is but a reflection of personality and character structure. The following clinical case study is presented in order to illustrate the complex and multifaceted relationships between alcoholism, sexuality, and identity.

Case 1. John W., a forty-three-year-old attorney, entered psychotherapy due to a severe "drinking problem." At the time of treatment engagement the patient was consuming approximately one-fifth of vodka each day. This pattern of drinking had been manifest for "a few years" according to the patient. The patient's wife had obtained a legal separation a few months earlier and she and the children, a fourteen-year-old son and an eleven-year-old daughter, were residing in the family house. The patient's father, also an attorney, had died as a result of alcoholism (cirrhosis) when the patient was thirty-six years of age.

Following medical detoxification the patient was seen in weekly outpatient psychotherapy for a period of four months. The patient was then seen in weekly out-patient family psychotherapy for nearly seven months. Additionally, the patient attended Alcoholics Anonymous on a regular basis (one or two times each week) and his wife became actively involved in Al-Anon. Within the confines of the psychotherapy relationship it very quickly became apparent that John had long struggled with identity and sexual conflicts. As an adolescent, John felt anxious about his "masculinity." He described himself as a "loner" during these developmental years. He was extremely uncomfortable and anxious over matters pertaining to dating and physical intimacy. John feared that his penis was "too small" and, in fact, this was a matter of great concern to him as an adult. While in undergraduate school, John managed to date occasionally and attempted sexual intercourse on four different occasions. The patient described each of these sexual encounters as "disastrous." On each occasion John ejaculated prior to removing his clothing and was then unable to achieve erection. One of the girls that he attempted to be intimate with laughed at him, which made matters much worse. Another girl, eventually to become his wife, was very understanding and supportive within the context of one of these sexual encounters. Soon John began to date her on a regular basis. Their dating relationship involved a good deal of drinking, heavy petting, and an active sexual involvement. The patient discovered that he was less inhibited sexually when intoxicated. After a few drinks John's concerns about the size of his penis seemed to "go away." Premature ejaculation was not a problem following a number of drinks. In order to avoid, while sober, sexual concerns associated with penis size and performance, John and his wife agreed to "limit" their sexual encounters to fellatio and cunnilingus.

After the initial two or three years of marriage the patient's sexual adjustment began to progressively deteriorate. The patient also began to drink more. He blamed his declining interest in sex and heavy drinking on the stresses associated with law school and eventually his legal practice. John felt that his masculinity was "boosted" as a result of being able to have children. When John was thirty-four he became sexually involved with an office secretary. According to the patient, this sexual liaison was limited to having his secretary give him a "blow-job" once or twice a week. This sexual relationship lasted for nearly two years. Between the age of thirty-six and forty-three John led a very promiscuous life-style. He would pick up prostitutes while out of town and attending professional meetings. On one occasion John initiated a menage á trois which, in his own terms, again proved disastrous. The patient's wife, Jane, eventually refused any form of sexual intimacy. Although she had considered an "affair" for many years, she did not act out this wish.

When John entered psychotherapy he was impotent. Even oral genital sex failed to produce an erection. At this time John described himself as being more interested in "drinking than screwing." In spite of being chronically intoxicated, the patient had been quite successful in the management of his legal practice. Indeed, John was both liked and respected by colleagues and associates. However, John perceived himself as a "failure" in every area of his life. As a father, husband, lover, and professional man the patient viewed himself as a failure. Clearly, John had developed a well-consolidated "failure identity" (Forrest, 1975). During the fourth individual therapy session John disclosed that he had "started believing" that he might be homosexual a few years earlier. The patient had developed a logic to support this belief. At the age of eleven, John had infrequently engaged in group masturbation with two male neighbors of about the same age. He had "always" been anxious about dating and sexual relations. He enjoyed a "good blow-job" more than genital intercourse. The patient had also read that many alcoholics are "latently" homosexual. In short, John's beliefs about himself and even his sexual identity were in the process of change. Most assuredly, the patient's sexual behaviors and beliefs about himself were directly influenced by his alcohol addiction. Impotence was the final step. The patient interpreted his own impotence to mean that he had no desire for women. In this regard, premature ejaculation was one thing. Impotence was another! John's personality also changed as he became progressively more addicted to alcohol. While John's underlying feelings of inadequacy and selfdoubt remained relatively constant, he attempted an acting-out solution to these struggles. His office affair, relationships with prostitutes, and promiscuous acting out can all be seen as neurotic attempts to be adequately masculine. Identity and sexual conflicts shaped John's acting-out adjustment solution.

Individual and family psychotherapy proved successful in the eventual resolution of John's impotence, premature ejaculation, and sexual acting-out. Sobriety is the first treatment goal which must be attained in cases such as this. Psychodynamic issues pertaining to the patient's feelings of inadequacy, guilt, fears of homosexuality, and anxiety about penis size were resolved. These secondary clinical issues were central to the sexual and identity conflicts of the patient. The addiction process actively synergized the sexual and identity conflicts of the patient. Eventually, John's alcoholism played a primary role in the development of sexual dysfunction and basic identity confusion.

This case study rather vividly demonstrates the interactive dynamics pertaining to alcoholism, sexuality, and identity as discussed in this chapter. Thus far in the chapter, intrapersonal and interpersonal factors have been aetiologically and psychodynamically related to the sexual and identity conflicts of the alcoholic. It is important to point out that psychological processes are but one important component of the alcoholism, sexuality, and identity interaction. At this juncture, it is relevant to briefly consider social and cultural realities which affect alcoholism, sexuality, and identity.

Modern society is ever changing. Social and cultural changes affect individuals as well as collective behavior. Sexual attitudes, beliefs, and values have changed rather drastically in America during the past fifteen years. Collectively, we have become more "open" with regard to the many issues associated with human sexuality. Sex is no longer a taboo subject. As noted in Chapter 1, American society has become overtly preoccupied with sex. American society is also obsessively preoccupied with alcohol and drinking. Traditional "male" and "female" identities appear to be in the process of change. At some point, social change becomes an all-encompassing process. Social change has resulted in attitudinal, belief, and value system evolution in the realms of alcohol, sex, and identity.

One major parameter of social change in America has occurred in the area of male and female roles. Male and female roles and role-appropriate behaviors are no longer clearly defined and socially delineated. We are presently in the process of experiencing "role fusion" in Western society. Society no longer expects or demands males to have their hair cut short. Clothing styles have moved in the direction of "unisex." Women wear pants and "three-piece" pantsuits. Women have assumed a major role in the American work force. The American military academies have begun to admit sizeable numbers of women. The "Women's Rights Movement" has evolved into a major social movement in this society. Men have assumed primary roles associated with parenting, housekeeping, and other domestic activities. In order to keep up with inflation and the high costs of living in America, most families have been forced to find employment for both spouses. Many women have assumed the family role of primary "breadwinner." Women have also actively entered the traditionally all male world of athletics and sports. Males no longer dictate the social experience of dating, courtship, and mating. Women are learning how to be assertive and aggressive in all of these areas of social interaction. In short, the list of social changes involving the issue of roles is virtually unending.

It is apparent that social role change in modern America has facilitated the surrender of traditional roles associated with masculinity and feminity. Generally speaking, women have gained a new and more positive identity as a result of these social changes (Steinmann and Fox, 1974). Some men have felt very threatened by recent role reversals. Indeed, many American males have felt castrated by these very social changes. The phenomena of changing identities in modern society is a topic which is poorly understood by the average person. This statement applies to males and females. As social roles and social role behaviors change in a culture, eventually identity is subject to modification. Quite simply, people begin to see themselves differently as a function of social role evolution and change. This process also results in behavioral change, perceptual change, affective change, and relationship change. All of these change-oriented processes become operational at the individual level, as well as on a collective basis. Social change and role modification usually occur quite slowly. These processes of change tend to initially involve only a limited segment of a society. The change process may then spread and generalize to include the entire society. People and societies very often fear change. Change creates anxiety, uncertainty, and ambiguity, and the change process requires that new behaviors and roles be learned. For these reasons, radical social change is most frequently resisted by the majority of people comprising a society. Identity change, as a function of cultural and social change, begins on an unconscious level. Individuals do not consciously recognize and understand their changing beliefs, values, and attitudes. In short, people do not realize that their basic identities are changing during the initial stages of the change process. Likewise, societies do not recognize social change until such change is monumental. The various and intricate factors associated with identity and social change may not be fully understood or appreciated for decades.

Our addictive society reflects individual and collective conflicts associated with the issue of identity change. The "drug crisis" of the late sixties and the seventies was, in part, the result of a collective identity crisis. Technological change, the "hippies and Yippies," the Vietnam War, contraception, environmental pollution, the threat of nuclear holocaust, economic instability, political corruption, minority group confrontation, the breakdown of the traditional family system, the "new" collective hedonism, intercity riots, and oil shortages are but a few of the more potent ingredients in the American identity crisis. The point to be emphasized in regard to these realities of social change is that our collective identity and individual identities have been altered and modified. Disruptions and changes in identity make it easier for individuals to seek out external, quick, easy solutions to the conflicts they experience as a result of personal and social identity evolution. Alcohol and other mood-altering drugs are external, fast-acting, and "easy" solutions to the problems of identity confusion, change, and evolution. More and more people in this society have turned to alcohol and drugs in order to "cope" with the stresses of modern life. Millions of Americans are alcohol and drug addicted. It is estimated that 3 million adolescents and children are alcohol addicted in the United States (Forrest, 1982a).

Social change and role evolution are present day realities that facilitate identity conflicts. Social and cultural changes do not, in a direct cause-and-effect function, cause clinical dependency. Social and cultural factors simply impact upon human beings in a plethora of ways, which foster and reinforce alcoholism and the other clinical dependencies. Today, various social and cultural factors are operating in a manner that makes it significantly easier for select individuals to choose a life-style involving alcohol addiction. In a congruent manner, social and cultural processes shape and determine individual and collective sexual behaviors, beliefs, and attitudes. Social factors more than tacitly constitute the reality of alcoholism as an interpersonal process.

Identity, human sexuality and perhaps even alcohol addiction are biologically determined. The physical reality of being either a male or female cannot be denied. Identity, in a physical and psychological sense, begins as a physical reality. Sexuality, within a biological and physical context, therefore determines identity. Most people accept and successfully come to grips with the reality of their biological and genetic being. Freud (1953) believed that "anatomy is destiny." Today, this statement continues to be valid in the strict physical sense, as well as generally valid within the context of interpersonal relationships and intrapersonal or psychological adjustment.

Alcohol addiction is believed by many researchers and clinicians to be genetically and biologically determined (Milt, 1969; Keller, 1972; Forrest, 1978a). Indeed, medical researchers have determined that physical factors can play a very important role in the aetiology of alcoholism (Haggard, 1944; Jellinek, 1945; Smith, 1950; Catanzaro, 1968; Delint, 1971; Evans, 1977). Family predisposition is an important reality in alcohol addiction (McCord and McCord, 1960; Paolino and McCrady, 1977; Lirette et al., 1977; Forrest, 1982a). Early investigations (Roe, 1945) in the field of alcoholism indicated that nearly one-half of the offspring of alcoholic parentage eventually developed severe drinking problems or chronic alcoholism. Recent research and clinical evidence pertaining to alcoholism in the offspring of alcoholic parentages (Chafetz, 1977; Ackerman, 1978; Wegscheider, 1978; Wilsnack, 1982) suggests even higher rates of substance abuse and alcoholism among the children of alcoholics. In general support of the viewpoint that alcoholism can be genetically and biologically determined, the American Medical Association recognizes alcoholism as a disease. The wisdom and experience of Alcoholics Anonymous is based on the belief that alcoholism is a disease. In spite of continuing heated controversy and debate surrounding the role of genetic and biological factors in the aetiology of alcoholism, research and clinical efforts in this realm have not clearly demonstrated the role of these factors as they relate to the addiction process. Perhaps our future research and clinical efforts in the alcoholism field will clearly delineate the role of physical factors in the development of alcohol addiction. Alcoholism, as we understand the disorder today, is the result of an "interaction effect" involving physical, psychological, interpersonal, social, and other variables (Forrest, 1978a; 1982a).

Physical identity, determined at the point of conception, remains a constant "given" for the duration of each of our lives. Physical identity dictates sexual identity and eventually sexual behavior. Paradoxically, physical identity remains for life a somewhat precarious reality. The precarious nature of physical identity is reflected via the sexual identities and sexual behaviors of human beings. Physical identity, as a "given," can always be modified and influenced by familial, educational, social, and other life processes. Physical trauma can occur at any point in life, and such an event may radically alter physical identity. The process of socialization as considered in this chapter shapes an individual's sense of physical being. The simple fact that an individual is "fat," tall, or very attractive impacts upon and in part determines physical identity and self-concept. Weight, height, and physical attractiveness can all influence dating and courtship behaviors, mate selection, and at some point sexual adjustment style. Education and religious preference as artifacts of the process of socialization shape the drinking behaviors and sexual adjustment of the individual (Forrest, 1975).

In spite of the physical reality of being male or female, many individuals in our society remain anxious and unsure of themselves as men and women. This is but one of the psychological dilemmas of modern living. As already discussed, the alcoholic is insecure with regard to both physical and psychological identity. Alcoholism is an interpersonal process. In part, interpersonal processes determine and maintain the alcoholic symptom choice. Aetiologically, alcohol addiction begins within the domains of identity conflict and ego pathology. The sexual adjustment of the alcoholic is shaped and determined by basic identity and the addiction process per se.

In this chapter, the interrelationships between alcoholism, sexuality, and identity have been explored. It is hypothesized that alcohol addiction and the sexual conflicts of the alcoholic develop as a result of identity defusion or ego pathology. Prior to the onset of alcoholism and disturbed sexuality, the addicted individual has sustained severe and chronic narcissistic injury. Narcissistic need and entitlement deprivation experiences create self-system fragmentation in the case of the alcoholic. Thus, basic identity disturbance, alcohol addiction, and sexual conflicts as considered in this chapter are interpersonally determined. The alcoholic experiences a chronic sense of personal inadequacy, inferiority, and worthlessness. Within the context of relationships with significant others the addicted person has experienced chronic rejection, unlove, and a lack of intimacy and closeness. As a re experience of disturbed intimacy during the initial epochs of life, the alcoholic is unable to consolidate an adequately defined sense of self. Alcoholics are people who have never satisfactorily resolved the many identity-oriented issues associated with the question "Who am I?" The alcohol addicted person has not experienced consistent consensual validation within the interpersonal realm. It is for these very reasons that the alcoholic remains interpersonally anxious and intrapersonally conflicted (Forrest, 1978a; 1982a).

Identity conflicts, alcoholism, and disturbed sexuality encompass a common denominator. Relationship disturbance is the common denominator in each of these modes of psychopathology. Identity defusion and fragmentation precipitate feelings of intense anxiety and facilitate a chronic sense of non-well-being. Alcoholism and sexual acting-out are neurotic solutions to these very dilemmas in living. It is important to point out that chronic alcoholism, although representing a neurotic compromise to identity and sexual conflicts, invariably exacerbates and synergizes these very sources of internal and interpersonal dissonance. Alcoholics always drive themselves into emotional and physical sickness. In this sense, an important by-product of the addiction process per se is always that of identity confusion and disturbed sexuality. Alcohol addiction causes identity pathology and ego defusion. Alcohol addiction results in a rather wide variety of male and female sexual dysfunctions. Chronic alcoholism, as well as alcohol abuse, can facilitate deviant sexual acting-out.

Hopefully, this chapter will help the reader synthesize the interaction effect of identity pathology, sexual disturbance, and alcohol addiction. In general, there is not a definitive cause-and-effect relationship between any of these three processes. In some clinical cases this may not be true. For example, short-term male impotence may be a direct consequence of chronic intoxication. It is the more subtle, underlying psychodynamic relationships between identity, sexuality, and alcohol addiction that remain clinically influential and yet less than definitive. Clinicians and therapists involved in the treatment of alcoholism, sexual dysfunction, and sexual deviation tend to be confronted with the various treatment realities of these less than definitive relationships between identity, sexuality, and alcohol addiction. The following chapters in this text are aimed at providing the reader with a better clinical understanding of the complex relationships involving identity, human sexuality, and alcoholism. In this respect, it is always important for the clinician to deal with the patient as a total person.

BIBLIOGRAPHY

Ackerman, R.J.: *Children of Alcoholics.* Holmes Beach, Florida, Learning Publications, 1978.

Arlett, A.H., and Wells, H.G.: The effect of alcohol on the reproductive tissues. *Journal of Experimental Medicine, 26(6)*:769-778, 1917.

Bowen, M.: *Family Therapy in Clinical Practice.* New York, Jason Aronson, 1978.

Busch, August: On azoospermia in healthy and sick men: Several observations on the pathological histology of male gonads. *Zeitschrift für Biologie, 18*:496-521, 1882.

Catanzaro, R.J.: *Alcoholism: The Total Treatment Approach.* Springfield, Charles C Thomas, 1968.

Chafetz, M.: The drug scene: Is there a safe way to drink? *Reader's Digest, pp. 100-103, July, 1977.*

Delint, J.: The status of alcoholism as a disease: A brief comment. *Br J Addict, 66*:108-109, 1971.

Evans, J.H.: *A Scientific Examination of the "Disease Concept" of Alcohol Dependency.* Paper, Psychotherapy Associates, P.C., Third Annual Advanced Winter Workshop, "Treatment and Rehabilitation of the Alcoholic," Colorado Springs, Colorado, February 2, 1977.

Forrest, G.G.: *The Diagnosis and Treatment of Alcoholism.* Springfield, Charles C Thomas, 1975.

Forrest, G.G.: *Alcoholism and the Reservation Indian.* Research and clinical paper compiled at the M.S.B.S. Research Project, Turtle Mountain Rehabilitation and Counseling Center, Belcourt, North Dakota, November, 1976.

Forrest, G.G.: *Group Psychotherapy Techniques for the Treatment of Alcoholism.* Lecture, Psychotherapy Associates, P.C. First Annual Southeastern "Treatment and Rehabilitation of the Alcoholic" Workshop, Savannah, Georgia, October 4, 1977.

Forrest, G.G.: *The Diagnosis and Treatment of Alcoholism.* Springfield, Charles C Thomas, Rev. 2nd Ed., 1978.

Forrest, G.G.: *Motivating Alcoholic Patients for Treatment.* Lecture, Fourth Annual Colorado Summer School on Alcoholism, Glenwood Springs, Colorado, June 11, 1978a.

Forrest, G.G.: *Alcoholism, Object Relations and Narcissistic Theory.* Lecture, Psychotherapy Associates, P.C. Fifth Annual Advanced Winter

Workshop, "Treatment and Rehabilitation of the Alcoholic," Colorado Springs, Colorado, January 29, 1979.

Forrest, G.G.: *Alcoholism, Identity and Sexuality*. Lecture, Psychotherapy Associates, P.C. Sixth Annual Winter Workshop, "Treatment and Rehabilitation of the Alcoholic," Colorado Springs, Colorado, February 4, 1980.

Forrest, G.G.: *Confrontation in Psychotherapy with the Alcoholic*. Holmes Beach, Florida, Learning Publications, 1982.

Forrest, G.G.: *The Teenage Drinkers*. New York, Atheneum, 1982a.

Freud, S.: *The Future Prospects of Psychoanalytic Therapy*. Collected Papers, Vol. II, London, Hobarth, 1953.

Gordon, G.G., Altman, R., and Southern, L.: Effect of alcohol (ethanol) administration on sex hormones in normal men. *N Eng Journ of Med, 295(15)*: 793-797, 1976.

Haggard, H.W.: Critique of the allergic nature of alcohol addiction. *Quart J Stud Alc*, pp. 4, 233-241, 1944.

Hartman, W.E., and Fithian, M.A.: *Treatment of Sexual Dysfunctions: A Bio-Psychological-Social Approach*. New York, Jason Aronson, 1974.

Jellinek, M.E.: Heredity and alcohol: Science and society. *Quart J Stud Alc*, pp. 104-113, 1945.

Kaplan, H.S.: *The New Sex Therapy: Active Treatment of Sexual Dysfunctions*. New York, Brunner/Mazel, 1974.

Keller, M.: The oddities of alcoholics. *Quart J Stud Alc*, pp. 33, 1147-1148, 1972.

Leiblum, S., and Pervin, L. (Eds.): *Principles and Practice of Sex Therapy*. New York, The Guilford Press, 1980.

Lirrette, H.F.J., Davis, J.T., Gheen, M.H., Montigros, P., and Tripp, J.: *Self-Esteem Investigation of Alcoholics and Their Non-Alcoholic Spouses*. Unpublished Masters Thesis, School of Social Work, University of South Carolina, Columbia, South Carolina, 1977.

McCord, W., and McCord, J.: *Origins of Alcoholism*. Stanford University Press, 1960.

Masters, W.H., and Johnson, V.E.: *Human Sexual Inadequacy*. Boston, Little, Brown & Co., 1970.

Menninger, K.: *Man Against Himself*. New York, Harcourt, Brace and World, Inc., 1938.

Milt, H.: *Basic Handbook on Alcoholism*. New Jersey, Scientific Aids Publications, 1969.

Paolino, T.J., and McCrady, B.S.: *The Alcoholic Marriage: Alternative Perspectives*. New York, Grune and Stratton, 1977.

Roe, A.: Children of alcoholic parents raised in foster homes. *Science and Society, Quart J Stud in Alc*, pp. 115-128, 1945.

Smith, J.J.: The endocrine basis of hormonal therapy of alcoholism. *NY State J of Med, 50*:1704-1706, 1711-1715, 1950.

Steinman, A., and Fox, D.J.: *The Male Dilemma*. New York, Jason Aronson, 1974.

Vraa, C.W.: *Treatment of the Human Sexual Dysfunctions*. Lecture, Psychotherapy Associates, P.C. Sixth Annual Advanced Winter Workshop, "Treatment and Rehabilitation of the Alcoholic," Colorado Springs, Colorado, February 5, 1980.

Wegscheider, S.: *The Family Trap—No One Escapes from a Chemically Dependent Family*. Lecture, Psychotherapy Associates, P.C. Fourth Annual Advanced Winter Workshop, "Treatment and Rehabilitation of the Alcoholic," Colorado Springs, Colorado, February 2, 1978.

Wilsnack, S.C.: *Alcohol and Issues in the Treatment of Alcoholic Women*. Lecture, Psychotherapy Associates, P.C., Eighth Annual Advanced Winter Workshop, "Treatment and Rehabilitation of the Alcoholic," Colorado Springs, Colorado, February 2, 1982.

Chapter 3
ALCOHOLISM AND
MALE SEXUAL DYSFUNCTION

IMPOTENCE

MALE impotence is basically an impairment of penile erection. Kaplan (1974) has noted that the term *impotence* is objectionable because it is both pejorative and inappropriate. This author suggests using the term *erectile dysfunction* rather than impotence. However, since the term impotence is widely used and accepted as meaning an impairment of penile erection, this term has been utilized in the present chapter. Impotence occurs when "the vascular reflex mechanism fails to pump sufficient blood into the cavernous sinuses of the penis to render it firm and erect" (Kaplan, 1974). In spite of feeling sexually stimulated and aroused, the penis of the impotent male does not become erect. Due to the dissociable nature of the ejaculatory and erectile reflexes it is not uncommon for the impotent male to achieve ejaculation.

Impotence can be caused by various physical and/or psychological factors. Brain and central nervous system impairment, direct physical trauma to the male genital apparatus, disease, and chronic alcohol abuse are physical factors that may result in impotence. Psychologically determined impotence is generally referred to as psychogenic impotence. Anxiety plays a central role in nearly all cases of psychogenic impotence (Masters and Johnson, 1966; 1970; Ellis, 1980; Vraa, 1982). There are many different patterns of male impotence. Hartman and Fithian (1974), Masters and Johnson (1970), and Peters (1979) report that some males are impotent when confronted with the task of intercourse,

34

but capable of attaining erection during masturbation or oral sex. Some males lose their erections when they expose their penis. Some males become impotent only when dominated, in terms of the physical position of a sexual act, by a woman.

When the male is unable to achieve even a partial erection with any partner, under all circumstances, "total" impotence has occurred. Secondary or partial impotence occurs when the male is unable to achieve a firm erection. Partial impotence is more common than total impotence. Kaplan (1974) places patients with erectile dysfunctions in two clinical categories: "patients who suffer from primary impotence have never been potent with a woman, although they may attain good erections by masturbating and have spontaneous erections in other situations. Patients with secondary impotence functioned well for some time prior to the development of their erectile dysfunction." Sex therapists report that the prognosis for both the treatment of male impotence and spontaneous remission of this disorder are directly related to the duration of the symptom (Kroop, 1977). Generally speaking, the prognosis is much better for secondary impotence than for primary impotence. Physical complications, endocrine disorders, and severe psychiatric problems are more frequently associated with primary impotence.

Secondary impotence occurs rather commonly among men. This form of male impotence may not be the result of severe physical or psychological problems. Kaplan (1974) estimates that nearly half of the male population experiences infrequent and short-term episodes of impotence. As such, impotence of this variety may be considered to be within the range of normal sexual behavior. Primary impotence is far less prevalent. It is important to recognize that erectile difficulties can occur in males of all ages. Impotence does not appear to be directly associated with such variables as education, race, religious affiliation, or socioeconomic class.

Alcoholism and Impotence

Chronic alcoholism results in male impotence (Lemere and Smith, 1973). Secondary impotence may follow even a singular instance of excessive alcohol intake (Masters and Johnson, 1970).

Research (Lemere and Smith, 1973) suggests that alcohol-induced sexual impotence is neurogenic in nature and frequently irreversible. Impotence resulting from chronic alcohol abuse may persist following many years of sobriety. It was found (Smith, Lemere, and Dunn, 1972) in a study involving 17,000 male alcoholic subjects that impotence after detoxification occurred in approximately 8 percent of this sample. Gradually, 50 percent of the impotent subjects returned to their previous level of sexual competence. Of the sample, 25 percent remained "relatively" impotent and 25 percent suffered total impotence. These results are consistent with another research investigation, which indicated that nearly one-fourth of a sample of treated alcoholics gave a history of impotence (Goodwin, Crane, and Gaze, 1971). Indeed, alcohol-induced impotence and sexual dysfunction is relatively common (Akhtar, 1977). Alcohol-induced impotence may not be the result of severe psychopathology or hormonal defect. Lemere and Smith (1973) indicate that alcohol-induced impotence is due to the destructive effect of alcohol on the neurogenic reflex area that serves the process of erection.

Alcohol and other drugs have been utilized in order to enhance sexual performance for thousands of years and in many different cultures (Gallant, 1968; Forrest, 1978). Yet, it is very obvious that the use and abuse of alcohol can often repress or impair sexual performance. Impotence due to chronic alcoholism may be permanent. It is medically difficult to point out the exact causes of alcohol-induced impotence. This is particularly true in the case of the older chronic alcoholic who suffers with primary impotence. Researchers (Fabre et al., 1973; Gordon, Altman, and Southern, 1976; Huttmen, Horkoven, and Nishamen, 1976) have indicated that alcohol affects sex hormone metabolism in males. Perhaps long-term ethanol ingestion per se effects testosterone metabolism in a fashion conducive to the development of impotence. Testicular atrophy due to chronic alcoholism may be another factor of importance in primary impotence.

Prior to the onset of alcohol abuse and addiction many male alcoholics have experienced impotence and other sexual difficulties (Clinebell, 1956; Kroop, 1977; Forrest, 1978; Forrest, 1982). Some alcoholics consciously decide to drink in order to cope with sexual conflicts and sexual dysfunction. Such a choice may obviously be made prior to becoming physiologically and psychologically addicted. The prealcoholic individual may be able to sustain a degree of psychological relief from drinking, which temporarily deters impotence. For example, the male who is quite anxious and threatened over the matter of penis size may find that a few drinks will extinguish this specific conflict on the level of conscious awareness. Rather than becoming anxious and impotent while being nude in the physical presence of a woman, such an individual might be able to attain an erection and complete coitus following the ingestion of three or four alcoholic beverages. Used in this manner, alcohol potentially is a deterrent to impotency. In terms of learning theory, this type of response set would tend to be repeated assuming, of course, that it continued to "work." Within this context, "work" simply means that as long as the process of ingesting ethanol resulted in anxiety extinction associated with penis size, to the extent of deterring impotence, the sequel of behavior would tend to be repeated. Unfortunately, "what alcohol gives, alcohol takes away!" Alcohol ingestion, alcohol abuse, and eventual alcohol addiction are not remedies for impotence. Drinking in order to deter impotence associated with concerns about penis size, performance anxiety, castration fears, and other psychological problems is not an effective solution. Alcoholic problem solving sometimes "works" on a short-term basis, but it never proves effective over an extended period of time. At some point, alcohol addiction dictates that impotence and sexual dysfunction must occur.

Impotence is always an emotionally threatening, frustrating, and depressing experience. Male identity and self-esteem are invested in the ability to achieve an erection (Ellis, 1980). Many males become depressed as a result of impotence. Depression can also cause impotence. These factors are generally important to the clinician who is involved in the treatment of impotent men. These same factors are even more germane to the treatment of the impotent male alcoholic. As discussed in Chapters 1 and 2, the alcoholic male drinks in order to establish an identity. Alcoholics have low self-esteem (Lirette et al., 1977). Underlying or secondary depression is central to the adjustment style and characterological makeup of the alcoholic (Forrest, 1982a). The alcoholic male who drinks in order to "be a man" and establishes some sense of positive self-esteem by drinking is "doubly" depressed and confused when impotence becomes a reality. For male alcoholics, the reality of impotence can be devastating. In addition to the depression, anxiety, loss of self-esteem, and identity fragmentation experienced by the impotent male alcoholic, feelings of anger, resentment, and hostility frequently predominate the overall adjustment pattern of these individuals. Severe marital conflicts can follow the onset of impotence in the alcoholic marriage. In this context, severe marital problems and perhaps chronic male-female relationship conflicts as well can contribute to the impotence of the male alcoholic. The following case demonstrates a number of the clinical aspects of impotence in the male alcoholic as discussed in this chapter.

CASE 2. Harold, a fifty-two-year-old practicing dentist, entered psychotherapy as a result of his anxiety about sexual relations. The patient reported that he was "impotent" during the initial treatment session. This patient and his wife were seen in weekly conjoint psychotherapy for nine months. At the time of treatment engagement, Harold had been totally abstinent from alcohol for a period of nine and one-half years. The patient had a history of some twenty years of alcohol abuse and alcohol addiction prior to establishing sobriety. Following a four-month psychiatric hospitalization for chronic alcoholism, the patient had joined Alcoholics Anonymous and continued to be totally sober. His wife was very active in Al-Anon.

During the second conjoint therapy session, Mrs. A. indicated that she and Harold had not engaged in sexual intercourse for over seven years. The couple had discussed this issue from time to time, but the general topic of sexuality was very threatening for both spouses. Mrs. A. indicated that she still considered herself "young" and sexually appealing. She had been desirous of engaging in sexual intercourse and other sexual behaviors for many years, but felt that it was better not to openly discuss these feelings with her husband since he was such a "poor performer." Over the years, Mrs. A. had fantasized about having an "affair" but in reality she was uncomfortable with this alternative. Rather than involving herself sexually with other men, Mrs. A. instead became very active in the church and Al-Anon, and she devoted much of her time to being an Alateen sponsor. She described these outside involvements as "compensations" for a "poor sex life."

Harold was depressed and guilty about being impotent. However, sexual conflicts and problems had been central to Harold's life for as long as he could remember. As a child and during adolescence the patient was told that sex was dirty and evil. As a Catholic, the patient was taught that masturbation was a "sin" that could lead to insanity or physical weakness. The patient had no physical contact or involvement with women prior to the age of twenty-four. His initial sexual experiences with women came while in the armed forces and involved infrequent contacts with prostitutes. While in his sophomore year in college, Harold experienced two homosexual contacts with a fraternity brother. On both occasions, Harold and his fraternity brother performed fellatio on each other. The patient reported being uncomfortable, guilty, depressed, and anxious about his homosexual experiences. He recalled being a premature ejaculator in these encounters and vividly remembered having had one prostitute laugh at him for this reason.

At the age of thirty-four Harold married Mrs. A., who had formerly been married. The couple recalled having intercourse once or twice a month during the initial years of their marriage. They had never attempted mutual masturbation, oral genital sex, anal sex, or other varieties of sexual behavior. The early years of this marriage involved heavy drinking and rather chronic intoxication upon the part of Harold. Harold was rarely ever able to sustain an erection after vaginal penetration. At this time, Mr. and Mrs. A. did not ever openly discuss their sexual relationship. Over the years, Mr. and Mrs. A. progressively avoided sexual intimacy more and more. Both were afraid of sexual intimacy. They were extremely uncomfortable with even talking about sexuality. After years of sexual conflict and a virtually "sexless" marriage, Mr. and Mrs. A. mutually decided to seek out professional help in order to change their sexual relationship.

Conjoint psychotherapy and sexual therapy with this couple eventually proved successful. Several weeks of therapy were devoted to exploring Mr. A.'s early sexual experiences, irrational beliefs about human sexuality (Ellis, 1979), and anxieties pertaining to sexual behavior. This patient had believed for the entirety of his adult life that sex was dirty, evil, and somehow sinful. He also felt sexually inadequate and perceived himself as a gross failure in terms of sexual performance. Another source of sexual anxiety for Mr. A. was his fear of homosexuality. Following a few months of psychodynamically oriented psychotherapy, behavioral sex therapy techniques were utilized to treat the patient's genital and castration anxiety, premature ejaculation, and impotence. At the point of treatment termination the patient and his wife were having sexual intercourse once or twice a week. The patient's self-esteem was greatly improved and the marital relationship was radically improved. Many of Mr. A.'s depressive conflicts were resolved. Human sexuality was no longer a topic that produced feelings of anxiety, guilt, depression, and frustration for Mr. and Mrs. A.

This clinical case presentation demonstrates that the impotence of some male alcoholics can be treated successfully. It is clinically significant that Mr. A. had an extended history of sexual difficulties. The patient had also been impotent following several years of abstinence from alcohol. Didactic sex education played an important role in Mr. A.'s recovery from impotence. Psychodynamically oriented conjoint therapy and behavioral sex therapy techniques were also essential to the successful management of this case.

Alcohol addiction is but one cause of impotence. In my clinical experience, the alcoholic is frequently impotent as a result of a combination of factors. The impotent alcoholic patient should have a complete medical examination prior to the initiation of psychotherapy or sexual counseling. In some cases, a neurological workup may be indicated. Some of the physical factors that contribute to impotence in the alcoholic patient are diabetes or blood sugar pathology, chronic or acute stress; physical exhaustion or fatigue, hepatic problems, endocrinological problems, and neurological disease. The psychological factors that contribute to the impotence of the alcoholic are complex, interrelated, and varied. Performance anxiety, concerns about penis size, irrational learning and conditioning experiences in the realm of human sexuality, castration anxiety, unresolved hatred and rage for women, fears of intimacy, and apprehension centering around the issue of control are but a few of the more common psychological factors that contribute to the impotence of the alcoholic.

Aside from physical illness, disease, and neurological or organic causation, impotence always involves faulty learning. The social learning experiences of the alcoholic contribute greatly to impotence and distorted or pathologic sexuality. Alcoholics have been taught and conditioned to fear sexual intimacy. Many alcoholics have learned to avoid or fear all forms of sexuality. Learning plays a crucial role in the case of the impotent alcoholic who is phobic with regard to the female genitals. The promiscuous or acting-out alcoholic learns a style or set of behaviors, which may or may not prove effective in terms of managing sexual conflicts. Performance anxiety is always a matter of learning and conditioning. Feelings of anxiety or anger associated with relationships involving women and sexuality are based upon social learning experiences and conditioning. In short, the social and interpersonal learning experiences of the alcoholic contribute greatly to the overall problem of impotence. While primary impotence in the case of the alcoholic is often directly attributed to the physical effects of chronic or acute intoxication, secondary impotence tends to encompass the effects of alcohol ingestion in combination with faulty learning experiences.

Basic Treatment Strategies

Sex therapists and behavioral scientists involved in the treatment of sexual dysfunction (Ellis, 1980) advocate a rather wide range of specific treatment modalities for impotence. Kaplan (1974), summarizing the clinical data on the treatment of impotence, suggests that "brief, symptom-focused forms of treatment which actively intervene to modify the patient's sexual behavior are superior to lengthy, reconstructive insight therapy which essentially ignores the immediate antecedents of sexual problems. These data further indicate that brief conjoint treatment techniques are also superior to office behavioral approaches which rely exclusively on relaxation and desensitization procedures. Inclusion of the sexual partner in therapy also seems to improve prognosis."

Few sex therapists work with alcoholic patients (Forrest, 1980b). Indeed, the impotent alcoholic has received little attention in the clinical and research literature. A precursor to all effective psychotherapeutic work with alcohol-addicted clients is that of abstinence from alcohol (Forrest, 1975; 1976; 1978a; 1979b; 1980c; 1982). Psychotherapy with the alcoholic begins with sobriety. This same position applies to sex therapy and sexual counseling with the impotent alcoholic. It is axiomatic that sex therapy with the drinking and impotent alcoholic is destined to failure. Therefore, the therapists involved in the treatment of sexual dysfunction must be generally versed in the treatment of alcoholism if they are to function effectively with alcoholic patients manifesting sexual dysfunctions. Following the establishment of sobriety, sexual counseling and sex therapy may be undertaken. Equally important, the impotent alcoholic must remain sober during the course of sex therapy. Impotent patients who have an extended history of alcohol abuse rather than alcohol addiction must also attain abstinence prior to and during sex therapy. It can be efficacious to suggest that the impotent alcoholic seek out psychotherapy for his addiction per se prior to or during the course of sex therapy. Likewise, a commitment to Alcoholics Anonymous, an Antabuse maintenance program (Knauert, 1979), a religious group, or some other variety of ongoing supportive psychotherapy can contribute to the effectiveness of sex therapy with the impotent alcoholic.

Due to the direct physical effects of chronic alcoholism, it is recommended that sex therapy with the impotent alcoholic be initiated from sixty to ninety days after medical detoxification. It is an utter waste of time and clinically inappropriate to begin sex therapy with the impotent alcoholic prior to the completion of detoxification. It is also clinically unsound to begin sex therapy with alcoholic patients during the initial days and weeks of sobriety. In addition to the direct physical effects of chronic alcohol ingestion on the sexual apparatus and human body in general, the alcoholic often suffers in the areas of general health and nutrition, diet, and physical exercise. The overall physical health of the deteriorated thirty-five- or forty-year-old chronic alcoholic may be such that the patient is barely ambulatory during the initial week or two following alcohol withdrawal. The drinking chronic alcoholic may eat very little for weeks or months at a time. Alcohol addicted persons tend to exercise very little on a regular basis (Forrest, 1979c). All of these factors can play an active and important role in the impotence of the alcoholic. The overall lifestyle of the alcoholic can be a determining factor in the causation of impotence. Programs providing comprehensive alcoholism services frequently fail to adequately take into account the role of holistic treatment and recovery. Exercise, nutrition, diet, and other life-style and health variables may actively contribute to the impotence of the alcoholic.

It is generally believed (Masters and Johnson, 1970; Kaplan, 1974; Vraa, 1978; Ellis, 1980; Vraa, 1982) that impotence is the result of anxiety occurring at the point of sexual intercourse. Anxiety extinguishes the erectile response. Therefore, a basic objective of sex therapy for impotence is to extinguish anxiety. Many factors can operate to help diminish or deter anxiety that results in impotence. However, as indicated in Chapter 2, the problem of anxiety is central to alcoholism as well as impotence. In this sense, the relationship between alcoholism and impotence is doubly complex.

Following a few weeks of sobriety, nutritional stabilization, and the active implementation of a program of exercise, sex therapy for impotence is appropriately initiated. Sex therapy should be adjunctive to conjoint psychotherapy and possibly patient and spouse involvement with the Alcoholics Anonymous community. Sex therapy should be conducted after the patient has completed a medical evaluation and workup. Assuming there is no medical or neurological basis for the patient's impotence, the initial sex therapy session should be devoted to discussing with the patient and spouse sexual and marital relationship issues. The couple is told that the erectile problem is functional. The patient is assured that his sexual apparatus is not physically impaired or abnormal. Alcoholism is discussed as a central ingredient in the patient's impotence. It can be psychologically helpful to indicate to the couple that impotence, in the case of the alcoholic, is frequently a direct consequence of intoxication or chronic intoxication. Such a treatment strategy creates realistic optimism, while at the same time reinforcing sobriety. An immediate treatment goal is to facilitate one erection and a subsequent successful coital experience for the impotent patient (Kaplan, 1974). Successful accomplishment of this task results in sexual and relationship changes, which reinforce subsequent adaptive behaviors while extinguishing anxiety and other variables supporting the patient's impotence.

The couple is instructed to abstain from intercourse and ejaculation during the first week of sex therapy. However, the therapist instructs the couple to caress each other and encourages physical contact short of coitus. It is important to suggest to the couple that they not concern themselves about eliciting an erection. These strategies alleviate pressure and anxiety. Usually, the couple finds during this time that erections will occur. When the patient's confidence has been reestablished via the ability to achieve erection, a variety of specific sex therapy techniques can be explored to reinforce continued adaptive sexual performance. Usually, it is important to teach the couple to employ the "squeeze method" (Masters and Johnson, 1970) to help extinguish the patient's fear of losing his erection "forever." This procedure involves instructing the wife or partner to squeeze, at the apex of erection, the patient's penis until the erection abates. By practicing this technique the patient learns that he can again become erect in a short period of time. Obviously, this technique helps build patient confidence and reduces performance anxiety. Rather than employing the squeeze technique, the wife can simply be instructed to manually or orally stimulate the patient's penis to erection and then discontinue these behaviors until the erection recedes. These techniques should be repeated several times during a lovemaking session. Direct penile insertion is not to be attempted during this phase of treatment.

As Peters (1979) has pointed out, the sex therapist must consistently explore the destructive sexual fantasies and cognitions of each spouse throughout the process of sex therapy. Ellis (1971; 1979) has indicated that irrational beliefs and irrational self-dialogue can contribute to faulty sexual behavior and impotence. Irrational sexual beliefs are very often destructive in terms of sexual performance. The beliefs that "my penis is not hard enough," "she is not satisfied," "this behavior is sick," and "I can't climax until she does" are examples of potentially irrational and destructive self-dialogue. When one or both partners report irrational sexual ideation of this variety, the sex therapist directly challenges and disputes these beliefs.

Patients frequently need the sex therapist to approve of their sexual fantasies and behaviors. The therapist may eventually find it helpful to give the couple permission to engage in sexual behaviors they have individually or mutually wanted to try out for many years. In such cases one or both spouses may have equated this "secret" variety of sexual behavior as abnormal or deviant. Along these lines, the impotent alcoholic sometimes needs to be told to focus only upon his own sexual needs. Overconcern with the sexual satisfaction of the patient's wife can contribute to impotence. Both husband and wife must ultimately take responsibility for their personal sexual behavior. A naturally satisfying sexual relationship requires giving, sensitivity, and awareness upon the part of both partners.

After several days of sharing physical intimacy without intercourse, erectile confidence is usually reestablished. At this point, the sex therapist explores with the couple any number of stimulating varieties of coitus. The first attempt at intercourse can be critical in the treatment of impotence. Successful coitus at this point usually generalizes into a more rewarding and richer sexual adjustment for the patient and his wife. Gross erectile dysfunction at this juncture usually results in reinitiating the treatment procedures previously considered. Dynamically oriented psychotherapy, in combination with the behavioral strategies already discussed, may be indicated following continued erectile dysfunction. Relatively easy, nondemanding varieties of sexual intercourse are suggested during this stage of treatment. The issue of prolonged intercourse is not important at this juncture, and the patient may be instructed to complete vaginal penetration and ejaculate as soon as he is ready. Some patients respond well to the use of specific sexual fantasy material in order to complete coitus during this phase of treatment.

These initially supportive and reassuring treatment strategies are utilized to facilitate a developing capacity for anxiety-free sexual functioning. It is important for the patient to develop an ever-increasing degree of self-confidence in the realm of sexual functioning. Practice and continued successful sexual responding are basic to the process of maintaining potency. Couples should be encouraged to maintain an active sexual relationship once the patient's impotence is in remission. Effective, mutually stimulating and rewarding sexual encounters require practice!

The wife of the alcoholic frequently plays an important role in the onset and continuation of impotence. This situation is not uncommon in cases of impotence in nonalcoholics. However, this particular clinical issue is much more common and dynamically significant in the case of the impotent alcoholic. Resentment, anger, rage, and retaliation are very often psychodynamically related to the destructive sexual behaviors of the wife. Wives of alcoholics attack "the addicted spouse" in response to the emotional hurt and pain that evolves as a result of alcoholic behavior and alcohol-facilitated marital and familial transactions. As the alcoholic deteriorates into the middle and later stages of the addiction process (Forrest, 1975), sexual performance usually declines. Some wives verbally attack their addicted husbands with the reality of their sexual inadequacy. Messages such as "you can't even get it up," "you're not a man," and "you couldn't get any even if you wanted to" are examples of the destructive verbal exchanges that take place between the wife and impotent alcoholic. These messages clearly reinforce impotence and sexual conflict. They are also castrative. The impotent alcoholic may respond to these confrontations by attempting one or numerous extramarital affairs in order to "prove" to himself and his wife that he can "cut the mustard." Guilt can be associated with marital and sexual adjustments of this type. The wife sometimes consciously realizes that she is reinforcing the patient's impotence and thus becomes guilty. The alcoholic experiences guilt as a consequence of sexual promiscuity and acting-out. Impotence creates feelings of guilt.

For these and myriad other clinical reasons, it is almost always important for the impotent alcoholic and his wife to be involved in relationship psychotherapy in addition to sex therapy. Alcoholic marriages tend to be severely conflicted. Impotence is but one important clinical issue in a disturbed marital relationship. Oedipal conflicts, identity and sexual pathology, feelings of inadequacy and inferiority, depression, interpersonal anxiety, anger and resentment, and low self-esteem are clinical issues which usually pertain to both the alcoholic and nonaddicted spouse. Sometimes both spouses are alcohol dependent. Clearly, all of these factors can be related to impotence.

Summary

In this section impotence was defined. The psychological and physical factors that contribute to impotence were discussed. Anxiety is central to impotence. Primary and secondary impotence were delineated. Chronic or acute alcohol ingestion can result in impotence. It was suggested that chronic alcoholism sometimes results in neurogenic impotence, which may be irreversible. The psychological makeup of the impotent alcoholic was touched upon. A clinical case study demonstrating the relationship between alcoholism and impotence was presented. The sexual conflicts of the alcoholic frequently serve as precursors to the addiction symptom choice. Social learning experiences pathologically contribute to the sexual problems of the alcoholic. Specific treatment techniques for the impotent alcoholic were outlined. Sex therapy is appropriately initiated after the alcoholic has been sober for at least four months. It is inappropriate to initiate or continue treatment for impotence when the alcoholic is intoxicated or drinking. Brief, behavioral oriented strategies of treatment for impotence are recommended. It is strongly recommended that the alcoholic couple be actively engaged in relationship psychotherapy in adjunct to sex therapy. Treatment of the impotent alcoholic should be holistic—to include an emphasis upon diet and nutrition, exercise, and possibly other medical and physiological measures. Alcoholic patients should complete a medical examination prior to beginning sex therapy and psychotherapy. A basic goal of sex therapy for impotence is to extinguish anxiety. The actual process of sex therapy for impotence includes noncoital pleasuring and intimacy exercises; possible utilization of the "squeeze technique"; the use of sexually stimulating fantasy, cognitive training, confidence and esteem building, and sexual experimentation; permission giving transactions upon the part of the sex therapist; controlled coital activities; and self-centered sexual responding. A more dynamically oriented relationship therapy as a part of the process of sex therapy is advocated in the treatment of the impotent alcoholic. Finally, it is suggested that patient and spouse involvement in Alcoholics Anonymous and Al-Anon can facilitate the process of alcoholism recovery and improved sexual functioning.

Abstinence from alcohol is essential to the successful treatment of impotence in the case of the alcoholic. In some cases the use of testosterone can be a helpful treatment adjunct. Research data dealing with the effectiveness of sex therapy in the treatment of the impotent alcoholic is lacking. However, the clinical experience of this author indicates that a long-term (one year or more) resolution of impotence is to be expected in approximately 70 percent of these cases entering therapy and remaining sober. Patients who are successfully treated for impotence and then resume alcoholic drinking patterns most typically become impotent again.

It is important for the sex therapist to remain creative, innovative, and imaginative in his or her clinical work with the impotent alcoholic. Sex therapy strategies with the impotent alcoholic should be pragmatically determined.

PREMATURE EJACULATION

Premature ejaculation or ejaculato praecox occurs when the male is unable to control his ejaculatory reflex. As a result, orgasm occurs almost immediately after sexual arousal. It is difficult to provide a specific definition of premature ejaculation. Clinicians have employed a variety of diagnostic criteria in assessing premature ejaculation. Masters and Johnson (1966; 1970) diagnose a man as a premature ejaculator if he experiences orgasm prior to his wife or sexual partner more than 50 percent of the time. According to sex therapists, the diagnosis of premature ejaculation is contingent upon the amount of time that elapses between vaginal penetration and ejaculation. Some sex therapy clinics define premature ejaculation as the occurence of orgasm thirty seconds after vaginal entry; others have extended this interim to one and one-half minutes or two minutes, and some clinics even employ the criteria of number of thrusts (Kaplan, 1974). The majority of premature ejaculators reach orgasm prior to or immediately following vaginal entry (Perelman, 1980).

It is clinically unrealistic to rely upon any of the singular diagnostic criteria thus far discussed in order to diagnose premature ejaculation. It is important to point out that women vary considerably with regard to time and thrusts required to reach orgasm. Premature ejaculators vary considerably with regard to prematurity. Some premature ejaculators will ejaculate at the sight of their nude spouse or partner. There is considerable variation in even the partner-response criterion of Masters and Johnson (1966; 1970). Almost all of the definitions of premature ejaculation rely upon the "time of sexual responding" in order to make this diagnosis. Kaplan (1974) has suggested that "prematurity cannot be defined in quantative terms because the essential pathology in this condition is not really related to time. Rather, the crucial aspect of prematurity is the absence of voluntary control over the ejaculatory reflex, regardless of whether this occurs after two thrusts or five; whether it occurs before the female reaches orgasm or not. Prematurity can thus be said to exist when orgasm occurs reflexly, when it is beyond the man's voluntary control once an intense level of sexual arousal is attained." This author asserts that ejaculatory control is established when the male can tolerate high levels of sexual excitement, which characterize the plateau state of the sexual response cycle and not ejaculate reflexly.

Obviously, premature ejaculation is not a unitarily diagnosed sexual dysfunction. Premature ejaculators exhibit a diversity of individual features, in terms of sexual dysfunction, personality, sexual adjustment style, and life-style. Various "types" of premature ejaculators have been discussed in the clinical literature dealing with sexual dysfunction. Type A (Kaplan, 1974) premature ejaculators are described as young, having a high sex drive with no erectile difficulties, but these individuals manifest a clinical history of never being able to establish good ejaculatory control. The type B premature ejaculator (Kaplan, 1974) is described as being older, having erectile difficulties, and premature ejaculation in this group tends to occur following a history of good control. Type B premature ejaculators often appear to manifest a form of impotence.

Premature ejaculation is felt to be the most common of the male sexual dysfunctions. This is a common sexual disorder among males. As many researchers and clinicians have pointed out (Masters and Johnson, 1970; Kaplan, 1974; Kroop, 1977; Perelman, 1980; Vraa, 1982), a diversity of males experience premature ejaculation. Educational, socioeconomic, and racial factors do not appear to relate to the incidence of premature ejaculation. The type or quality of the marital relationship has no direct clinical impact upon the incidence of this disorder. Many premature ejaculators are clearly not disturbed in a psychological or psychiatric sense.

A variety of psychological and physical factors have been associated with prematurity. Disease of the posterior urethra, pathology involving the nerve pathways, multiple sclerosis, and other neurological disorders can result in premature ejaculation. For these reasons, it may be appropriate for the sex therapist to refer the premature ejaculator for neurological and urological evaluations prior to initiating treatment. This decision is indicated in the case of patients who have a history of good ejaculatory control and suddenly experience a loss of control in combination with other health problems.

Many different psychological explanations of premature ejaculation have been advanced in the clinical and research literature. The more traditional psychodynamic and psychoanalytically oriented theories of prematurity suggest that the premature ejaculator is afraid of women or the vagina, angry, sexually ambivalent, and regressively fixated. Relationship disturbance may be associated with prematurity. Family systems theorists and transactional theorists stress the importance of relationship, communication, and interpersonal factors in the aetiology of premature ejaculation. Performance anxiety can play a crucial role in prematurity. Social learning theory advocates stress the importance of faulty conditioning and learning experiences in the development of prematurity. The clinical experience of the author suggests that many premature ejaculators do indeed have a history of faulty learning in the realm of sexual relationships. Early sexual encounters in the backseat of an automobile, being "caught in the act," and other situational occurrences of the "hurry up and get it over with" variety are frequently reported by premature ejaculators. In situations such as these, the man has been conditioned to ejaculate rapidly. Conditioning and learning experiences involving sexual intimacy are very affectively involved and subject to generalization. Premature ejaculation may become a learned behavioral set. Covert and secondary learning factors may also operate to reinforce the pattern of prematurity.

Today's commercial market of erotic publications and sexual devices has certainly capitalized upon the widespread problem of prematurity. In viewing premature ejaculation as a problem caused by excessive sensitivity to sexual stimulation, the commercial market of erotic sexual devices has developed many anesthetic salves, ointments, and mechanical devices, which are purportedly "guaranteed" to deter prematurity. These methods have not proven effective in the establishment of ejaculatory inhibition and control. It is apparent that the personal sense of anxiety and psychological threat that accompanies the loss of ejaculatory control has created a multimillion dollar industry, which promises a solution to this form of sexual dysfunction. Many of our present "sexual myths" surrounding the matter of performance reinforce the commercial marketing and sales of devices that supposedly facilitate ejaculatory control.

Premature ejaculation can most assuredly create anxiety and conflict in the marital relationship. Some couples are unable to discuss the matter of the husband's prematurity. The wife of the premature ejaculator may feel upset, anxious, inadequate, and angry. Many of these wives feel sexually frustrated and unsatisfied. Many men who consistently suffer from premature ejaculation are depressed, guilty, and anxious. Few premature ejaculators seek out professional help. Sometimes secondary impotence develops as a reaction to premature ejaculation. It is for these reasons that sex therapy, conjoint psychotherapy, and other strategies of treatment are indicated for the amelioration of prematurity. Premature ejaculation is a sexually oriented relationship problem that facilitates other relationship difficulties and conflicts.

Alcoholism and Premature Ejaculation

Alcohol-induced sexual dysfunction is fairly common (Akhtar, 1977). Research evidence and clinical experience rather consistently indicate that the physiological effect of alcohol on sexual performance can cause premature ejaculation (Neshkov, 1969; Todd, 1973; Williams, 1976; Wilson, 1977). The ability of the alcoholic to ejaculate is sometimes severely impaired (Powell, Viamontes, and Brown, 1974). Research evidence also indicates that alcohol ingestion results in a diminished interest in heterosexual relationships (Akhtar, 1977). Studies dealing with the effects of alcohol on male sexual arousal indicate that penile size, duration of erection, and other indicators of arousal generally diminish following alcohol ingestion (Farkas and Rosen, 1975; Briddell and Wilson, 1976; Rubin and Henson, 1976). It appears that alcohol abuse and alcoholism can cause premature ejaculation as well as retarded ejaculation. Within this context, the issue of retarded ejaculation will be discussed in the third part of this chapter.

In clinical practice it is rather common to treat alcoholic and alcohol-abusing, premature ejaculators who early in their drinking careers somewhat successfully utilized alcohol as a deterrent to prematurity (Vraa, 1977; Forrest, 1978; 1982a). As a central nervous system depressant, alcohol potentially inhibits the ejaculatory response. Some alcoholics report a generally enhanced sexual response following the ingestion of ethanol. This pattern occurs most typically during the early and middle stages of alcoholism. The inhibition of premature ejaculation or a better controlled ejaculatory response can be but one area of gain associated with drinking during early stages of the addiction process. Transient escape from performance anxiety, a loosening of sexual inhibitions, sexual assertiveness, and improved self-confidence are other areas of reported gain associated with imbibing. Users and abusers of other drugs and chemicals tend to report similar experiences in this realm (Smith, 1972). The self-reports of alcoholics and other drug addicts and substance abusers regarding addiction and human sexuality are subject to distortion, inaccuracies, and fallacy. In spite of this reality, short-term or intermittantly improved ejaculatory control may be associated with the use of alcohol.

The type A premature ejaculator, as discussed earlier, tends to derive the most gain in the area of using and abusing alcohol as a means of managing prematurity. Such patients, even when they are floridly alcoholic, are often capable of attaining full erection. They may be able to ejaculate as many as three or four times in the course of an evening's sexual encounter. Older premature ejaculators, in accord with the type B model already briefly considered, tend to be increasingly impotent as they attempt to utilize alcohol as an agent of ejaculatory regulation. Alcohol addiction eventually inhibits the type B patient's ability to become erect, sustain an erection, and ejaculate.

Sexual dysfunction, in the case of the alcoholic and alcohol abuser, is very often a progressive disorder. This situation pertains to premature ejaculation. The young, sexually active, and erectile competent alcoholic eventually conditions himself into impotence via the addiction process. By using alcohol as an agent to control ejaculation, the addicted person further reinforces the alcoholic symptom choice. As the addiction process evolves into the stage of physical dependency, the problem of premature ejaculation becomes progressively more pathologic. Premature ejaculation is but a developmental stage of sexual dysfunction for many alcoholic persons. The alcoholic derives a good deal of generalized gain from drinking during the early stage of the addiction process. These sources of gain reinforce further drinking and an increasing psychological dependence upon alcohol. During the early stages of the addiction process this gain is frequently in the realm of regulating prematurity. As suggested in the first part of this chapter, eventually alcohol and intoxication take away the gain related to prematurity.

Some type A alcoholic premature ejaculators report that drinking only a "few" drinks will not result in an enhanced ability to control the ejaculatory response. Such individuals continue to experience prematurity after consuming two or three alcoholic beverages. This situation usually pertains to the first attempt at coitus. Therefore, these select alcoholics often consciously decide to consume several alcoholic drinks prior to intercourse. Premature ejaculation can thus play an important role in the reinforcement of the alcoholic symptom choice. The case of Mr. R. demonstrates the problem of Type A premature ejaculation in the alcoholic.

Case 3. The patient, Mr. R., entered individual psychotherapy following his wife's decision to initiate a legal separation. During the initial few individual therapy sessions Mr. R. indicated that he "had been drinking too much" for nearly ten years. The patient was a forty-six-year-old retired Air Force command sergeant major. Since retiring some three years earlier the patient had not been employed. The patient's wife was successfully employed as an executive secretary with a large corporation. Each of the spouses had been married before. At the time of treatment engagement, the wife's fourteen-year-old son was residing with the couple. The son had a history of school failure, truancy, and severe conflicts with the patient. This family system had been intact for nearly nine years.

After four individual therapy sessions, at the suggestion of the author, the patient was seen in weekly conjoint therapy with his wife for a period of six months. The sexual relationship of the couple was not generally explored during the early weeks of conjoint therapy. During the initial three or four conjoint sessions Mrs. R. recalled vivid accounts of the patient's drinking behavior over the past several years. For this duration of time, Mr. R. had consumed ten to twelve "mixed drinks" each evening. About two years before entering conjoint psychotherapy, Mrs. R. had started attending Al-Anon on a weekly basis. She believed that the patient was an "alcoholic." The patient completely terminated his drinking behavior after the third individual therapy session. In the fourth month of conjoint therapy Mr. R. drank to the point of intoxication on one occasion. Presently, the patient has been totally abstinent for a period of two and one-half years. This patient did not choose to participate in Alcoholics Anonymous and at the point of therapy termination he perceived himself as a "problem drinker" who had "decided to do something about my drinking."

During the sixth conjoint therapy session, Mrs. R. brought up her feelings of sexual frustration. In a very supportive and nonthreatening manner, Mrs. R. indicated that she was "tired" of being sexually excited during foreplay only to have Mr. R. ejaculate immediately upon vaginal entry. The patient was very uncomfortable with the general topic of sex. After this issue was openly discussed by Mrs. R., the patient looked at the floor and remained silent. After a few minutes, the patient verbalized that "this" was a topic that "makes me feel bad." Within the following three or four conjoint therapy sessions Mr. R. became increasingly able to discuss his long-standing problem with premature ejaculation. According to the patient, his first wife became sexually involved with another man and eventually divorced him as a result of his prematurity. The patient disclosed that he had "always" been a premature ejaculator. His earliest sexual encounters were with prostitutes and these relationships occurred at the age of seventeen. This was shortly after the patient joined the Air Force. The patient's first wife, whom he married at age twenty-two, eventually became very angry and resentful about the issue of prematurity. She also laughed and joked a good deal about the patient's prematurity with friends and others outside of the marital relationship. The patient's present wife reported that prematurity had been a problem throughout their marriage.

In spite of the problem of prematurity, the patient had "always" been capable of having intercourse on two or three occasions each night. Furthermore, Mr. R. could usually ejaculate two or three times per occasion of lovemaking. For these reasons, Mrs. R. felt generally happy with their sexual relationship over the first two or three years of marriage. Likewise, Mr. R. believed that his ability to experience multiple orgasms with no erectile difficulties compensated, "over the long run," for his problem with premature ejaculation. The patient verbalized a sense of "uncomfortableness" with his prematurity that dated back to his earliest sexual experiences. He also stated that as a late adolescent, he usually had "two or three" drinks to deter premature ejaculation. During the early years of his first marriage, Mr. R. frequently drank to the point of near stuperous intoxication prior to attempting coitus. Under these circumstances the patient was sometimes unable to ejaculate. Since he experienced no difficulty establishing and maintaining a full erection while intoxicated, the ability to perform coitus for an extended period of time without ejaculation was a very rewarding experience in these situations of intoxication. In the absence of a "few" drinks, Mr. R. stated that he was rarely, if ever, able to have coitus for more than a "few seconds" without reaching orgasm. This situation pertained to the first marriage.

As the patient deteriorated into florid alcohol addiction, his overall sexual performance progressively declined. For two or three years prior to treatment involvement Mr. R. was a maintenance drinker. From time to time the patient experienced erectile dysfunction. Prior to these experiences of erectile dysfunction, at the age of forty-three, the patient had not been impotent. For several months prior to being in treatment, Mr. R. was usually capable of becoming erect, but ejaculation occurred prior to vaginal entry. At that time the patient was unable to achieve another erection following one ejaculation. On several occasions Mr. R. suggested that he was "getting older" and that age must be responsible for his prematurity. Both Mr. and Mrs. R. were extremely anxious and unhappy with their sexual relationship when they entered therapy. The patient was no longer able to "treat" his prematurity via the method of heavy drinking. His wife was "fed up" with the drinking and the problem of premature ejaculation. Clearly, Mr. R. was anxious, depressed, guilty, and embarrassed about his prematurity. He believed that he had a "drinking problem" but denied being alcoholic.

Shortly after entering therapy Mr. R. decided to terminate his drinking. This decision was, at this point, obviously designed to deter Mrs. R.'s decision to leave the patient. After a few months of conjoint therapy the patient decided that the decision not to drink had to be his own and "for myself." The patient learned to discuss and deal with the issue of sexuality and human sexual behavior within the context of conjoint psychotherapy. After a number of conjoint therapy sessions, which were focused upon the drinking behavior of the patient and the marital relationship dynamics pertaining to the couple, the treatment emphasis shifted to the patient's problem of premature ejaculation. Following some ten hours of specific behavioral sex therapy training for prematurity, the patient was able to consistently engage in coitus without ejaculation for seven to ten minutes. The matter of prematurity and other sexual issues continued to be focal in the ongoing treatment process. The drinking behavior of the patient also continued to be a focal issue in therapy. Relationship conflicts between Mr. and Mrs. R. constitued the major area of therapeutic work during the final months of therapy. This couple was seen in weekly conjoint therapy for nine months.

This clinical case study demonstrates many of the sexual conflicts of the alcoholic. The patient was obviously a premature ejaculator prior to becoming an alcohol abuser. As the patient became progressively more alcohol dependent, the problem of prematurity was exacerbated. At the point of treatment engagement, the patient was alcoholic, intermittently impotent, and a consistent premature ejaculator. This patient had somewhat successfully utilized alcohol to deter his prematurity for many years prior to entering conjoint psychotherapy. The alcoholic very often learns to rely upon alcohol in order to cope with sexual conflicts. Eventually, "alcoholic problem solving" no longer works. Alcohol abuse and alcoholism are not effective or rational solutions for premature ejaculation.

As indicated in the first part of this chapter, faulty learning and conditioning experiences contribute greatly to the problems of sexual dysfunction. While it is unclear why the premature ejaculator has not learned to voluntarily control the orgasm reflex, it is apparent that a diversity of learning and conditioning factors contribute to this dysfunction. In this case, the early coital experiences of the patient were pathologic and perhaps frankly supportive for the development of premature ejaculation. Sexual relations with prostitutes, a wife that was castrative in the face of the patient's prematurity, and being "laughed at" as a result of this problem are all pathological social learning experiences, which in all probability reinforced this patient's sexual dysfunction.

Kaplan (1974) has speculated that the premature ejaculator has failed to acquire ejaculatory control because "he has not received, or, rather, not allowed himself to receive, the sensory feedback which is necessary to bring any reflex function under control." She points out that treatment techniques which rapidly and effectively bring orgasm under voluntary control have at least one common denominator: "they all foster the patient's perception of the erotic sensations that arise from his genitals during intense excitement, which automatically triggered the ejaculatory reflex in the past, and so teach him to exercise voluntary control over the reflex at this point." In this context, learning plays an important role in prematurity. However, learning encompasses the ability to self-regulate biological functions involving basic reflex discharges.

The alcoholic premature ejaculator is anxious and apprehensive about the issue of intimate sexual contact. Psychodynamically speaking, prematurity is a defense against sexual intimacy. As noted earlier, alcoholic males are often angry and enraged in their relationships with women. Certainly, a number of experiences of being laughed at and made fun of following premature ejaculation could be expected to foster feelings of anger and hostility. The experience of having a wife initiate a divorce or seek·out another lover as a result of one's prematurity would likewise create feelings of rage and anger. Pathologically, the alcoholic premature ejaculator controls his spouse or lover through the medium of prematurity. As humiliating, embarrassing, and depressing as prematurity may be, it is nevertheless a method whereby the spouse is controlled. Alcoholics are frequently afforded intermittent or secondary gain as a result of their prematurity.

It is important for the clinician and sex therapist to recognize that in the case of many alcoholics the ingestion of alcohol can, at least intermittently, deter premature ejaculation. As a central nervous system depressant, alcohol blocks the individual's perceptions and awareness of genital excitement and thus inhibits the ejaculatory reflex. This "blocking effect" is both physiological and psychological. Therefore, within the treatment relationship, the clinician must deal with the paradoxical and yet ultimately destructive aspects of the alcoholic's use of alcohol as a deterrent to premature ejaculation.

Basic Treatment Strategies

A primary goal in the treatment of premature ejaculation is obviously that of facilitating the patient's control of the ejaculatory reflex. Sex therapists utilize a variety of treatment techniques in order to accomplish this fundamental treatment goal (Masters and Johnson, 1970; Kaplan, 1974; Hartman and Fithian, 1974; Perelman, 1980; Vraa, 1982). The Cornell treatment program (Kaplan, 1974) assumes that an enhanced sensory feedback awareness of preorgastic arousal will result in patient ejaculatory continence. According to this model, the patient does not exert a special effort to control orgasm. Rather, the patient is taught and conditioned to repeatedly focus his attention on prolonged intense levels of sexual arousal and stimulation. Ejaculatory control follows. Other treatment models utilize the "stop-start" method, the "squeeze" technique, and an aggregate of other behavioral interventions.

The alcoholic premature ejaculator should be referred to a physician for a complete physical examination prior to the initiation of sex therapy. As indicated in the first part of this chapter, in some cases it is appropriate to refer the patient for neurological and/or psychiatric examination. Psychological testing can also be most helpful in determining the possible role of psychological and personality factors in the patient's prematurity. The spouse or lover of the patient should be seen for clinical evaluation and testing prior to beginning treatment.

During the initial treatment session an extensive review of the patient's history of prematurity is conducted. The patient's history of alcohol abuse, addiction, and drinking behavior is also discussed. It is very important for the clinician to stress the importance and role of sobriety in the effective treatment process. This point must be clearly delineated to both spouses. Sobriety is one of the most essential prerequisites to successful and effective clinical work with alcoholic premature ejaculators. Throughout the treatment process the patient is required to be abstinent from alcohol. Early in treatment the clinician attempts to establish a relationship between the patient's prematurity and pattern of drinking. In some cases, such a relationship does not appear to exist. In other cases, such as the one of Mr. R., it is quite obvious that the patient has long used and abused alcohol for the conscious purpose, among other purposes, of establishing ejaculatory continence or control. Consistently, such patients initiate sex therapy and treatment for their alcoholism when alcohol no longer "works." This simply means that the alcoholic premature ejaculator frequently enters therapy or is forced into some type of rehabilitation program when he has reached the point of being grossly dysfunctional. At this point, the patient is experiencing serious interpersonal, social, possibly medical and legal, sexual, and probably vocational difficulties that are directly related to his alcohol addiction. When the patient's sexual performance is being pathologically influenced by his alcoholism and when the patient verbalizes that he has utilized alcohol over the years as a deterrent to premature ejaculation, it is crucial for the clinician or sex therapist to point out that this procedure of "self-treatment" will no longer work. This position needs to be reinforced and considered throughout the treatment process.

Psychotherapy with the alcoholic patient involves an active exploration of alternative behaviors and alternative life-styles (Forrest, 1979c; Silverstein, 1980). The same can be said of the process and goal of sex therapy with the addicted premature ejaculator. Alcohol addiction is not an effective treatment regimen for prematurity.

The clinician or sex therapist attempts to explain the goals and objectives of the treatment process to the patient and his spouse in the initial hour or two of therapy. It is helpful to instill an optimistic expectancy set on the part of the patient and spouse. However, the clinician must be realistic in terms of conveying treatment outcome expectancies. The patient and his wife must be committed to the treatment process. In the experience of the author, effective resolution of the alcoholic's premature ejaculation can be expected to occur following ten to fifteen hours of weekly sex therapy and counseling. When working with the alcoholic premature ejaculator in conjoint therapy (Forrest, 1978), sex therapy for prematurity is very often only one phase of the overall treatment process. As suggested earlier, relationship conflicts and pathology tend to be associated with the prematurity and other sexual difficulties of the alcoholic couple. Resolution of the alcoholic's prematurity can facilitate the process of relationship change and growth. In some cases involving an alcoholic marital dyad, relationship change is the basic precursor to improved sexual functioning. For these reasons, it is very important for the clinician to be experienced and well trained in alcoholism as well as sexual counseling when working with alcoholic premature ejaculators.

It is recommended that the treatment of premature ejaculation be initiated after the alcoholic has been totally abstinent from alcohol for at least four to six months. It is clinically inappropriate to attempt treatment for this dysfunction while the alcoholic is drinking, going through detoxification, or immediately after having been detoxified. It is also generally recommended that the patient discontinue taking psychotropic medication and/or Antabuse prior to beginning therapy for premature ejaculation. This same clinical position is recommended for alcoholic patients entering therapy for impotence or retarded ejaculation. Psychotropic medication can clearly affect sexual performance and the sexual response. Antabuse may or may not physiologically inhibit or impair sexual performance, but some patients do report problems in the areas of impotence, premature ejaculation, and retarded ejaculation after beginning an Antabuse maintenance program (Knauert, 1979b).

After the initial sex therapy session, assuming that the treatment relationship has not previously included a specific focus on sexual functioning, the therapist teaches the couple either the "squeeze technique" (*see* Chapter 2) or the "stop-start" method. Both of these procedures work well in the treatment of prematurity. The training and experience of the clinician will dictate which particular treatment strategy is employed. The primary goal of therapy at this point is to teach the couple to engage in sexually stimulating behaviors, which simply bring the husband to erection. The wife or lover may manually or orally stimulate her partner to full erection. Prior to orgasm, the patient is instructed to tell his partner to stop all stimulating and erotic behaviors. When the orgastic sensation subsides, but prior to loss of erection, the patient asks his partner to again stimulate him. This procedure, referred to as the "stop-start" method, should be repeated a number of times (at least three or four times). The therapist should also instruct the patient to attend to his penile sensations while being stimulated by his partner. The patient is advised that he can be sexually "selfish" during this phase of treatment. He is not to be concerned with distracting thoughts, the behaviors of his wife, or other matters.

When the patient has successfully completed this procedure at least three times, the couple is instructed to continue erotic stimulation to orgasm. Prior to the stage of ejaculation, the therapist suggests to the patient that he need not worry about the matter of controlling his orgasm. By practicing the "squeeze technique" or the "stop-start" method, as discussed in this section, the patient quickly learns that he is able to establish ejaculatory continence. After practicing the "stop-start" method several times and subsequently continuing this procedure to orgasm on four or five occasions, the couple is told to proceed with vaginal intercourse. Attempts at coitus at this point do not involve a good deal of bodily movement. The wife or partner is told to assume a superior position and she is responsible for thrusting during this stage of treatment. The stop-start method is employed in the context of coitus. The patient is instructed to tell his partner to stop thrusting when he experiences the preorgastic level of stimulation. Upon reaching this level of arousal, both partners stop all sexually stimulating behavior. Thrusting is discontinued by the patient's partner. The penis remains inserted in the vagina until preorgastic sensation subsides. Active coitus is resumed when the level of preorgastic stimulation has fully terminated.

Successful coital experiences with the female in a superior position are the basis for attempting intercourse in other positions. The male superior position is mastered last, as it is usually most difficult for the male to control orgasm in this position. The couple may be instructed to complete intercourse while lying on their sides. Rear entry may be attempted. Other positions of mutual choice are eventually suggested by the clinician. As the patient achieves ejaculatory control in a growing variety of sexual positions, the couple is told to continue practicing the "stop-start" method from time to time in their sexual encounters. Following the termination of sex therapy, the couple will find it advantageous to continue practicing the stop-start technique on a monthly basis.

During the treatment process it is important for the sex therapist to consistently explore the wife's role in the ejaculatory dysfunction. Her feelings about sex and the patient, her beliefs and attitudes in these areas, and the totality of the marital relationship are grist for the treatment process. It is also clinically germane to integrate the topic of alcoholism and the patient's addiction in each of the previously mentioned contexts. The sex therapy treatment process is somewhat frustrating for some wives. The clinician can suggest that the couple work out an agreement whereby the patient will sexually stimulate the wife or partner to orgasm before or after he has ejaculated. Such an arrangement is based upon the assumption that the wife or partner is orgastic. Assuming that the wife is orgastic, the patient can utilize manual, oral or, perhaps mechanical techniques to meet the sexual and erotic needs of his spouse. In cases involving a preorgastic or otherwise sexually dysfunctional wife or partner the clinician will find it therapeutically efficacious to focus primarily upon the patient's premature ejaculation problem. When patient ejaculatory control has been consistently and satisfactorily established, the focus of treatment is shifted to the wife.

Frequently, in the treatment of alcoholic premature ejaculators, the spouse is angry and resentful about the patient's prematurity dysfunction. Many wives tend to feel that "it's his problem." Likewise, such wives often view the patient's alcohol addiction as "his problem." Severe marital and relationship conflicts are basic to most of these marriages. It has been the experience of the author that in marriages of this type, the problem of prematurity may be very successfully treated, but divorce or separation may well also occur following successful treatment. The alcoholic marriage tends to be conflicted in many areas (Forrest, 1975; 1982a). For these reasons, it is recommended that in most cases involving an alcoholic premature ejaculator specific sex therapy interventions should comprise but one phase in the ongoing treatment process. Clinicians working with the sexually dysfunctional alcoholic soon realize that conflicted sexuality is but a symptom of a conflicted relationship. More specifically, the alcoholic's problem of prematurity often involves a number of basic difficulties associated with the matter of male-female relationships. The spouse of the alcoholic (Forrest, 1982a) is consistently conflicted and disturbed in her relationships with males in general. Initially, the basic relationship disturbances of the alcoholic premature ejaculator and his spouse must be therapeutically resolved. Long-term resolution of prematurity is contingent upon this factor and sobriety. When these two criteria are achieved, it is realistic to expect a 75 to 80 percent success rate in the treatment of alcoholic premature ejaculators. Following successful treatment for prematurity, any further regressions into chronic intoxication can be expected to once again exacerbate the patient's premature ejaculation problem. In order to reduce the chances of such a regressive process, the therapist can suggest that the patient and his spouse involve themselves in intermittent long-term supportive psychotherapy or the Alcoholics Anonymous community.

Summary

Premature ejaculation has been defined and clinically described in this section. A number of etiological factors that contribute to prematurity have been considered. Two primary "types" of premature ejaculators were discussed. Alcohol addiction and alcohol abuse can create or contribute to the problem of prematurity. Many alcoholics have learned to utilize alcohol as an ejaculatory inhibiting agent. While the procedure of ingesting alcohol in order to inhibit the ejaculatory reflex may "work" for some alcoholics for a few months or years, eventually this methodology of "self-treatment" fails. A clinical case study that elucidates the various dynamics of alcoholism and premature ejaculation was presented. Strategies of sex therapy and psychotherapy with alcoholic premature ejaculators were discussed. Specifically, the "stop-start" method was outlined and explored as a strategy of intervention to be employed during the various stages of treatment for prematurity. The "squeeze" technique may also be utilized quite effectively in the treatment of this dysfunction (Perelman, 1980). As was indicated in the treatment of impotence, it is inappropriate to attempt to treat the prematurity of the alcoholic who is intoxicated or continuing to drink. The treatment of prematurity is initiated after the alcoholic has been totally abstinent for at least a number of months. Although not stressed in this section, it is important and helpful for the clinician to stress "holistic" health care in his or her treatment efforts with alcoholic patients.

It is suggested in this section that the treatment of prematurity is most successful when initiated as a specific phase of relationship psychotherapy. The alcoholic marriage is often diffusely pathognomonic and, thus, relationship changes involving other than merely sexual behavior and performance are essential to effective treatment. Therapists and clinicians who deal with alcoholic premature ejaculators require training and clinical skills in the areas of alcoholism and human sexuality. The wife of the alcoholic may perceive the patient's prematurity as "his problem." Such a stance is frequently associated with feelings of anger, resentment, and hostility. Sobriety, improved sexual functioning, and relationship modification and growth are the essential treatment goals in clinical work with the alcoholic premature ejaculator and his wife. Briefly, behaviorally oriented strategies of intervention are usually effective in the treatment of premature ejaculation. Abstinence and relationship change, in the case of the alcoholic premature ejaculator, require additional ongoing psychotherapy. Therapy for prematurity involves more than simple sex therapy interventions with the alcoholic patient.

RETARDED EJACULATION

Retarded ejaculation has been referred to as ejaculatory incompetence by Masters and Johnson (1966; 1970). Kaplan (1974) defines retarded ejaculation as a "specific inhibition of the ejaculatory reflex." In this condition, the patient retains his erectile capacity. The ability to ejaculate is impaired. Patients who experience retarded ejaculation respond to sexual stimulation by attaining erection. However, direct sexual stimulation is ineffective in facilitating the orgastic reflex. As Kaplan (1974) points out, this condition vividly demonstrates the biphasic nature of the male sexual response.

Many patients who suffer from retarded ejaculation have been unable to reach orgasm during intercourse and other varieties of direct sexual stimulation for many years. These individuals may be capable of engaging in coitus for more than an hour at a time without achieving orgasm. In some cases, the patient experiences retarded ejaculation only within the context of intercourse. Manual, oral, anal, or other varieties of sexual stimulation may result in appropriate or rapid ejaculation for such individuals. Some patients experience retarded ejaculation only when having intercourse with their wives or another particular woman. A rather consistent clinical observation of the author (Forrest, 1979d) is that alcoholic retarded ejaculators frequently rely upon masturbation following intercourse in order to reach orgasm. Obviously, the severity of this disorder varies greatly. Very rarely, patients do report having never experienced orgasm.

Kaplan (1974) places retarded ejaculators in two clinical categories: (1) "those who suffer from 'primary' retarded ejaculation, and (2) those whose retarded ejaculation is secondary. Primary retarded ejaculators date their awareness of this difficulty from their first attempt at sexual intercourse. While the great majority of patients in this category have never achieved orgasm during coitus, they are able to achieve extravaginal orgasm. In contrast, the patient who suffers from secondary retarded ejaculation enjoyed a period of good ejaculatory functioning before his problem began. Very commonly in such cases, retarded ejaculation has an acute onset after the patient experienced a specific trauma, such as being discovered in forbidden sexual behavior and/or being severely punished for sexual activity. In other cases, no specific precipitating event can be identified."

Kaplan also describes another variety of retarded ejaculation as "partial ejaculatory incompetence." In essence, partial ejaculatory incompetence occurs when the patient is sexually stimulated to firm erection and interested in sex. Following stimulation, the patient senses impending orgasm but then responds with an essentially nonpleasurable seepage of seminal fluid. Some patients describe this occurrence as "coming without knowing it." Masters and Johnson (1970) and Kaplan (1974) refer to this dysfunction as "split" ejaculatory retardation and suggest that possibly organic as well as psychological factors contribute to its aetiology.

Retarded ejaculation is rarely caused by physical or organic processes. Physical illness is infrequently associated with retarded ejaculation. However, diabetes that is untreated can relate to ejaculatory disturbance. Neurological disease affecting the ejaculatory apparatus can also impair ejaculation. Psychological and interpersonal factors consistently play an important role in the aetiology of retarded ejaculation. A diversity of psychological issues can be associated with the problem of retarded ejaculation. Castration fears, anger, marital discord, traumatic experiences such as the discovery of a wife's infidelity, and faulty learning factors can contribute to ejaculatory disturbances.

Masters and Johnson (1966; 1970) report that retarded ejaculation is a relatively rare form of sexual dysfunction. These authors found that only 17 of 510 couples treated for sexual dysfunction involved retarded ejaculation. Mild forms of this dysfunction may be highly prevalent according to other sex therapists (Kaplan, 1974; Apfelbaum, 1980; Vraa, 1982). This disorder is rather common among drinking alcoholics. Retarded ejaculation is a relatively rare variety of sexual dysfunction among patients who have terminated their drinking behavior (Forrest, 1980b).

Alcoholism and Retarded Ejaculation

As indicated in the first and second part of this chapter, alcohol-induced sexual dysfunction is relatively common. Akhtar (1977), in a research investigation of sexual disorders in males admitted to an alcoholism addiction treatment unit, reported definite sexual disorders in libido, the erectile apparatus, and the ejaculatory mechanism. In comparing the results of this investigation with the findings of Masters and Johnson (1970), Akhtar (1977) reported that the extent of ejaculatory incompetence was "strikingly smaller" in the Masters and Johnson study. According to Akhtar (1977), retarded ejaculation is but one of the many sexual dysfunctions that alcoholics experience as a result of chronic intoxication. Todd (1973) suggests that cirrhosis of the liver in the male alcoholic makes the elimination of female hormones impossible. Furthermore, this process results in a buildup of large amounts of female hormones causing breast enlargement, loss of muscle tone, a loss of body hair, and atrophy of the testicles. Todd (1973) indicates that problems with premature ejaculation, retarded ejaculation, and impotence are inevitable. It has been reported that the specific ability to ejaculate is most influenced by alcohol ingestion (Powell, Viamontes, and Brown, 1974). Alcohol ingestion inhibits the ejaculatory response. The physiological effect of alcohol on sexual performance includes retarded ejaculation (Williams, 1976). Intoxication and chronic alcohol ingestion physically affect the central nervous system and the ejaculatory reflex. The physical and physiological effects of intoxication upon the sexual behavior and sexual performance of the male alcoholic are both short-term and permanent (Lemere and Smith, 1973). Acute intoxication (Vraa, 1982) may result in ejaculatory inhibition.

In clinical practice (Forrest, 1978; 1980; Peters, 1979; Byers, 1979; Vraa, 1982) it is rather common to encounter alcoholic patients who report a history of ejaculatory inhibition subsequent to ingesting a number of alcoholic beverages. These patients tend to report that on many occasions, over the years, retarded ejaculation has been a problem. More specifically, such patients usually indicate that retarded ejaculation only occurs when they are grossly intoxicated or drinking heavily. Retarded ejaculation is a relatively rare variety of sexual dysfunction in the case of alcoholics who have been totally abstinent for several months or years. This clinical data clearly indicates that intoxication and heavy drinking inhibit the ability to ejaculate. When the intoxicated alcoholic experiences an inability to ejaculate, he may engage in any variety of sexual behavior in order to reach orgasm. Retarded ejaculation or a totally inhibited ability to ejaculate is frustrating as well as a source of fear and anxiety for the alcoholic. Wives of alcoholic retarded ejaculators sometimes learn to fear and disdain this form of sexual dysfunction. In response to his inability to reach orgasm, the intoxicated alcoholic may sexually abuse or physically harm his wife or partner. The wife of one alcoholic retarded ejaculator indicated that her husband, on one occasion, blamed her for his inability to ejaculate. She was told that her vagina was "too loose." Her intoxicated husband then forced her to perform oral sex on him for nearly an hour. When this variety of sexual behavior failed to produce an orgasm, the husband inserted his unlubricated and erect penis fully into her anus with one thrust. This episode resulted in the medical hospitalization of the patient's wife.

A total inability to ejaculate, in spite of being able to attain and maintain a firm erection, can be viewed as a form of impotence. Not surprisingly, a rather widespread myth regarding sexual performance is that the wife or partner of the alcoholic retarded or inhibited ejaculator is very sexually satisfied and happy with her sexual "state of affairs." In the clinical experience of the author, nothing could be further from the truth. The wife of the alcoholic retarded ejaculator tends to believe that she is somehow responsible for her husband's ejaculatory dysfunction. Aside from the physical abuse or discomfort that she may be forced to experience as a result of her husband's retarded ejaculation, the wife of the alcoholic retarded ejaculator often feels sexually inadequate. These wives perceive their husband's inability to ejaculate as a personal validation of impotence. The alcoholic retarded ejaculator may not feel impotent as a result of his ejaculatory inhibition. However, his wife may believe that she is totally inadequate in a sexual sense and thus "impotent" due to the ejaculatory problem of the alcoholic husband. Alcoholic retarded ejaculators consistently blame their wives or partners for their ejaculatory inhibitions. This situation contributes to the wife's feelings of sexual inadequacy and ultimately reinforces the patient's ejaculatory dysfunction. Severe and chronic sexual conflicts of this variety may result in primary impotence in the alcoholic and frigidity in the wife.

A few alcoholic retarded ejaculators report that early in their pathological drinking histories, they consciously drank in order to inhibit ejaculation. Some of these patients were premature ejaculators (*see* the first part of this chapter) prior to establishing a pattern of retarded ejaculation. The procedure of drinking in order to inhibit ejaculation sometimes proves generally effective for a number of years. Unfortunately, many alcoholic patients who in part drink for this reason eventually find themselves experiencing problems with retarded ejaculation or impotence. Alcoholism is a progressive disorder. In a congruous fashion, the sexual problems and dysfunctions of the alcoholic tend to become progressively more pathologic. It has been the clinical observation of the author that many alcoholics progress through three stages of alcohol-related and eventually alcohol-determined sexual dysfunction: (1) premature ejaculation and drinking in order to "control" prematurity, (2) alcohol-induced retarded ejaculation, and eventually (3) alcohol-determined impotence. Chronic alcohol addiction results in a progressively disturbed pattern of sexual functioning.

Retarded ejaculation is a common problem for drinking alcoholics. This disorder also occurs when the alcoholic has been abstinent from alcohol for a number of months or even following years of sobriety. The problem of retarded ejaculation following months or years of abstinence from alcohol, in the case of the alcoholic patient, can be quite difficult to treat (Forrest,

1980b). Relatively few alcoholic patients enter sex therapy under these circumstances. The following clinical case presentation demonstrates the problem of retarded ejaculation in the alcoholic patient who has achieved prolonged sobriety.

Case 4. Tom W., a thirty-two-year-old alcoholic, initiated therapy as a result of ejaculatory inhibition. At the time of treatment engagement, the patient had been totally abstinent from alcohol and all other mood altering chemicals for a period of nearly four years. Prior to these four years of abstinence, the patient had been a daily drinker and regular abuser of a wide variety of mood-altering drugs. Tom began his addiction career at the age of seventeen. At the age of twenty-six the patient married a woman who was some six years his elder. Mrs. W. had previously been married and had two children by her first husband. The marital relationship between Tom and his wife was stable and relatively conflict free. They were the parents of one child. The patient had adopted Mrs. W.'s two children. Tom had been successfully employed as a mid-level manager by a large corporation for about seven years. His wife was a student.

This couple was seen in conjoint therapy on six occasions. The patient had attended Alcoholics Anonymous several times a week for the duration of his sobriety. Mrs. W. was actively involved in Al-Anon. During the initial treatment session, Mrs. W. indicated that the couple decided to enter therapy as a result of her unhappiness with Tom's retarded ejaculation problem. As Mrs. W. put it, "I'm not putting myself through this anymore." According to both spouses, sexual intercourse was no longer a mutually stimulating and enjoyable experience. In order to ejaculate, Tom consistently "needed" to have intercourse for "an hour or so." Often, extended periods of coital and oral-genital activity failed to bring the patient to orgasm. In these situations Tom would ultimately retire to the bathroom and masturbate to orgasm. The patient and his wife were extremely frustrated and threatened by the retarded ejaculation problem. Tom stated that he felt "guilty" about being a retarded ejaculator and verbalized fear that his ejaculatory inhibition might be the physical result of alcohol and drug addiction. In a related manner, Mrs. W. expressed the belief that "maybe something is wrong with me—maybe Tom doesn't find me sexually stimulating and exciting." She was also quick to add that she had experienced this problem in her first marriage. Mrs. W.'s first husband had also been a retarded ejaculator. In her first marriage, Mrs. W.'s husband would regularly "force" her to have anal intercourse for extended intervals of time after he had failed to reach orgasm through genital and oral stimulation. Although Mrs. W. initially enjoyed her sexual relationship with this husband, she soon learned to dislike their sexual adjustment style. It was within this context that she stated "I'm not putting myself through this anymore."

The second treatment session with this couple centered around a discussion of masturbation. As married adults, both Mr. and Mrs. W. masturbated once or twice each week. Both believed that something was "wrong" about masturbating, particularly since they were "married." They also felt guilty about masturbating. As Tom put it, "I feel like hell about stroking the mule (meaning masturbating)—after all, I'm married, I've got children—I'm not a sixteen-year-old kid." Furthermore, Tom described himself as psychologically "sick" due to his need to masturbate. At this juncture, an important therapeutic intervention was simply that of assuring Tom and his wife that masturbation is an acceptable and appropriate expression of sexual behavior for adults within the context of marriage! The couple responded to this intervention by indicating that it was good to know they weren't "crazy" or "sex deviates." Likewise, both indicated that it was "good" to finally be able to talk about their "sexual problem" with a professional person.

At the beginning of the third conjoint therapy session Tom stated that his problem with retarded ejaculation had "gone away." The patient's wife agreed that each time they had engaged in coitus during the week Tom was able to have an orgasm within four to six minutes after vaginal penetration. While both partners were quite openly happy and enthusiastic about the patient's radically improved sexual functioning, both expressed a sense of disbelief that such improvement could occur so rapidly. At this point in the treatment process Mr. and Mrs. W. began to talk about a number of relationship dynamics, which they mutually felt contributed to Tom's problem of ejaculatory inhibition. Within this context, the issue of "control" was discussed at length. Although Tom denied having consciously thought of controlling his wife through the medium of retarded ejaculation, his wife asserted that she had considered this "psychological" possibility many, many times. The patient soon agreed that this "might" be true, stating "I can now see how my sex problem did control your feelings, even if I wasn't aware of this fact before." The couple again brought up the issue of masturbation. Both needed further reassurance that masturbation wasn't "abnormal" or deviant within the context of marriage. Mrs. W. openly expressed her feelings of frustration, guilt, and sexual inadequacy which were associated with Tom's inhibited ejaculation.

The remaining three treatment sessions substantiated the reality of Tom's enhanced sexual functioning. Tom shared with the therapist the feeling that Mrs. W. had "taught me everything I know about sex." The issue of Tom's alcohol and drug abuse history became a focal point in the treatment process. As a young adult Tom had experienced a number of sexual problems. Feelings of inadequacy, anxiety, and shyness made it difficult for him to approach women. Tom indicated that he was "afraid" of women during this developmental juncture. His initial attempts at intercourse were accompanied by problems of secondary impotence. However, Tom discovered that drinking or "doing drugs" enhanced his sexual performance. When intoxicated Tom was able to complete intercourse and sustain a full erection for "an hour or so at a time." He felt good about this for a number of years. During the initial months of marriage Tom's problem of ejaculatory inhibition was rarely a source of conflict. The couple assumed that with "more sobriety" Tom would no longer experience retarded ejaculation. After several months of avoiding this issue, Tom decided that "the problem was not going to go away, on its own." At this point, the couple decided to seek out professional help. In this case, therapy proved successful and relatively easy. During a six-month follow-up consultation, after treatment termination, the couple indicated that they had not experienced subsequent problems with retarded ejaculation.

This case study demonstrates a rather easy, quick, and successful treatment outcome. The patient's ejaculatory inhibition went into remission after only three conjoint therapy sessions. These sessions were limited to a treatment format involving traditional dynamically oriented psychotherapy. Specific sex therapy and behavioral therapy techniques were not utilized in the management of this case.

It is significant that this patient had been totally abstinent from alcohol and other drugs for a period of four years prior to entering therapy for his problem of retarded ejaculation. The patient had experienced other sexual performance problems and conflicts as an adolescent and young adult. His earliest attempts at intercourse, in the absence of chemical intoxication, resulted in impotence. Like so many alcoholic patients who enter therapy as a result of sexual dysfunction, the patient had learned to use alcohol as an agent to enhance his sexual performance. After drinking or ingesting other drugs the patient found that impotence was no longer a problem. Indeed, as the patient described it "I felt like some kind of sexual superman after getting drunk and having intercourse nonstop for an hour or two." Eventually, the patient developed a clear-cut retarded ejaculation problem. This dysfunction did not go into remission after the patient terminated his addiction career. Rather, the patient's retarded ejaculation problem soon became a serious issue which threatened the marital relationship. The patient's wife became emotionally conflicted as a result of the ejaculatory inhibition problem and seriously questioned her attractivelness, feminity, and ability to be sexually exciting and stimulating.

It is apparent that alcohol abuse and alcohol addiction can cause retarded ejaculation. However, as indicated with regard to the other male sexual dysfunctions, a combination of factors can facilitate the onset of retarded ejaculation. For these reasons, it is generally appropriate for the sex therapist or clinician to refer the patient who is experiencing retarded ejaculation to a physician for a complete medical examination prior to the initiation of sex therapy. It is a truism that few physical illnesses specifically cause ejaculatory inhibition. Diabetes that is undiagnosed and untreated can precipitate ejaculatory problems. Some of the psychotropic medications and antihypertensive drugs do impair ejaculation. These may be important factors for the therapist to consider in the case of alcoholic retarded ejaculators, as physicians often pre- scribe such medications to alcoholics. As indicated in cases of im- potence and premature ejaculation, neurological disease can play a pathologic role in the aetiology of ejaculatory dysfunction. Kap- lan (1974) indicates that the "tactile sensory perception of the penis, the antonomic nervous outflow, and the ejaculatory reflex centers in the spinal cord must all be intact for good ejaculatory functioning."

A plethora of psychological factors can be associated with re- tarded ejaculation. Psychodynamic and psychoanalytic theory speculates that the retarded ejaculator fears castration by the va- gina and thus experiences ejaculatory inhibition. Oedipal conflicts are seen as contributing to ejaculatory dysfunction by the psycho- analyst. In the clinical experience of the author, the alcoholic re- tarded ejaculator tends to be angry at his wife and, indeed, angry at women in general. Thus, ejaculatory inhibition, in the case of the alcoholic, can often be viewed as an expression of the patient's rage and anger toward women. Alcoholics are also afraid of losing control (Forrest, 1980d). Alcoholics attempt to rigidly control themselves, their wives, and their world. Paradoxically, the alco- holic is always diffusely out of control. The drinking behavior and alcoholic modus operandi of the addicted person is but one indi- cator of pathology in the realm of personal control. The alcoholic retarded ejaculator is afraid of "losing control" or "letting go" in his sexual encounters. Orgasm is an ultimate form of losing control and requires an ability to let go sexually. Guilt associated with sexual intercourse plays a role in the ejaculatory inhibition of some alcoholics. An "unfinished" or incomplete sex act, in the form of intercourse without orgasm, is irrationally interpreted as an exoneration from the "sin" of engaging in sexual intimacy by some alcoholic retarded ejaculators.

As indicated in earlier chapters, conditioning and learning experiences actively shape the sexual adjustment of the alcoholic. Very often the sexual experiences of the alcoholic retarded ejaculator have been pathological. An extended history of faulty learning experiences, which combine alcohol and sex, is central to the social history of most alcoholics. As has also been noted earlier, many alcoholics learn that they can in reality or fantasy directly improve their sexual performance through the medium of alcohol ingestion. These learning and conditioning experiences eventually prove faulty and reinforce further sexual dysfunction.

Basic Treatment Strategies

Most treatment strategies currently employed for the modification of retarded ejaculation are behavioral in approach. The alcoholic retarded ejaculator is a candidate for sex therapy after attaining total abstinence from alcohol. As in the case of alcoholics who are impotent or premature ejaculators, sex therapy with alcoholic retarded ejaculators should not be initiated until the patient has been sober for several months. Additionally, the alcoholic retarded ejaculator must be committed to total abstinence while undergoing sex therapy. It is appropriate to refer the alcoholic retarded ejaculator for a complete physical examination prior to beginning treatment.

In Chapters 2 and 3, it is indicated that alcoholic patients require "holistic" treatment. Treatment for retarded ejaculation, in the case of the alcoholic, is most efficaciously conducted after the patient has been treated for other medical complications and has established a proper nutritional diet, a regular exercise program, and sustained sobriety through a psychotherapy relationship or Alcoholics Anonymous. Sex therapy and sexual counseling are very often part of the holistic treatment that alcoholic patients require.

Initially, in the treatment of the alcoholic retarded ejaculator, the sex therapist actively reinforces the patient's existing ejaculatory capacity. During the early therapy sessions the patient is instructed to have sex via any variety of sexual behavior *except* genital intercourse. All this time, the patient is also told not to attempt to ejaculate during these sexual activities. The couple may engage in mutual masturbation, oral-genital stimulation or other forms of mutual sexual pleasuring. It can be helpful for the clinician to point out to the patient and his wife that stimulation of the wife to orgasm is permissible throughout the treatment process.

Following these instructions, which generally encompass the initial two to five treatment sessions, the patient is told to proceed to orgasm via these stimulating noncoital behaviors. The therapist needs to suggest to the patient that it is important to attempt to ejaculate in situations that are most apt to result in success. Some patients are inhibited and embarrassed about masturbating in the presence of their wives. Such individuals are instructed to proceed with masturbating in private when they feel stimulated to the point of being able to achieve ejaculation. With other patients, the wife is a welcomed participant in masturbation or oral-genital activities which lead to ejaculation.

Kaplan (1974) and Masters and Johnson (1970) indicate that ejaculation facilitated by the patient's spouse or partner is a paramount indicator of treatment progress in the therapy of retarded ejaculation. This general position is also germane to the treatment process of the alcoholic retarded ejaculator. When the alcoholic retarded ejaculator has reached the point of consistently being able to ejaculate via autoerotic and precoital sexual behaviors, he is instructed to proceed with stimulation by his wife or partner to ejaculation. The patient's wife may employ manual, oral, anal, verbal, or other erotic techniques to help stimulate the patient to ejaculation. It is helpful for the sex therapist and couple to openly discuss the particular sexual behaviors that the patient finds stimulating and arousing. Sexual imagery techniques can be employed by the patient, in adjunct to the stimulating sexual behaviors of the partner, to facilitate the ejaculatory response.

After a number of successful ejaculatory experiences involving stimulation by the wife or partner, the couple is instructed to engage in active penile stimulation in close proximity to the entrance. Kaplan (1974) suggests that the patient be stimulated to the point of impending orgasm by his wife and then proceed to vaginal penetration just prior to ejaculating. In the event that the patient fails to ejaculate utilizing this procedure he is told to withdraw his penis and the wife again orally or manually stimulates him to the stage of impending ejaculation. Vaginal insertion is again initiated at this point.

With practice the patient is soon able to penetrate the vagina prior to the point of impending ejaculation. The ability to then engage in sexual intercourse for several minutes and ejaculate in the vagina on a consistent basis is indicative of a resolution of the patient's retarded ejaculation (Apfelbaum, 1980).

As was indicated earlier in the chapter in the sections dealing with the treatment of impotent alcoholics and alcoholic premature ejaculators, it is important for the clinician to implement dynamically oriented psychotherapy in adjunct to specific sex therapy techniques. This is also applicable in the effective management of most alcoholic-retarded ejaculators. Anger, resentment, and other destructive affects are central to the adjustment style of the alcoholic and his wife. Power struggles and continuous relationship conflicts involving control are basic to the alcoholic marriage. Some alcoholics and their wives attempt to angrily control each other through tactics of manipulation and deception. These psychodynamically oriented conflicts are very often basic to the alcoholic's retarded ejaculation problem. Preconsciously, if not consciously, many alcoholic retarded ejaculators feel that they can control or "get even" with their wives by "holding back" sexually. In such cases, retarded ejaculation serves the explicit purposes of control and retaliation.

The problem of retarded ejaculation may also involve a number of sadomasochistic dimensions in the alcoholic marriage. The patient who must engage in intercourse for extended periods of time, perhaps as long as an hour or more, sometimes inflicts physical discomfort and pain upon his wife. Psychologically, the process of engaging in sexual intercourse for such extended time intervals is also sadomasochistic. Wives of alcoholic retarded ejaculators learn to disdain intercourse. The wife of one alcoholic retarded ejaculator stated that she felt as though her husband was trying to "kill her" when they had intercourse. Frequently, the alcoholic retarded ejaculator blames his wife for his ejaculatory inhibition. On several occasions one patient had told his wife that having intercourse with her was "like sticking my penis in a bucket of lard." Indeed, it is little wonder that the wives of many alcoholic retarded ejaculators tend to feel sexually inadequate, insecure, and inhibited. It is clearly apparent that the alcoholic retarded ejaculator sadomasochistically victimizes himself in transactions of this variety. As the patient blames and projectively attacks his wife, the sexual relationship further deteriorates. Thus, the alcoholic retarded ejaculator punishes himself as well as his wife. Anger and sadomasochism are often basic pathological ingredients in the sexual adjustment style of the alcoholic retarded ejaculator and his wife.

Behaviorally oriented sex therapy techniques are not clinically appropriate for the resolution of relationship conflicts of the types just discussed. The alcoholic retarded ejaculator most typically manifests serious psychological and relationship conflicts in addition to the problem of retarded ejaculation. Successful treatment of the alcoholic retarded ejaculator encompasses clinical interventions, which facilitate modified sexual performance, sobriety, relationship change, and psychological growth and integration. Sex therapists and clinicians involved in the treatment of alcoholics with sexual dysfunction problems must aim their treatment efforts at the total person. It is my belief (Forrest, 1978; 1980; 1982) that most alcoholics who seek out therapy for sexual dysfunction should be treated holistically. Alcoholics with impotence, premature ejaculation, and retarded ejaculation problems typically manifest a plethora of other problems that directly contribute to the specific sexual dysfunction. Clinicians who attempt to treat alcoholics with sexual dysfunction problems and sexual conflicts soon discover that these patients must be treated holistically.

Summary

Retarded ejaculation and the various psychological and physical factors that cause this sexual dysfunction were discussed in this section. The retarded ejaculator responds to sexual stimulation but experiences significant difficulty ejaculating. Primary- and secondary-retarded ejaculators were considered. Retarded ejaculation may be a relatively rare variety of sexual dysfunction. Chronic or acute alcohol ingestion can cause retarded ejaculation. A case study was included in this section in order to clearly demonstrate the association between retarded ejaculation and alcoholism. This interesting case study involved a nondrinking or "recovered" alcoholic who initiated sex therapy as a result of retarded ejaculation.

In this section, sex therapy techniques and strategies were elucidated for working with alcoholic retarded ejaculators. Sex therapy techniques and sexual counseling should always be conducted in accord with the specific needs of the patient. In many respects every alcoholic retarded ejaculator is different and unique. The clinician must continually be cognizant of these issues.

Abstinence from alcohol is a basic precursor to effective sex therapy with the alcoholic retarded ejaculator. Alcoholic retarded ejaculators should be totally abstinent from alcohol for a period of no less than four to six months prior to undertaking sex therapy and sexual counseling. In addition to being abstinent from alcohol the patient should be on a properly balanced diet, involved in a regular program of physical exercise, and involved in relationship psychotherapy or Alcoholics Anonymous prior to initiating treatment for retarded ejaculation. A thorough medical examination may be indicated for the alcoholic patient prior to beginning sex therapy for retarded ejaculation. Early in the treatment process the clinician actively reinforces the patient's existing ejaculatory capacity. Initially, the patient is instructed to engage in any variety of sexual behaviors except genital intercourse. During this stage of therapy the patient is supportively told not to attempt to ejaculate during these stimulating sexual interactions. After two to five days of successfully practicing these procedures, the patient is instructed to proceed to orgasm through noncoital sexual behavior. The patient's wife or partner is encouraged to actively stimulate the patient throughout the treatment process. However, genital intercourse is avoided early in treatment. The next stage of sex therapy for the alcoholic retarded ejaculator involves active penile stimulation in close proximity to the vaginal entrance. During this stage of therapy the wife stimulates the patient to the point of impending orgasm, in close proximity to her vagina, and then the patient completes vaginal penetration at the point of ejaculation. Eventually, the patient is able to enter the vagina prior to impending orgasm and ejaculates in the vagina following several minutes of genital intercourse (Apfelbaum, 1980).

The treatment format for retarded ejaculation discussed in this section is behaviorally oriented. In addition to this basic treatment format for alcoholic retarded ejaculators, the clinician will frequently find it therapeutically appropriate and efficacious to utilize sexual imagery training, cognitive restructuring, and relaxation therapy. As already indicated, dynamically oriented relationship psychotherapy can often be an integral part of successful sex therapy with the alcoholic retarded ejaculator. Marital and family relationships involving an alcoholic tend to be diffusely conflicted and pathological. In most cases, the clinician is confronted with the task of treating the alcoholic patient's sexual dysfunction in addition to his relationship and intrapsychic conflicts. Sex therapy with the male alcoholic is very often doomed to failure in the absence of a therapeutic resolution of the patient's basic intrapersonal and interpersonal psychopathology prior to the initiation of sexual counseling and treatment for sexual dysfunction. Alcoholics Anonymous can be a viable treatment adjunct for the global relationship pathology of some alcoholics who enter sex therapy due to retarded ejaculation.

Clearly, alcohol abuse and alcoholism facilitate and actively create a variety of male sexual dysfunctions. Impotence, premature ejaculation, and retarded ejaculation can be alcohol related or alcohol determined (Masters and Johnson, 1970; Lemere and Smith, 1973; Paredes, 1973; Kaplan, 1974; Akhtar, 1977; Vraa, 1978; 1982; Forrest, 1978; 1982). The treatment of alcoholic patients experiencing sexual dysfunction and sexual problems can be difficult and challenging. The issue of the patient's alcoholism or alcohol abuse is a primary clinical concern which the sex therapist must manage effectively as a part of the ongoing treatment process. Somewhat redundantly, the matter has been emphasized in each of the four sections considered in this chapter. The basic strategies of sex therapy discussed in each section will provide the clinician with a repertoire of treatment techniques for working with the sexually dysfunctional male alcoholic patient.

LOW SEXUAL DESIRE AND AROUSAL DYSFUNCTIONS

Psychotherapists have long recognized that human beings seem to differ with regard to desire for sexual relations and stimulation needed for sexual arousal. Freud (1962) asserted that the human sexual drive, or libido, is determined by body physiology, constitution, and heredity. Kinsey et al. (1948) believed that some individuals experience a diminished sexual desire because they "never were equipped to respond erotically." Therapists and sex researchers have also indicated that cultural, social, learning, conditioning and psychological factors can be related to low sexual desire and arousal problems.

Masters and Johnson (1970) discuss the problem of low sexual desire as it relates to women who "are rarely orgastic and usually are aware of little or no physical need for sexual expression." Masters and Johnson (1970) do not refer to the problems of low desire and arousal in males. Clinicians and sex therapists seem to have historically believed that gender differences between males and females result in a stronger "sex urge" in males. Kaplan (1974) notes that people have varying sexual urges and "cravings for sexual expression."

Kaplan (1977; 1979) refers to low sexual desire and arousal problems as "hypoactive sexual desire." According to Kaplan (1977), low desire disorders involve an impairment of the desire phase of the sexual response cycle. She indicates that the desire for sexual activity originates in the brain and is dependent upon testosterone. Thus, sexual desire is decreased by central nervous system depressants and testosterone or estrogen imbalance. Kaplan (1977; 1979) uses the following diagnostic categories of low sexual desire: (1) primary hypoactive sexual desire refers to a basic lack of sexual desire throughout the individual's life; (2) secondary hypoactive sexual desire refers to individuals who have previously experienced satisfactory sexual desire, but these persons have become uninterested in sex; (3) situational hypoactive sexual desire refers to persons who experience a lack of sexual desire and arousal in some situations, but not others; and (4) global hypoactive sexual desire refers to a current lack of sexual desire that is pervasive and not related to situational factors (stress, illness, etc.).

Low sexual desire and arousal problems quite simply refer to a lowered or decreased interest in sexual relations and difficulty becoming sexually aroused. The individual who is not desirous of having coitus or engaging in other sexual activities may also experience arousal difficulties. Such an individual may not become sexually aroused by erotic stimuli. It is difficult for such persons to become sexually aroused and/or sustain sexual arousal. Low sexual desire is essentially a diminished desire for sexual relations. Sexual arousal difficulties refer to the person's inability or difficulty in becoming and/or sustaining sexual arousal.

It is very difficult to clinically define low sexual desire and arousal deficit. Is frequency of sexual intercourse the basic criterion for diagnosing this dysfunction? Are there clinically significant differences associated with engaging in sexual relations on a weekly or monthly basis in contrast to a yearly basis? Obviously, these issues are related to diagnosing low sexual desire and arousal dysfunctions.

The Kinsey data (Kinsey et al., 1948; 1965) are somewhat helpful in evaluating low sexual desire from the perspective of the larger population. With regard to married women, it was found (Kinsey et al., 1965) that women are more sexually active after marriage. Yet, this increase in sexual activity steadily declined after the age of twenty. Over three-quarters of the male subjects in this study experienced sex between one and six times per week. However, nearly one-fourth of the sample either was extremely active in sexual outlets or extremely inactive. For example, one male averaged twenty or more ejaculations per week while another man had ejaculated only once in thirty years. Kinsey et al. (1948) identified nearly 200 males who manifested a low frequency of sexual outlet. These men were under thirty-six years of age. They experienced sexual outlet on an average of once in two weeks or less for a period of five years or more. There are no data (Kinsey et al., 1965) on female sexual outlet responding. The number of low outlet males increases after age thirty-five. Low sexual outlet tended to be associated with religious preference (Catholics and Orthodox Jews), less education, and late onset of first ejaculation. Kinsey et al. (1948) described low sexual outlet males as sexually "apathetic" and "inhibited."

LoPiccolo (1980) points out that data of this type may not be a valid measure of sexual desire. Frequency of sexual behavior may not be a measure of desire. Specific norms for sexual responding are not often available. These norms must take into account a variety of factors such as age, race, geographical location, socioeconomic class, religion, and specific sexual activity (coitus, masturbation, oral sex, etc.).

In a recent investigation of non-emotionally disturbed couples (Frank, Anderson and Rubinstein, 1978), it was found that 35 percent of the wives and 16 percent of the husbands complained of "disinterest" in sex. Over one-fourth of the women and 10 percent of the men experienced being "turned off" by sex. One-third of these couples engaged in sexual intercourse two to three times each month or less. LoPiccolo (1980) reports that 63 percent of men and 37 percent of women in therapy for sexual dysfunction indicated that low sexual desire is a problem. It is suggested (LoPiccolo, 1980) that low sexual desire is often associated with (1) depression, (2) Catholicism, (3) sexual dysfunction, (4) aversion to oral-genital sex, (5) aversion to female genitals, (6) masturbation conflicts, and (7) marital problems. Kaplan (1977) indicates that these patients tend to be psychologically injured, vulnerable, and rigidly defensive.

Perhaps the most pragmatic approach to the diagnosis of desire and arousal dysfunctions involves the belief and feelings of the couple relative to their sexual adjustment style. In some cases, both spouses indicate that they are dissatisfied with the frequency of sex in their marital relationship. More commonly, one partner is quite dissatisfied with the frequency of sexual relations experienced within the marital relationship. The other partner may feel that the quantity of sexual expression in the marriage is satisfactory or even too frequent. One spouse may identify the other as "not interested in sex." Both partners may agree that low desire is a sexual problem in their marital relationship. Severe marital and sexual conflicts can be associated with the consistent pattern of one spouse desiring seuxal relations and the other "refusing" or not being interested in sex.

Clinicians and sex therapists must evaluate each case of low desire and arousal on an individual basis. A lack of sound research data and clinical expertise in these areas often makes it difficult accurately to diagnose and properly treat these couples. With the sexual "enlightenment" of the past two decades many people have developed unrealistic expectations in the realms of sexual desire and performance. A few patient's believe that "something is wrong" if they are not desirous of sexual relations four or five times each week. Some women feel they are sexually inadequate if they fail to reach orgasm on every occasion of coitus or sexual relations. In sum, a patient's or couple's complaint of low desire or low arousal may or may not be clinically valid. The sex therapist must be aware of these variables as he or she attempts to evaluate and treat problems of low desire and arousal.

LoPiccolo (1980) and LoPiccolo and Heiman (1978) provide a number of excellent criteria for the diagnosis and assessment of the low desire and low arousal dysfunctions. Problems of low desire and arousal (LoPiccolo, 1980) should be evaluated in terms of (1) the couple's and individual's actual sexual behavior (frequency of coitus, oral sex, masturbation, etc.), (2) the couple's and individual's desired frequency of engaging in various sexual behaviors, (3) emotional and physiological response to sexual stimulation, (4) psychophysiological functioning, to include the effects of alcohol, drugs, illness, and stress, (5) neuroendocrine/hormonal components of sexual functioning (testosterone, estrogen, diabetes and thyroid workups), (6) psychological variables (anxiety, depression and overall personality assessment), and (7) marital satisfaction and marital relationship factors.

There are a number of clinically relevant differences between sexual desire and sexual arousal. In general terms, desire refers to the frequency with which a person wants to have sexual relations. Arousal refers to the extent to which a person becomes sexually excited and stimulated. A plethora of physiological and psychological variables is associated with sexual arousal. Arousal can be measured physiologically. Heartbeat, blood pressure, GSR and pulse are indicators of physiological arousal. Psychological data and self-reports can also be used to assess arousal. Many aspects of sexual arousal remain subjective. Psychological and physiological indicators of sexual arousal can really be reflections of anxiety or anger! It should also be noted that physiological and psychological indicators of sexual arousal, i.e. erections and vaginal swelling and lubrication, sometimes occur in the absence of sexual feelings (Zilbergeld, 1978). Thus, it may be difficult for the clinician accurately to assess problems of arousal. Nonetheless, the seven evaluation criteria outlined in the previous paragraph can be very helpful in the assessment of arousal problems. Arousal problems are most commonly seen in combination with marital relationship conflicts and sexual dysfunction problems.

The aetiology of low sexual desire and arousal dysfunctions appears to be multifaceted. As touched upon earlier, biological, constitutional, genetic, and physiological factors may be related to desire and arousal problems (Kinsey et al., 1948; Freud, 1962; Masters and Johnson, 1966, 1970). Research (Carney, Bancroft, and Mathews, 1977) suggests that the androgens play an important role in facilitating sexual responsiveness in men and women. Yet, as LoPiccolo (1980) states, "there is relatively little that can be said with certainty about the relationship between the levels of the various hormones and the level of sexual desire."

A diversity of psychological factors is associated with desire and arousal dysfunctions. Anxiety is a primary ingredient in most, if not all, human sexual dysfunctions. Anxiety can cause problems of sexual desire and arousal. Indeed, the intensely anxious individual experiences low sexual desire and marital difficulties in the realm of becoming adequately aroused. Performance anxiety is also related to desire and arousal problems. Depression results in a decreased interest in sexual relations (Lobitz and Lobitz, 1978). Moderate to severe depression in males frequently causes decreased desire for sex and an inability to become aroused. Guilt, marital conflicts, power and control issues, and fears of sexuality and intimacy can also be associated with disorders of desire and arousal.

Learning and conditioning variables can contribute to the development and maintenance of low desire and arousal dysfunctions. Faulty learning may begin within the patient's family of origin. As children, many sexually dysfunctional patient's have been told that sex is evil or "dirty," masturbation will result in mental illness, and coitus should only take place when procreation is desired. Many parents avoid discussing issues associated with human sexuality in the presence of their children. Some parents tell their daughters that all boys are "animals" and "out to get one thing." The warped and parataxic nature of messages such as these can be devastating to the sexual adjustment of children and adolescents. Pathological learning, conditioning, reinforcement, and overlearning can create and maintain low desire and arousal dysfunctions. It is only rational to expect adults who have been taught to deny their sexual urges and feelings to be uninterested in sexual relations. These people will also experience difficulty becoming sexually "turned on" and aroused.

Pathologic social learning and conditioning experiences precipitate the development of irrational beliefs, thoughts, and value systems pertaining to sexual behavior. Some patients believe that they "should not" desire sex on a regular basis. They feel guilty or psychologically upset about becoming sexually aroused. Furthermore, distorted beliefs and irrational self-dialogue can alter the person's awareness and perceptions of the physical experience of sex (Heiman and Morokoff, 1977). In turn, a vicious circle is created whereby current perceptions and cognitions of the physical experiences of sexual desire and arousal distort and alter future sexual expectations, cognitions, and belief systems! In sum, myriad social, familial, psychological, physical, and situational variables can contribute to the development and maintenance of the desire and arousal dysfunctions.

Alcoholism, Low Sexual Desire and Arousal Dysfunctions

Much of the research and clinical literature dealing with alcoholism, alcohol abuse, and sexual behavior seems to focus upon problems associated with alcohol-facilitated sexual acting-out and promiscuity (Clinebell, 1956; Blum and Blum, 1969; Williams, 1976; Forrest, 1978, 1982). However, alcoholism researchers and clinicians (Levine, 1955; Blane, 1968; Wilson and Lawson, 1976; Vraa, 1982) have also clearly indicated that alcohol addiction and alcohol abuse result in a diminished interest in heterosexual relationships and a loss of interest in sexual relations. Male sexual arousal, as indicated by penile size, duration of erection, and ejaculatory competence, is generally diminshed following alcohol ingestion (Farkas and Rosen, 1975; Briddell and Wilson, 1976; Rubin and Henson, 1975; Vraa, 1982). These issues have been discussed in the earlier sections of this chapter. Unfortunately, precise research investigations have not been conducted that indicate the percentage of alcoholics and problem drinkers who experience problems of desire and arousal. In fact, very little has been written about problems of desire and arousal in alcoholics and problem drinkers.

It can realistically be said that "what alcohol giveth, alcohol taketh away." During the early and middle stages of the addiction process (Forrest, 1978), the alcoholic often manifests "pseudo-hypersexuality." At these junctures in the developmental process of alcohol addiction, the alcoholic may appear to be a hypersexual person. Promiscuity, sexual acting-out, and an apparent absence of sexual dysfunction characterize the sexual adjustment style of many alcoholic persons who have not reached the later stages of the addiction process. As these individuals begin to progress into the later stages of alcoholism, they invariably begin to manifest florid problems of desire and arousal. Intoxication and heavy drinking may well mask the sexual problems and dysfunctions of many alcoholics during the earlier stages of alcoholism. Most alcoholic persons manifest florid sexual dysfunction in the stage of chronic alcoholism (Forrest, 1978).

There are exceptions to these clinical observations regarding the process of alcohol addiction and sexual dysfunction. Some alcoholics and problem drinkers experience marked desire and arousal dysfunction very early in their drinking careers or even prior to the onset of pathological drinking. It is important to point out that both male and female alcoholics and problem drinkers experience desire and arousal dysfunctions. Women alcoholics seem to manifest desire and arousal dysfunctions much sooner in their alcoholic careers than their male alcoholic counterparts. Acute intoxication may render the male alcoholic physically incapable of sexual arousal. This situation can also apply to the woman alcoholic.

Alcoholism can be viewed as "a marriage to the bottle." The alcoholic is literally "in love" with alcohol and the bottle. Alcoholism is also an erotic experience (Forrest, 1978; 1982a). In many respects, alcoholism and problem drinking are highly eroticized patterns of adjustment. As the addicted person becomes progressively more dependent upon alcohol he or she tends to become progressively less interested in coitus and sexual relations. As a result of the physiological and psychological consequences of chronic intoxication, the alcoholic is progressively less able to become sexually aroused. Eventually, the alcoholic is unable to function sexually. Sex and eroticism via intoxication and the bottle becomes a neurotic compensation for sexual desire and arousal deficits. In actuality, alcohol dependence is a defense against sexual desire, arousal, and intimacy.

The spouse of the alcoholic may very often manifest problems of low desire and arousal. A diversity of psychological and relationship factors contributes to the spouse's lack of interest in sex and arousal deficit. Some of these individuals, particularly wives, have been verbally and physically abused by the alcoholic. Alcoholic husbands may have raped or sexually abused their spouses on many occasions. The nonaddicted spouse rationally learns to be disinterested and nonaroused by the alcoholic behaviors, smells, and inadequate or inappropriate sexual advances of the addicted partner. These couples often do not "practice" effective patterns of sexual interaction. They tend to lose sexual interest in each other and do not find the other spouse to be sexually arousing and stimulating. The alcoholic may urinate, deficate, or throw-up on the nonaddicted spouse while they are sleeping together. In short, there is a plethora of sexual learning and conditioning experiences that may quite understandably contribute to the nonaddicted spouse's problems of low sexual desire and arousal.

When the alcoholic has finally established sobriety and the couple enters conjoint therapy or sex therapy, it is rather common for both spouses to be experiencing low sexual desire and arousal dysfunctions. In these situations, extended marital therapy is appropriately initiated. It can also be rather surprising to discover that the nonaddicted spouse has continued, perhaps for many years, to be desirous of having more frequent sex with the alcoholic spouse. These spouses tend to be easily aroused and do not report arousal problems. However, they are often quick to indicate that they do not find their drunken spouse sexually arousing and stimulating. They do not wish to have more frequent sexual relations with an intoxicated spouse!

The case of Roy Q. demonstrates how problems of low sexual desire and arousal are associated with chronic alcoholism. Although the patient's wife was never seen in treatment, she was identified by the patient as an alcoholic. It was apparent that she also manifested low sexual desire and arousal dysfunction.

Case 5. Roy Q., a forty-seven-year-old insurance executive, entered individual psychotherapy as a result of marital problems and "having too many drinks." The patient had been married for twenty-six years and was the father of two children. He was a very wealthy and successful insurance executive.

In the initial therapy hour, Roy stated, "I'm sick and tired of my wife dinging off the walls." The patient also felt that he was drinking too much. Each night he consumed "four or five" double martinis. He had been drinking several drinks daily for a period of fifteen years. When asked about his current sexual relationship with his wife, Roy simply replied by stating, "what sexual relationship?" During this session, Roy also indicated that his wife was an alcoholic. She had received residential treatment for alcoholism some six months earlier and was actively attending Alcoholics Anonymous. The patient's wife had been totally abstinent from alcohol since entering residential treatment.

The patient had grown up in a large, metropolitan city in the Midwest. His parents were divorced when he was six years old. The patient and his older sister grew up with their biologic mother. She remarried when the patient was eleven. The patient's mother had repeatedly indicated that his father was a "damned drunk." After graduating from high school Roy joined the Army. He did not date in high school and described himself as "insecure and uncomfortable with girls" at this time in his life. The patient was not sexually active while in the military. He was very "religious" and had attended the Catholic church weekly since early childhood. The patient indicated that he had been "picked on" by his high school peers and military peers. After getting out of the service, Roy held several sales positions. Within two years of the time he left the service he entered the insurance field. In a very short time, Roy became a very successful salesman. Roy met his wife during the course of his first sales position. She was one of the company secretaries. Initially, she refused to date the patient. Roy had persisted in asking his wife to go out for dinner for nearly six months before she finally accepted. During this time, she referred to Roy as a "dip." After a few months of dating they were married.

The patient described the early years of his marriage as being relatively conflict free. During the fourth individual therapy session, Roy told the therapist that the major "thing" he would like to have been able to have changed over the past ten years of his marriage was his "sex life." He then told the therapist that he had not engaged in any form of sexual activity for ten years. He denied having engaged in coitus, oral sex, masturbation, etc. with his wife or any other woman for a period of ten years. The patient seemed to be very sad as he discussed these matters with the therapist. During the fifth therapy session, Roy recalled that eight or nine years earlier he, in fact, had picked up a prostitute at a sales convention being held in a large eastern city. She had performed fellatio on him. The patient felt extremely guilty about this episode when it occurred and he had continued to feel guilty about this incident for ten years!

During his early years in the sales profession, the patient had developed the "habit" of having "one or two" mixed drinks with his lunch. Quite often, these drinks were a part of having "business" lunches with clients and colleagues. The patient would then have several drinks before, with, and after his evening meal. His wife only drank in the evenings for many years and did not drink alcoholically until the latter "eight or ten" years of the marriage. It was clinically significant that the patient recalled that the onset of his wife's pathological drinking corresponded with the termination of their sexual activities. Early in the marriage, there were no significant sexual problems. The patient indicated that he and his wife engaged in coitus and a variety of other sexual behaviors "at least once or twice a week" during the first ten years of marriage.

The patient's wife apparently progressed from a routine of regular "social" drinking to florid alcohol dependence in a matter of months. Between the tenth and eleventh years of their marriage, Roy would come home three or four evenings a week and find his wife acutely intoxicated and stuporous. Roy began to drink more heavily at this time. The marital relationship deteriorated. The couple began to argue and fight almost every evening. They began sleeping in separate bedrooms. Their children avoided Mr. and Mrs. Q. as much as possible. The children did not bring friends and playmates to the Q. home. Upon graduating from high school, both children went away to college and returned home for short visits only once or twice each year. This pattern of drinking, marital and family living persisted until Mrs. Q. entered an alcoholic treatment center some nine years later. In spite of these various conflicts and difficulties, Mr. Q. managed to earn well over 100,000 dollars each year in his sales profession.

Roy indicated that he and his wife had not even "talked" about sex in several years. The topic of sex seemed to be a verboten issue between Mr. and Mrs. Q. Over the years, Roy had thought a great deal about sex and fantasized about having sexual relations with his wife and other women. He believed that masturbation was "wrong and somehow sinful" and therefore struggled against his masturbation impulses and desires. He believed that extramarital affairs were sinful. His severe guilt feelings associated with one extramarital sexual encounter validated his feelings and beliefs about the "evil" nature of extramarital sex! In short, Mr. and Mrs. Q. had repressed their sexual impulses, feelings, and needs for nearly ten years. Apparently, neither spouse felt any real desire to have sex. The patient had not experienced sexual arousal in several years. The couple had not experienced sexual relations with each other or with extramarital partners for many years.

At the point of treatment engagement, the patient was determined to stop drinking. He began taking Antabuse. The initial ten therapy sessions were devoted to exploring the patient's resentful, angry feelings toward his wife and their avoidance of sex. At this point, they were unable to watch television in the same room for any longer than an hour without becoming involved in an argument. The therapist suggested conjoint therapy to Mr. Q. on several occasions. When the patient attempted to discuss this matter with his wife, he met with refusal on her part. She indicated that she had "her own recovery program and didn't need a damned shrink." However, as the patient continued to be sober, the marital relationship slowly began to improve. The couple began to watch television together, and they occasionally began to go out for dinner together. They began to talk to each other. The frequency of marital arguments and "shouting matches" began to lessen.

Roy indicated to the therapist that he wanted to start having sexual relations with his wife. He began a regular exercise program, stopped smoking, and started eating well-balanced meals. After about three months of holistic treatment, the patient began to have morning erections. The therapist suggested to Roy that he begin to discuss openly his sexual feelings and desires with his wife. This was a most difficult task for the patient. His initial attempts at discussing sexual issues with his wife were unsuccessful. Nevertheless, Roy persisted in his attempts to express verbally to his wife that he was desirous of having sexual relations. When the issue of sex was brought up, both spouses reacted by blaming the other for their sexual problems and lack of sexual activity. With direct suggestion, encouragement, and support, the patient was soon able to stop blaming his wife and simply listen to her angry, blaming verbalizations.

After eighteen individual therapy sessions, Roy and his wife went on a five week trip to Germany to visit their daughter. The patient was smiling and elated at his first therapy session after returning from Germany. He reported to the therapist that he and his wife had engaged in intercourse for the first time in ten years! Moreover, they had been having sex "two or three times" each week. Their initial attempts at coitus had been difficult. Roy experienced both erection and ejaculatory problems. His wife was anxious and did not lubricate adequately. Yet, as they continued to have sexual relations, their sexual dysfunctions improved.

This patient continued to be seen in outpatient psychotherapy for over one year. Presently, the patient has been totally abstinent from alcohol for over three years. The marital relationship continues to be radically improved. Follow-up data at eighteen months after therapy termination indicated that the couple was engaging in sexual intercourse and other sexual activities "once or twice" each week. The patient's low desire and arousal dysfunctions were resolved.

This case study of low sexual desire and arousal dysfunction in the alcoholic is typical. Many alcoholics and problem drinkers suffer with problems of low sexual desire and arousal. The patient's wife, also an alcoholic, seemed to manifest low sexual desire. This couple had not engaged in any sexual activity for a period of ten years. Both spouses had been drinking alcoholically for nearly ten years. Once the patient entered psychotherapy, the issues of low sexual desire and sexual abstinence within the marital relationship became focal issues in the treatment process. The patient had thought about having sex, fantasized about sexual relations, and even desired sex for several years. Yet, he had been unable to discuss these thoughts, feelings, and desires with his wife. The patient had not experienced intense sexual arousal in years.

Treatment proved globally successful in this case. The patient completely terminated all drinking. He initiated a number of positive health and behavioral changes in other areas of his life. After several weeks of therapy and sobriety, the patient began to be aware of feelings of sexual arousal. With a good deal of therapist support and encouragement, the patient was soon able to communicate to his wife that he was desirous of having sexual relations. Eventually, the couple was able to resume an active and rewarding sexual adjustment. Follow-up indicates that the couple has continued to be sober and sexually active.

Basic Treatment Strategies

The physiological and psychological effects of chronic alcohol addiction and acute intoxication include low sexual desire and arousal dysfunctions. Alcoholism and problem drinking are very often the direct causes of desire and arousal dysfunctions in both men and women. It should be pointed out that low sexual desire and arousal dysfunction is not a predominately male disorder. Male and female alcoholics experience desire and arousal problems.

It is essential for the alcoholic or alcohol abuser who manifests low sexual desire and/or arousal dysfunctions to be totally abstinent from alcohol for at least four to six months prior to beginning sex therapy. In many of these cases, extended individual and/or conjoint therapy is a prerequisite to effective sex therapy. As indicated in earlier sections of this chapter, it is clinically inappropriate to begin sex therapy with alcoholic or problem drinking patients who are still drinking, being detoxified, or receiving inpatient treatment for alcoholism.

Low sexual desire and arousal dysfunctions can also be related to the overall life-style adjustment of the alcohol abusing person. Many of these patients are in very poor physical health. They do not eat regularly. They eat improperly balanced diets. Their sleep patterns tend to be disturbed. They do not exercise on a regular basis. As such, many of these patients are chronically anxious, depressed, or stressed (Della-Giustina, Brooks and Forrest, 1978; Della-Giustina and Forrest, 1979). For these reasons, the sexually dysfunctional alcoholic patient is in need of holistic treatment.

Very early in the treatment process, the clinician must point out to these patients that their drinking behavior is diminishing their desire for sexual relations and impairing their ability to become sexually aroused. Indeed, it is irrational for the drinking alcoholic to expect to be able to become properly aroused. Chronic alcoholic patients lose their desire for sexual relations. These factors form a physical basis for low desire and arousal dysfunctions. The addiction process and alcohol ingestion constitute a physical basis for low sexual desire and arousal dysfunctions in the alcoholic and alcohol abuser. As touched upon earlier, the physical basis of desire and arousal dysfunctions in alcoholics may also include nutrition, exercise, and other general health maintenance factors. The therapist must also realize that hormonal deficits (LoPiccolo, 1980) may be associated with the patient's low desire and/or arousal dysfunction. This factor is an important reason for referring the patient to a physician for a complete medical evaluation prior to beginning sex therapy. Many, if not most, alcoholic patients who manifest sexual dysfunction should be referred for a complete medical workup before sex therapy is initiated.

Depression and anxiety are frequently key ingredients in problems of low desire and arousal. The therapist needs to accurately assess the overall and current affective adjustment style of the alcoholic patient with low desire and/or arousal dysfunction. As a group, alcoholic persons tend to experience chronic anxiety, depression of an endogenous nature, and general affective disturbance (Forrest, 1978; 1979b; 1980a; 1982). These individuals behave in a neurotic manner that actually fosters depression, anxiety, guilt, and confusion. Obviously, affective disturbance is but one physical and psychological "side effect" of chronic alcohol addiction or even acute intoxication. The therapist must begin to help the patient understand and modify his or her irrational patterns of self-defeating behavior (Ellis, 1979). Alcoholic and problem drinking patients can be taught to stop making themselves drug dependent, anxious, depressed, guilty, sexually dysfunctional, and generally conflicted! Alcoholic women are especially prone to affective disturbance, which in turn can be related to low sexual desire and arousal dysfunctions. Relationship psychotherapy and behavioral sex therapy, rather than psychotropic medication, are usually the treatments of choice for alcoholic and/or problem drinking patients who manifest desire and arousal problems.

Low sexual desire and arousal dysfunction in alcoholic and/or problem drinking persons is almost always associated with marital relationship conflict. The alcoholic marriage is pervasively conflicted (Paolino and McCrady, 1977; Forrest, 1978; 1979b; 1982a). Patterns of relating, communicating, and emoting are distorted in these families. Low desire and arousal problems constitute a relationship pattern that involves relating, communicating, and emoting. Low desire and arousal dysfunctions can be viewed as defenses against relationship and sexual intimacy. These dysfunctions also involve marital relationship issues pertaining to control, dominance, power, and independence/dependence. Although both spouses in the alcoholic marriage tend to be angry and resentful, it is often the partner who manifests low sexual desire and/or arousal dysfunction who is explosive, enraged, and hostile. Whenever marital rape or other forms of sexual abuse and assault have occurred in the alcoholic marriage and/or alcoholic family system, sexual problems and dysfunction can be expected to occur in most, if not all, of the family members.

The children of alcoholics experience problems of desire and arousal. The therapist needs to be well aware of all of these relationship issues in his or her clinical work with alcoholic persons manifesting low sexual desire and/or arousal dysfunction. In some cases of low desire and/or arousal dysfunction, extended conjoint therapy is a precursor to sex therapy. In other cases, the clinician will need to deal with the relationship conflicts and pathology of the couple as a part of the ongoing sex therapy process.

Quite commonly, the alcoholic who voluntarily enters outpatient sex therapy for low sexual desire and/or arousal dysfunction has been totally abstinent from alcohol for several years. Many of these patients are active in Alcoholics Anonymous. Some have been in psychotherapy before. Their marital relationships may not be severely conflicted, and the nonaddicted spouse in these marriages may be eager to begin conjoint sex therapy. Therapy is usually effective in these cases, and it is realistic to expect the treatment process to involve ten to fifteen sessions. The patient who reports a history of low desire and/or arousal dysfunction prior to the onset of heavy drinking does not present such a favorable treatment prognosis. Typically, such patients describe themselves as having never been "all that interested, or turned on by sex." In cases involving long-term sexual repression and chronic desire and/or arousal dysfunction, the therapist can expect less favorable treatment outcomes. It is also realistic for the clinician to expect the therapy process to be more dynamically oriented and, thus, far more lengthy.

When the alcoholic patient has been sober for several months or years, the marital relationship is not grossly dysfunctional, and the patient and/or couple has not experienced desire and/or arousal dysfunction since early adolescence, the clinician can begin the therapy process by exploring the patient's (couple's) basic beliefs and attitudes regarding human sexuality. Most of these couples are in need of basic sex information and education. They often believe that all sexual feelings, desires, and urges are evil and somehow "wrong." Many have been taught that masturbation, oral sex, anal sex, and other varieties of human sexual behavior are deviant or sinful. These patients struggle with cognitions, beliefs, and impulses, which, in effect, tell them to engage in many forms of sexual behavior. Most of these patients and their spouses feel guilty and anxious about their sexual impulses and desires. The therapist must challenge and dispute (Ellis, 1979; 1980) the irrational sexual beliefs of the patient. The therapist must also provide the couple with a wealth of sex education information. These interventions need to be accomplished with a good deal of therapist support and encouragement. Some of these patients and their spouses simply need to be given therapist permission to experience sexual desire and arousal.

It is essential that the sex therapist help the couple begin to engage in more stimulating and arousing sexual behaviors. This essential treatment task can be accomplished through the use of various sex therapy techniques. The therapist may encourage the patient and spouse to begin an active program of masturbation. Nondemanding pleasuring is a good procedure for the couple to begin practicing. Massages, rub-downs and nongenital caressing are helpful procedures for the couple to practice between early therapy sessions. Body awareness exercises, genital exploration, "letting go" exercises, imagery training, and improving the actual sexual techniques of the couple are also methods for enhancing levels of sexual desire and arousal.

Desire and arousal demands by the nondysfunctional spouse must be extinguished. In essence, these are issues that are associated with performance demands. Rather commonly, low sexual desire and arousal dysfunctions in the alcoholic are related to or associated with another sexual dysfunction. Alcoholic patients sometimes become disinterested in coitus and other sexual activities after an extended history of premature ejaculation, orgastic dysfunction, or some other form of dysfunction. Thus, problems of desire and arousal may be defenses against another dysfunction. The patient attempts to maintain his or her self-esteem and sense of sexual adequacy by avoiding intercourse and sexual intimacy. In such cases, the therapist will initially be forced to treat the patient and/or couple for desire and/or arousal dysfunction. The sex therapist will be faced with the treatment task of helping the patient and/or couple resolve the underlying sexual dysfunction once this barrier to effective sexual functioning has been overcome.

Chronically inhibited and sexually repressed alcoholic patients with low sexual desire and/or arousal dysfunction are sometimes very difficult to treat. The therapist can employ sexual assertion techniques with these patients. It is sometimes quite beneficial to show these patients explicit films that depict a diversity of human sexual activities. The sex therapist may suggest that the couple view a pornographic movie from time to time. This particular treatment strategy can be very threatening to alcoholic patients who are overly religious, dogmatic, and rigidly asexual. Therapist skill, sensitivity, and training are crucial factors that determine the effectiveness of using erotic stimuli within the treatment process. These same general issues must be considered in suggesting that the patient masturbate or employ vibrators and other erotic devices to overcome desire and arousal problems. Some alcoholic patients are even threatened by the suggestion of trying different sexual positions or expressing themselves verbally during sexual relations.

As Zilbergeld and Ellison (1980) indicate, it is important for the therapist to help the couple identify sexual behaviors and situations that they experience as erotic and sexually arousing. The couple must develop more effective patterns of sexual communication. Indeed, most of these patients are in need of multimodal therapeutic interventions (Kaplan, 1979; Lazarus, 1980). Social skills training, assertiveness training, relaxation therapy, sex therapy, relationship therapy and/or conjoint therapy, imagery training, rational emotive therapy, and hormonal treatment are but a few of the strategies of intervention that can be used effectively with the alcoholic patient who manifests low sexual desire and/or arousal dysfunction.

Conjoint sex therapy is the treatment format of choice with alcoholic and/or problem drinking patients who manifest low sexual desire and arousal dysfunctions. However, sex therapy and sexual counseling with only the primary patient can prove beneficial. In the experience of the author, the spouse who is identified (the identified patient) as having low desire and/or arousal dysfunction may not end up being the patient who is being treated for this dysfunction! It is not always the alcoholic or alcohol abusing spouse who manifests desire and arousal problems. The spouse of the alcoholic has often experienced desire and/or arousal dysfunction for years. Both spouses may have an extended history of low sexual desire and/or arousal dysfunction. For these reasons, sex therapy interventions with the patient experiencing desire and arousal dysfunctions should be initiated with more than the simple goal of raising or increasing the identified patient's desire for sex and ability to become sexually aroused. The apparently nondysfunctional spouse may have a long history of sabotaging the identified patient's desire for sex and ability to become aroused. Thus, low sexual desire and arousal dysfunctions are always a manifestation of relationship disturbance.

Comparatively little is known about the treatment of low sexual desire and arousal dysfunctions. Even less is known about the treatment of these dysfunctions among alcoholic and alcohol abusing persons. Therefore, a step-by-step oriented treatment format for the patient with sexual desire and/or arousal dysfunctions has not been developed. Clinicians and sex therapists (LoPiccolo, 1980) even question whether or not problems of desire and arousal constitute a separate category of human sexual dysfunction! Alcoholics, alcohol abusers, and their nonabusing spouses are literally plagued with low sexual desire and arousal problems. The children of alcoholics also experience desire and arousal difficulties. The treatment interventions outlined in this section of the chapter have been found useful and effective in the treatment of male and female alcoholics manifesting low sexual desire and arousal dysfunctions.

Summary

Behavioral scientists have long realized that the realm of individual differences encompasses the desire for sexual relations and the capacity to become sexually aroused. Desire and arousal problems seem to have been primarily associated with males (Kinsey et al., 1948; Freud, 1962; Masters and Johnson, 1966; 1970). It has been suggested that physiological, constitutional and hereditary factors are related to these particular differences in sexual behavior.

The various diagnostic categories of "hypoactive sexual desire" (Kaplan, 1977; 1979) were outlined in this chapter. Low sexual desire and arousal problems refer to a lowered or decreased interest in sexual relations and difficulty becoming sexually aroused. Low sexual desire is often accompanied by arousal difficulty and vice versa. As indicated earlier in this chapter, it is difficult to define the low sexual desire and arousal dysfunctions. The Kinsey data (Kinsey et al., 1948; 1965) are explored so as to ferret out baseline information pertaining to the frequency of sexual activities engaged in by the general male population. Data of this variety (LoPiccolo, 1980) do not constitute valid measures of sexual desire. Recent research (Frank, Anderson and Reubinstein, 1978; LoPiccolo, 1980) suggests that problems of low sexual desire and arousal are relatively common even among non-emotionally disturbed couples. The sex therapist must evaluate the beliefs and feelings of the couple relative to low desire and/or arousal dysfunction.

These dysfunctions can be associated with emotional stress, depression, anxiety, marital problems and relationship pathology, hormonal problems, and social learning and conditioning factors. Some patients with low desire and/or arousal dysfunction have been taught that they "should not" desire sex on a regular basis. In sum, low sexual desire and arousal dysfunctions appear to be multivariantly determined.

A good deal of the alcoholism literature focuses upon the role of alcohol in sexual acting-out and promiscuity (Clinebell, 1956; Forrest, 1978; 1982). Alcoholism researchers and clinicians (Levine, 1955; Wilson, 1977; Forrest, 1978; Vraa, 1982) have also indicated that alcoholism and alcohol abuse result in a diminished interest in heterosexual relationships and a diminished desire for sex. Male sexual arousal is generally diminished following alcohol ingestion. Male and female alcoholics frequently seem to manifest a "pseudohypersexual" adjustment during the early and middle stages of the addiction process. Alcoholic persons in the later stages of the addiction process are often disinterested in sex. Most of these individuals are not capable of sexual arousal and adequate sexual functioning. This may be due to the physical and emotional effects of chronic intoxication.

Some alcoholics and problem drinkers manifest low sexual desire and/or arousal dysfunctions prior to the onset of their addiction or very early in the addiction process. The spouse of the alcoholic very often experiences low sexual desire and/or arousal difficulties. Even the children of the alcoholic tend to manifest a plethora of sexual problems. The case study presented in this section of the chapter elucidates the role of alcoholism in low sexual desire and arousal dysfunctions.

Alcoholism and alcohol abuse are often the direct causes of low sexual desire and/or arousal dysfunctions. Therefore, abstinence from alcohol is a basic precursor to the effective treatment of alcohol abusing patients who manifest these sexual dysfunctions. Sex therapy with the alcoholic patient who is experiencing low sexual desire and/or arousal dysfunctions is not initiated until the patient has been totally abstinent from alcohol for a period of no less than four to six months. In many of these cases, extended individual and/or conjoint psychotherapy is a prerequisite to sex therapy. Alcoholic patients tend to maintain poor nutritional habits. They may not exercise on a regular basis. Some experience sleep disturbance. The alcoholic's over-all poor pattern of health maintenance (Wooddell, 1979) can contribute to sexual desire and arousal problems.

The emotional adjustment of the alcohol abusing patient may also contribute directly to desire and arousal difficulties. These patients are depressive, anxious, guilty, and disturbed in their heterosexual relationships. As Kaplan (1979), LoPiccolo (1980), and Zilbergeld and Ellison (1980) indicate, these psychological factors seem to be consistently related to sexual desire and arousal problems. A number of basic (Sena, 1980; Forrest, 1980d) counseling techniques and more advanced therapeutic interventions (Forrest, 1982a) for helping the sexually dysfunctional alcoholic overcome his or her emotional problems were discussed in this chapter.

The therapist must help the couple begin to engage in more sensuous and arousing sexual behaviors. Basic sex education and information are sometimes essential to this treatment task. Treatment techniques for alcoholic patients with desire and/or arousal dysfunctions include masturbation training, nongenital caressing, massage, genital exploration, imagery and relaxation training, and "letting go" exercises. The therapist must help the patient and/or couple overcome performance demands.

Conjoint sex therapy is perhaps the treatment format of choice for working with alcoholic and/or alcohol abusing patients manifesting low sexual desire and/or arousal dysfunctions. However, individual sex therapy can also be an effective treatment modality in some of these cases. Chronically inhibited and sexually repressed alcoholic patients with desire and/or arousal dysfunctions can be very difficult to treat. It is important for the clinician to bear in mind that low sexual desire and/or arousal dysfunctions are always a manifestation of relationship disturbance.

Very little is known about the treatment of low sexual desire and/or arousal dysfunctions in alcoholic and alcohol abusing persons. Indeed, comparatively litttle is known about these general dysfunctions. Perhaps desire and arousal problems do not constitute a separate category of human sexual dysfunction. Clearly, a great deal of further research and clinical exploration is needed in the areas of alcoholism, alcohol abuse, and the low sexual desire and arousal dysfunctions.

BIBLIOGRAPHY

Akhtar, M.J.: Sexual disorders in male alcoholics. In Madden, Walker, and Kenyon (Eds.): *Alcoholism and Drug Dependence*. New York, Plenum Press, 1977.

Apfelbaum, B.: The diagnosis and treatment of retarded ejaculation. In Leiblum, S., and Pervin, L. (Eds.): *Principles and Practices of Sex Therapy*. New York, The Guilford Press, 1980.

Blane, H.T.: *The Personality of the Alcoholic: Guises of Dependency*. New York, Harper and Row, 1968.

Blum, E.M., and Blum, R.H.: *Alcoholism: Modern Psychological Approaches to Treatment*. San Francisco, Jossey-Bass, Inc., 1969.

Briddell, D.W., and Wilson, G.T.: Effects of alcohol and expectancy set on male sexual arousal. *Journ of Abnormal Psychology, 85(2)*:223-234, 1976.

Byers, A.P.: *Clinical Hypnosis Training*. Lecture, Psychotherapy Associates, P.C. Fifth Annual Advanced Winter Workshop, "Treatment and Rehabilitation of the Alcoholic," Colorado Springs, Colorado, February 2, 1979.

Carney, A., Bancroft, J., and Mathews, A.: The Combination of Hormonal and Psychological Treatment for Female Sexual Unresponsiveness: A Comparative Study. Unpublished Manuscript, 1977.

Clinebell, H.J., Jr.: *Understanding and Counseling the Alcoholic*. Nashville, Abingdon, 1956.

Della-Giustina, V.E., Brooks, J.D., and Forrest, G.G.: Stress management techniques for the practicing dentist. *GA J Dentistry*, 18-20, Aug., 1978.

Della-Giustina, V.E. and Forrest, G.G.: Depression and the dentist. *GA J Dentistry*, 15-17, Aug., 1979.

Ellis, A.: Rational emotive treatment of impotence, frigidity and other sexual problems. *Prof Psychology, 2*:346-349, 1971.

Ellis, A.: *Rational Emotive Therapy Training*. Lecture, Psychotherapy Associates, P.C. Fifth Annual Advanced Winter Workshop, "Treatment and Rehabilitation of the Alcoholic," Colorado Springs, Colorado, February 1, 1979.

Ellis, A.: Treatment of erectile dysfunctions. In Leiblum, S., and Pervin, L. (Eds.): *Principles and Practice of Sex Therapy*. New York, The Guilford Press, 1980.

Fabre, L.F. et al.: Abnormal testosterone excretion in men alcoholics. *Quart J of Stud on Alc, 34(1)*:57-63, 1973.

Farkas, G.M., and Rosen, R.G.: Effects of alcohol on elicited male sexual response. *Journ of Stud on Alc, 37(3)*:265-272, 1975.

Forrest, G.G.: *The Diagnosis and Treatment of Alcoholism*. Springfield, Charles C Thomas, 1975.

Forrest, G.G.: *Alcoholism and the Reservation Indian*. Research and clinical paper compiled at the M.S.B.S. Research Project, Turtle Mountain Rehabilitation and Counseling Center, Belcourt, North Dakota, November, 1976.

Forrest, G.G.: *The Diagnosis and Treatment of Alcoholism*, Rev. 2nd ed. Springfield, Charles C Thomas, 1978.

Forrest, G.G.: *Motivating Alcoholic Patients for Treatment*. Lecture, Fourth Annual Colorado Summer School on Alcoholism, Glenwood Springs, Colorado, June 11, 1978a.

Forrest, G.G.: Negative and positive addictions. *Family and Community Health, 2(1)*:103-112, 1979b.

Forrest, G.G.: Setting alcoholics up for therapeutic failure. *Family and*

Community Health, 2(2):59-64, 1979c.

Forrest, G.G.: *Psychotherapy with the Alcoholic Patient.* Lecture, Psychotherapy Associates, P.C. Intensive One Day Seminar, Denver, Colorado, June 2, 1979d.

Forrest, G.G.: *Alcoholism, Identity and Sexuality.* Lecture, Psychotherapy Associates, P.C. Sixth Annual Advanced Winter Workshop, "Treatment and Rehabilitation of the Alcoholic," Colorado Springs, Colorado, February 4, 1980b.

Forrest, G.G.: *How to Live with a Problem Drinker and Survive.* New York, Atheneum, 1980c.

Forrest, G.G.: Psychotherapy with the Alcoholic. Pre-Convention Workshop. American Personnel and Guidance Association Annual Convention, Atlanta, GA, March 24, 1980d.

Forrest, G.G.: *Confrontation in Psychotherapy with the Alcoholic.* Holmes Beach, Florida, Learning Publications, 1982.

Forrest, G.G.: *Alcoholism, Narcissism and Psychopathology.* Holmes Beach, Florida, Learning Publications, 1982a.

Frank, E., Anderson, C. and Rubinstein, D.: Frequency of sexual dysfunction in "normal couples." *N Engl J Med, 229(3)*:11-115, 1978.

Freud, S.: *Three Essays on the Theory of Sexuality* (J. Starchey, Ed.). New York, Avon Books, 1962. (Originally published, 1905).

Gallant, D.M.: The effect of alcohol and drug abuse on sexual behavior. *Medical Aspects of Human Sexuality, 2(1)*:30-31, 36, 1968.

Goodwin, D.W., Crane, J. Bruce, and Guze, S.B.: Felons who drink: An 8-year follow-up. *Quart J of Stud Alcohol, 32(1)*:136-147, 1971.

Gordon, G.G., Altman, K., and Southern, L.: Effect of alcohol (ethanol) administration on sex hormone metabolism in normal men. *N End J of Med, 295(15)*:793-797, 1976.

Hartman, W.E., and Fithian, M.A.: *Treatment of Sexual Dysfunctions: A Bio-Physical-Social Approach.* New York, Jason Aronson, 1974.

Heiman, J.R. and Morokoff, P.: *Sexual Arousal and Experience as Correlates of Sexual Malaise.* Paper presented at American Psychological Assoc. Meeting, San Francisco, CA, 1977.

Huttmen, M.O., Horkoven, M., and Nishamen, P.: Plasma testosterone concentrations in alcoholics. *J of Stud on Alcoholism, 37(9)*:1165-1177, 1976.

Kaplan, H.S.: *The New Sex Therapy: Active Treatment of Sexual Dysfunctions.* New York, Brunner/Mazel, 1974.

Kaplan, H.S.: Hypoactive sexual desire. *Journal of Sex and Marital Therapy, 3*:39, 1977.

Kaplan, H.S.: *Disorders of Sexual Desire.* New York, Brunner/Mazel, 1979.

Kinsey, A.C., Pomeroy, W.B., and Martin, C.E.: *Sexual Behavior in the Human Male.* Philadelphia, W.B. Saunders, 1948.

Kinsey, A.C. Pomeroy, W.B., Martin, C.E., and Gebhard, P.H.: *Sexual Behavior in the Human Female.* New York, Pocket Books, 1965.

Knauert, A.P.: *Differential Diagnosis of Alcoholism*. Lecture, Psychotherapy Associates, P.C. Fifth Annual Advanced Winter Workshop, "Treatment and Rehabilitation of the Alcoholic," Colorado Springs, Colorado, January 28, 1979.

Knauert, A.P.: The treatment of alcoholism in a community setting. Family and Comm Health. *J of Health Promotion and Maintenance, 2(1)*:91-102, May 1979b.

Kroop, M.: *Sex Therapy Counseling Techniques*. Second Annual Sex Therapy Workshop, Department of Counseling and Guidance, University of North Dakota, Grand Forks, North Dakota, May 3, 1977.

Lazarus, A.A.: Psychological treatment of dyspareunia. In Leiblum, S. and Pervin, L. (Eds.): *Principles and Practice of Sex Therapy*. New York, The Guilford Press, 1980.

Lemere, F., and Smith, J.W.: Alcohol-induced sexual impotence. *Amer J of Psychiatry, 130(22)*:212-213, 1973.

Levine, J.: The sexual adjustment of alcoholics: A clinical study of a selected sample. *Quart J of Stud on Alc, 16(14)*:675-680, 1955.

Lirrette, H.F.J., Davis, J.T., Gheen, M.H., Montigros, P., and Tripp, J.: *Self-Esteem Investigations of Alcoholics and Their Non-Alcoholic Spouses*. Unpublished Masters Thesis, School of Social Work, University of South Carolina, Columbia, South Carolina, 1977.

Lobitz, W.C. and Lobitz, G.K.: Clinical assessment in the treatment of sexual dysfunctions. In LoPiccolo, J. and LoPiccolo, L. (Eds.): *Handbook of Sex Therapy*. New York, Plenum Press, 1978.

LoPiccolo, L.: Low sexual desire. In Leiblum, S. and Pervin, L. (Eds.): *Principles and Practices of Sex Therapy*. New York, The Guilford Press, 1980.

LoPiccolo, L. and Heiman, J.: Sexual assessment and history interview. In LoPiccolo, J. and LoPiccolo, L. (Eds.): *Handbook of Sex Therapy*. New York, Plenum Press, 1978.

Masters, W.H., and Johnson, V.E.: *Human Sexual Inadequacy*. Boston, Little, Brown, & Co., 1966.

Masters, W.H., and Johnson, V.E.: *Human Sexual Inadequacy*. Boston, Little, Brown & Co., 1970.

Neshkov, N.S.: The state of spermalogenesis and sexual function in those who abuse alcohol. *Vrachebnoe Delo (Kiev)*, No. 2, pp. 130-131, 1969.

Paolino, T.J. and McCrady, B.S.: *The Alcoholic Marriage: Alternative Perspectives*. New York, Grune and Stratton, 1977.

Paredes, A.: Marital-sexual factors in alcoholism. *Medical Aspects of Human Sexuality*, April, 1973.

Perelman, M.A.: Treatment of premature ejaculation. In Leiblum, S., and Pervin, L. (Eds.) *Principles and Practices of Sex Therapy*. New York, The Guilford Press, 1980.

Peters, J.E.: *Behavioral Treatment of Alcoholism Related Sexual Dysfunc-*

tions. Lecture, Psychotherapy Associates, P.C. Fifth Annual Advanced Winter Workshop, "Treatment and Rehabilitation of the Alcoholic," Colorado Springs, Colorado, January 29, 1979.

Powell, B.J., Viamontes, J.A., and Brown, C.W.: Alcohol affects on the sexual potency of alcoholic and non-alcoholic males. *J on Alc and Related Addictions, 10(1-2)*:78-80, 1974.

Rubin, H.B. and Henson, D.E.: Voluntary enhancement of penile erection. *Bulletin of the Psychonomic Society, 6,* 158-160, 1975.

Rubin, H.B. and Henson, D.E.: Effects of alcohol on male sexual responding. *Journal-Psychopharmacology, 47(2)*:123-124, 1976.

Sena, D.A.: *Basic Counseling Skills Training.* Lecture, Psychotherapy Associates, P.C. Sixth Annual Advanced Winter Workshop, "Treatment and Rehabilitation of the Alcoholic," Colorado Springs, Colorado, February 4-5, 1980.

Silverstein, L.M.: *Motivating Alcoholics for Treatment.* Lecture, Psychotherapy Associates, P.C. Sixth Annual Advanced Winter Workshop, "Treatment and Rehabilitation of the Alcoholic," Colorado Springs, Colorado, February 7, 1980.

Smith, J.W., Lemere, F., and Dunn, R.B.: Impotence and alcohol. *Northwest Medicine, 71*:523-524, 1972.

Todd, W.H.: Truth about sex and alcohol, *Memorial Mercury, 13(4)*:15-16, 1973.

Vraa, C.W.: *Sex Therapy Training.* Lecture, Psychotherapy Associates, P.C. Third Annual Advanced Winter Workshop, "Treatment and Rehabilitation of the Alcoholic," Colorado Springs, Colorado, January 28, 1977.

Vraa, C.W.: *Alcoholism and the Treatment of Sexual Dysfunction.* Lecture, Psychotherapy Associates, P.C. Fourth Annual Advanced Winter Workshop, "Treatment and Rehabilitation of the Alcoholic," Colorado Springs, Colorado, February 3, 1978.

Vraa, C.W.: *Sex Therapy Training.* Lecture, Psychotherapy Associates, P.C. Eighth Annual Advanced Winter Workshop, "Treatment and Rehabilitation of the Alcoholic," Colorado Springs, Colorado, February 2, 1982.

Williams, K.H.: *Overview of Sexual Problems in Alcoholism.* Workshop on Sexual Counseling for Persons with Problems, Pittsburgh, Pennsylvania, January 1976.

Wilson, G.T.: Alcohol and human sexual behavior. *Behavior Research and Therapy, 15(3)*:239-252, 1977.

Wilson, G.T. and Lawson, D.M.: Effects of alcohol on sexual arousal in women. *J of Abn Psy, 85(5)*:489-497, 1976.

Wooddell, W.J.: Liver disease in alcohol-addicted patients. *Family and Community Health, 2(2)*:13-22, Aug., 1979.

Zilbergeld, B.: *Male Sexuality.* New York, Bantam, 1978.

Zilbergeld, B. and Ellison, C.: Desire discrepancies and arousal problems. In
    Leiblum, S. and Pervin, L. (Eds.): *Principles and Practice of Sex Therapy*.
    New York, The Guilford Press, 1980.

Chapter 4
ALCOHOLISM AND
FEMALE SEXUAL DYSFUNCTION

FRIGIDITY

GENERAL sexual dysfunction in women is most typically referred to as "frigidity" (Masters and Johnson, 1970; Kaplan, 1974; Kroop, 1977; Vraa, 1982). Women who are frigid report a lack of sexual stimulation and sexual feelings. They are very often disinterested in sex or actually repulsed at the thought of having sexual intercourse and engaging in other varieties of intimate sexual behavior. The frigid woman can also be accurately described as nonorgastic or preorgastic. Kaplan (1974) suggests that women who are frigid can be classified as either suffering from primary frigidity or secondary frigidity. According to this author, "the woman who suffers from primary frigidity has never experienced erotic pleasure with any partner in any situation," while the woman who suffers from secondary frigidity "has responded at one time to sexual stimulation to some extent." Many women who suffer from secondary frigidity experienced sexual arousal and stimulation prior to being married. Following marriage and a refocusing of sexual behaviors to the specific realm of intercourse, such women find themselves no longer capable of sexual arousal, excitement, or stimulation.

The frigid woman may show no physiological evidence (genital vasocongestion) of sexual excitement in response to direct sexual stimulation (Hartman and Fithian, 1974; Peters, 1979). Other dysfunctional women (Barbach, 1980) may partially respond to direct sexual stimulation with light lubrication. A few women are able to experience orgasm in the absence of significant lubrication. Sex therapists (Vraa, 1982) report that some patients are frigid and unable to adequately lubricate with their husbands but are easily aroused and stimulated to orgasm by lovers or males other than their husbands.

According to Kaplan (1974), female sexual arousal "is a visceral reaction." The female sexual response consists of the dilation of the genital vasculature. Kaplan (1974) indicates that "genital vaso-congestion, with the consequent engorgement of the labial valvae and perivaginal tissues, is produced by the relaxation of the smooth muscles which regulate the calibre of the genital blood vessels. In addition, smooth muscle reactions of the vagina and uterus cause vaginal ballooning and uterine elevation, which are also characteristic of female sexual arousal."

Frigidity is generally felt to be caused by a combination of emotional factors. However, physical factors such as clitoral adhesions and inadequate pubococcygeal muscle strength and contractions have been aetiologically associated with the female sexual dysfunctions (Masters and Johnson, 1966; 1970; Kaplan, 1974; Hartman and Fithian, 1974). Hartman and Fithian (1974) suggest that orgastic failure is sometimes due to clitoral adhesions, which deter or inhibit the preorgastic rotation and retractions of the clitoris. Vraa (1982) points out that many sex therapists and clinicians reject the position that clitoral adhesions play a crucial role in the aetiology of most cases of frigidity. There seems to be a rather consistent clinical consensus (Kaplan 1974) that poor tone of the pubococcygeal muscle is related to many cases of female sexual inadequacy and frigidity. The pubococcygeal muscle is involved in orgastic discharge and is believed to contain both the motor and sensory elements of the female orgasm. Patients can be taught to strengthen the pubococcygeal and other perineal muscles by practicing tightening and relaxing exercises. Once the patient's perineal muscle tone improves, orgastic response sometimes follows. Kaplan (1974) reports that by instructing totally inorgastic patients to tighten their perineal and abdominal muscles an initial orgasm may be facilitated.

A variety of psychological factors have been associated with frigidity and the female sexual dysfunctions. Kaplan (1974) very astutely points out that there are three essential prerequisites to the adequate female sexual response: "(1) a woman cannot respond unless she is properly stimulated, (2) she must be sufficiently relaxed during lovemaking to be able to respond to this stimulation and to abandon herself to the experience, and (3) even if these first two conditions are met, the woman's sexual functioning will still be impaired if she suffers from a specific learned inhibition of her orgastic response." It is rather apparent that relationship conflicts are consistently associated with frigidity. Quite commonly, males fail to understand and appreciate the role of adequate stimulation in female sexual functioning. Frigidity, in the case of some women, is the direct result of inadequate stimulation. Faulty sexual learning experiences and an inability to relax during intercourse are interpersonal factors that often directly facilitate frigidity. Communication difficulties or a lack of communication regarding sexual responding contribute to the sexual dysfunctions of many women.

Social and cultural factors sometimes contribute to the problem of frigidity. Fear, shame, and guilt are powerful factors which adversely affect the sexual behaviors and sexual adjustments of many women. Some women experience unconscious guilt relative to their sexual desires, needs, and impulses. In general, women in our culture have historically been conditioned to avoid, deny, and repress assertive and aggressive sexual behaviors. As a result of social changes during the past decade or so, women have been "given permission" by society to be sexually assertive. Social changes in the realm of human sexuality have contributed to the sexual problems of many females as well as many males.

A variety of intrapersonal conflicts can be associated with the problem of frigidity. Unresolved oedipal conflicts, deep-seated fears of penile penetration, a fear and/or denial of femininity, penis envy, and masculine strivings are reported in the psychoanalytic literature as being causative factors in frigidity.

The dynamic or intrapersonal conflicts of the frigid woman almost always become manifest in the interpersonal realm. Women who avoid sexual intimacy as a result of the unconscious equation "sexual intercourse with a male equals sexual intercourse with my father" very quickly experience rather serious interpersonal struggles. In general, the sexual response of women is closely related to the quality of relationship she maintains with her husband or lover. Such may not be the case with many males.Women find it difficult to "let go" or abandon themselves to the sexual experience when they feel unloved, unimportant, and not respected. The sexual experience of the woman is based upon mutual respect, caring, and trust. Women who are either afraid or uncomfortable with their lovers invariably find it difficult to respond to sexual stimulation. Frigidity is a relationship problem. The female sexual dysfunctions do not occur in a vacuum. Regardless of her internal conflicts and struggles, the frigid woman experiences a sexual relationship disturbance.

At present we do not have accurate statistics and data relative to the incidence of frigidity among women in general. Relatively little data is available on the incidence of different patterns of sexual functioning in women. However, Kinsey (Kaplan, 1974) reported that 30 percent of the women in his investigation of female sexual behavior did not experience orgasm early in marriage. Only 10 percent of this sample of nonorgastic women continued to be nonorgastic following ten years of marriage. Vraa (1982) indicates that roughly 85 percent of all women in our society are able to reach orgasm by some means. Perhaps less than 50 percent of women reach orgasm during sexual intercourse. Direct clitoral stimulation is essential to female orgasm and in the case of many women such stimulation often requires more than basic coitus. In the clinical experience of the author (Forrest, 1980a), less than 15 percent of the women entering psychotherapy report being "frigid." As is indicated later in this chapter, the percentage of alcoholic women who report being frigid is considerably larger than the figure for "women in general" who enter therapy.

As indicated in Chapter 3 dealing with male sexual dysfunctions and alcoholism, men generally tend to feel that erectile failure or inadequacy is catastrophic. By contrast, many women seem to accept their frigidity. Such women are not acutely anxious or emotionally upset over the matter of being frigid. Most assuredly, there are observable differences between men and women in the areas of emotions and cognitions associated with sexual dysfunction! However, some women feel quite depressed, anxious, and threatened as a result of being frigid. Alcoholic women are consistently insecure and anxious over the matters of identity, femininity, and sexual adequacy (Wilsnack, 1973; Barbach, 1980; Forrest, 1980a, 1982a). Intensive psychotherapy with frigid women, who on the surface appear to have adaptively accepted their frigidity, consistently reveals underlying feelings of inadequacy, depression, guilt, and anger. These women tend to be self-depreciating. They soon find themselves feeling very angry and hostile toward husbands or lovers who enjoy sex, experience intense sexual stimulation, and have orgasms.

Men respond in a variety of ways to a frigid wife or lover. Some men accept the fact that their wife or lover is frigid. Indeed, many males expect women to be frigid, sexually inhibited, nonresponsive, and sexually nonassertive. However, many males are insecure and very threatened about their partner's frigidity and lack of sexual responsiveness. Such men tend to believe that they are somehow responsible for their wives' frigidity. In these sexual relationships the husband may eventually blame, confront, and attack his wife over the matter of her lack of sexual responsiveness. Marital transactions of this variety actively reinforce her frigidity.

The frigid woman may engage in any variety of sexual behaviors without experiencing excitement and stimulation for a lifetime. Unlike the sexually dysfunctional male, her sexual dysfunction may not be behaviorally apparent. Some women who are frigid appear to have "good" marriages and they do not evidence psychological disturbance. Social, cultural, religious, and familial factors are often associated with marital and sexual adjustment styles involving the frigid woman.

Alcoholism and Frigidity

Alcoholic women experience myriad sexual and identity problems. Wilsnack (1973) points out that women drink alcoholically in order to feel feminine. Extensive research dealing with the woman alcoholic (Wilsnack, 1973; 1982) consistently indicates that female alcoholics are overly concerned about their adequacy as women. As this same author suggests, drinking offers the alcoholic woman a transient escape from sex role conflicts. On a conscious level alcoholic women appear to be no less feminine than nonalcoholic women, but unconsciously (Wilsnack, 1973) alcoholic women experience significant conflicts about their adequacy as women. Masculine traits in the unconscious levels of personality are theorized as the causative factors associated with the sex role and identity conflicts of many alcoholic women.

In accordance with this research evidence and theoretical viewpoint, Wilsnack (1973; 1982) has found that "seventy-eight percent of alcoholic women but only thirty-five percent of nonalcoholic women who were married had suffered some kind of obstetrical or gynecological disorder." Alcoholic women have problems in the areas of conception, many have a history of repeated miscarriages, and permanent infertility is far more often a problem for the addicted woman. Wilsnack (1973) reports that 26 percent of alcoholic wives are unable to have children, as contrasted with 4 percent of nonalcoholic wives. Fetal alcohol syndrome is closely associated with the drinking behavior of alcoholic women. Alcoholic women frequently give birth to children that are mentally defective or physically deformed, or they are bearers of other congenital birth defects. It is only in recent years (Knauert, 1980) that physicians have discovered the devastating relationship between alcoholism or heavy drinking by pregnant mothers and the subsequent pattern of giving birth to physically and/or mentally defective offspring. Research (Medhus and Hansson, 1976) even suggests that alcoholic women are more often treated for venereal disease than nonalcoholic women.

There is relatively little data available concerning the relationship between alcoholism in women and resulting specific sexual dysfunctions (Vraa, 1982; Wilsnack, 1982). This situation is very much in contrast to the relative wealth of research and clinical data dealing with the onset and incidence of impotence, premature ejaculation, and retarded ejaculation in male alcoholics. However, several authors (Gallant, 1968; Corrigan, 1974; Wilson and Lawson, 1976; Cerul, 1976; Malloy, 1976; Wilson, 1977; Vraa, 1982; Wilsnack, 1982) report that alcoholic women do experience frigidity in combination with their alcoholism and alcohol abuse. Wilson and Lawson (1976) in an interesting investigation of the effects of alcohol on sexual arousal in women report a negative linear relationship between increasing levels of alcohol consumption and sexual arousal as measured by vaginal pressure pulse recording. Measures of vaginal pressure pulse were obtained by a vaginal pho-toplethysmograph. In this study, sixteen university women re-ceived, in counterbalanced order, four doses of alcohol prior to viewing a control film and an erotic film. Eight of the subjects in the investigation were told that alcohol would increase their sexual arousal in response to the erotic film, while the other eight sub-jects were told that ethanol would decrease their sexual arousal. It was clinically significant that the majority of women in this study reported heightened sexual arousal with increasing levels of intox-ication. However, the vaginal pressure pulse readings of the women subjects indicated a physiological decrease in sexual arousal with increasing levels of intoxication. In effect, the women's subjective estimates of increased sexual stimulation and arousal following in-creasing levels of alcohol consumption and intoxication were "di-ametrically at odds" with their actual measured physical patterns of sexual responding.

This investigation (Wilson and Lawson, 1976) presents findings that very clearly indicate a reinforcing relationship between alco-hol consumption and perceived sexual arousal among women. In essence, these results support Wilsnack's (1973; 1982) position that drinking enhances feelings of femininity upon the part of the alcoholic woman. Many frigid alcoholic women drink in order to feel feminine, sexually aroused, and stimulated. In the case of some frigid alcoholic women, intoxication serves the purpose of denying, blocking, or avoiding the reality of being sexually frigid. The process of drinking alcoholically in order to deny sexual frigidity may reflect a conscious choice or decision-making pro-cess upon the part of some alcoholic women. More commonly, it has been the experience of the author that most alcoholic women who are frigid do not consciously associate their pathological drinking with the process of attempting to deny being frigid.

Approximately 20 percent of alcoholic women (Forrest, 1980a) who enter outpatient psychotherapy for alcohol addiction eventually report either being "frigid" or they describe their sex-ual feelings and behaviors in terms of the various clinical symp-toms and signs discussed earlier in this chapter as being indicative of frigidity. Clinical research has not indicated that the physical effects of chronic intoxication in women directly causes physiological and biological organismic changes which in turn cause frigidity (Vraa, 1982). This data is rather in contrast to that pertaining to the male alcoholic. As indicated in the chapters dealing with alcohol addiction and the male sexual dysfunctions, chronic alcohol ingestion in the male often results in neurologic, metabolic, and a variety of other basic physical changes, which directly cause erectile difficulties and ejaculatory problems. Perhaps future clinical researchers will be able to demonstrate that frigidity in the alcoholic woman is but another physical consequence of chronic intoxication.

Sex therapists and counselors have long indicated that a by-product of alcoholism can be frigidity. Alcohol abuse and chronic alcohol addiction in women can cause frigidity (Williams, 1976; Cerul, 1976; Berenson, 1976; Wilson, 1977; Vraa, 1982). As indicated earlier in this chapter, a diversity of psychological factors (Forrest, 1982a) contribute to the frigidity of the alcoholic woman. Many alcoholic women act out sexually while under the influence of alcohol and give the appearance of being very heterosexual and in "need" of a great deal of sexual gratification. Frequently, the promiscuity and diffuse sexual acting-out of the alcoholic woman is a defense against fears of inadequacy as a woman, unattractiveness, and intrusive homosexual fears. As Wilsnack (1973; 1982) suggests, such women often feel "unfeminine." An extended history of intoxication, promiscuous acting-out, and severe heterosexual conflicts will not contribute to the resolution of the alcoholic woman's underlying identity conflicts. Alcoholic women sometimes make themselves sexually frigid as a result of their long-term alcoholic behavior patterns. As the addicted woman overlearns to utilize alcohol and intoxication as a method for feeling feminine, attractive, and sexual, she invariably begins to act out sexually in any number of self-defeating or destructive ways. A number of extramarital affairs, "one night stands," perhaps "group sex" experiences, and even contracting venereal disease become the behavioral and transactional realities that actively facilitate and create the problem of frigidity for some alcoholic women. As the alcoholic woman consistently "sets" herself up to be sexually used and manipulated by men, she also "sets" herself up to dislike herself and more importantly she conditions herself to be frigid. The pattern of drinking in order to feel and behave sexually and then being used and rejected soon becomes a vicious circle. Alcoholic women who become caught up in this process eventually feel frigid, asexual, angry, and enraged at men in general. They also learn to hate and despise themselves.

The following case study quite lucidly demonstrates the many interrelated factors associated with alcoholism and frigidity.

> CASE 6. Debbie M., a twenty-seven-year-old woman in the process of a second divorce, entered outpatient psychotherapy as a result of "a drinking problem." During the initial therapy session the patient indicated that she had been hospitalized several times in the past four or five years for "alcoholism" treatment. In fact, she had received extended (thirty to sixty days) inpatient care for her alcoholism on seven different occasions during the three-year period of time prior to entering outpatient therapy. The patient indicated that she had "tried" Alcoholics Anonymous several times, she had been placed on "several" Antabuse maintenance programs by her parents, employers, and prior therapists and that all of these measures aimed at fostering recovery had failed. It was apparent that Debbie had made numerous attempts to recover. She seemed to have tried "everything" in her attempts to stop drinking! Yet, it was also obvious that she had never really committed herself to an ongoing program of treatment and recovery. Rather than "working" in an extended psychotherapy relationship, Alcoholics Anonymous, or even within the context of an Antabuse maintenance program, Debbie had a long history of "trying" any number of treatment modalities for a few weeks or months and then terminating these efforts at recovery. The result was always the same—Debbie ended up drunk and in trouble again!
>
> The patient described herself as an "Army brat." Debbie's biologic parents divorced when she was three years old. Debbie had grown up with her mother. The mother had remarried when Debbie was nearly five years old. According to the patient's mother, the parental divorce was due to alcoholism upon the part of the biologic father. The patient had one sibling, a "half-brother" who was some six years younger. Debbie's stepfather was a retired Army officer. The family had moved on numerous occasions during the patient's formative years.
>
> Debbie first began to "experiment" with alcohol at the age of fourteen. On several occasions she became inebriated to the point of either "passing out" or "getting sick at the stomach" at this age. Shortly after her fourteenth birthday, the patient got drunk at a party, had intercourse with a boy she had met for the first time, and became pregnant. After discussing the matter of being pregnant with her parents, Debbie

decided to have an abortion. At the age of sixteen Debbie dropped out of high school and married a twenty-year-old soldier. The marriage came about after a two-month period of dating and courtship. Thirteen months later the patient gave birth to a son. This marriage lasted for three-and-a-half years. During this time, the patient as well as her husband drank a great deal. Severe marital problems, physical and verbal assaults, and mutual drunkenness and intoxication characterized the marital relationship. Finally, the patient initiated a divorce. Debbie and Johnny, her son, returned to the parental home. Shortly thereafter, Debbie obtained a job as a receptionist and clerk-typist with a large local corporation. In order to "control" her drinking, Debbie decided at this time to only drink on weekends. After several "affairs" and relationships with different men, Debbie decided to "move in" and live with Joe, a fireman. At this time, Debbie was twenty-two years old and Joe was twenty-seven. In spite of many difficulties and almost constant arguing, Debbie and Joe were married four months after they had decided to live together. The patient continued to drink heavily during the course of this marriage. Joe was a nondrinker. Finally, after some five years of marriage Debbie again initiated a divorce.

Prior to beginning psychotherapy with the author, Debbie had led a very promiscuous life-style. The patient had been sexually active at age fourteen. Pregnancy, abortion, and a series of sexual relationships with many different males constituted much of the patient's adolescent adjustment style. Debbie had a virtual unending number of affairs during the brief course of her first marriage. Alcohol and intoxication were central to these affairs. During her final two years of marriage to Joe, the patient established a consistent pattern of "binge-drinking" and sexual acting-out. At this time, Debbie would drink very little for several weeks and then go on a drinking spree, which would last for a week or two. These periods of acute intoxication were consistently terminated by arrest, hospitalization, or placement in a detoxification center. Debbie was either "fired" or "lost" seven different jobs during the five years that she and Joe were married. Alcoholism was the primary factor in all of these job losses.

While caught up in the process of a "binge" Debbie would, in her own words, "*always* manage to pick up a fuck for the night." On several occasions Joe had found Debbie in a motel room, drunk, and in bed with a complete stranger that she had "picked up" at a bar or lounge. The only times that Debbie acted out sexually were when she was drinking alcoholically and in the midst of an alcoholic binge. The following is an example of the patient's pattern of binge-drinking and sexual acting-out: While attending a family reunion one Sunday afternoon during the summer, Debbie and Joe became engaged in a rather heated argument. According to Debbie, her parents soon "sided" with Joe in the argument. Finally, Debbie became so upset and angry "at Joe and her family" that she left the family reunion and stopped for a "few" drinks at a local bar. Needless to say, in rather short order Debbie was drunk! After a few hours of drinking, talking, and dancing with a man that she had met at the bar, Debbie suggested that they get a motel room. Debbie and her male companion stayed in the motel for three days. Both were acutely intoxicated for the entire period of time. Debbie "came to" three days later, her male companion was gone, and she remembered little of what had occurred for this period of time other than, in her words, "doing a lot of drinking and screwing." The patient managed to return home and was promptly taken to a local detoxification center by her husband.

After several individual therapy sessions the patient began to openly discuss her long-term disinterest in sex. She stated that she had "never really liked or enjoyed sex." In spite of her overdetermined flight into heterosexual acting-out, Debbie revealed that she had never experienced an orgasm. In this regard, she stated that she had "tried everything"—genital sex, oral sex, anal sex, group sex, vibrators, threesomes, and so forth. Debbie stated "I guess that deep down I've always kinda hated sex—I don't even like being touched sexually unless I've been drinking." It eventually became apparent to the patient that even intoxication failed to result in a sense of sexual excitement and stimulation.

The patient was able to remain totally abstinent for a period of some five months while in therapy. Early in the therapy process she continued her pattern of pathological sexual acting-out, but in the absence of drinking and intoxication. Eventually, Debbie discontinued her promiscuous sexual behavior. She continued to be anxious and concerned about her inability to "feel" sexually responsive after five months of sobriety and following an active involvement in psychotherapy. The patient discontinued therapy at this point due to taking a job in another state. Unfortunately, follow-up data on the patient's long-term progress in the areas of continuing in therapy, alcohol addiction, and sexual frigidity is not available.

The case of Debbie illustrates very well the problems of frigidity and orgastic dysfunction in the alcoholic woman. A seriously conflicted sexual and identity adjustment during adolescence, in this case, precipitated a disturbed early adult sexual adjustment style. Alcohol addiction compounded the patient's sexual problems. This patient eventually developed a pattern of rather bizarre sexual acting-out while intoxicated. After numerous attempts at treatment and rehabilitation, Debbie was finally able to establish sobriety within the context of a psychotherapy relationship. It became readily apparent to both the patient and therapist that sexual acting-out and promiscuity were a defense against frigidity. In spite of her extended history of sexual relations with many different males, Debbie was sexually unresponsive and "uncomfortable" within the context of intimate sexual encounters. In fact, after the patient was able to establish several months of sobriety, she continued to verbalize great concern over her inability to "feel" sexually responsive. It is obvious that alcohol-facilitated sexuality is not a solution to the problem of frigidity. In this case, alcoholism clearly compounded the patient's many sexual and identity conflicts.

Basic Treatment Strategies

In accord with the therapy strategies discussed in the earlier chapter dealing with the treatment of sexually dysfunctional male alcoholics, it is of paramount clinical importance that frigid alcoholic women be sober prior to the initiation of sexual counseling and sex therapy. It is clinically inappropriate to begin sex therapy with the frigid alcoholic woman who is in the process of "drying out" or being detoxified. Extended sobriety and an ongoing commitment to psychotherapy are basic precursors to the undertaking of sex therapy with the frigid alcoholic woman. It is usually recommended (Forrest, 1980a; Vraa, 1982) that sex therapy with the frigid alcoholic woman be initiated after the patient has been committed to a psychotherapy relationship and totally abstinent from alcohol for a period of at least fifteen to eighteen weeks.

Prior to beginning sex therapy, the frigid alcoholic woman should usually be referred for a complete medical examination. The medical examination includes evaluation of the pubococcygeal muscle and checking for clitoral adhesions (Vraa, 1982). Alcoholic women frequently manifest a wide variety of nutritional, medical, and general health problems associated with their patterns of alcohol consumption. Obstetrical and gynecological problems are common in the case of alcoholic women (Wilsnack, 1982). In a few cases, the sex therapist and patient may have reason to suspect venereal disease. Alcoholic males and females who act out sexually are much more prone to contacting a venereal disease than are those alcoholic males and females who do not behave promiscuously. Obviously, whenever there is a question of possible venereal infection the patient is immediately referred for a medical examination.

It is physically and psychologically helpful for the patient to be actively involved in a holistic program of recovery prior to beginning sex therapy. The alcoholic woman, whether she be a housewife or skid-row resident, tends to eat irregular and improperly balanced nutritional meals, lacks involvement in a program of consistent exercise, and is almost always depressed and psychologically conflicted. Indeed, it is not surprising that so many alcoholic women are "frigid" and sexually dysfunctional. Therapists and counselors must teach the alcoholic woman to like herself. Alcoholic women also need to learn how to respect themselves. In the case of the alcoholic woman, very often liking and respecting oneself encompasses the ability to simply "like and respect" oneself as a *woman*. Many alcoholic women seem to be unable to feel good about themselves as women. In order to like and respect herself, feel better about being a woman, and feel more feminine, some alcoholic women will need to gain or lose weight, pay more attention to clothing, makeup, and personal appearance. For the alcoholic woman, the process of changing self-oriented perceptions and feelings begins with sobriety. Beyond sobriety, the addicted woman progressively teaches herself to feel more adequate, feminine, and sexually responsible by behaving differently, more rationally, and adaptively in each of these areas. Holistic treatment strategies simply help the alcoholic woman recover more quickly as a result of facilitating growth and change in a number of different areas of living, behaving, perceiving, and feeling.

A general goal of sex therapy with sexually dysfunctional women is that of helping such women to "let go" or abandon themselves to the sexual experience. Sex therapists and counselors facilitate this goal by "creating a nondemanding, relaxed, and sensuous ambience which permits the natural unfolding of the sexual response during lovemaking" (Kaplan, 1974). This author indicates that the "systematic prescription of various sensuous and erotic experiences has proven highly effective in removing some of the immediate obstacles to sexual functioning."

An initial strategy of sex therapy utilized with the frigid woman is that of nondemanding pleasuring. Kaplan (1974) refers to this set of prescribed sex therapy tasks as "the sensate focus exercises." This particular treatment technique was developed by Masters and Johnson (1970). In accord with this treatment technique, the therapist instructs the couple in the initial session to abstain from sexual intercourse for several days. During this period of abstinence from intercourse the couple are instructed to limit their sexual behaviors and interactions to body touching, caressing, and massage. The wife is told to practice these techniques on the husband first; then the husband is instructed to practice the same techniques on the wife. The procedure of having the wife caress, touch, and massage the husband first allows her to more fully concentrate on the eventual feelings and sensations that occur as a result of his caressing her. In this way, she does not have to worry about her adequacy in the matter of stimulating her husband, but can better concentrate upon her own feelings and bodily sensations while being caressed. In the case of some women, this procedure helps extinguish anxiety and guilt related to the matter of feeling and believing that they must adequately stimulate their husband or lover before they can be concerned about their own sexual feelings, sensations, and responding. This technique also teaches the woman that she can expect to be sexually stimulated in the sense of being caressed and touched. Obviously, this procedure facilitates sexual relationship changes in cases where the husband may have actually reinforced the wife's frigidity by being concerned only with his own sexual stimulation and orgasm (Barbach, 1980).

Rather commonly, the utilization of caressing and touching techniques over a period of four or five days will result in the patient's first feelings of arousal and stimulation. In cases where the patient reports no heightened sense of stimulation and arousal, the clinician should explore the explicit sexual behaviors and relationship interactions which have occurred as the couple practiced the caressing, touching, and massage tasks. The couple is instructed to continue practicing these behaviors until the patient begins to experience arousal and sensuous, erotic feelings. This procedure extinguishes the patient's need to have an orgasm. The patient also learns to be assertive and responsible for her own sexual pleasure. Very often the husband becomes a catalyst in the treatment process as he enjoys these sexual exercises and thus actively reinforces the patient's newly discovered sexual enjoyment.

After the patient has experienced consistent feelings of pleasure, arousal, and erotic stimulation as a result of the touching and caressing exercises, the sex therapist suggests that the couple begin to engage in "light" genital stimulation. In this context, light genital stimulation refers to the husband's touching and caressing of the patient's breasts and nipples, clitoral region, and vaginal entrance. The husband is told to avoid intense stimulation of the patient. At this point, he is not to be concerned with direct stimulation of the patient's clitoris and intensive modes of stimulation are not appropriate. Rather, the couple is instructed to enjoy nondemanding, non-performance-oriented modes of sexual pleasuring. Sexual performance is not the goal of this stage of therapy. Developing the abilities to be sexually intimate, loving, mutually sensitive, and enjoying sex as a form of fun are the goals associated with this stage of the treatment process.

During this stage of sex therapy many couples report "falling in love again." The alcoholic woman who, perhaps for the first time in her life, begins to experience sexual stimulation and arousal is logically elated and romantic. Many husbands who are able to share in this process tend to feel excited, happy, and close to their wives. Aside from sobriety, the ability to genuinely feel sexually responsive is a major issue in the overall recovery process for many alcoholic women who are sexually dysfunctional. This is most assuredly a synergistic model of recovery. Sobriety very consistently precipitates healthy global relationship changes and growth, which in turn facilitate adaptive changes in the explicit realm of sexuality and sexual responding, which then creates even more generalized adaptive relationship changes.

Following a series of successful and rewarding experiences utilizing the techniques of genital stimulation, as just discussed, the patient is ready to have intercourse. The goal of intercourse is not that of stimulating the patient to orgasm. The clinician should make this point clear to the couple. Following the genital stimulation exercises, the patient is instructed to initiate intercourse. It is after the patient has achieved a state of arousal and stimulation via the "light" genital stimulation techniques that *she* is told to proceed to the stage of coitus. The couple is told to engage in intercourse in a mutually nondemanding manner. In other words, the rigorous thrusting varieties of coitus aimed at facilitating orgasm are actively discouraged by the sex therapist. The patient is instructed to concentrate and focus upon the sensory stimulation she is experiencing in the clitoral and vaginal areas during lovemaking. It may be easier for the patient to more fully concentrate upon her sensory awareness of sexual excitement and stimulation if intercourse is conducted in the female superior position during this stage of the treatment process. Couples should be encouraged to "experiment" and discover for themselves which positions are more pleasurable and stimulating.

The stage of engaging in intercourse without pressure to "perform" or reach orgasm, referred to as nondemanding coitus, should be practiced by the couple for fifteen to thirty minute intervals. In the event that the patient's husband experiences the urge to ejaculate prematurely or very early during the nondemanding coitus exercises, the couple is told to discontinue genital stimulation until the husband's ejaculatory sensations subside. Actually, this procedure can be repeated any number of times during the course of a lovemaking session. This technique is somewhat similar to the "stop-start" procedure discussed in Chapter 3. When the patient feels the desire to more actively engage in intercourse, with the explicit goal of achieving orgasm, she is told to openly communicate this desire to her spouse. The couple is then encouraged to continue intercourse to the point of orgasm or sexual satisfaction.

At this point in the treatment process the patient is capable of experiencing adequate sexual arousal, stimulation, and frequently orgasm. In essence, the patient is no longer "frigid." It is very important for the patient to be able to maintain an ongoing pattern of successful sexual responding. The couple is actively encouraged to practice the caressing, touching, and massage exercises. Additionally, it is advantageous for the couple to periodically practice the "light" genital stimulation and nondemanding coitus exercises. By practicing these various sexual behaviors and interactions the couple is better able to maintain and reinforce the gains that were evidenced during the actual sex therapy process. Kaplan (1974) summarizes the positive sources of treatment gain associated with the utilization of these specific sex therapy techniques as follows: "(1) because the woman is relieved of the pressure of having to produce a response, these exercises are not apt to mobilize her defenses and anxiety, and so she is often able to experience unimpeded erotic enjoyment, (2) the therapeutic effectiveness of these exercises derives in large measure from the fact that they are specifically structured to evoke sexual excitement in the woman, and (3) inevitably, in the process of implementing these sexual tasks, the patient and her husband become more perceptive and sensitive to each other's sexual needs and reactions."

The marital relationship involving an alcoholic wife is often diffusely conflicted. Alcoholic wives have often been physically and psychologically abused by their husbands and significant others. The alcoholic woman is also sadomasochistic (Forrest, 1982a). Not only does she masochistically punish herself through the medium of the addiction process, but invariably the alcoholic woman inflicts a great deal of emotional and perhaps even physical pain upon those comprising her interpersonal world. The sex therapist must always be aware of these clinical issues in his or her treatment relationships with frigid alcoholic women. It is inappropriate to attempt to initiate sex therapy procedures for frigidity when the alcoholic woman is involved in a seriously disturbed sadomasochistic marriage or "live-in" relationship. Such couples are appropriately referred for extended conjoint and/or individual therapy prior to entering treatment for the woman's frigidity. It is "crazy" to expect the alcoholic woman to be sexually responsive and stimulated by a husband who constantly belittles her and is physically and psychologically abusive.

Many *women* who are married to an alcoholic report being "frigid" (Forrest, 1980a; Vraa, 1982). As the husband becomes increasingly dysfunctional and behaviorally inappropriate, as a result of the addiction process, the wife develops frigidity. Attempting to make love to an intoxicated, possibly impotent, and abusive husband or "lover" over a period of several months or years logically can result in frigidity. Women who are married to an alcoholic frequently indicate that they cannot stand the "alcoholic smell" of their husbands. Even this seemingly unimportant factor can eventually play an important role in the sexual adjustment and sexual feelings of the woman who is married to an alcoholic. Sex therapists and counselors who begin treatment relationships with sexually dysfunctional male alcoholics should always explore the sexual adjustment of the spouse or partner prior to undertaking the sex therapy process.

Infrequently, alcohol-addicted and/or "other" drug-abusing prostitutes initiate sex therapy as a result of frigidity. Typically, such women are expensive "call girls." They tend to be rather intelligent, in their early twenties, sometimes well educated, attractive, and "successful" in their profession. These women frequently complain of "situational frigidity." Commonly, such women report that they previously enjoyed sex and have been orgastic. Such women have often abused alcohol and other drugs since the time of middle adolescence. Prior to contacting a therapist in order to receive treatment for frigidity, these women have established a pattern of maintenance drinking and drug use. Patients of this variety should receive treatment for their alcoholism and substance abuse. Following this stage of treatment, the patient should be involved in extended dynamic psychotherapy. It is clinically most appropriate to begin sex therapy with these patients *after* they have received treatment for their addictions and other emotional problems.

A basic precursor to effective sex therapy and counseling with the frigid alcoholic woman is a reasonably intact and stable relationship with a man. Unfortunately, most alcoholic women are not involved in stable, loving, and healthy marital or living arrangements. With sobriety, time, and work in psychotherapy, the alcoholic woman can change. Her relationships with other people become more healthy and stable. Certainly, her relationships with men, to include the husband or lover, will become more healthy and rewarding. It is the observation of the author (Forrest, 1982a) that most alcoholic women who recover from alcoholism do not continue to persist in "sick" sadomasochistic marital relationships. Sex therapy is an integral part of the total recovery process in the case of alcoholic women who are frigid or otherwise sexually dysfunctional.

Summary

Frigidity has been defined and discussed in this section. The frigid woman is unable to feel sexually stimulated and responsive. Primary and secondary forms of frigidity were outlined. The fundamental physical and psychological processes essential to female sexual arousal were also discussed. Some sex therapists (Hartman and Fithian, 1974) believe that physical factors, mainly clitoral adhesions, tend to be a significant factor in the aetiology of frigidity. A number of psychological factors are associated with frigidity. It is important that the woman be adequately stimulated in order to be sexually responsive. Relaxation during lovemaking, the absence of an overdetermined need to "perform," and a healthy marital relationship are factors which contribute greatly to optimal female sexual responding. Faulty learning experiences, culturally and socially dictated roles, beliefs, and behaviors, and intrapersonal conflicts can operate to facilitate female frigidity (Barbach, 1980).

Alcohol abuse and alcohol addiction have been associated with frigidity in the clinical and research literature (Cerul, 1976; Wilson, 1977; Vraa, 1982). Alcoholic women (Wilsnack, 1973; 1982) experience a plethora of sexual, obstetrical, and gynecological problems. The addicted woman often manifests significant identity and sexual conflicts prior to the onset of alcoholism (Forrest, 1980b; 1982a). Alcoholism clearly compounds the sexual and identity problems of the female alcoholic. It is the position of the author that some alcoholic women in effect make themselves frigid. A case study is included in this section in order to demonstrate a number of the more typical clinical issues associated with alcoholism and frigidity in women. Sexual acting-out facilitated by intoxication adds to the identity and sexual conflicts of many alcoholic women.

Strategies of sex therapy and sexual counseling specific to the treatment of frigid alcoholic women are presented in this section. It is imperative that the frigid alcoholic woman be totally abstinent from alcohol for an extended period of time before initiating sex therapy. In addition, the patient's marital relationship should be relatively healthy. The husband should be a willing partner in the sex therapy process. If the marital relationship is severely conflicted and pathological, extended individual psychotherapy and/or conjoint therapy is a precursor to sex therapy interventions. The clinician must actively explore all of these issues with the patient prior to undertaking sex therapy. Sex therapy with the severely depressed, or otherwise seriously disturbed, frigid alcoholic woman consistently fails. Likewise, in these cases, treatment failure is closely associated with severe relationship disturbance.

An initial task in the therapy process with the frigid patient involves the utilization of nondemanding pleasuring techniques. Sexually dysfunctional women need to be taught to "let go" and abandon themselves to the sexual experience. During the first few days of the treatment process the couple is instructed to limit their physical relations to caressing, touching, and massage. Physical contact, intimacy, and communication not involving intercourse are the important ingredients in this stage of therapy. The couple practices these behaviors until the patient begins to experience a sense of stimulation and sexual arousal. It is productive to instruct the patient to focus and concentrate upon her bodily sensations and physical respondency during these exercises. When the patient reports feeling sensual and sexually aroused, the therapist instructs the couple to begin engaging in "light" genital stimulation. This phase of therapy involves the husband's touching and caressing of the patient's nipples, clitoral region, and vaginal entrance. At this point, the goal of treatment is for the couple to learn how to enjoy nondemanding, non-performance-oriented modes of sexual pleasuring. Intense stimulation of the patient is not a part of this phase of treatment. Many couples report feeling "closer together" and a renewed sense of being "in love" during this phase of therapy. After the couple has successfully practiced the techniques of light genital stimulation, the clinician suggests that they begin to have intercourse. The therapist emphasizes that the goal of intercourse is not to stimulate the patient to orgasm. The patient is told to initiate intercourse. Rigorous thrusting during coitus is discouraged. Intercourse is nondemanding and not performance oriented. It may be helpful for the sex therapist to suggest that the couple practice the "stop-start" method during intercourse. At this point the patient becomes capable of feeling sexually stimulated, excited, and aroused and is thus no longer frigid. The couple is told to practice the nondemanding pleasuring exercises from time to time. This procedure reinforces and synergizes the sexual responding of the patient.

The wives of many alcoholic males are frigid and sexually dysfunctional. Typically, these women develop frigidity as the alcoholic progresses into the middle and late stages (Forrest, 1978) of the addiction process. Alcoholism can literally destroy the sexual adjustment of the alcoholic as well as that of the nonaddicted spouse. It is suggested that the sex therapist not attempt to treat alcoholic prostitutes who are frigid. Recovery from alcoholism involves the total person. Optimal recovery, in the case of most alcoholic women, includes overcoming sexual "hang-ups" and sexual dysfunction problems. Alcohol abuse and alcohol addiction are not solutions to the problem of frigidity. Most frigid alcoholic women suffer from "secondary" frigidity. Clinicians who are trained and experienced in the treatment of alcoholism and sexual dysfunction can usually treat the frigid alcoholic within the context of ongoing relationship psychotherapy.

ORGASTIC DYSFUNCTION

Orgastic dysfunction refers to the specific inability of the woman to achieve an orgasm or "climax." Most sex therapists (Vraa, 1982) and sex researchers (Masters and Johnson, 1966; 1970; Hartman and Fithian, 1974; Kaplan, 1974; 1977; Barbach, 1980) agree that orgastic problems are the most common variety of "sexual dysfunctions" reported by women.

There is considerable controversy among sex therapists and clinical researchers over the issue of orgastic dysfunction. Historically, clinicians (Fenichel, 1945) have tended to view orgastic dysfunction as either frigidity or a special variety of frigidity. Recently, sex therapists (Kaplan, 1974; Ellis, 1979; Barbach, 1980; Vraa, 1982) tend to express the belief that orgastic dysfunction is a specific category or syndrome of sexual dysfunction. Orgastic dysfunction is not simply a type of frigidity. Psychoanalysts (Reich, 1945; Fenichel, 1945; 1953; Stekel, 1967) and psychotherapists have long espoused that frigid and sexually dysfunctional women are emotionally disturbed. Some of these authors (Reich, 1942) purport that the inability of a woman to achieve orgasm causes her to become emotionally disturbed and pathological. Reich (1942; 1945; 1953) believed that the fundamental cause of all emotional disturbance, in the case of men as well as women, is either an inability to experience orgasm or achieving only a partial or "blocked" orgasm. In the experience of the author (Forrest, 1980a) orgastic dysfunction in women does not necessarily create emotional problems. Furthermore, it is inappropriate to label a woman "emotionally disturbed" or "sick" simply because she is nonorgastic. Indeed, Kaplan (1974) indicates that an inability to achieve orgasm may represent a "normal" varient of female sexual responding and functioning.

Women with orgastic dysfunction problems can be classified (Kaplan, 1974) as suffering from "primary" or "secondary" orgastic dysfunction. Women who have *never* experienced an orgasm are diagnosed as suffering from primary orgastic dysfunction. Women who have been able to experience an orgasm but, for whatever reasons, become unable to reach orgasm are diagnosed as suffering from secondary orgastic dysfunction. In cases of primary orgastic dysfunction, the woman has not been able to reach orgasm by any means. Many women are able to reach orgasm infrequently. These women may, from time to time, experience orgasm through manual, oral, or genital stimulation. Some women seem to "lose" the ability to be orgastic. Such women manifest secondary orgastic dysfunction.

Unlike the frigid woman, orgastically dysfunctional women do not disdain or abhor sexual relations. Orgastically dysfunctional women very often enjoy sex, experience sexual stimulation and arousal, and are capable of loving relationships. Their sexual and interpersonal relationships with men are usually healthy and enjoyable. For the most part, they do not avoid sexual encounters and they do not feel "afraid" of sexual intimacy. Most orgastically dysfunctional women are loving and sensuous. Most typically, their desire for sex is not inhibited or lacking. Their repertoire of sexual behaviors and sexual responding is not constricted or pathologic. These women "feel" sexual and they are not sexually anesthetic. Usually, they lubricate quite adequately and their overall physiological and psychological set toward sex is conducive to proper sexual responding. In spite of these various factors, the orgastically dysfunctional woman experiences severe difficulty in the explicit realm of reaching orgasm. Some orgastically dysfunctional women are unable to reach a climax. In spite of adequate stimulation, appropriate vasocongestive functioning, and a psychological "set" that encompasses healthy sexual feelings, beliefs, and cognitions, the inorgastic or "preorgastic" woman is unable to reach orgasm (Barbach, 1980).

Women vary considerably with regard to the capacity to achieve orgasm. A few women report (Masters and Johnson, 1970; Vraa, 1982) being able to reach orgasm without any direct physical stimulation. These women are able to reach orgasm by simply fantasizing about making love or engaging in some form of sexual behavior. Orgasm follows direct stimulation of the breasts or after a few coital thrusts in the case of some women. Most orgastic women are able to reach orgasm during intercourse. In many cases, these women are orgastic in the male superior position. Some women who experience orgasm via intercourse are only able to do so in the female superior position. Nearly half (Vraa, 1982) of all orgastic women require direct manual or oral stimulation, aside from or in addition to coitus, in order to reach orgasm. Among the orgastically dysfunctional women are those who require extended periods of direct clitoral stimulation in order to climax. These women may reach orgasm during as few as one in 100 lovemaking encounters. The orgastically dysfunctional woman's spontaneous use of fantasy, manual and oral lovemaking techniques, and even mechanical devices usually do not enhance her ability to reach orgasm. It is estimated (Kaplan, 1974) that only 10 percent of the female population manifests primary orgastic dysfunction.

It is important for sex therapists and clinicians to have an understanding of the basic physiological and psychological processes involved in the female orgasm. The female orgasm has been conceptualized as a "reflex" by some sex researchers and clinicians (Masters and Johnson, 1966; 1970; Kaplan, 1974). According to Kaplan (1974) the "sensory input which generally triggers the reflex appears to derive mainly from sensory nerves, probably tactile and pressure fibers, whose endings are located in the clitoris." Like most reflexes, sensory stimulation and input from other anatomical areas can facilitate discharge. Thus, kissing, caressing, and direct stimulation of the nipples and other erogenous zones can result in orgastic discharge. Lower neural centers as well as high centers play an important role in facilitating the orgastic reflex. Kaplan (1974) states that "the motor outflow from the orgastic reflex centers of the female orgasm goes to the circumvaginal muscles and the muscles of the pelvic viscera, which respond with reflex spasms during orgastic discharge. Deep pressure receptors in those vaginal muscles, and perhaps visceral sensory nerves in the pelvic organs as well, transmit the orgastic sensations to the sentient brain." According to this model, the female orgasm is reflexive in nature. Sensory stimulation, which facilitates the orgasm reflex, derives essentially from the clitoral sensory nerves. The motor component of the orgasm reflex is associated with the circumvaginal muscles.

Only in recent years (Masters and Johnson, 1966; 1970) has the female orgasm been investigated physiologically and anatomically. Comparatively little is known about the female orgastic response. Sex researchers have not determined basic concepts of orgastic responding for women. Strict criteria for the measurement of stimulus intensity and duration relative to female orgastic responding have not been developed. Clinicians do not agree (Vraa, 1982) about the psychopathology of orgastic dysfunction. Indeed, many sex therapists (Kaplan, 1974) do not feel that women who are unable to reach orgasm are ipso facto emotionally disturbed. Orgastic dysfunction in women may represent a pattern of "normal" sexual behavior and "normal" sexual responding.

A plethora of myths, irrational beliefs, and social misconceptions surround the matter of female sexual responding. People somehow continue to believe that a woman *must* reach orgasm by intercourse if she is truly sexually responsive and orgastic. It is believed by some that a woman should reach orgasm every time she has coitus. Furthermore, some couples actually feel guilty because they are unable to reach simultaneous orgasms during intercourse. Often, such couples state to the sex therapist that they *should* be able to "come together" more frequently. These "performance-oriented" sexual expectations are clearly unrealistic and mythical. Yet, such myths, irrational beliefs, and misconceptions contribute to the sexual problems and dysfunctions of many women in our culture. One of the most common "complaints" expressed by women to their sex therapists is that of being sexually responsive and stimulated but unable to consistently reach orgasm via intercourse. Many of these women believe that the only "real" orgasms are those which occur as a result of coitus. In fact, some of these women feel guilty because they are so easily stimulated to orgasm by manual or oral methods and unable to reach orgasm by coitus. This situation is a double-bind. The woman who believes that it is "not right" to reach orgasm by oral or manual stimulation, and yet has easily experienced orgasm by these methods, eventually finds herself in a double-bind. She is in an even more difficult double-bind if she rarely experiences orgasm by intercourse.

The sex counselor is a sex educator. In cases such as those just described, the therapist must often provide the patient with basic sex education information. Some women simply need to be told that it is unlikely that they will reach orgasm on every coital occasion. Others need to be given "permission" to masturbate to orgasm. Frequently, patients neeed to be reassured that masturbation and oral sex are not deviant or perverse. In clinical practice it is not uncommon to encounter women who are initially afraid to "admit" that they are orgastic when stimulated orally or manually. These women tend to believe that they are emotionally "sick" or sexually disturbed because they are consistently orgastic by oral or manual stimulation rather than by intercourse. Alcoholic women are especially apt to have these irrational and unfounded beliefs.

A few women who enter sex therapy due to orgastic dysfunction do so as a result of "not being able to reach both clitoral and vaginal" orgasm. Based upon Freudian theory, many people have believed in two separate "types" of female orgasm: clitoral and vaginal. The extensive physiological research of Masters and Johnson (1970) dealing with the female orgasm clearly demonstrates that there are not two "types" of female orgasm. The female orgasm is clitoral. When a patient indicates that she is unable

to experience vaginal orgasm it is important for the sex therapist
to dispel the myth of vaginal orgasm. This simple information dis-
pels the anxieties of many women who believe themselves to be
sexually inadequate or dysfunctional because they do not experience "vaginal orgasm." Kaplan (1974) stresses that the specific
form of sexual behavior determines the intensity of clitoral stimulation and that stimulation of the clitoris is essential to the "pro-
duction of the female orgasm." While vaginal stimulation is exciting and erotic, such activity is of little consequence in the matter
of facilitating the female orgasm.

In the absence of physical pathology all women are capable
of orgastic responding. Clitoral adhesions (Hartman and Fithian,
1974), gynecological diseases, and neurologic impairments can be
associated with orgastic dysfunction. Chronic alcohol addiction
can result in physiological and neurological impairments. These
impairments may also be associated with orgastic dysfunction
(Vraa, 1982). However, physical factors are rarely associated with
orgastic dysfunction. Women who are orgastically dysfunctional
experience a great deal of difficulty "letting go." The orgastically
dysfunctional woman, like all sexually dysfunctional individuals,
may manifest any variety of psychological problems that cause
sexual problems. Conditioning, learning, and relationship factors
can be closely associated with the orgastic dysfunction of some
women. The orgastically dysfunctional alcoholic is sometimes
afraid to reach orgasm. These women are afraid of (1) losing
control, (2) "letting go," (3) being controlled sexually and interpersonally by a male, and (4) as a result of these dynamic issues,
the patient is afraid to experience orgasm. Furthermore, many
orgastically dysfunctional alcoholics irrationally believe that they
do not "deserve" to have orgasms. In fact, such women may become anxious and feel guilty following very sensuous and stimulating sexual encounters. Early in the sex therapy process, the therapist must give such patients "permission" to be orgastic.

When a woman has voluntarily and consistently inhibited her
orgastic reflex on several occasions, she soon finds that she has
lost her ability to voluntarily control her orgasm. The orgastic
reflex seems to involve an intensely affective learning and conditioning experience. Orgastic inhibition appears to become almost

automatic after a woman has voluntarily inhibited her orgastic reflex several times (Kaplan, 1974). This learning-theory-oriented explanation of orgastic dysfunction is rather simplistic. Yet, this learning theory paradigm readily applies to the social, interpersonal, and sexual conditioning experiences of many alcoholic women who are orgastically dysfunctional.

In spite of the various psychological and interpersonal variables that play an active role in the aetiology of orgastic dysfunction, it must again be emphasized that orgastic dysfunction may well represent a "normal" variant of female sexual functioning. Alcoholic women who are orgastically dysfunctional are not "crazy" or "sick" simply as a result of their sexual dysfunction. However, some women do become unhappy and somewhat depressive as a result of long-term orgastic dysfunction. A few women become angry and even reject sexual intimacy due to their consistent inability to reach orgasm. Alcoholic women who have been orgastically dysfunctional for several years tend to reach a point where they begin to reject men and avoid sexual intimacy. These women feel they have "tried everything, and nothing works" and therefore "give up" on the belief that they will one day be able to reach orgasm. At the other end of the continuum, a great many women appear to accept their inability to reach orgasm. These women do not avoid sexual intercourse and sexual intimacy. They are not clinically depressed, anxious, and hostile as a result of their orgastic dysfunction. Clearly, such women enjoy the nonorgastic experiences associated with human sexuality.

Alcoholism and Orgastic Dysfunction

Alcohol addiction and alcohol abuse are clearly associated with orgastic dysfunction in women (Cerul, 1976; Williams, 1976; Berenson, 1976; Wilson, 1977; Vraa, 1982). Clinical experience (Malloy, 1976; Williams, 1976; Peters, 1979; Forrest, 1980a) in the realm of sexual counseling with alcoholic women clearly indicates that a significant number of these women are orgastically dysfunctional. Williams (1976) suggests that the physiological effect of alcohol on sexual performance can cause frigidity and orgastic dysfunction. According to Wilson (1977), orgastic dysfunction is associated with alcohol abuse. Secondary orgastic dysfunction and intermittent periods of frigidity (secondary frigidity) are very common sexual problems among alcoholic women. In the clinical experience of the author, approximately 70 to 80 percent of alcoholic women who enter psychotherapy report symptoms of secondary orgastic dysfunction. Less than 15 percent of the alcoholic women who enter sexual counseling report having never experienced an orgasm.

Many alcoholic women have experienced orgastic dysfunction prior to the onset of their alcoholism. Indeed, the alcoholic woman learns to "use" alcohol in order to feel feminine (Wilsnack, 1973; 1982) and sexual. In therapy, the alcoholic woman may report that her early sexual experiences did not result in orgasm or intense arousal. Many alcoholic women state that they "felt nothing" during their initial coital experiences or while being "petted" or manually stimulated by a boyfriend. Eventually, such women begin to believe that "something is wrong" with them sexually. This belief system may lead to a chronic sense of uncomfortableness or anxiety within the context of sexual relationships. Alcohol ingestion can reduce or inhibit feelings of anxiety and stress. Alcoholic women very often learn to utilize alcohol in order to inhibit their feelings of anxiety, which are explicitly associated with coitus and sexual encounters. More specifically, some alcoholic women condition themselves to avoid intense anxiety associated with their inability to reach orgasm by drinking before and during sexual encounters. In cases such as this, the patient's orgastic dysfunction serves the addiction process. As a result of being intoxicated the patient is more comfortable with her sexuality. She is less apprehensive and anxious about the many issues associated with sexual intimacy. In the case of some alcoholic women who are orgastically dysfunctional, the paramount issue of being unable to reach orgasm is no longer a major source of threat once the woman is intoxicated. Once this general learning paradigm has been practiced and overlearned for a number of months or years, the patient has pathologically conditioned herself to depend upon alcohol as a tool for coping with sexual conflicts. Obviously, this process further reinforces and synergizes the woman's alcohol addiction.

Alcoholic women, like their male counterparts, very often engage in sexual intercourse and various sexually intimate behaviors while intoxicated or after imbibing. The pattern of drinking heavily before, during, and after sexual intimacy is very typical for the alcoholic woman. A woman alcoholic in therapy recently stated "every time I've had sex in the past six years, I've been drinking— whether it was with my husband, boyfriend, or a pickup." Even in the case of alcoholic women who are not sexually promiscuous, the pattern of drinking before and during sexual relations eventually becomes a manifest reality. The alcoholic wife of a physician stated "we only have sex after I have a *few* drinks—it's been that way for years." This woman had never been involved in a single extramarital affair in twenty-one years of marriage. Prior to entering therapy, she had consumed over a pint of vodka daily for more than three years.

When women engage in coitus or other intensive forms of sexual behavior after drinking several alcoholic beverages, their perceptual awareness of bodily and psychological stimulation is impaired. Intoxicated or "drunk" women do not "feel" sexually stimulated. Alcohol causes physiological and cortical changes in the human being which inhibit sexual responding, sexual "feelings," and even sexual thinking. The alcoholic woman is literally anesthetized by alcohol. In view of these clinical realities, it is only logical that alcoholic women should eventually find themselves orgastically dysfunctional. The alcoholic woman is "out of touch" with her sexual feelings. These women, primarily as a result of intoxication and the addiction process, lose the ability to sexually respond and sexually "feel." The many affairs and polymorphous sexual acting-out of some alcoholic women represent masochistic attempts to "feel" sexual stimulation. Such transactions soon become sadistic in nature, as the alcoholic woman unconsciously attempts to punish her husband or lover for his inability to provide her with adequate sexual gratification and stimulation.

A few alcoholic women report being able to reach orgasm only when they are intoxicated. One such patient was easily aroused and stimulated to orgasm after drinking or when she felt very depressed. In these cases the woman is able to relax, "let go," and abandon herself to the sexual experience only after drinking. Alcohol ingestion and enhanced sexual responding become pathologically associated in these situations. Paradoxically, the patient may respond more adequately after drinking. However, the pattern of depending upon alcohol in order to reach orgasm or complete the sexual act is clearly pathological. As the woman progresses into the middle and later stages of the addiction process (Forrest, 1978) the pattern of relying upon alcohol as a means of facilitating sexual responding becomes increasingly pathologic. At some point in the addiction process this procedure "breaks down" completely. The sexual pathology of many alcoholic women develops as follows: (1) drinking in order to be intimate and sexual during late teens and early adulthood, (2) drinking in order to be orgastic or avoid the reality of being orgastically dysfunctional during early adulthood and the early years of marriage, and (3) becoming frigid and grossly sexually aberrant or dysfunctional as a result of chronic alcohol addiction during middle adulthood and the later years of life.

The case of Laura exemplifies the problem of orgastic dysfunction in the alcohol addicted woman.

CASE 7. Laura B., the wife of a successful dentist, entered psychotherapy as a result of alcoholism, abuse of prescription drugs, and depression. The patient was a twenty-nine-year-old college graduate and had been married for over five years. Severe marital problems were not basic to the family relationship. The couple had one child, a four-year-old daughter. At the time of treatment engagement Laura had been totally abstinent from alcohol and all other drugs for a period of ten months. She was attending Alcoholics Anonymous two or three times each week.

The patient had grown up on a farm in western North Dakota and was the youngest of three children. Her father, a veterinarian, was described as "loving, but cold and aloof" by the patient. Laura felt that her mother was also "aloof and hard to talk to." The parents rarely argued, the family system was apparently stable, and Laura's older brother and sister were leading "normal" adult lives. During the initial therapy session, Laura emphasized the point that her parents "never kissed, never touched, and *certainly* never talked about sex" while she was growing up. In spite of being successful in her struggle to live a chemically free life-style, the patient decided to enter psychotherapy as a result of "still feeling depressed and having a lousy self-concept." She did not indicate that she was sexually conflicted or orgastically dysfunctional during the initial three therapy sessions. Indeed, the area of sexual functioning and sexual behavior was little touched upon early in treatment.

After completing a rather extensive psychosocial history on the patient, it became obvious that she felt rejected, unloved, and unimportant within the context of her family of origin. As these issues were being discussed at length during the third therapy session, Laura again brought up the matter of her parents' physical avoidance of each other. She stated that it was "little wonder that I felt physically and emotionally rejected." Within the context of the fourth therapy session an exploration of the patient's dating history and pattern of male-female relating was initiated. Laura very clearly indicated that it had always been difficult for her to "feel comfortable" in dating relationships. She stated that she had long recognized that she "felt inferior to men." During high school Laura dated "two or three" boys but was never sexually active. While in college Laura was involved in several short-term relationships with different men. None of these relationships were sexually oriented. After college graduation the patient taught in an elementary school located in Nebraska. Shortly after taking her first teaching position the patient met her husband. Laura and Jim dated for nearly two years before deciding to get married. During the first few months of their courtship the couple engaged in virtually no intimate sexual behaviors. A few months prior to marriage they became sexually intimate and began to have intercourse on a regular basis. It was at this time that Laura began to "drink a few glasses of wine" in order to "get in the mood for sex." However, the patient indicated that she enjoyed her sexual experiences with Jim, she felt sexually aroused and stimulated, had no difficulties lubricating, and perceived Jim as an "excellent lover."

The patient was quite excited and happy about getting married. She stated that "my father never really accepted me until I married Jim." However, she became increasingly anxious and apprehensive as the wedding date approached. Prior to the wedding, the patient consulted a local physician because of her feeling of acute uneasiness and anxiety. He immediately prescribed Valium. Within a month after being married the patient became severely depressed. She stayed in bed until noon, cried constantly, gained some fifty pounds in a period of seven months, drank every evening and avoided social contacts. At the urging of her local physician, Laura made an appointment with a psychiatrist who practiced in a larger city some sixty-five miles away. The psychiatrist placed Laura on an antidepressant medication and saw her in weekly outpatient psychotherapy for a period of five months. Laura "lost all interest in sex" at this time.

The patient became pregnant some fourteen months after getting married. Upon finding out that she was pregnant Laura stopped drinking. She also stopped smoking and began an exercise program, and her

depressive symptoms began to go into remission. Once again she began
to enjoy sex and on a number of occasions she reached orgasm. The patient experienced orgasm when her husband stimulated her orally. However, she stated in therapy that she "intellectually knew better, but
somehow felt that oral sex was bizarre or deviant." She had engaged in
oral sex and indeed was orgastic when stimulated orally, but felt guilty
about engaging in this form of "perverse" sexual behavior. The family
moved to a large city in Colorado following the birth of a healthy
daughter.

Almost immediately after moving to Colorado Laura began to
drink again. For a few weeks she "drank socially" and was usually
able to limit her pattern of consumption to less than four drinks per
evening. Soon she was drinking "a couple of drinks" in the mornings.
Once again she consulted a physician for her "nerves" and was prescribed Valium. Again, she became disinterested in sex and felt herself
"slipping into a deep depression." The patient's husband suggested
that she enter psychotherapy or perhaps "try" Alcoholics Anonymous.
Laura decided to attend Alcoholics Anonymous. She began attending
A.A. several times a week and within a period of three weeks she had
stopped drinking and discontinued her prescribed psychotropic medication.

The many clinical issues that were discussed with the patient during the context of the third and fourth therapy sessions indicated sexual conflicts in the areas of (1) a generally inhibited experiential sexual
history, (2) possible situational frigidity associated with alcohol and
drug abuse, and (3) definite situational orgastic dysfunction associated
with alcohol and drug abuse. The patient also was lacking in basic sex
education information and techniques of sexual behavior. The patient
was seen in nine individual therapy sessions. During these sessions the
focus of treatment consisted of (1) an exploration of the many historical and present dynamic factors associated with the patient's alcohol
addiction, (2) support and self-esteem building, (3) basic sex education
(giving the patient permission to masturbate and engage in oral sex),
(4) reinforcing the appropriateness of behaving in sexually assertive
ways, and (5) reinforcing all varieties of sexual intimacy in the absence
of alcohol or mood-altering chemicals.

Following individual psychotherapy, the patient and her husband
were seen in conjoint therapy on eight occasions for the explicit purpose of treating the patient's orgastic dysfunction. In these conjoint
sessions the couple openly explored their sexual feelings, experiences,
and desires. Specific sex therapy techniques were utilized in order to
resolve the patient's secondary orgastic dysfunction. Between the
first and third conjoint therapy sessions the couple was instructed to
practice extended caressing and nondemanding sexual pleasuring *prior*
to engaging in intercourse. For this couple, it was important for the

therapist to stress the mutual practice of kissing, caressing, and fondling, to be followed by mutual masturbation, and then the husband intensely stimulated the patient orally prior to coitus. By the fifth conjoint session the husband was able to stimulate the patient to near orgasm by utilizing these precoital stimulation methods and then bring her to full orgasm during coitus. The final conjoint session involved teaching both partners to manually utilize direct clitoral stimulation while engaging in intercourse in order to facilitate the orgastic reflex. The patient was also instructed to contract her vaginal and abdominal muscles when she felt herself beginning to reach orgasm and then to "relax and let go" at the point of impending orgasm.

This patient continued to be seen in weekly outpatient psychotherapy for a period of six months. She did not enter therapy for the specific purpose of changing her orgastic dysfunction. Sex therapy was conducted with the patient as one dimension of the overall treatment process. In a matter of weeks she was able to become consistently orgastic and, in fact, became capable of reaching multiple orgasms. A follow-up interview conducted two years after the completion of psychotherapy indicated that the patient had continued to be orgastic. At that point, she had also continued to be totally abstinent from alcohol and other drugs. Her depressive symptoms remained in remission.

This clinical case demonstrates that some alcoholic women with orgastic dysfunction can be treated easily and successfully. The patient grew up in a family system that avoided physical contact and feeling-oriented transactions. She was sexually inhibited and had avoided sexual intimacy during adolescence and early adulthood. Like so many alcoholic women, Laura eventually learned to use alcohol in order to be intimate and sexual. The patient had experienced periods of time in which she was orgastic. However, as she became progressively dependent upon alcohol and other drugs, a number of sexual problems developed. Transient frigidity became a reality for the patient. She soon developed orgastic dysfunction.

It is apparent that Laura needed basic sex education in order to overcome her orgastic dysfunction. She was sexually nonassertive and had been reluctant to assume the degree of responsibility required to help her reach orgasm. This case study involved a relatively healthy marital relationship. The overall sexual adjustment style of the couple was functional and generally healthy at the point of treatment engagement. Sex therapy was one focal dimension of the ongoing psychotherapy process with Laura. Certainly, the fact that Laura had been totally abstinent from alcohol for several months prior to entering therapy expedited a successful treatment outcome. Follow-up contact with the patient indicated that the symptoms of orgastic dysfunction, alcohol addiction, and depression continued to be in remission.

Basic Treatment Strategies

Alcoholic women with orgastic dysfunction can be difficult to treat (Forrest, 1979; Bratter, 1979). Sex therapy should not be initiated with the orgastically dysfunctional alcoholic woman who is uncommitted to sobriety. It is clinically inappropriate to attempt to treat the sexual problems of alcoholic women who are still drinking or in the process of being detoxified. In most cases of orgastic dysfunction, sex therapy should be undertaken after the patient has been abstinent from alcohol for a period of at least four to six months. Hopefully, the patient has been involved in intensive psychotherapy and/or Alcoholics Anonymous prior to beginning sex therapy and sexual counseling. Antabuse maintenance (Knauert, 1979) is not a deterrent to the process of sex therapy with orgastically dysfunctional women.

During the initial treatment session the clinician should investigate the recent medical history of the orgastically dysfunctional alcoholic patient. If the patient has not completed an extensive physical examination, including an "ob-gyn" examination, within the past six months, immediate referral should be made to a physician for these purposes. It is also important for the therapist to evaluate the patient's overall health maintenance adjustment. Within the context of the initial two treatment sessions the therapist should determine if the patient is eating properly and exercising on a regular basis. In general, alcoholic women do not maintain good overall health and living habits. It is important for the patient to develop proper eating habits, sleeping patterns, and a consistent exercise program. Drinking alcoholics abuse themselves. Recovering alcoholics must learn to "like themselves," and this includes learning how to take care of themselves. Therapists who advocate holistic "self-care" early in the development of their treatment relationships with alcoholic women soon discover that their patients improve more rapidly and globally. Sexual functioning is enhanced as a result of holistic health management.

Prior to beginning intensive sex therapy and sexual counseling with the orgastically dysfunctional woman, the clinician must explore the marital relationship. In the event that the marital relationship or living relationship is severely conflicted and psychodynamically sadomasochistic, sex therapy should not be initiated. Such couples will need to undergo extensive individual and/or conjoint therapy prior to beginning sex therapy. All marriages involving a drinking alcoholic are conflicted. Most marriages involving a sober alcoholic are difficult and somewhat conflicted. Some marriages or "living together" relationships involving a sober alcoholic are severely conflicted and bizarre. For these reasons, it is imperative for the sex therapist who works with alcoholic women with sexual dysfunctions to be well trained and clinically experienced in the area of alcohol addiction as well as human sexual behavior.

According to Kaplan (1974) the "primary objective in the treatment of orgastic dysfunction is to diminish or extinguish the involuntary overcontrol of the orgastic reflex." In accord with this primary treatment objective, the actual treatment process (Kaplan, 1974) consists of "teaching the patient to focus her attention on the premonitory sensations, but to allow them to proceed to their natural conclusion, free of control."

Since the treatment of orgastic dysfunction varies somewhat according to whether the patient manifests primary orgastic dysfunction, secondary orgastic dysfunction, or the inability to reach orgasm via intercourse, the therapist must be concerned with the issue of accurate differential diagnosis in the initial treatment sessions. Many alcoholic women who report having never experienced orgasm are surprisingly lacking in basic sex information and not at all knowledgeable with regard to their personal sexual anatomy and sexual functioning. In cases of primary orgastic dysfunction, treatment can be very effective and easy. Conjoint sex therapy is an appropriate and rapid method for treating some alcoholic women who have never reached orgasm. Conjointly discussing techniques of clitoral stimulation, feelings and irrational beliefs surrounding sexual behavior, and teaching simple relationship enhancement techniques (Tinker, 1980) may be sufficient to result in orgastic functioning for some orgastically dysfunctional alcoholic women. In retrospect, the clinician may doubt that cases of this variety represent primary orgastic dysfunction.

Some alcoholic women with primary orgastic dysfunction have "tried everything" in order to reach orgasm. Such patients have unsuccessfully tried masturbation, oral sex, mirrors, "groupies," vibrators, and any variety of other sexual behaviors as a means of experiencing orgasm. Kaplan (1974) states that these women have "true orgastic dysfunction." The most crucial step in the treatment of such women is that of facilitating the initial orgastic experience. The therapist explains to the patient that she is capable of reaching orgasm. In order to become orgastic the patient must be adequately stimulated. She must also be able to overcome the psychological factors that have historically inhibited her ability to reach orgasm. Dynamically oriented psychotherapy, as a part of the sex therapy process, is often required to elucidate the various psychological factors involved in the patient's orgastic inhibition. The simple reality that the patient has "tried everything" in order to reach orgasm, while *intoxicated*, may be a dynamically explorable issue in therapy, which quite readily leads to the resolution of orgastic inhibition.

In the event that these basic strategies of intervention do not result in the patient's ability to reach orgasm the treatment format must be modified. The decision to modify the treatment format can usually be made after eight to ten unsuccessful conjoint sex therapy sessions. When the patient is unable to reach orgasm with her husband, via mutual masturbation and other forms of direct external stimulation, the treatment format is shifted to self-stimulation. The sex therapist instructs the patient to practice masturbating under the most relaxing and pleasurable circumstances. Some patients are most comfortable masturbating while alone in the house. Soft music, the use of erotic fantasy, taking a relaxing shower, and arranging to be uninterrupted can be helpful factors as the patient masturbates. Some alcoholic women believe that masturbation is deviant, evil, and embarrassing. Obviously, in such cases the therapist must help the patient overcome these misconceptions and irrational beliefs (Ellis, 1980). The patient is able to overcome her uncomfortableness with masturbation by *practicing* this very form of sexual behavior. Kaplan (1974) suggests telling the patient to contract her abdominal and perineal muscles when she feels highly stimulated during masturbation. Many patients become orgastically functional following the practice of solitary masturbation. It is important that the patient be given permission to masturbate several times a week during this stage of treatment. She should be instructed to masturbate to the point of orgasm or, in the event that she is unable to reach orgasm by self-stimulation, she is told to practice masturbating for fifteen to thirty minutes per occasion (Barbach, 1980).

Should the patient fail to reach orgasm by masturbation, she is instructed to use a vibrator for self-stimulation. The vibrator provides intense clitoral stimulation. As some alcoholic women believe that the use of a vibrator for self-stimulation is "weird" or deviant, the therapist should explore these issues openly with the patient. Some sex therapists (Vraa, 1982) indicate that a few women reach orgasm the first time they use a vibrator. These women are able to "let go" and allow themselves to be fully stimulated by the vibrator. However, other clinicians (Kaplan, 1974) indicated that some women must stimulate themselves with the vibrator for nearly an hour in order to experience their first orgasm. This same author reports that a few women become "hooked" on the vibrator and are unable to reach orgasm by other methods of stimulation. The therapist must be aware of these dilemmas and pitfalls. It is important for the therapist to encourage the patient to practice a variety of methods of stimulation rather than relying totally upon the vibrator.

In many cases it is therapeutically efficacious for the sex therapist to teach the patient to use distraction during stimulation. The patient is told to practice thinking and concentrating upon something other than her stimulation and orgastic sensations. Thus, she may be instructed to fantasize about erotic experiences involving someone else during intercourse or masturbation. Some women are able to concentrate upon their vaginal sensations during intercourse, to the extent of not focusing upon the experience of impending orgasm, and thereby reach orgasm. Many orgastically dysfunctional women are literally obsessed with the issue of having an orgasm and become so preoccupied with their sexual responding that they actually inhibit the orgastic reflex. This pattern must be modified. The "orgasm watcher" (Kaplan, 1974) is caught up in a pattern of sexually and orgastically self-defeating behavior.

At the other end of the continuum, some alcoholic women have made themselves so anxious over the matter of being orgastically dysfunctional that they are totally unable to concentrate upon their feelings and bodily responding during coitus or clitoral stimulation. Such women are too distracted during stimulation. Relaxation training, sensate focus exercises, and the use of erotic fantasy are methods the sex therapist can utilize in order to help the patient extinguish anxiety, which inhibits stimulation awareness.

Kaplan (1974) indicates that "the orgastic discharge involves clonic contractions of the pubococcygeal and circumvaginal muscles. The orgastic reflex can be inhibited by overrelaxation or, in rare instances, by spastically contracting the pelvic muscles." According to this author, the sex therapist must encourage the patient to thrust actively and "contract her vaginal and abdominal muscles when she feels the sensations of impending orgasm." The patient can employ these techniques during coitus or while masturbating or using the vibrator.

After the patient reaches her first orgasm it becomes progressively easier for her to reach subsequent orgasms. Typically, she requires less stimulation and shorter periods of stimulation in order to experience orgasm. Once the patient has experienced several orgasms by self-stimulation, conjoint sex therapy is initiated. At this point, the goal of treatment is that of helping the patient establish orgastic functioning within the context of a sexual *relationship*. The husband attempts to stimulate the patient to orgasm during this stage of treatment. This task can be accomplished in a number of ways. The husband may be instructed to stimulate his wife manually or with a vibrator after coitus. The patient is told to be selfish during these exercises. She may employ any or all of the forementioned techniques in order to reach orgasm with her partner. Practice is essential to the success of this final stage of treatment.

Skilled sex therapists and researchers (Masters and Johnson, 1970; Kaplan, 1974; Barbach, 1980; Vraa, 1982) report that the vast majority of primary orgastically dysfunctional women develop the capacity to experience orgasm when treated with these basic procedures. A smaller percent of primary orgastically dysfunctional alcoholic women receiving treatment develop the capacity to reach orgasm.

Most women who are orgastically dysfunctional experience secondary or "situational" orgastic dysfunction. These women, as discussed earlier, have previously been able to reach orgasm but they develop orgastic inhibition. Frequently, anxiety inhibits or "blocks" the orgastic reflex of the woman with secondary orgastic dysfunction. Many of these women are able to reach orgasm by manual or oral stimulation. However, they are preorgastic upon intercourse. Kaplan (1974) indicates that there are "millions" of women who are orgastic, but these same women are nonorgastic during intercourse "unless they receive simultaneous clitoral stimulation." In some cases, orgastic inhibition is caused by relationship conflicts, poor or inadequate lovemaking techniques, and internal psychological problems. Women who are afraid of pregnancy may experience situational orgastic dysfunction. However, many women do not appear to manifest any of these aetiological symptoms. After failing to reach coital orgasm on several occasions, most women eventually "expect" to be coitally nonorgastic.

Treatment of the coitally preorgastic woman (Kaplan, 1974; Vraa, 1982) involves the resolution of internal and/or relationship pathology in addition to the utilization of specific sex therapy strategies of intervention. The sex therapist initially explores the marital relationship and the patient's beliefs, feelings, and internal "set" toward sex and sexual behaviors. Interventions of this variety facilitate orgastic functioning for some women. When these strategies of intervention do not result in the patient's ability to achieve coital orgasm, the clinician teaches the couple specific lovemaking techniques, which will enhance the patient's level of precoital arousal. It is very important for the patient to be highly stimulated and aroused prior to engaging in coitus. Adequate foreplay is a precursor to attempts at intercourse. When the patient becomes highly aroused during foreplay, the husband is told to initiate coitus slowly and to proceed with slow thrusting movements. After several minutes of intercourse, the husband removes his penis from the patient but continues to manually or orally stimulate her clitoris. Intercourse is again initiated. This style of lovemaking is practiced until the patient feels an impending orgasm. At this point, she is instructed to begin thrusting actively, exert abdominal and vaginal muscular control, and "let go." The patient soon discovers that she is more aware of her physical responding during sex. Thus, she can assume an active role in the experience of coital orgasm.

Another useful technique in the treatment of women who are situationally or coitally inorgastic involves teaching the patient to more fully experience her erotic vaginal sensations during intercourse. Kaplan (1974) points out that "there are two sources of sensory input from the vagina, and these produce distinctly different erotic sensations. Tactile stimulation of the outer third of the vaginal skin and adjacent labia minor produces specific sexual sensations." In order to develop the patient's sensitivity and awareness to vaginal stimulation the sex therapist suggests that the couple practice manual and oral caressing and exploration of this area. Upon intercourse, the patient attempts to concentrate on the pleasurable vaginal sensations created by the erect penis inside her vagina. While practicing this technique the woman is responsible for nondemanding thrusting. This procedure is continued until the patient becomes much more aware of her vaginal sensations during stimulation.

A consistently effective technique in the treatment of coitally preorgastic women is that of teaching the couple to practice clitoral stimulation during coitus. Clitoral stimulation during intercourse can be performed by the patient's husband or by the patient. The therapist instructs the couple to have intercourse in the female superior position. The husband then stimulates the patient's clitoris manually while his penis is inserted in the patient's vagina and during coitus. Other coital positions can also be utilized for the purpose of combining intercourse and manual clitoral stimulation. The husband is instructed to thrust slowly and simultaneously to stimulate the patient's clitoris manually until she is on the verge of reaching orgasm. At this point, the patient tells the husband that she is approaching orgasm and then begins to thrust actively until she experiences orgasm. The husband discontinues clitoral stimulation immediately prior to the patient's experiencing orgasm. With consistent practice, over a three- to four-week period of time, the patient becomes progressively less dependent upon clitoral stimulation to reach orgasm. Should the patient fail to reach orgasm after the husband has discontinued clitoral stimulation, the procedure is repeated. This is most likely to occur during the initial few practice sessions of combined clitoral and coital stimulation.

Many women readily develop the ability to be coitally orgastic when they stimulate themselves clitorally during intercourse. This procedure seems to produce the best results when the patient is comfortable masturbating in front of her husband and when he finds her autoerotic stimulation personally exciting and stimulating. In short, the patient stimulates her clitoris manually during intercourse. At the point of impending orgasm she discontinues manual stimulation and begins active coital thrusting to the point of reaching orgasm. As this procedure is repeated, the patient progressively becomes less reliant upon clitoral self-stimulation in order to reach orgasm.

A number of rather specific psychological factors impede the orgastically dysfunctional alcoholic woman from achieving orgasm. Alcoholic women tend to feel guilty about sex. Many of these women believe that sex is somehow dirty or "wrong." Orgastically dysfunctional alcoholic women are afraid to "let go" in their sexual relationships. They tend to "hold back" in their sexual encounters. It is for these very reasons that alcoholic women consistently report (Forrest, 1980a) that they have overused and abused alcohol in order to be sensuous and sexual. The sex therapist must help the alcoholic woman overcome these factors in treatment. Some alcoholic women need to spend several months in intensive individual and/or conjoint psychotherapy prior to beginning sex therapy. The marital relationships of many, if not most, alcoholic women contribute to the development of sexual problems and sexual dysfunctions (Skynner, 1976; Paolino and McCrady, 1977). In these marital situations, extended conjoint therapy is a precursor to effective sex therapy and sexual counseling.

Frequently, the nonalcoholic wives of addicted men are orgastically dysfunctional. Some of these women were orgastically dysfunctional prior to the onset of their husband's alcoholism. Most develop orgastic dysfunction as the marital relationship becomes increasingly pathological and as the husband progresses into the middle and later stages (Forrest, 1978) of the addiction process. These women learn to fear sex with an intoxicated husband. One patient stated that her husband would come home drunk and "try to fuck my brains out." She avoided sexual intimacy with her husband out of fear. This patient developed coital dysfunction, followed by generalized orgastic dysfunction, and finally frigidity.

Summary

Orgastic dysfunction is a problem experienced by millions of women. The orgastically dysfunctional woman is unable to reach orgasm. Women who have never experienced orgasm suffer from "primary" orgastic dysfunction. Some women are situationally unable to reach orgasm. These women manifest "secondary" orgastic dysfunction. Many women are unable to experience coital orgasm. It is important to point out that orgastic inhibition is not necessarily indicative of emotional disturbance or severe pathology. A few decades ago, psychotherapists mendaciously tended to believe that all orgastically inhibited women were neurotic. Many orgastically dysfunctional women enjoy sex, feel stimulated, and lubricate adequately.

Relatively little is known about the female orgastic response. The "reflex" model of female sexual responding was explored in this chapter. It is important for the sex therapist to have a thorough understanding of the physical and psychological factors associated with female sexual responding. The female orgasm is clitoral. The concept of "vaginal orgasm" is essentially a myth. In the absence of physical pathology, all women are capable of reaching orgasm. Psychological and relationship conflicts are most commonly responsible for orgastic dysfunction. Orgastically dysfunctional women encounter difficulty "letting go," relaxing, and abandoning themselves to the sexual experience.

Alcoholism and alcohol abuse actively contribute to the orgastic dysfunctions of many women (Cerul, 1976; Wilson, 1977;

Vraa, 1982). Williams (1976) suggests that one physiological effect of alcoholism on women can be orgastic dysfunction. The vast majority of alcoholic women who enter psychotherapy report having experienced secondary orgastic dysfunction. Many of these women manifest orgastic dysfunction and other sexual problems prior to the onset of their alcohol addiction. Alcoholic women drink in order to avoid sexual and identity conflicts. More specifically, some alcoholic women condition themselves to avoid intense anxiety associated with their inability to reach orgasm by drinking before and during sexual encounters. Orgastically dysfunctional alcoholic women tend to feel that they are inadequate and somehow not really a whole woman as a result of their inability to achieve orgasm. One such alcoholic patient stated that she had been searching for the big "O" (meaning orgasm) since she was seventeen years old. As the alcoholic woman drinks more and more, she loses the ability to perceive and feel herself respond sexually. Eventually, the alcoholic woman becomes so anesthetized by alcohol that she is physically and psychologically incapable of orgastic responding. The case presentation included in this section elucidates the many recondite clinical issues associated with alcoholism and orgastic dysfunction.

Sex therapy and sexual counseling with the orgastically dysfunctional alcoholic woman begins with total abstinence from alcohol. Sex therapy is initiated after the patient has been sober and committed to psychotherapy, Alcoholics Anonymous, or some other program of recovery for at least four to six months. The therapist may want the patient to complete a physical examination prior to beginning sex therapy. A gynecological examination should be completed by all patients manifesting present or historic "ob-gyn" problems. It is also therapeutically efficacious for the patient to be actively involved in a regular exercise program, nutritionally stabilized, and vegetatively regulated at the onset of treatment. The patient should not be taking psychotropic medication while undergoing sex therapy.

The clinician must accurately evaluate the marital relationship during the initial one or two therapy sessions. It is generally inappropriate to attempt conjoint sex therapy with severely disturbed couples. In such cases, the couple may be referred for extended marital therapy prior to beginning conjoint sex therapy.

The treatment strategies discussed in this section vary somewhat based upon the differential diagnosis of "primary" or "secondary" orgastic dysfunction. Kaplan (1974) states that "the primary objective in the treatment of orgastic dysfunction is to diminish or extinguish the involuntary over-control of the orgastic reflex." In many cases of secondary orgastic dysfunction, the utilization of direct clitoral stimulation, proper lovemaking techniques, therapist support and "permission," dissemination of basic sex education information, and the therapeutic resolution of irrational sexual feelings and beliefs will result in the patient's ability to reach orgasm. In the event that the use of these procedures does not result in orgastic functioning, the patient is taught techniques of self-stimulation (Barbach, 1980). In order to reach orgasm, the patient must be adequately stimulated and also psychologically capable of "letting go" or abandoning herself to the sexual experience. Intense clitoral stimulation via masturbation or use of the vibrator may be sufficient to produce orgasm. Some patients must be additionally taught to use cognitive techniques, muscle control, and relaxation in order to achieve orgasm. In the event that the patient is able to achieve orgasm only through autoerotic stimulation, strategies for enabling the patient to generalize her orgastic functioning to the marital relationship are discussed. Treatment of the situationally or coitally inorgastic woman was considered. Such women require somewhat different treatment than the totally inorgastic woman. Brief conjoint psychotherapy and/or individual psychotherapy may be essential to the resolution of the inhibition of the coitally inorgastic woman. Techniques to enhance the patient's level of sexual arousal are basic to the treatment of coitally and situationally inorgastic women. Vaginal focusing and direct clitoral stimulation during intercourse are essential sex therapy tasks that the therapist teaches the couple. Group therapy techniques are quite effective in the treatment of anorgasmic women (Barbach, 1980).

It is imperative that the orgastically dysfunctional alcoholic woman be committed to sobriety before, during, and following the sex therapy process. Intensive individual psychotherapy and marital therapy (Forrest, 1978) may be required in order to get the patient and couple "ready" for sex therapy. Many alcoholic women have been sexually used, abused, and even raped. It is relatively easy to understand why so many alcoholic women have sexual problems. Likewise, it is only logical and rational that the wives of so many alcoholic males are sexually dysfunctional and conflicted. Most orgastically dysfunctional alcoholic women respond favorably to sex therapy. Holistic recovery dictates improved sexual functioning for the alcoholic woman. A few patients remain coitally preorgastic after treatment. In these few cases it is important for the therapist to point out to the patient that she is not sexually inadequate or sexually sick. The husband is not inadequate or sexually a failure. These couples must be helped in the realm of accepting their particular pattern or style of sexual functioning.

VAGINISMUS

Vaginismus is a condition in which it is very difficult, if not impossible, for the woman to complete intercourse. Upon insertion of the penis into the vagina, "the vaginal introitus literally snaps shut so tightly that intercourse is impossible and even vaginal examinations must frequently be conducted under anesthesia" (Kaplan, 1974). Masters and Johnson (1966; 1970) and other sex therapists (Kaplan, 1974; Kroop, 1977; Vraa, 1982) consistently indicate that the woman who suffers from vaginismus suffers from no anatomical abnormality. The genitalia of these women are not physically different from those of women who are sexually fully functioning.

Kaplan (1974) indicates that vaginismus is "due to an involuntary spasm of the muscles surrounding the vaginal entrance, specifically of the sphincter vaginae and levator ani muscles, which occurs whenever an attempt is made to introduce an object into the vaginal orifice." A pelvic examination (Masters and Johnson, 1970) is often felt to be essential to the accurate diagnosis of vaginismus. Vaginismus does not occur as a result of physical obstruction in the vagina.

A number of physical factors have been associated with vaginismus in the sex therapy literature (Masters and Johnson, 1970; Hartman and Fithian, 1974). These physical factors include endometriosis, pelvic infections, a rigid hymen, and physical complications resulting from childbirth. Physical complications such as these result in coital pain. Rather than directly causing vaginismus, physical problems of this variety create a psychological "set," which reinforces the development of vaginismus. Any form of physical pathology of the pelvic organs that causes pain at the point of vaginal penetration or during intercourse can facilitate the development of vaginismus. Learning and conditioning factors very clearly play an important role in the aetiology of vaginismus. Kaplan (1974) states "vaginismus is a conditioned response which probably results from the association of pain or fear with attempts at or even fantasies of vaginal penetration. The original noxious stimulus may have been physical pain or psychological distress."

Various psychological factors can play an important role in the aetiology of vaginismus. Vraa (1982) concludes that many of the women who enter sex therapy for this dysfunction have grown up in rigid, overly religious family systems. Rape (Masters and Johnson, 1970) seems to play an important psychological role in the vaginismus of some women. In the experience of the author, incest can be directly related to the problem of vaginismus. Alcoholic women who have been sexually abused by fathers, step-fathers, or brothers experience a greater number of sexual problems, including vaginismus, than alcoholic women who have not been subjected to these traumatic experiences. Furthermore, vaginismus appears to occur more frequently in alcoholic women who have experienced consistent *attempts* at seduction by fathers, step-fathers, or brothers. In these cases, frank sexual encounters (intercourse, masturbation, and oral sex) have not actually taken place between the patient and any of her male family members. Yet, these sexual transactions involving the alcoholic woman with vaginismus and a male family member take place at the conscious or preconscious levels of awareness. Such erotic patterns of family interaction do not take place at the unconscious level of awareness. This position pertains to the patient, the primary family member involved in the sexual transaction, and other family members as well. These familial patterns are referred to as "covert incest" in Chapter 5.

Vaginismic patients do not manifest one basic personality configuration. There are a multiplicity of psychological and interpersonal factors related to the development of vaginismus (Leiblum, Pervin, and Campbell, 1980). However, the common denominator in this dysfunction seems to be a psychological fear of penile penetration and coitus. Obviously, any number of social learning mechanisms can be involved in the development of the patient's fear of intercourse. Some vaginismic patients consciously fear injury by the phallus. This fear is understandable in the case of patients who have been raped or sexually assaulted. Faulty social learning and conditioning experiences appear to be germane to most cases of sexual dysfunction in women. Vaginismus is no exception. However, some vaginismic patients do not have a history of being sexually assaulted or psychologically traumatized. By the same token, some vaginismic patients do not appear to be emotionally disturbed or "sick."

Psychoanalytic theory (Fenichel, 1945; 1953; Reik, 1974) rather consistently suggests that vaginismic women unconsciously hate men. Furthermore, this hatred of men is expressed via the symbolic castration of the man (Fenichel, 1945) by the vaginismic response or reflex. In effect, the man is castrated when he is unable to have coitus with the vaginismic woman. Freud (1953) believed vaginismus to be a manifestation of hysteria. Some sex therapists (Vraa, 1982) continue to perceive vaginismus as a "conversion-like" symptom. The clinical experience of recent sex therapists (Masters and Johnson, 1970; Kaplan, 1974; Leiblum, Pervin, and Campbell, 1980) does not seem to substantiate the psychoanalytic theory of vaginismus. Although some vaginismic patients manifest a hatred of men, penis envy, and so forth, most do not.

Vaginismus can create many psychological problems for the patient and her husband. The couple usually become increasingly upset and conflicted as they unsuccessfully persist in their attempts to have intercourse. The husband and wife may feel sexually "frustrated" early in their marriage and during courtship, but the very devastating impact of vaginismus upon the marital and sexual adjustment of the couple is not fully manifest until the couple has been married for a few years. At this point, they have "tried everything" and given up. Consultation with the family physician, the use of various lubricants, "talking," and attempts at prolonged foreplay have not resulted in the amelioration of the patient's vaginismus. The alcoholic woman with vaginismus may have even "gone on the wagon" for a few weeks as a "last ditch" effort to overcome her sexual dysfunction. When all else has failed, the couple may initiate sex therapy. By this time, the patient is in all probability determined to avoid all forms of sexual intimacy. She is morbidly afraid of sex. Indeed, her underlying problem of vaginismus may well have precipitated a more frigid type of sexual adjustment style. She feels anxious, inadequate, angry, and hurt, and the issue of being deserted or abandoned by her husband or lover may be a paramount source of threat. The husband feels increasingly frustrated as he experiences failure after failure in his attempts to penetrate the patient. He cannot "understand" her tightly shut vagina. Eventually, many husbands begin to angrily blame the vaginismic wife for her sexual dysfunction. Husbands who are sexually anxious and sexually threatened actively contribute to the patient's sexual dysfunction by their blaming and rejecting attitudes. These husbands soon develop sexual dysfunction. They may become impotent. Some develop prematurity or retarded ejaculation. Rather commonly, the clinician is confronted with the task of treating a vaginismic wife and a sexually dysfunctional husband.

In short, vaginismus can facilitate the development of severe marital problems. Vaginismus seems to result in more severe marital and relationship conflicts than even frigidity or orgastic dysfunction. These couples become sexually dysfunctional. The patient is guilty about her inability to have intercourse. The husband feels guilty about his inability to stimulate the patient. Both become depressed. After a few years, and in some cases only a few months, both spouses avoid sexual intimacy. They stop talking about sex. The husband may become sexually dysfunctional. The husband may begin an extramarital affair in order to meet his sexual needs and reassure himself of his sexual adequacy. It is not surprising that vaginismus is a key factor in unconsummated marriages.

It is difficult to estimate the exact prevalence of vaginismus among women (Leiblum, Pervin, and Campbell, 1980). Certainly, this form of sexual dysfunction is far less prevalent among women than frigidity or orgastic dysfunction. Kaplan (1974) states that this disorder is "relatively rare." Even less is known about the prevalence of vaginismus among alcoholic women. In the experience of the author, very few alcoholic women report being vaginismic. Perhaps as many as four to six out of every 100 alcoholic women who enter therapy due to a sexual dysfunction manifest vaginismus. However, symptoms very similar to vaginismus are common among alcoholic women. Many alcoholic women report marked pain associated with coitus. In such cases, it is important for the sex therapist to clinically and diagnostically differentiate between true vaginismus and painful intercourse or dyspareunia. Rarely is the alcoholic woman unable to have intercourse as a result of a tightened and constricted vaginal introitus. Some alcoholic women tend to have a long history of successfully completing intercourse *with* pain. Such a history may be indicative of dyspareunia. Other alcoholic women eventually manifest a phobic avoidance of coitus as a result of the pain they experience during intercourse. Effective sex therapy interventions with the alcoholic woman may be contingent upon the clinician's ability to differentially diagnose vaginismus, painful intercourse, coital phobia, and other psychopathologies associated with the patient's inability to have sexual intercourse.

Alcoholism and Vaginismus

Vaginismus is one of the sexual dysfunctions experienced by alcoholic women (Vraa, 1982). Wilson (1977) suggests that alcohol abuse can lead to sexual problems and vaginismus in women. However, Wilson (1977) also points out that this finding is "confusing correlation with cause." At this time, there is a very definite lack of unequivocal research and clinical data indicating that alcohol is the causative agent in vaginismus and the other female sexual dysfunctions. Research (Curlee, 1968; Mulford, 1977) indicates that women progress into alcoholism more rapidly than men; and women are more likely to be motivated to drink heavily as a result of personal crises than men. Research evidence (Jones, 1975; Jones and Jones, 1976; Belfer and Shader, 1976) even suggests that the menstrual cycle may affect women's susceptibility to the influence of alcohol. In spite of the vast number of research studies that have been conducted on alcoholic women, the fact remains that little has been done in the explicit area of investigating the sexual functioning and sexual adjustment of alcoholic women.

Clinicians (Corrigan, 1974; Williams, 1976; Cerul, 1976; Berenson, 1976; Malloy, 1976; Forrest, 1980a) tend to consistently report a high incidence of sexual dysfunction among alcoholic women. Yet, clinicians do not usually report precise statistical or research data in the area of alcoholism-related female sexual dysfunction. Cerul (1976) does indicate that among female alcohol abusers, the major categories of sexual dysfunction seen in therapy are orgasmic dysfunction and vaginismus. Data is not presented (Cerul, 1976) indicating the percentage of vaginismic alcoholic women entering therapy in comparison with orgastically dysfunctional alcoholic women entering therapy. The clinical experience of the author over the past ten years does not support Cerul's (1976) position regarding the high incidence of vaginismus among alcoholic women. As indicated earlier, the therapy experiences of the author with alcoholic women over a period of several years suggest that less than 10 in 100 alcoholic women manifest vaginismus.

Vaginismus can be more difficult for the sex therapist or counselor to diagnose than frigidity or orgastic dysfunction. An error which some sex therapists and clinicians tend to make is that of consistently diagnosing pain with coitus as vaginismus. Many alcoholic women experience pain during intercourse. Sex therapists and clinicians who are not medically trained will need to refer the alcoholic patient who complains of pain during attempts at coitus for a pelvic examination (Masters and Johnson, 1970) in order to confirm the diagnosis of vaginismus. Alcoholic women with vaginismus report that they have been unsuccessful in their attempts to complete intercourse. On occasion, the patient's husband or lover may have been able to insert the tip of his penis in her vagina. One vaginismic patient's husband expressed his disbelief about her sexual dysfunction as follows: "I can't understand how she can be so tight—there must be something physically wrong." Alcoholic women who are vaginismic want to experience complete intercourse. They may feel sexual, want to have coitus, lubricate properly, and feel stimulated or "turned on." In spite of appearing to be physically and psychologically "ready" to have coitus, the patient's vaginal introitus snaps shut when coitus is attempted. Many alcoholic women with vaginismus report that their earliest coital experiences were very painful. Commonly, these patients first attempted intercourse at thirteen or fourteen years of age. A few alcoholic women have been sexually assaulted by male family members (fathers, step-fathers, brothers or step-brothers, uncles, etc.) during childhood. Such women have been sexually traumatized.

Most vaginismic alcoholic women have not been sexually abused by male family members during childhood or adolescence. However, covertly incestuous sexual dynamics have often been operational within the alcoholic woman's family of origin. Sexually dysfunctional alcoholic women are uncomfortable with the sexuality involved in their familial relationships. Psychodynamically, vaginismus may be a defense against incest and incestuous impulses. In the case of alcoholic women who are vaginismic, vaginismus is sometimes rooted in an adaptive defense against an incestuous sexual relationship. Many, if not most, alcoholic women have grown up in emotionally disturbed family systems. The disturbed family system is also sexually pathologic (Bowen, 1978). Sometimes the alcoholic patient consciously remembers very well being approached sexually by her father or some other family member. More commonly, sexual impulses and sexual transactions within the family system have been denied and repressed by the alcoholic woman who is vaginismic. In order to avoid sexual intimacy with a family member, the patient develops vaginismus. These dynamic issues eventually play a pathological role in mate selection, the marital relationship, and sexual relations. The alcoholic woman may marry a man who is unconsciously very similar to her own father (Forrest, 1978; 1982a), thus experiencing severe marital problems and also becoming vaginismic in order to avoid sexual intimacy with the symbolic father or other family member.

Alcoholic women who are vaginismic often report having experienced a great deal of pain and difficulty with their initial attempts at coitus. It appears that these women have been vaginismic since adolescence. This pattern and style of sexual adjustment is rather consistent in the case of alcoholic women who suffer this particular sexual dysfunction. A second pattern of sexual responding in alcoholic women involves the onset of vaginismus after several months or years of marriage. Most alcoholic women who are in the first category consciously decide to drink prior to attempts at coitus. In fact, many of these women develop a consistent pattern of heavy drinking prior to all sexually intimate encounters. In psychotherapy these patients reveal that alcohol helps them relax and results in partially successful, less painful coital experiences. The process of drinking heavily in order to cope with vaginismus provides some psychological and physical relief for the patient, but eventually most of these women become floridly frigid. This occurs during the middle and later stages of the addiction process (Forrest, 1978). Alcoholic women who "fit" the second pattern seem to also develop vaginismus during the middle and later stages of alcoholism. Severe marital conflicts, possibly a number of marital failures, alcohol-facilitated sexual acting-out, and a long history of sexual abuse and manipulation by males are all very often factors that contribute to the development of "late onset" vaginismus. Understandably, these women are enraged at men. They are also unhappy, depressed, and angry at themselves.

The case of Annie M. illustrates rather well the multiple conflicts and pathology of the alcoholic woman who is vaginismic.

Case 8. Annie M., a thirty-nine-year-old woman, entered psychotherapy as a result of "sex problems" and marital difficulties. The patient had been married for some eighteen years and was the mother of three children. Her husband was a colonel in the Air Force. At the time of treatment engagement Annie had been totally abstinent from alcohol for six years. The patient described herself as an "alcoholic," having been hospitalized several times for alcohol withdrawal and rehabilitation prior to achieving sobriety. She had consumed more than a pint of vodka daily for three and one-half years during her alcoholic history. At the time of treatment engagement Annie was attending Alcoholics Anonymous "two or three" times per week.

During the initial few hours of individual psychotherapy Annie spent a great deal of time emoting and discussing the marital relationship. The patient's husband had physically abused and assaulted her on a regular basis since the early months of their marriage. She had "attended counseling" with several military chaplains over the years as a result of the marital abuse and discord. On one occasion both Annie and her husband had been "ordered" into marital therapy by the husband's commanding officer. This occurred following an incident that took place in an Air Force housing facility. On this occasion the patient was thrown out of their apartment and cast into the streets without any clothing on. To make matters worse, the patient's husband had broken her nose and two ribs. He then proceeded to throw her out and locked the door. The air police were summoned by a neighbor and the entire matter was brought to the attention of the husband's commanding officer who "forced" the couple to seek marital therapy with a post chaplain.

As she discussed her present marital situation, Annie was quick to point out that her husband treated her "just like my father." The patient's father, a career army first sergeant, had been physically and verbally abusive toward her as a child and adolescent. She described her father as cold, demanding, aloof, and perfectionistic. He was also a heavy drinker. The patient's mother was an alcoholic. Annie perceived her mother as passive, inadequate, and depressed. Annie had a sister and a brother. She was three years older than her sister and five years older than her brother. According to the patient, neither sibling was a problem drinker or alcoholic. Both were married, employed, and reasonably happy. Annie described her family as "screwed up." Throughout adolescence the patient remembered fearing her father. All of the family feared the father. On a rather consistent basis he would physically and psychologically abuse the patient's mother. A specific fear of the father involved his episodic late-night visits to the patient's bedroom. Annie stated that her father began coming into her bedroom at night when she was thirteen or fourteen years old. The father was always intoxicated on these occasions. Sometimes he would merely "pass out" on her bedroom floor. Sometimes he would awaken her and want to "talk." On a few occasions Annie's father had stumbled into her bedroom, completely intoxicated, and attempted to get into her bed. When the patient attempted to discuss her fears and feelings about these transactions with her mother, she was told "that's just your father—he was drunk, but he'd never really do anything to harm you." The father manifested similar behaviors with Annie's younger sister.

At age sixteen Annie began to date. Although her parents were generally unconcerned about the fact that she was dating, they were very concerned about her not getting pregnant. Her father reminded her over and over again that "all boys were out to get one thing—sex." During her junior year in high school Annie became sexually involved with a classmate. Annie recalled in therapy that they had "petted" several times each week for two or three months prior to attempting coitus.

The patient's boyfriend had tried to stimulate her manually on numerous occasions. Each of these attempts at manual stimulation had
failed. Annie stated that even manual stimulation was impossible due to
"the pain." Furthermore, her vagina became so constricted that the
boyfriend was unable to insert his finger inside her. Annie was emotionally upset about her inability to respond to manual stimulation. She
wondered what was wrong and thought that she might be physically
"deformed." In spite of these difficulties the couple decided that they
were "in love" and that they should have sexual intercourse. Annie described her first attempt at coitus as a "disaster." Penile insertion was
impossible. The pain associated with attempted coitus was unbearable.
The couple attempted to have intercourse on many occasions and the
outcome was always the same—failure. Annie remembered feeling
frustrated, inadequate, and embarrassed. Her boyfriend felt frustrated
and eventually he became resentful and overtly angry. Finally, the patient's boyfriend terminated their relationship. Annie felt deeply hurt,
rejected, and angry. Drinking was not associated with the patient's
sexual behavior during this relationship.

After this relationship the patient dated a number of males but
did not become sexually involved with any of them until she met her
husband at the age of twenty-two. The patient had, during the interim,
graduated from high school and worked as a secretary with two ac-
counting firms. She drank "socially" and had not experienced any difficulties as a result of her drinking behavior. Annie met her husband at
a Friday afternoon "happy hour." At the time, her husband was a second lieutenant in the Air Force. He was stationed at a nearby Air Force
base and was in the process of finishing training as a fighter pilot. The
couple dated several nights a week for a period of six months. Heavy
petting became a part of their relationship, but Annie did not allow her
husband to manually stimulate her vaginal area. Her husband "taught"
her how to perform oral sex on him and soon their sexual relationship
centered around her giving him several "blow-jobs" each week. Joking-
ly, the patient's husband would often tell her that she gave the best
"blow-jobs in town." During their courtship, Annie realized that Charlie
had a "bad temper" and that he tended to treat her cruelly. As graduation from flight training approached, the couple began to discuss the
possibility of marriage. Two weeks prior to Charlie's graduation, they
decided to get married.

The wedding night was the first time that Annie and Charlie had
tried to have intercourse. Needless to say, their attempts at coitus were
unsuccessful. Charlie was not angry at Annie when she was unable to
have intercourse during the early weeks of marriage. Rather, he was sur-
prised and unable to understand why "it wouldn't go in." The patient
had all of her previous beliefs and fears regarding her inability to function sexually confirmed. She expected to be unable to have intercourse

with Charlie and had avoided intercourse prior to marriage for this very reason. Although she "knew" that there was something "seriously wrong" with her sexually, Annie was not about to disclose this belief to her husband during the early months of their marriage.

After several months of marriage Charlie began to become increasingly resentful about not being able to complete coitus. The couple tried using lubricants, prolonged foreplay, and drinking a "few" drinks in order to complete intercourse. All of these measures failed. The patient consulted a physician about her sexual dysfunction. After finding no physical basis for her dysfunction, he recommended that she try to "relax" while having sex. During the second year of their marriage Charlie became so angry after an unsuccessful attempt at coitus that he hit the patient in the face with his fist, resulting in a "black eye." The marital relationship progressively deteriorated. Constant physical and verbal attacking became the relationship modus vivendi of this couple. They avoided all sexual intimacy for months at a time. The couple did conceive three children, much to their mutual amazement. According to Annie, full penile penetration during coitus had been possible on only "ten or fifteen" occasions in eighteen years of marriage.

The patient's husband had been on three "tours" of overseas military duty. On these occasions the patient drank heavily, "forged" checks, and engaged in extramarital sex. She was vaginismic on every occasion that extramarital coitus was attempted. Consequently, Annie "limited" her extramarital sexual relationships to fellatio and cunnilingus. She was able to reach orgasm by oral stimulation on a few occasions. Heavy drinking was consistently associated with orgastic success. This was also a very frustrating matter as she became even more desirous of having intercourse. She fantasized of being coitally stimulated to orgasm. Annie stated that she "had always" avoided masturbation as she felt this mode of sexual behavior was "dirty or somehow perverse."

Early in therapy it became apparent that conjoint treatment was indicated. Unfortunately, the patient's husband would not initially participate in treatment. On numerous occasions the patient's husband indicated to her that "once you've gotten your head screwed on, I'll think about seeing the shrink with you." Annie was seen in weekly outpatient psychotherapy for six months prior to any conjoint contacts with the couple. Finally, the patient's husband agreed to "come in" as a means of improving their sexual relationship. At this point, the patient felt that the marital relationship was generally improved. During the initial conjoint therapy session Charlie asked the therapist "how would you like to try living with that dumb son-of-a-bitch?" Charlie attended six conjoint therapy sessions and then terminated treatment feeling that he did not "have a problem." Needless to say, the marital relationship was so severely conflicted that it was both clinically inappropriate and impossible to begin sex therapy with this couple.

Annie continued in outpatient psychotherapy. Four months after the last conjoint therapy session she initiated a legal separation. Charlie was "shocked," angry, and depressed by the legal separation. He was also embarrassed and concerned about the impact of a marital separation on his military career. A divorce followed some nine months later. Following the legal separation Annie began to feel less depressed, she obtained a job as a legal secretary, and her self-concept improved rather radically. The children were happy about the separation and the oldest son, a junior in high school, commented several times "you should have left him years ago."

For the most part, the issue of Annie's vaginismus was explored very little in therapy from the time that conjoint treatment was discontinued until the divorce was completed. However, in psychotherapy the patient had rather consistently dealt with many of the dynamic, psychogenic, and affective components of her sexual dysfunction over a period of more than a year. A few weeks after the patient's divorce was final, specific sex therapy procedures were initiated as a part of the ongoing treatment process. The overall treatment format was quite simple. During three treatment sessions the focus of discussion was masturbation. The patient was encouraged to explore her vaginal region in front of a mirror, given permission to masturbate, and very directly told that she could not be "cured" unless she was willing to insert "something" in her vagina. With some difficulty, the patient was able to begin exploring her vaginal and clitoral areas. She agreed to "try" inserting something in her vagina. This issue was discussed at length in two therapy sessions. Annie was most comfortable using her well-lubricated index finger for this purpose. The patient was taught to utilize deep relaxation techniques, in combination with erotic imagery, while inserting her finger in her vaginal orifice. Within two weeks the patient was able to insert two fingers in her vagina and bring herself to orgasm without pain. The use of these behavioral sex therapy strategies resulted in a complete amelioration of the patient's vaginismus.

A successful outcome in the area of sex therapy was but one dimension of the overall effectiveness of treatment with this patient. Annie married a high school administrator some four years after her divorce. They have experienced no sexual problems and the patient has been totally nonvaginismic during eighteen months of marriage. The couple engage in coitus and a wide variety of other sexual behaviors two or three times each week. Annie has remained totally abstinent from alcohol and other mood altering drugs.

The case of Annie demonstrates well the multifaceted conflicts of the vaginismic woman with alcoholism. Annie had grown up within an alcoholic family system. Her alcoholic mother was certainly a pathologic role model. Her father was abusive and evidenced clear-cut sexual pathology. The patient's earliest sexual encounters were conflicted. Annie had been vaginismic throughout adolescence and adulthood. Her marital relationship was severely disturbed. Heavy drinking did not improve Annie's sexual functioning. However, she was less afraid and less phobic with regard to attempting coitus while intoxicated. In this regard, alcohol offered the patient a neurotic solution to her vaginismic dysfunction. Conjoint sex therapy failed in this case. Indeed, the marital relationship was pathologic to the extent of precluding the utilization of effective conjoint strategies of intervention. Divorce was an adaptive and healthy choice upon the part of this patient. Individual sex therapy, as a part of the ongoing process of psychotherapy with this patient, resulted in a complete extinction of the vaginismic response. The patient eventually actualized very significant generalized gains as a function of relationship psychotherapy and sex therapy.

Basic Treatment Strategies

Alcoholic women with vaginismic dysfunction should be referred for a thorough medical and "ob-gyn" examination prior to beginning sex therapy. A few patients who manifest vaginismic symptoms are suffering from physical pathology. These patients may require direct medical care or perhaps surgical treatment. Historically, the "treatment of choice" in cases of intractable vaginismus was to "enlarge the introitus surgically by means of an adequate perineotomy, with or without division of the perineal muscles" (Kaplan, 1974). The surgical treatment of vaginismus was usually successful in terms of enlarging the vagina and thus making intercourse without pain possible. However, surgical treatment for vaginismus very often results in psychological complications, which compound the patient's sexual problems.

Sex therapy is appropriately initiated after ruling out an organic basis for the patient's vaginismic responding. Alcoholic women should not be treated for vaginismus prior to the establishment of four to six months of total abstinence from alcohol. As pointed out in earlier chapters, it is clinically inappropriate to begin sex therapy and sexual counseling with alcoholic patients who are actively drinking or not committed to a sober life-style. Sex therapy should not be undertaken while the patient is being detoxified or treated within a short-term rehabilitation program. Additionally, prior to initiating treatment for vaginismus, it is desirable for the patient to be committed to (1) an active program of total health maintenance and (2) relationship psychotherapy. The alcoholic woman benefits most from a holistic treatment approach. A program of regular exercise, nutritional and diet stabilization, conjoint therapy and/or individual psychotherapy, an active involvement in Alcoholics Anonymous, and perhaps even a commitment to some form of religious or spiritual program of recovery, make up the ingredients in any holistic treatment program for alcoholic persons.

Frequently, conjoint therapy is a precursor to effective sex therapy. Alcoholic women who are vaginismic tend to be involved in conflicted marriages. Severe marital discord is one significant contributing factor in vaginismus (Leiblum, Pervin and Campbell, 1980). Sex therapists and counselors should not attempt to treat vaginismic alcoholic women who are involved in a severely pathologic marital relationship. Such couples need to be referred for extended marital therapy (Forrest, 1978) and/or individual psychotherapy before sex therapy is initiated. The alcoholic woman with vaginismus is most efficaciously treated by a conjoint sex therapy approach. However, as demonstrated by the case of Annie, individual sex therapy interventions can be very effective with the alcoholic vaginismic patient. Sexually dysfunctional alcoholic women have experienced globally conflicted relationships with their fathers or surrogate fathers, lovers, and husbands. Successful treatment of the sexually dysfunctional alcoholic woman may eventually result in divorce or marked adaptive changes in the patient's generalized style of heterosexual relating.

The treatment of vaginismus is relatively simple. Behaviorally, the essential goal of treatment is that of modifying the vaginismic response. Kaplan (1974) states that the treatment of vaginismus "consists of the progressive in vivo deconditioning of the involuntary spasm of the muscles which guard the vaginal entry." The successful treatment of vaginismus encompasses (1) modification or extinction of the conditioned vaginal response, and (2) behavioral and dynamic resolution of the patient's phobic fear or avoidance of vaginal penetration. It is critically important for the patient to overcome her fears and anxiety associated with vaginal penetration. Indeed, the sex therapist's initial and primary task in the treatment of vaginismic women is that of helping the patient resolve her phobic avoidance of vaginal entry. Once this treatment task has been accomplished, it is usually easy to extinguish the dysfunctional conditioned vaginal response.

Sex therapists (Masters and Johnson, 1970; Kaplan, 1974; Leiblum, Pervin, and Campbell, 1980; Vraa, 1982) vary somewhat with regard to the utilization of treatment formats aimed at modifying the vaginismic response and the anxiety or phobic behavior associated with vaginismus. In the experience of the author, it is clinically most appropriate to spend three to six conjoint therapy sessions with the alcoholic vaginismic patient and her husband discussing and focusing upon the patient's explicit fears and anxiety associated with vaginal penetration. It is helpful for the clinician to explain to the patient, as well as her husband, how she has psychologically and physically conditioned herself to be vaginismic. The sex therapist supportively reassures the patient that she will quickly overcome her pattern of vaginismic functioning with therapy. Very often, the husband of the vaginismic patient also needs to be assured that treatment can radically improve the couple's sexual adjustment. Many of these husbands have "given up" and believe that their vaginismic wife cannot be helped. A few believe that they are somehow responsible for her vaginismus. These issues must be considered and hopefully resolved during the initial three to six sex therapy sessions. Treatment cannot proceed until the patient has essentially resolved her phobic avoidance of vaginal penetration. She must also be psychologically "ready" to attempt vaginal dilatation. Therapist-provided didactic sex education, suggestion, reassurance, and support are often sufficient to enable the patient to overcome her morbid fear of vaginal entry. In some cases, the therapist will need to implement specific strategies of behavioral therapy (Wolpe, 1958). Vaginismus always involves a very significant phobic element. Therefore, the use of relaxation training (Wellman, 1980), systematic desensitization, imagery training, hypnosis, and covert desensitization techniques are appropriate treatment modalities for the resolution of the phobic aspects of vaginismus and dyspareunia (Lazarus, 1980). It is not appropriate to use tranquilizers and antianxiety medications in order to extinguish the phobic elements of the alcoholic woman's vaginismic disorder. It is too easy for these patients to develop a "cross addiction." Kaplan (1974) feels that the vaginismic patient is ready to begin the vaginal dilatation phase of sex therapy when she "can calmly imagine, while sitting in the therapist's office, being penetrated during intercourse."

The vaginal dilatation phase of treatment is begun by instructing the couple to visually and manually explore the patient's genital area. Coitus is not attempted until the final stage of therapy. Masters and Johnson (1970) suggest that the patient, with the help of her husband, conduct a pelvic examination. This procedure permits the couple to mutually explore the patient's vaginal entrance and genital area, thus validating that the patient is not anatomically "deformed" or abnormal. The conjoint treatment approach also facilitates communication and a feeling of shared commitment to the therapy process. Healthy relationship changes often occur more quickly in cases where conjoint therapy is appropriate. As indicated earlier in this chapter, it has been the experience of the author that many alcoholic women with vaginismus are involved in marital relationships that preclude the husband's participation in the early stages of treatment. Many of these husbands simply "refuse" to participate in sex therapy and/or relationship psychotherapy. Under these circumstances, the alcoholic woman with vaginismus can be successfully treated. This point needs to be emphasized. When the patient's husband refuses to enter sex therapy or, a somewhat similar situation, where the marital relationship is severely conflicted, the patient is treated on an individual basis. This treatment format is in accord with the belief held by some sex therapists (Peters, 1979) that it is generally appropriate to exclude the vaginismic patient's husband from the early treatment sessions.

After having successfully completed the vaginal and genital exploration exercise, the patient is ready to begin the in vivo desensitization phase of therapy. In some cases, the couple will need to practice the vaginal and genital exploration exercise three or four times before the vaginismic patient is "comfortable" enough to move on to the desensitization procedure. Sex therapists (Masters and Johnson, 1970; Kaplan, 1974; Leiblum, Pervin, and Campbell, 1980; Vraa, 1982) use a variety of desensitization procedures for the treatment of vaginismus. For example, Masters and Johnson (1970) employ a desensitization procedure that involves the use of rubber or glass catheters. This is a very common treatment procedure for vaginismus. The patient is initially dilatated with a very thin (wire-thin) catheter; a graduated series of catheters are inserted into the patient's vagina until she is able to tolerate the insertion of a catheter that has the circumference of an erect penis. In order to facilitate the desensitization process, some patients may need to retain a catheter intravaginally for an extended period of time. Intercourse is initiated when the patient has reached the point of being able to tolerate penile sized catheters without pain or trepidation. Using this procedure, Masters and Johnson (1970) report that most vaginismic patients are ready to attempt coitus after no more than ten dilatation experiences.

Some women do not feel comfortable with even the *idea* of inserting a mechanical device in their vagina. In general, alcoholic women seem to prefer self-dilatation over mechanical means of dilatation. This is a very individual matter and the sex therapist must openly discuss this issue with the patient. Patients who are not threatened and guilty about masturbation tend to respond most favorably to self-dilatation. The procedure can be easily accomplished by the patient and her husband in the privacy of their bedroom. The sex therapist instructs the patient to gently insert her well-lubricated finger into her vagina. This procedure may be accomplished in a step-by-step or progressive desensitization fashion. Initially, only the tip of the finger is inserted in the vagina. When this procedure is completed without pain or anxiety, the patient proceeds to insert a more extended length of her finger into her vagina. Eventually, she is able to fully insert her finger into her vagina without precipitating the vaginismic reflex. At this point, the patient is told to keep her finger inserted in her vagina for several minutes. Success in this exercise very actively facilitates the patient's commitment to treatment. She is then instructed to begin moving her finger in and out of her vagina in a coital like manner. Movement of the finger within the vagina is conducted slowly and gently.

After the patient is able to accommodate her finger in her vagina without pain, fear, and anxiety, she is then instructed to insert two fingers in her vagina. Additionally, she is told to begin to more actively move and rotate her fingers within her vagina. This procedure teaches the patient that she can actually expand and stretch her vagina without incurring the vaginismic reflex. Relaxation and fantasy techniques can be utilized in order to help the patient further relax her vaginal muscles and synergize treatment gains. This procedure is practiced daily for three to six days, depending upon the overall progress of the patient. With practice, the patient is soon able to voluntarily relax her vaginal muscles at the point of inserting her finger into her vagina.

The couple is clinically ready to attempt coitus when the patient is clearly able to insert, thrust, and rotate two fingers in her vagina for several minutes. It is imperative that the sex therapist accurately assess the coital "readiness" of the patient. Intercourse should not be attempted until the patient has successfully completed the previously discussed treatment tasks. The first attempt at coitus is very important. A good deal of therapist support and encouragement are essential to this phase of therapy. Successful coitus without pain or anxiety is the final stage of sex therapy with the vaginismic patient. Prior to attempting intercourse, the couple is told to proceed slowly with the task, and they are not encouraged to thrust actively during the initial attempts at coitus. The patient is "in control" of the husband's penile insertion. The couple must communicate openly about the patient's feelings and vaginal sensations during the early coital experiences. The husband is told to amply lubricate his penis prior to initiating coitus. The patient is then instructed to gently insert the tip of her husband's penis in her vagina. After allowing the tip of the penis to be vaginally inserted for one or two minutes, the patient signals her husband to slowly proceed to full penile penetration. The couple may proceed with slow and gentle thrusting at this stage of therapy, but this decision must be based upon the patient's overall response to coitus. This procedure is practiced on several occasions before the couple proceeds to active coital thrusting to orgasm. Should the patient become somewhat phobic or vaginismic during the coital stage of treatment, she must immediately make this known to her husband. In such cases, the final stage of treatment will require further intervention upon the part of the therapist. The couple will need to repeat and practice the tasks involved in the coital phase of therapy.

The clinician must consistently encourage the patient to "hang in there" and work through her pattern of vaginismic responding. Kaplan (1974) similarly states "the therapeutic maneuver which has proven most useful in treating vaginismic patients is the advice and encouragement to *stay with your unpleasant feelings.*" The patient is told throughout therapy that "pain" will be associated with "getting better."

Many sex therapists (Masters and Johnson, 1970; Hartman and Fithian, 1974; Kaplan, 1974; Vraa, 1982) suggest that the patient's husband insert his finger in the patient's vagina during the dilatation phase of therapy. Such a technique works well with some alcoholic couples. The clinician and couple will need to reach a joint decision on this treatment issue early in the treatment process. When this matter was discussed with one couple in therapy, the husband stated that he "couldn't" insert his finger in his wife's vagina. This husband had never in twenty-two years of marriage touched his alcoholic wife's genitals. Through self-insertion the patient readily overcame her vaginismic dysfunction. The husband, in response to the therapy process, decided that he wanted to be able to stimulate his wife manually. However, he was so phobic of the patient's genitals that he was initially only able to stimulate her manually while wearing a rubber glove. The husband was also successfully treated in this case. The therapist who works with alcoholic sexually dysfunctional patients must always be alert to the profound clinical and treatment implications associated with "secondary" complications of this type.

The wife of the alcoholic is often "somewhat" vaginismic. Upon close clinical scrutiny, these women are rarely vaginismic. Rather, they are coitally phobic. During the early months and years of marriage, the vast majority of these women have not been vaginismic or coitally phobic. They became sexually dysfunctional much later in marriage. Frequently, the onset of their grossly dysfunctional sexual responding occurs when the husband enters the middle stages (Forrest, 1978) of the addiction process. Vaginismic and coitally phobic women who are married to an alcoholic have experienced consistently pathologic patterns of sexual relating. Their alcoholic husbands sometimes "rape" them. The addicted husband comes home in an intoxicated state, verbally and perhaps physically abuses the wife, and then expects her to have intercourse. Alcoholic husbands tend to avoid or "omit" foreplay. They literally attempt to "jump on" their wives, who are not adequately stimulated, lubricated, or "psychologically ready" to have coitus. When the sexual relationship deteriorates, the alcoholic belittles and blames his vaginismic or partially phobic wife. As a result, she becomes even more sexually inhibited and dysfunctional.

Experiences of this variety involve traumatic and pathological conditioning and faulty learning. Such women are conditioned to be vaginismic or phobic. They learn to detest the smell of alcohol and many associate the smell of alcohol with sex. Such association patterns are pathologic. In the case of many women who are married to a chronic alcoholic, vaginismus and/or coital phobia eventually precipitate frigidity. Counselors and sex therapists need to be aware of these clinical issues. Some alcoholic women are vaginismic. Just as often, the wife of the alcoholic is vaginismic or otherwise sexually dysfunctional. The wife of the alcoholic is frequently also in need of sexual counseling and sex therapy.

Summary

Vaginismus is a variety of sexual dysfunction, which involves an inability upon the part of the woman to complete coitus. Attempts to insert the penis in the patient's vagina immediately result in vaginal constriction and severe pain. Vaginismic women do not manifest an anatomical aberration. However, physical factors are sometimes associated with the onset of vaginismus. Any form of physical pathology of the pelvic organs that results in pain at the point of vaginal penetration or during intercourse can facilitate the development of vaginismus. A diversity of psychological factors are aetiologically associated with vaginismus. Some alcoholic women with vaginismus have been raped by their fathers or step-fathers. More typically, these women have grown up in family systems that rigidly avoid the overt discussion of sex, and yet unconsciously and covertly such families are incestuous.

The vaginismic woman manifests a psychological fear of penile penetration and coitus. Some of these patients consciously fear injury by the phallus. They irrationally believe that the penis will "tear" their vagina apart. Psychoanalysts (Fenichel, 1945) assert that vaginismus is unconsciously associated with the woman's hatred of men and her desire to castrate men.

Vaginismus can result in severe marital problems. The woman feels depressed, confused, angry, and guilty about being vaginismic. Many of these women state "I can't understand what's wrong with me." The patient's husband feels sexually frustrated. Some husbands blame themselves for the patient's inability to have coitus. Alcoholic women drink in order to overcome their pattern of vaginismic responding. Commonly, alcoholic women with vaginismus have experienced severe pain during their earliest attempts at coitus. These women learn to use alcohol in combination with sex in order to overcome coital pain, vaginismic sexual responding, and a generalized anxiety or uncomfortableness associated with sexual intimacy. The alcoholic vaginismic woman may even "go on the wagon" for a few weeks as a means of "curing" her vaginismus. When such attempts at self-treatment for sexual dysfunction fail, she begins to drink more pathologically.

Very few alcoholic women are vaginismic. However, many alcoholic women experience a good deal of pain (dyspareunia*) associated with coitus. Coital phobia is rather common among alcoholic women. These are important clinical issues. The sex therapist must be able to accurately diagnose the patient's sexual dysfunction and then implement appropriate strategies of treatment. The differential diagnosis of vaginismus and coital phobia can be difficult and, indeed, a pelvic examination may be essential to this procedure.

---

*Dyspareunia refers to painful intercourse or coital discomfort. The basic difference between vaginismus and dyspareunia is that insertion of the penis is usually impossible in the first condition but possible with pain and discomfort in the latter condition. The treatment techniques discussed in this chapter for vaginismus are generally applicable in cases of dyspareunia.

Sex therapists (Cerul, 1976; Wilson, 1977; Vraa, 1982) clearly indicate that vaginismus is one of the primary sexual dysfunctions experienced by alcoholic women. Cerul (1976) suggests that vaginismus and orgastic dysfunction are the most common sexual dysfunctions among alcoholic women entering sex therapy. Researchers (Wilson, 1977) seem to indicate that alcohol abuse can lead to the onset of vaginismus. In the experience of the author, vaginismus is a rather rare form of sexual dysfunction among alcoholic women. Nonmedically trained sex therapists will need to refer patients that appear to be vaginismic to a physician for pelvic examination prior to beginning sex therapy. Some alcoholic women who are vaginismic have manifested this form of sexual dysfunction since adolescence. However, other alcoholic women seem to develop vaginismus after several months or years of marriage and following the onset of their alcohol addiction. Intoxication helps extinguish the anxiety and pain associated with vaginal penetration. It is for these reasons that alcoholic women with vaginismus drink heavily prior to attempts at sexual intercourse. However, many alcoholic women who are vaginismic develop frigidity during the middle and later stages of the addiction process (Forrest, 1978). In this respect, alcoholic women can make themselves sexually dysfunctional via the addiction process. A case study was included in this section in order to demonstrate the various problems of the alcoholic woman with vaginismus.

The vaginismic woman should complete a pelvic examination and thorough medical examination. Prior to beginning sex therapy, alcoholic women need to be totally abstinent from alcohol for a period of no less than four to six months before entering sex therapy for vaginismus. It is clinically inappropriate to begin sex therapy with the vaginismic patient who is still drinking or involved in a detoxification program. Additionally, it is desirable for the patient to be committed to relationship psychotherapy and a program of holistic health care prior to undertaking sex therapy. If the patient is involved in a seriously conflicted marital relationship, conjoint therapy and/or individual therapy will be a basic prerequisite to successful sex therapy interventions.

The basic goal of sex therapy with these patients is to modify the vaginismic response. The initial conjoint therapy sessions involve an open discussion of the patient's fears and anxieties associated with vaginal penetration. An initial goal of therapy is to help the patient overcome her phobic avoidance of vaginal penetration. A variety of behavioral therapy techniques can be used in order to reach this treatment goal. Vaginal dilatation is used to extinguish the pathological vaginal response. The couple is encouraged to examine the patient's vaginal opening and genital area. When this sexual task has been successfully accomplished, vaginal dilatation is initiated. Alcoholic women seem to prefer self-dilatation over mechanical means of dilatation. This procedure involves inserting one finger in the vagina, then two fingers, and finally vaginal rotating and stretching exercises. Strategies of penile insertion and other techniques of stimulation are also discussed. The sex therapist must be encouraging, supportive, and yet confrontive (Forrest, 1982) throughout the treatment process with alcoholic vaginismic women. As indicated in this section, individual sex therapy with the alcoholic woman who is vaginismic is often appropriate and successful.

The wife of the alcoholic may be vaginismic or coitally phobic. As their husbands become progressively alcohol dependent, these women develop vaginismus or other sexual dysfunctions. Clinicians who work with alcoholics need to openly explore the sexual adjustments of both spouses. It is relatively easy to treat the alcoholic woman who is vaginismic. In order to maintain sobriety, grow, and actualize her fullest potential as a human being, the alcoholic woman with vaginismus must effectively resolve her sexual dysfunction and sexual problems. In the case of the alcoholic woman, sexual "recovery" can only take place after sobriety is established.

BIBLIOGRAPHY

Barbach, L.: Group treatment of anorgasmic women. In Leiblum, S., and Pervin, L. (Eds.): *Principles and Practice of Sex Therapy*. New York, The Guilford Press, 1980.

Belfar, M.L., and Shader, R.I.: Premenstrual factors as determinants of alcoholism in women. In Greenblatt, Milton, and Schuckit, Marc A. (Eds.): *Alcoholism Problems in Women and Children*. New York, Grune and Stratton, 1976.

Berenson, D.: *Sexual Counseling with Alcoholics*. Workshop on Sexual Counseling with Alcoholic Problems. Pittsburgh, Pennsylvania, January, 1976.

Bowen, M.: *Family Therapy in Clinical Practice*. New York, Jason Aronson, 1978.

Bratter, Thomas E.: *Reality Therapy Training*. Lecture, Psychotherapy Associates, P.C. Fifth Annual Advanced Winter Workshop, "Treatment and Rehabilitation of the Alcoholic," Colorado Springs, Colorado, February 1, 1979.

Cerul, M.: *Basic Considerations in Sexual Counseling*. Workshop on Sexual Counseling for Persons with Alcoholic Problems, Pittsburgh, Pennsylvania, January 1976.

Corrigan, E.M.: Women and problem drinking. *Journal of Addictive Diseases, 1(2)*:215-222, 1974.

Curlee, J.: *Comparison of Male and Female Patients at an Alcoholism Treatment Center*. Doctoral dissertation, Ann Arbor, Michigan, University Microfilms, No. 69-11, 378, December, 1968.

Ellis, Albert: *Rational Emotive Therapy Training*. Lecture, Psychotherapy Associates, P.C. Fifth Annual Advanced Winter Workshop, "Treatment and Rehabilitation of the Alcoholic," Colorado Springs, Colorado, February 1, 1979.

Ellis, Albert: Treatment of erectile dysfunctions. In Leiblum, S., and Pervin, L. (Eds.): *Principles and Practice of Sex Therapy*. New York, The Guilford Press, 1980.

Fenichel, O.: *The Psychoanalytic Theory of Neuroses*. New York, Norton, 1945.

Fenichel, O.: *The Collected Papers of Otto Fenichel*, 1st Series. New York, Norton, 1953.

Forrest, G.G.: *The Diagnosis and Treatment of Alcoholism*. Springfield, Charles C Thomas, Rev. 2nd Edition, 1978.

Forrest, G.G.: *Motivating Alcoholic Patients for Treatment*. Lecture, Fourth Annual Colorado Summer School on Alcoholism, Glenwood Springs, Colorado, June 11, 1978a.

Forrest, G.G.: Setting alcoholics up for therapeutic failure. *Family and Community Health, 2(2)*:59-64, August, 1979.

Forrest, G.G.: *Alcoholism, Identity and Sexuality*. Lecture, Psychotherapy Associates, P.C. Sixth Annual Advanced Winter Workshop, "Treatment and Rehabilitation of the Alcoholic," Colorado Springs, Colorado, February 3, 1980a.

Forrest, G.G.: *How to Live with a Problem Drinker and Survive*. New York, Atheneum 1980b.

Forrest, G.G.: *Confrontation in Psychotherapy with the Alcoholic*. Holmes Beach, Florida, Learning Publication, 1982.

Forrest, G.G.: *Alcoholism, Narcissism and Psychopathology*. Holmes Beach,

Florida, Learning Publications, 1982a.

Freud, S.: *The Future Prospects of Psychoanalytic Therapy*. Collected Papers, Vol. II, London, Hobarth, 1953.

Gallant, D.M.: The effect of alcohol and drug abuse on sexual behavior. *Medical Aspects of Human Sexuality, 2(1)*:30-31, 1968.

Hartman, W.E., and Fithian, M.A.: *Treatment of Sexual Dysfunction: A Bio-Psychological-Social Approach*. New York, Jason Aronson, 1974.

Jones, B.: Alcohol and women: Intoxication levels and memory impairment as related to the menstrual cycle. *Alcohol Technical Reports, 4(1)*:4-10, 1975.

Jones, B., and Jones, M.: Alcohol effects in women during the menstrual cycle. *Annals of the New York Academy of Sciences, 273*:576-587, 1976.

Kaplan, H.S.: *The New Sex Therapy: Active Treatment of Sexual Dysfunctions*. New York, Brunner/Mazel, 1974.

Knauert, A.P.: *Differential Diagnosis of Alcoholism*. Lecture, Psychotherapy Associates, P.C. Fifth Annual Advanced Winter Workshop, "Treatment and Rehabilitation of the Alcoholic," Colorado Springs, Colorado, January 28, 1979.

Knauert, A.P.: *Issues in the Treatment of Alcoholism*. Lecture, Psychotherapy Associates, P.C. Sixth Annual Advanced Winter Workshop, "Treatment and Rehabilitation of the Alcoholic," Colorado Springs, Colorado, February 7, 1980.

Kroop, M.: *Sex Therapy Counseling Techniques*. Second Annual Sex Therapy Workshop, Department of Counseling and Guidance, University of North Dakota, Grand Forks, North Dakota, May 3, 1977.

Lazarus, A.: Psychological treatment of dyspareunia. In Leiblum, S., and Pervin, L. (Eds.): *Principles and Practice of Sex Therapy*. New York, The Guilford Press, 1980.

Leiblum, S., Pervin, L., and Campbell, E.: The treatment of vaginismus: Success and failure. In Leiblum, S., and Pervin, L. (Eds.): *Principles and Practice of Sex Therapy*. New York, The Guilford Press, 1980.

Malloy, E.S.: *Strategies in Sexual Counseling in Alcoholic Marriages*. Proceedings of a Workshop on Sexual Counseling for Persons with Alcoholic Problems. Pittsburgh, Pennsylvania, University of Pittsburgh, Medical School, October, 1976.

Masters, W.H., and Johnson, V.E.: *Human Sexual Response*. Boston, Little, Brown & Co., 1966.

Masters, W.H., and Johnson, V.E.: *Human Sexual Inadequacy*. Boston, Little, Brown & Co., 1970.

Medhus, A., and Hansson, H.: Alcohol problems among female gonorrhea patients. *Scandinavian J of Social Medicine, 4(3)*:141-143, 1976.

Mulford, H.A.: Men and women problem drinkers: Sex differences in patients served by Iowa's community alcoholism centers. *J of Stud on Alcoholism, 38(9)*:1624-1639, 1977.

Paolino, T.J., and McCrady, B.S.: *The Alcoholic Marriage: Alternative Perspectives.* New York, Green and Stratton, 1977.

Peters, J.E.: *Behavioral Treatment of Alcoholism Related Sexual Dysfunctions.* Lecture, Psychotherapy Associates, P.C. Fifth Annual Advanced Winter Workshop, "Treatment and Rehabilitation of the Alcoholic," Colorado Springs, Colorado, January 29, 1979.

Reich, W.: *The Discovery of the Orgone: The Function of the Orgasm.* Vol. I. New York, Orgone Institute Press, 1942.

Reich, W.: *The Murder of Christ: The Emotional Plague of Mankind.* New York, The Noonday Press, 1953.

Reich, W.: *Character-Analysis.* 2nd Edition. New York, Orgone Institute Press, 1945.

Reik, T.: *Of Love and Lust.* New York, Jason Aronson, 1974.

Skynner, A.C.R.: *Systems of Family and Marital Psychotherapy.* New York, Brunner/Mazel, 1976.

Stekel, W.: *Compulsion and Doubt.* New York, Washington Square Press, 1967.

Tinker, R.H.: *Relationship Enhancement Techniques and Video-Therapy with Alcoholics.* Lecture, Psychotherapy Associates, P.C. Sixth Annual Advanced Winter Workshop, "Treatment and Rehabilitation of the Alcoholic," Colorado Springs, Colorado, February 8, 1980.

Vraa, C.W.: *Sex Therapy Training.* Lecture, Psychotherapy Associates, P.C. Eighth Annual Winter Workshop, "Treatment and Rehabilitation of the Alcoholic," Colorado Springs, Colorado, February 2, 1982.

Wellman, L.: *Relaxation Therapy Training.* Lecture, Psychotherapy Associates, P.C. Sixth Annual Advanced Winter Workshop, "Treatment and Rehabilitation of the Alcoholic," Colorado Springs, Colorado, February 7, 1980.

Williams, K.H.: *Overview of Sexual Problems in Alcoholism.* Workshop on Sexual Counseling for Persons with Alcohol Problems, Pittsburgh, Pennsylvania, January, 1976.

Wilsnack, S.C.: Femininity by the bottle. *Psychology Today*, pp. 39-43, April, 1973.

Wilsnack, S.C.: *Alcohol and Issues in the Treatment of Alcoholic Women.* Lecture, Psychotherapy Associates, P.C. Eighth Annual Advanced Winter Workshop, "Treatment and Rehabilitation of the Alcoholic," Colorado Springs, Colorado, February 2, 1982.

Wilson, G.T.: Alcohol and human seuxal behavior. *Behavior Research and Therapy, 15(3)*:239-252, 1977.

Wilson, G.T., and Lawson, D.M.: Effects of alcohol on sexual arousal in women. *J of Abnormal Psy, 85(5)*:489-497, 1976.

Wolpe, J.: *Psychotherapy by Reciprocal Inhibition.* Stanford, California, Stanford University Press, 1958.

Section II
ALCOHOLISM AND
SEXUAL DEVIATION
An Overview

DEVIANT SEXUAL BEHAVIOR

IN the first section of this text the various behavioral and psychodynamic interrelationships between alcohol addiction and the human sexual dysfunctions were examined. Alcoholism was defined. The major forms of human sexual dysfunction were clinically defined, described, and delineated. The role of alcohol addiction and alcohol abuse in the aetiology of each of the human sexual dysfunctions were considered. Finally, specific strategies of sex therapy were outlined for the treatment of alcoholic persons manifesting each of the major human sexual dysfunctions.

Section II of this text encompasses an exploration of the role of alcoholism and alcohol abuse in the aetiology of several forms of deviant sexual behavior. The various important clinical issues related to alcoholism and incest, alcoholism and homosexuality, alcoholism and child molesting or pedophilia, alcoholism and rape, alcoholism and exhibitionism, and alcoholism and sadomasochism are explored in this section of the book. Sexually deviant behavior has been the topic of many researchers and clinicians. Yet, very few studies have been conducted in the explicit realm of alcoholism and sexual deviation. Sexual deviation has remained an area of social interest for centuries. Sexual deviants and "perverts" have long been the subject of clinical investigation and research. It is only in recent years that behavioral scientists have become cognizant of the fact that many deviant sexual acts are precipitated by intoxication or alcohol addiction upon the part of the sexually deviant person. Indeed, many "perverts" are unable to act out their sexually deviant behavior in the absence of alcohol ingestion or intoxication.

There is considerable professional controversy and disagreement over the nature of deviant sexual behavior. According to Vraa (1982), whenever two adults mutually agree to participate in any form of sexual behavior the term *deviant* is inappropriate. Hatterer (1970) indicates that homosexual behavior upon the part of two mutually consenting adults may be considered deviant simply on a statistical basis. Homosexual behavior is statistically abnormal. Cameron (1963) states that "sexual deviations or perversions are patterns of sex behavior which do not culminate in heterosexual intercourse when this outcome is permissible and objectively possible." The sexual deviant may engage in sexual behavior with a member of the same sex when members of the opposite sex are available. However, there remains considerable controversy over these viewpoints. The American Psychiatric Association (Barlow and Wincze, 1980) recently removed homosexuality from its list of deviant sexual behaviors. Some people become sexually stimulated and excited by contact with an inanimate object, such as a shoe or underclothing, rather than a live person. Most would agree that such a pattern of sexual responding is atypical or deviant.

Historically, sexual deviation has been viewed as immoral and unnatural. Homosexuality and intercourse with animals are "forbidden" acts according to Christian, Moslem, and Judaic scriptures. For hundreds of years these acts have been punishable by death throughout many cultures. In recent Western culture, the trend has been to abolish legal punishments for sexual deviation involving mutually consenting adults. Within the United States sexually deviant behavior which is conducted in public is punishable by law. Our current legal system very actively punishes adults who "use" or involve minors in any sexually deviant manner. It is only within the last decade or so that the vast majority of Americans have learned that masturbation and oral and anal modes of sexual behaviors are not deviant or abnormal. However, in some states legal doctrine continues to view oral, anal, and other forms of normal heterosexual behavior between a married couple and practiced within the privacy of the bedroom as criminal. Counselors and sex therapists are often "sex educators" in the sense that they need to explore and dispel the many irrational beliefs (Ellis, 1980) that their patients have learned during the process of socialization. Sexuality continues to be shrouded in myth, taboo, and ignorance.

The "mixture" of sex and alcohol is potent and very often catastrophically destructive. As indicated throughout the various chapters in the first section of this book, one outcome of combining alcohol and sex is sexual dysfunction. Alcohol as a causative or precipitating variable in sexual deviance is but another tragic reality, which psychologically devastates the lives of millions of Americans each year. We are only now beginning to realize that alcohol abuse and alcohol addiction relate to the issues of sexual deviation and sexually deviant patterns of behavior. At present, we do not possess adequate research data pertaining to the roles of alcohol abuse and alcoholism in the aetiology of sexual deviation. In juxtaposition to this reality, we do not fully understand the roles of sexually deviant and sexually dysfunctional behavior in the development of alcohol abuse and alcohol addiction. Quite simply, we are only now beginning to conduct extensive and systematic research in the area of alcoholism and human sexuality. Alcohol abuse can result in sexually deviant acting-out. By the same token, sexual deviation or "sex problems" can lead to alcohol abuse and eventually addiction. The eminent sex researcher Kinsey (1953) stated "it is not so difficult to explain why a human animal does a particular thing sexually. It is more difficult to explain why each and every individual is not involved in every type of activity." Intoxication results in a generalized loss of personal control. The intoxicated person is less in control of his or her motor functions, cognitive abilities, thought processes, feelings, and behavior. As such, the alcoholic or intoxicated individual is not fully in control of sexual feelings, thoughts, impulses, and behaviors. Therefore, it is only logical and rational to expect that alcohol-induced patterns of behavior will include an enhanced probability of sexually deviant acting-out.

Alcohol addiction and sexual deviation are major social and health problems throughout the world. It is only now that we are collectively concerning ourselves with the many interrelationships between alcoholism and sexual deviation. In this respect, the chapters included in this section of the text represent but a beginning point. Hopefully, the material in these chapters will generate further research and clinical study in the area of alcoholism and sexual deviation.

BIBLIOGRAPHY

Barlow, D.H., and Wincze, J.P.: Treatment of sexual deviations. In Leiblum, S., and Pervin, L. (Eds.): *Principles and Practices of Sex Therapy*. New York, The Guilford Press, 1980.

Cameron, N.: *Personality Development and Psychopathology: A Dynamic Approach*. Boston, Houghton Mifflin Co., 1963.

Ellis, A.: Treatment of erectile dysfunctions. In Leiblum, S., and Pervin, L. (Eds.): *Principles and Practices of Sex Therapy*. New York, The Guilford Press, 1980.

Hatterer, L.J.: *Changing Homosexuality in the Male*. New York, McGraw-Hill, 1970.

Kinsey, A.C. et al.: *Sexual Behavior in the Human Female*. Philadelphia, Saunders, 1953.

Vraa, C.W.: *Sex Therapy Training*. Lecture, Psychotherapy Associates, P.C. Eighth Annual Advanced Winter Workshop, "Treatment and Rehabilitation of the Alcoholic," Colorado Springs, Colorado, February 2, 1982.

Chapter 5
ALCOHOLISM
AND HOMOSEXUALITY

HISTORIANS report that homosexuality has been considered a "problem" in most, if not all, societies for thousands of years. The homosexual is a matter of concern in the written documents of most civilizations and societies. A great deal has been written about homosexuality over the centuries. In recent decades, behavioral scientists have investigated the origins of homosexual behavior. Indeed, the homosexual has been a subject of considerable clinical and research interest during the past fifty years. In fact, overt homosexuality is still poorly understood by clinicians, therapists, and the various behavioral science professions. The general public does not understand homosexuality. Many people seem to fear the homosexual. In general, homosexuality in women is considered to be somewhat of a joke. In our culture, female homosexuality is not accepted or viewed as socially acceptable and appropriate behavior. Yet, the female homosexual tends not to be feared and perceived as a criminal or bizarre deviant. Somewhat to the contrary, the male homosexual often tends to be viewed as a "pervert" or criminal. Men seem to be more threatened than women over the matter of homosexuality.

There are numerous clinical definitions of homosexuality. Cameron (1963) indicates that overt homosexuality is "an adult preferring sex relations with his or her own sex, in spite of the availability of potential partners of the opposite sex." This author (Cameron, 1963) does not consider the homosexual behavior of young children, adolescent "experimenters," or people segregated from members of the opposite sex for extended periods of time to be indicative of homosexuality. Today, there is a great deal of controversy among clinicians regarding the use of the term "latent" homosexuality. Many clinicians believe that everyone has latent homosexual trends. This position can be associated with Freud's (1953) bisexual theory of man. According to Freud (1953), homosexuality is the expression of a universal trend in all human beings, stemming from a biologically determined bisexual predisposition. There can be little doubt that men and women have a great deal in common. This statement applies to anatomy, physiology, personality, feelings, cognitions, and behavior.

Hatterer (1970) states that homosexual phenomena "can appear along a continuum containing hundreds of gradations, from a fleeting and brief attraction and erotic arousal by another male to an automatic, unceasing, and fanatically compulsive pursuit of homoerotic contacts to the point of orgasm." In defining male homosexuality Hatterer (1970) asserts the presence of one common denominator: "that the male (or female) experiences active or passive sexual arousal by another male (or female) at some level of consciousness—in dream, in fantasy, in impulse, or in act."

A more "popular" definition (Bergler, 1956) of homosexuality is simply that "a homosexual is a person who derives sexual excitement and satisfaction from a person of his or her own sex in contradistinction to a heterosexual, who is sexually attracted only to members of the opposite sex." Bergler (1956) views homosexuality as a "neurotic disease" and asserts that "specific neurotic defenses and personality traits that are partly or entirely psychopathic are specifically and exclusively characteristic of homosexuals." Bergler (1956) also refers to homosexuality as a "curable illness."

Over the past decade or so clinical opinions and social beliefs about homosexuality have evolved or changed in the direction of viewing this form of sexual behavior from a more socially oriented perspective. Fewer people tend to perceive the homosexual as a "diseased" or bizarrely perverted person. The American Psychiatric Association (Barlow and Wincze, 1980) recently removed homosexuality from its list of deviant sexual behavior. Even the legal consequences for engaging in homosexual behavior have undergone a slow process of modification in the United States and throughout many countries of the world. In most modern societies, homosexuality is considered a crime or legal matter when practiced in public, when mutual consent is not involved, or when children or young adolescents are seduced by adults. In America, the Gay Liberation Movement has been very active in advocating equal rights and nondiscrimination-oriented social practices for homosexuals. The gay movement has done a great deal to dispel many of the distorted myths surrounding the homosexual and homosexual behavior. Homosexuals have historically been persecuted or alienated in most societies. Homosexuals continue to be feared or disdained in the United States. Quite commonly, we are exposed to the messages of a few well-known celebrities asserting that homosexuals are "sick," deprived individuals who sexually prey upon young children and adolescents. The homosexual teacher has been a subject of considerable controversy and debate among parents, educators, and the lay public. All of these factors seem to indicate that homosexuality continues to be poorly understood by the general public as well as behavioral scientists.

Social scientists have long questioned the validity and appropriateness of labeling homosexuality as a "perversion" or sexual deviation. In view of the rather pervasive incidence of homosexuality in most societies, this ambivalence about viewing homosexual behavior as a "sexual deviation" appears to be quite logical and understandable. Ford and Beach (1951) investigated the incidence of homosexual behavior in seventy-six different societies. The results of this study are helpful in assessing the cultural aspects of homosexuality as a deviation or perversion. These researchers (Ford and Beach, 1951) found that 67 percent (48) of the seventy-six societies (other than the United States) considered homosexual behavior to be "normal and socially acceptable" for certain members of the community. In twenty-eight of the seventy-six societies adult homosexual behavior was "totally absent, rare, or carried on only in secrecy." These authors (Ford and Beach, 1951) point out that 100 percent of the males in certain societies actively engage in both homosexual and heterosexual behavior. Kinsey et al. (1948) estimated that approximately 30 percent of the adult males in the United States have on one occasion or another been brought to orgasm as a result of having oral sex (fellatio) with another male. The findings of these various studies seem to indicate that some homosexual behavior occurs in most human societies. Homosexual behavior appears to occur more frequently among adolescents and males. Interestingly, Hatterer (1970) states that "cross-cultural and cross-species comparisons suggest that a biological tendency for inversion of sexual behavior is inherent in most, if not all, mammals including the human species. At the same time we have seen that homosexual behavior is never the predominant type of sexual activity for adults in any society or in any animal species."

Hatterer (1970) indicates that millions of men in contemporary American society have experienced homosexual thoughts and fantasies. Many of these men engage in overt homosexual behavior while many others do not. According to this same author, there are approximately 2.5 million, or more, practicing male homosexuals in the United States. Caprio (1954) indicates that 19 percent of women have had sexual contact with members of their own sex. This statistic was taken from the original Kinsey et al. (1953) study on *Sexual Behavior in the Human Female*. Among unmarried women, one in ten have experienced a homosexual relationship by the age of forty. Early studies (Hamilton and MacGowan, 1929; Davis, 1929) of homosexuality among women reported that 25 to 50 percent of women "admitted sexual intimacy with other women." Most experts in the field of homosexuality (Caprio, 1954; Hatterer, 1970; Vraa, 1982) believe that this form of sexual behavior is at least as common among women as it is among men. Researchers (Bergler, 1956) point out that homosexuality is often less apparent in women, and society seems to be less concerned with the homosexual behavior of women. Sexual inversion among women is much more difficult to detect than among men. In this realm, it is interesting that throughout history the legal codes of various cultures and societies have sharply distinguished between male and female homosexuality. Female homosexuality is not mentioned in the Hittite code. In the Bible and Talmud almost all references to homosexuality pertain to males. According to Caprio (1954) the Talmud characterizes female homosexuality as a "mere obscenity." Catholic codes condemn both male and female homosexuality but penalties are enforced only in the cases of male homosexuality. The

Catholic church frequently imposed the death sentence upon male homosexuals in medieval Europe. Only in Austria, Greece, Finland, and Switzerland are there specific statutes against female homosexuality (Caprio, 1954).

For these reasons, homosexuality has remained an enigma in much of American society. Only in recent years have male and female homosexuals begun to come "out of the closet." It is little wonder that homosexuals and people with homosexually oriented identity conflicts have been reluctant to identify themselves or seek therapy.

It is difficult to explain the origins of homosexual behavior. Indeed, there are many theories or explanations of homosexuality. A plethora of psychological theories of homosexuality have been developed by clinicians and behavioral scientists. Biological, sociological, and anthropological theories of homosexuality have been developed by many different behavioral scientists. Bieber et al. (1962) indicate that for a homosexual adaptation to occur in our time and culture, factors must combine to "(1) create an impaired gender-identity, (2) create a fear of intimate contact with members of the opposite sex, and (3) provide opportunities for sexual release with members of the same sex." Bieber et al. (1962) stress that homosexual adaptation is a result of "hidden but incapacitating fears of the opposite sex." In essence, this theory of homosexuality purports that the fear of heterosexuality determines the homosexual object choice. Psychodynamic theorists (Fenichel, 1945, Ovesey, 1963; Hatterer, 1970) associate homosexuality with unresolved oedipal conflicts. More specifically, the family style of interaction and relating is believed to foster the development of homosexual strivings. In these family systems, the mother is traditionally reported to be seductive and overly attached to the homosexual son. The father is aloof, removed from the son, and hostile. Bieber et al. (1962) found that severe psychopathology in the homosexual parent-child relationship was ubiquitous, and "similar psychodynamics, attitudes, and behavioral constellations prevailed throughout most of the families of the homosexuals." All of the parents of homosexuals were characterized as having severe emotional problems. The triadic interactions in these families (Bieber et al., 1962) were "disturbed and psychopathic." Homosexuality in the male can be viewed as a neurotic attempt to resolve oedipal conflicts involving the father.

Freud (1953), as touched upon earlier, postulated that all human beings are bisexual. Therefore, it was his belief that there is a homosexual component in everyone. Freud (1953) also pointed out the narcissistic dimension of homosexuality. The homosexual male loves himself (narcissism) as he sees himself in members of his own sex. Homosexuality is also an expression of infantile sexuality and a symbiotic attachment to the mother object. Freud (1953) viewed homosexuality as a reflection of an overdetermined identification with the mother object in adjunct to a morbid fear of the father. In accord with this viewpoint, Fenichel (1954) emphasized the castration fears of the male homosexual. The son fears his father to the extent that he is unable to properly identify with him. He also is afraid to love his mother because loving her will result in castration by the father. These dilemmas generalize, and the son is eventually unable to love and be sexually intimate with all women. Freudian theorists (Fenichel, 1945; 1953) point out that some homosexual males perceive their mothers as dangerous, frightening, and castrating. For these reasons, they are unable to be sexually and interpersonally intimate with women. Therefore, they seek out a homosexual relationship as a solution to these mother-son-oriented conflicts.

Lesbians, or female inverts, suffer from an overdetermined or unresolved Electra complex according to Freud (1953). These women are fixated or too much attached to their fathers. Freudian theory also emphasizes the role of penis envy in the development of female personality and the sexual problems of women. Psychoanalysts (Fenichel, 1953; Reik, 1974) suggest that the female homosexual is often unable to make a healthy heterosexual adjustment as a result of unconscious incestuous feelings toward her father or brother. In such cases, female homosexuality is seen as a defense against incest.

Cameron (1963) believes that a child of either sex "is likely to develop distortions in basic object relationships, including homosexuality, when the mother is strong and dominant in the home while the father is weak, ineffectual, or habitually neglectful of his children. A boy may be unable to identify with such a father and develop instead a feminine identification by default. A girl may be unable to take such a man as her love object. She may not only identify with her powerful mother but also take over her mother's attitudes of masculine domination, thus making her unfit to play a normal feminine role." The simple absence of a father or mother within the family constellation can result in role, identity, and sexual confusion. In view of the growing incidence of divorce and legal separation in the Western world, some might speculate that this factor alone will eventually result in an increase in homosexuality and sexual problems.

Biological theories of homosexuality suggest, as did Freud (1953) and Stekel (1929), that (1) all people are bisexual, thus homosexual, or (2) some people are "born" homosexual. We have already explored the first biologic perspective at some length. The second biologic model suggests that the homosexual person is homosexual at the time of birth, if not before. Perhaps homosexuality is determined at the time of conception. This model implies that each person is fated to be heterosexual or homosexual from the time of birth. Furthermore, this model implies that it is extremely difficult, if not impossible, to reverse the biologically determined sexual makeup of an individual. Thus, homosexuality is genetically determined. The male and female anatomy, physiology, and total physical makeups are dissimilar and yet paradoxically very much alike. A hormonal imbalance or endocrine disturbance may contribute to the constitutional makeup of the homosexual.

Some homosexual persons (Hatterer, 1970; Masters and Johnson, 1979; Vraa, 1982) state that they have "always known" they were "gay" or homosexual. Such individuals report that as young children they were very much aware of their same-sexed object preference. In adolescence and young adulthood these early self-perceptions and beliefs have been experientially and sexually validated. However, the heterosexuality or homosexuality of many, if not most, individuals does not fall into an "all or none" category. Hatterer (1970) indicates that only about one-half of the male population engage in exclusively heterosexual behavior and a very small percent engage in only homosexual behavior. Masters and Johnson (1979) have found that many homosexual persons think about and fantasize about heterosexual behavior. Moreover, heterosexual persons have homosexual thoughts and fantasies and some even experience homosexual desires or impulses. There is every reason to suspect a biologic factor in homosexuality. Possibly there is a genetic or biophysiological predisposition to homosexuality, but such theoretical positions remain to be scientifically proven or disproven. Interestingly, Bergler (1956) states "homosexuality is neither a biologically determined destiny, nor incomprehensible ill luck. It is an unfavorable unconscious solution of a conflict that faces every child." The conflict that faces every child, in Bergler's opinion, is that of resolving and giving up the narcissistic mother attachment.

Social learning theory emphasizes the role of conditioning, modeling, and faulty learning factors in the aetiology of homosexuality and other forms of aberrant sexual behavior. Thus, the homosexual male or female learns to be homosexual. Conditioning and faulty learning experiences within the family system shape the identity and sexual adjustment styles of children. When a male child is consistently exposed to an inadequate, passive, and effeminate father the child learns this same style of behavior, which in turn may evolve into a homosexual object choice. Daughters who grow up with overly aggressive, masculine, and domineering mothers will be more prone to homosexuality. Faulty learning and modeling experiences shape or determine homosexual behavior. Sexual pathology or deviation in a parent or other member of the family system may result in a homosexual object choice. A homosexual experience or other sexual traumas during childhood or adolescence can possibly shape and affect the occurrence of homosexual behavior. Social learning perspectives on the development of homosexuality are interpersonal in nature. Yet, the behavioral and social learning theorists (Forrest, 1978) are surprisingly similar to the psychodynamic and psychoanalytic schools of thought with regard to aetiological explanations of homosexuality.

Sociological and anthropological theories of homosexuality are generally vague and inconclusive. There is no doubt that the process of socialization radically affects the development of personality, sexuality, and behavior. However, the specific socialization processes that operate to cause homosexuality remain unknown. Sociologists and family therapists suggest that recent changes in the family structure (Satir, 1980) may impact upon the identities and sexual adjustments of children. Sociological investigations (Hatterer, 1970) seem to indicate that poverty and deprivation do not cause or explain homosexuality. Educational, racial, socioeconomic, intellectual, and other such demographic variables do not predict whether or not a given individual or group of individuals will be homosexual or heterosexual. Based upon clinical experience, Hatterer (1970) believes that a disproportionate percent of individuals in certain occupations or career areas tend to be homosexual. He mentions actors, artists, and musicians as being career groups which seem to involve a greater number of overtly homosexual and overtly bisexual persons. As touched upon earlier, anthropological studies of homosexual behavior indicate that this particular form of sexuality is characteristic of the human species. Throughout history homosexuality has been a matter of social concern and question in most cultures and societies. It is clinically significant that Ford and Beach (1951) found homosexual behavior to be "totally absent, rare or carried on in secrecy" in over 25 percent of the seventy-six different societies that they investigated. This finding is somewhat confusing. The clinical implications, meanings, and cultural implications associated with the words "totally absent, rare or carried on in secrecy" are significant. A few societies actively reinforce and advocate homosexual behavior. Quite simply, homosexuality is a variant of sexual behavior which occurs in the vast majority of peoples and cultures throughout the world. This has always been true.

Alcoholism Associated with Homosexuality

Several clinicians and researchers (Parker, 1959; Goodwin et al., 1971; Beaton and Guild, 1976; Hawkins, 1976; Small and Leach, 1977; Forrest, 1978; 1982a) suggest that the incidence of overt homosexuality, "latent" homosexuality, or sexual problems associated with homosexuality is greater among alcoholics than nonalcoholics. Parker (1959) conducted a psychometric investigation of the sex temperament of fifty male alcoholic individuals and fifty male moderate drinkers. This study indicated that the alcoholic group has a significantly lower degree of masculinity than the moderate drinkers. Parker (1959) considers deficient masculinity and/or "latent" homosexuality as an important aetiological factor in alcoholism. Among the alcoholic persons studied, mother's preference, broken marriages, odd-numbered ordinal positions, and possibly broken homes were associated with low masculinity. Alcoholics and moderate drinkers with a preponderance of male siblings evidenced lower masculinity than did the subjects with the opposite sibling distribution. Small and Leach (1977) report clinical findings and case history data relative to a sample of ten male homosexual alcoholics. These authors indicate that patients who are able to accept the need for abstinence are most likely to achieve successful sexual functioning, while patients who accept their homosexuality find it easier to achieve sobriety. Small and Leach (1977) conclude that homosexuality and alcoholism are "independent states" and that homosexuality need not be an obstacle to treatment for alcohol addiction.

Clinical investigations and demographically oriented studies (Beaton and Guild, 1976; Hawkins, 1976; Judd, 1977) generally support the position that gay alcoholics require somewhat different treatment than nongay alcoholics. Hawkins (1976) concluded from a study of lesbianism and alcoholism that there is a tremendous need for adequate social support systems involving nonalcoholic environments for the gay alcoholic and alcohol abuser. Homosexual alcoholism treatment centers have been established in several communities in the United States (Judd, 1977). Judd (1977) has found that negative judgmental attributes are held toward the gay alcoholic by many of the staff members of nongay alcoholism treatment agencies. She indicates that the presence of strong negative attitudes toward the gay alcoholic are reflected in the type, number, and quality of treatment services that alcoholic treatment agencies provide for homosexual alcoholics. It has been found (Hawkins, 1976) that certain social factors specifically contribute to alcohol abuse upon the part of homosexuals. These social factors include attitudes, values, and alienation. The "bar scene" in homosexual communities is felt to contribute to alcoholism and the abuse of alcohol among homosexuals.

There is very little research data available dealing with the incidence of overt homosexuality among chronic alcoholics. Hawkins (1976) found "no scientific data were found on the topic of lesbian alcohol abusers." It is generally concluded in the clinical literature (Forrest, 1978) that the issue of homosexuality is pertinent to the global pathology of some alcoholic persons, but statistical and research data in support of this viewpoint is lacking. In most studies of alcoholism and homosexuality (Small and Leach, 1977) a definition of "alcoholism" is either lacking or inadequate. Researchers (Goodwin, Crane, and Guze, 1971) do indicate that many convicted male felons are diagnosed "alcoholic" or "problem drinkers." In this investigation (Goodwin et al., 1971) about one-half of the blacks in a sample of 223 convicted male felons were diagnosed alcoholic. About 75 percent of the whites in this study were diagnosed alcoholic. Again, diagnostic criteria are not clearly delineated in this investigation. It is reported that the alcoholic subjects in this study (Goodwin et al., 1971) were "more often homosexual" than the nonalcoholic subjects. Unfortunately, no precise statistical data are presented to indicate the incidence of overt homosexuality within this research population. The authors conclude that untreated alcoholism among criminals has a different course and outcome than treated alcoholism among noncriminals. Rathod, Gregory, and Blows (1966) report that male alcoholic in-patients who have a history of truancy during childhood, criminal behavior before addictive drinking, or recurrently engaging in "homosexual practices" tend to relapse after treatment. In this study, alcoholism and "homosexual practices" are not defined. Sexual promiscuity before marriage, infidelity, and broken marriages also indicated a poor prognosis in this investigation (Rathod, Gregory, and Blows, 1966). Excessive drinking is reported (Saghir, Robins, and Walbran, 1970) to be more common among homosexual males than heterosexual males. Williams (1976) indicates that the alcoholic homosexual presents special sexual problems for the alcoholism therapist.

A recent six year follow-up study of convicted male felons (Martin, Cloninger, and Guze, 1978) involving the rate of criminal recidivism revealed that the most powerful predictors of recidivism were the diagnosis of drug dependence, antisocial personality, and a history of homosexuality. In this investigation (Martin, Cloninger, and Guze, 1978) it was found that alcoholism was *not* a predictor of criminal recidivism. In another study (Climent, Ervin,

Rollins et al., 1977) of incarcerated women it is reported that heterosexuals scored higher on alcoholism than did self-reported homosexuals and homosexuals known to the prison staff.

It is apparent that there is a good deal of conflicting research evidence within the realm of alcoholism and homosexuality. Clinicians and personality theorists also disagree on many issues in the area of alcohol addiction and homosexuality.

Alcoholics are rarely overt homosexuals (Forrest, 1978; 1982a). In clinical practice (Forrest, 1982a) the therapist can expect to encounter no more than three to six overt homosexual alcoholics in every 100 alcoholics. This clinical position is congruous with the research of Cameron (1963) indicating that none of forty-six alcoholic patients studied were "completely" homosexual, and only one engaged in more homosexual than heterosexual activity. However, male and female alcoholics have marked identity problems and they are quite anxious over the various matters associated with sexual and gender identity. Karl Menninger (1938) states "it is almost axiomatic that alcoholics, in spite of a great show of heterosexual activity, have secretly a great fear of women and heterosexuality in general, apparently regarding it as fraught with much danger." Menninger (1938) also points out that the homosexuality of many alcoholics is expressed only when they are intoxicated. He views alcoholism as not a disease but rather as a suicidal flight from disease, a disastrous attempt at a self-cure of an unseen inner conflict.

Many alcoholics consciously fear homosexuality. They are afraid that they "might be" homosexual. All alcoholics are preconsciously and unconsciously anxious over the issues of identity, adequacy as a person, and sexual adequacy. It for these reasons that analysts (Stekel, 1929) consistently indicate that "one dimension of the alcoholic paraphilia is a strong unconscious homosexual striving." Thus, it is understandable why so many personality theorists and clinicians have indicated that the alcoholic is a "latent homosexual." In part, alcoholics drink alcoholically in order to feel adequately male or female. Wilsnack (1973; 1982) has found that women drink alcoholically in order to feel feminine. Women alcoholics are concerned about their adequacy as women. Research (Wilsnack, 1973; 1982) suggests that alcoholic women experience significant conflict about their adequacy as women, stemming from the existence of masculine traits in the unconscious levels of their personalities. Alcoholic males (Forrest, 1978; 1980; 1982; 1982a) drink in order to secure a sense of masculine adequacy. The alcoholic has never been able to adequately resolve the identity-oriented quesiton "Who am I?" After drinking, the alcoholic male feels more powerful, adequate, assertive, and masculine. Alcohol addiction is a neurotic solution to severe identity conflicts. Alcoholism is partially a defense against homosexuality and underlying homosexual conflicts.

It is difficult to explain why so few alcoholic persons are overtly homosexual. However, it must be emphasized that alcoholism and homosexuality seem to exist together. A few alcoholic individuals are exclusively homosexual in object choice. These individuals manifest a clinical history of tissue dependance, maintenance drinking, hospitalization, or inpatient care for alcohol addiction, interpersonal problems associated with drinking, legal and vocational difficulties stemming from the use of alcohol, and other central clinical symptoms of primary alcoholism (Knauert, 1979). It is important that such matters be understood by the therapist so that his or her treatment efforts are appropriate and maximally effective.

There are a number of personality similarities between alcoholics and homosexuals (Forrest, 1982a). In some ways, this factor has been confusing to clinicians and therapists as well as the lay community. Yet, in working with all alcoholic patients, a clear understanding of these personality similarities between alcoholics and homosexuals is essential to accurate diagnostic assessment, the development of appropriate treatment plans and strategies, and the development of a clinical understanding of the very significant personality and behavioral differences between most alcoholics and homosexuals. According to Bergler (1956) the personality of the homosexual involves a mixture of the following elements: "(1) masochistic provocation and injustice-collecting, (2) defensive malice, (3) flippancy covering depression and guilt, (4) hypernarcissism and hypersuperciliousness, (5) refusal to acknowledge accepted standards in non-sexual matters, on the assumption that the right to cut moral corners is due homosexuals as compensation for their 'suffering,' and (6) general unreliability, also of a more or less psychopathic nature. The most interesting feature of this sextet of traits is its universality. Regardless of the level of intelligence, culture, background or education, all homosexuals possess it." Moreover, the homosexual is often anxious and depressed, the product of a distorted family system and the seeming victim of an overwhelming obsessive-compulsive disorder, homosexuality (Forrest, 1982a). Alcoholics and homosexuals often struggle "against" their compulsions. Some alcoholics "try everything" in order to stay sober. Some homosexuals constantly attempt to guard against their homosexual feelings, thoughts, impulses, and behaviors. Additionally, Bergler (1956) indicates that the unconscious bases for both criminality and homosexuality are similar in structure.

The global psychopathology of alcoholism and homosexuality is similar. An overdetermined oral character structure, regressive sexuality and sexual conflicts, sadomasochistic conflicts, "people problems," struggles with anxiety, depression, hostility and guilt, narcissistic and acting-out dilemmas, and alienation are but a few of the similar behavioral and dynamic facets of the psychopathology of alcoholism and homosexuality.

The case of John B. illustrates one rather common pattern of homosexual functioning among alcoholic males. It is clinically significant that this patient was not consciously aware of having homosexual impulses or thoughts prior to being involved in an alcohol-facilitated homosexual episode, which resulted in his entering psychotherapy.

CASE 9. John B., a thirty-four-year-old married city employee, was referred for evaluation and psychotherapy following a drunken episode during which he sexually assaulted an eighteen-year-old male coworker. The patient had been married for fifteen years and was the father of three children. During the initial clinical interview John denied having had prior homosexual relations. He did indicate that drinking had been a "problem" for several years. At the age of twenty-three John was discharged from the Army after three unsuccessful attempts at rehabilitation. John indicated that his wife had told him on several occasions prior to their marriage that she would not marry him because of his "alcoholism." He was able to stop drinking for "two or three" weeks at a time during their courtship and while in the Army.

John had grown up in a small rural community in Nebraska. His father was an alcoholic. Life on the farm and family living were difficult for the patient. According to John, the parents argued and "fought all the time" and his two older brothers used to "kick hell out of me." John described his father as a physically overpowering man who was "one hell of a barroom fighter." Once or twice a week John's father would come home drunk and proceed to verbally attack or "kick hell out of anyone he could." John felt "trapped" within the family. He feared his father and his brothers as well. He was unable to talk to his mother. The patient described his mother as depressed and "afraid of my father." John's older brothers were five and three years older than himself.

During the initial three or four therapy sessions John was very reluctant to talk about the sexual assault. He stressed that he had "never done anything like this before." The patient did indicate that his brothers "used to" engage in "weird" sexual practices. As an early adolescent the patient had, on several occasions, observed his brothers having a "circle jerk." By this, the patient meant that his brothers would masturbate together. The goal of this activity was to see who could reach orgasm first. The brothers continually attempted to get John to masturbate with them. Furthermore, they would repeatedly "goose" him and squeeze his testicles. The latter activity was conducted under the auspices of playing "squirrel," a game which the patient described as centering around the covertly homosexual objective of "grabbing a nut (meaning testicle) and running." John repeatedly denied any personal involvement in these covert homosexual practices of adolescence.

The patient began to date while in his senior year of high school. He also began to "get drunk" at this time, although he initiated drinking in the eighth grade. By the time John was a senior in high school, both of his brothers had moved out of the family home and the oldest brother was married. At this time John's father consumed roughly one-fifth of vodka each day. His father was "dried out" several times and "sent" to the state hospital for "alcoholism treatment" for two months during John's senior year of high school. John indicated that while in high school he "always" tried to have sex with the girls that he dated, but that he was unsuccessful in his efforts at seduction. Three weeks after graduating from high school John joined the Army. John was in the service for some five years and hoped to make it his career. Unfortunately, the patient became a maintenance drinker within the first two years of duty. While on "leave" from active duty, John returned home and met his wife. They met at a local nightclub and as might be expected, both were drinking heavily on this occasion. After leaving the bar intoxicated, the couple went "parking." Before having intercourse, Sharon, the patient's eventual wife, proceeded to suck the patient's penis to orgasm. Although John had experienced oral sex with a prostitute shortly after joining the Army, he had never experienced oral sex or other forms of sexually intimate behavior with a nonprostitute. This experience was well remembered by the patient. He indicated that the couple engaged in oral sex "two or three times a week since we started dating." The patient's wife had told him on many occasions that she would rather "suck than fuck."

While in the Army John encountered a number of difficulties as a result of drinking and drunkenness. A few months after being in the Army John was "approached" by a homosexual first sergeant. Apparently, the sergeant had attempted to fondle the patient's penis in a bar. Both were drinking heavily, but John knew very well what was taking place. Not only did he resist the seductive behaviors of the sergeant, but he proceeded to severely assault the sergeant. In this regard, John stated "one thing I never could stand is a fag." Due to intoxication, the patient missed work or reported to work late several times. He was financially penalized for these alcohol facilitated behaviors. In addition, John had been "busted" (meaning reduced in rank) twice during his five years of military service. He was also "passed over" for promotion during this time. The last several months of military service were difficult for the patient to "remember." He was moved from one unit to another. When not in treatment or confinement, he was chronically intoxicated. At this time, John stayed away from home. All of his drinking was done in bars with "the guys." From time to time he would manage to pick up a woman and they might spend the night together in order to have sex. On other occasions, the patient only wanted to get drunk and "get a quickie" or a "blow-job in the front seat of the car."

During these early years of marriage the patient's wife had a number of sexual relationships with John's friends as well as other men. She openly described her sexual encounters with these various men to the patient. Needless to say, the marital relationship was severely conflicted. Mutual physical and verbal confrontations were basic to the marital adjustment. The coup de grace for John's military career involved a rather bizarre sexual transaction between him and his wife. After drinking for several hours at a local bar one summer evening, John returned home and initiated sexual relations with his wife. The patient's wife had also been drinking, but apparently she was not "drunk." When John failed to reach orgasm after nearly an hour of various forms of sexual relations, he "forced" his wife to lean out of the window of their apartment while they had anal intercourse. He had also inserted a wine bottle in his wife's vagina. The couple lived in military housing, which meant that a number of neighbors lived in very close physical proximity to their apartment. One of these neighbors witnessed the patient's wife hanging out of the window nude and out of concern for her welfare called the military police. When the military police arrived they found

John "passed out" and nude on the bedroom floor. Within a few weeks after this incident, the patient was given a "general" discharge from the Army. John was unable to recall the specific events of this evening but he did indicate that he had been "drunk" when the military police arrived.

After being discharged from the service John was able to secure employment as a maintenance worker for the city. He did well at this job and was soon promoted to a maintenance supervisor. The couple had three sons and the overall marital relationship improved. John "learned how to control" his drinking. He developed a pattern of limiting his drinking to the weekends. On Friday evening after work, John would drink a "few" beers with work associates and then stop by the liquor store, purchase a "case or two" of beer and go home. He stopped drinking vodka and other "hard liquors." By and large, he also discontinued drinking in bars and nightclubs. Nevertheless, the patient would literally drink all weekend. He would drink "one or two six packs" on Friday night, begin drinking early Saturday morning, drink until late in the evening, and again initiate drinking on Sunday morning. He began "tapering off" on Sunday afternoon and night and returned to work on Monday morning. John indicated that he wasn't really sober until Tuesday or Wednesday of each week!

Following four or five individual therapy sessions, the patient began to anxiously discuss the general issue of homosexuality. John stated that for years he had consciously "worried about" the possibility of being homosexual. He was afraid of homosexuals. When confronted with anyone who seemed to manifest homosexual characteristics, John became angry, volatile, and physically assaultive. In therapy, John vividly recalled a recurrent dream. In this dream the patient was being chased by a man with a butcher's knife. The patient remembered having this same dream over and over again since the age of ten or twelve. He would often awaken in the middle of the night sweating, agitated, and panicky when having this dream. In therapy, the patient also began to be less defensive about the homosexual assault. He clearly remembered drinking with the victim, an eighteen-year-old male employee, for several hours on a Friday evening. They had gone from work to a local bar with three other male employees. After drinking several drinks the patient and male employee left the bar and went to a motel room. The patient "vaguely" remembered going to the motel room. They continued to drink at the motel room. John did remember drinking with the employee in a motel room. According to the legal testimony of the male employee, John became enraged and assaulted the male companion when it was suggested that John perform fellatio on him. This occurred after the male employee had performed oral sex on John. The employee had also allowed John to perform anal sex with him. When the employee suggested that John "suck him," a violent physical assault followed. During this assault, John broke the man's nose, several ribs, knocked out a tooth, and caused internal injuries. The man was hospitalized for over three weeks. John had "no recall" of the physical assault or homosexual transactions that took place between the two men.

Early in therapy, John indicated that he felt that the "real homosexual" in a male homosexual relationship was the person who "took it in the ass" or the one who "did the suckin'." After the therapist had pointed out several times that the real fact of this matter was that both men were involved with each other sexually and this relationship was not heterosexual, as a woman was not involved, John began to perceive himself as bisexual. However, John continued to be apprehensive about the issue of homosexuality. He was especially fearful of going to prison. Actually, John's successful persistence in treatment was a court ordered alternative.to incarceration. According to the legal arrangements in this case, John was to be seen in weekly psychotherapy for no less than eighteen months. Additionally, the patient was to be placed on a monitored Antabuse maintenance program for two years and he was encouraged to attend Alcoholics Anonymous. John successfully completed therapy. At this time he has been totally abstinent from alcohol for nearly six years. He also attends Alcoholics Anonymous regularly and takes Antabuse weekly. John has not experienced another homosexual relationship since entering therapy. While in therapy it was suggested to the patient that several marital therapy sessions might be beneficial to the couple. John's wife refused to participate in therapy. However, after the patient had been in therapy for nearly two years and actively involved in Alcoholics Anonymous for the same length of time, she decided to begin attending Al-Anon. She continues to attend Al-Anon once or twice each week.

The case of John B. is not atypical. Counselors and clinicians employed in comprehensive alcoholic treatment centers encounter patients like John on a rather regular basis. While acutely intoxicated, such patients act out homosexually. In some cases, the patient has a long history of homosexual acting-out while under the influence of alcohol. In other cases, the patient has never previously experienced an overt homosexual relationship. In this case, it is clearly apparent that the patient had long struggled with unconscious, preconscious, and even conscious homosexual strivings. The patient's adolescent family relationship was highly homoeroticized. His sexual relationship within the context of marriage was primarily pregenital. Even the patient's dream content reflected his homosexual conflicts. John feared homosexuality. He did not recall sexually assaulting a male employee. John believed that this was due to being in an alcoholic "blackout." Treatment was globally successful in this case. Not only did the patient establish long-term sobriety and terminate his homosexual acting-out, but more importantly he was able to resolve his overall sexual pathology.

Another "typical" case involving alcoholism and homosexuality is that of the patient who has been chronically alcoholic for years and simultaneously consistently an overt homosexual for years or perhaps a lifetime. Such individuals are also seen rather regularly within the context of comprehensive alcoholic treatment centers. As will be discussed later in this chapter, these patients require different strategies of therapeutic intervention as a part of the successful overall rehabilitation process.

Basic Treatment Strategies

There is a very consistent agreement among experienced clinicians and therapists who work primarily with homosexuals that homosexuality is often "curable" (Caprio, 1954; Bergler, 1956; Hatterer, 1970; Ellis, 1979). Likewise, the alcoholic can almost always benefit from psychotherapy and treatment (Forrest, 1978; 1982a). It is important to point out that therapy is beneficial and successful in many of these cases involving alcoholism and homosexuality. As Bratter (1979; 1980) so poignantly indicates, psychiatrists, psychologists, and other behavioral scientists have long tended to believe that alcoholics cannot be successfully treated. Likewise, as Hatterer (1970) points out, change agents have also felt that homosexuals cannot be "cured" or benefited from psychotherapy. These patients do change adaptively as a result of psychotherapy and rehabilitation. Perhaps these viewpoints are more congruous with the recent APA position that homosexuality is not a sexual deviation (Masters and Johnson, 1979).

An initial treatment goal in the case of all alcoholic persons who are homosexual or homosexually conflicted is that of helping the patient achieve total sobriety. In many of these cases, detoxification or hospitalization will be the first step in the treatment process. Some patients need residential treatment in order to establish a period of abstinence conducive to initiating other more global personality and life-style changes. The homosexual or homosexually conflicted alcoholic should be treated like all other alcoholic persons, with the notable exception of implementing an eventual treatment focus in the area of the patient's homosexuality or homosexual conflicts. The patient's alcoholism must be treated first. As indicated in earlier chapters, an initial medical examination or other direct interventions may be indicated early in the treatment process. Holistic treatment interventions are indicated in the treatment of all alcoholic persons. Therefore, the homosexually conflicted alcoholic patient should be actively involved in an ongoing program of exercise, in Alcoholics Anonymous, nutritionally stabilized, and possibly engaged in other adjunctive treatment modalities when intensive psychotherapy is initiated. The total person must recover. As such, the homosexual dimension of some alcoholic persons constitutes but one aspect of those persons, which must be resolved or adaptively changed as a function of the treatment process.

The homosexual alcoholic does present a number of special treatment problems or different clinical considerations. First, the therapist must accurately discern and evaluate the drinking behavior of the homosexual. While alcohol addiction and homosexuality do coexist, many patients who are overtly homosexual or homosexually conflicted are problem drinkers (Forrest, 1978) or reactive alcoholics (Forrest, 1978; Knauert, 1979) rather than primary alcoholics. In the case of people with drinking problems, differential diagnosis can be of the utmost importance in psychotherapy and in the development of sound treatment plans (Knauert, 1980). Treatment tactics and prognosis will vary according to the drinking history and style of the patient. The clinician must also be able to accurately assess the patient's homosexual pathology. The early therapy sessions with homosexually conflicted alcoholics usually reveal a great deal about the patient's motivation for therapy. Early in therapy, the therapist and patient must jointly decide upon the issue of working toward a heterosexual adaptation upon the part of the patient. Just as the therapist and patient must commit themselves to the process of alcoholism recovery, in some cases involving homosexually conflicted alcoholics, a mutual commitment to the patient's recovery from homosexuality is basic to the undertaking of psychotherapy. In this sense, treatment and therapy are aimed at the resolution of two addictions or addictive life-styles, alcoholism and homosexuality. The homosexual alcoholic suffers from a dual addiction.

There are no precise clinical signs that indicate that the clinician and patient should work toward the goal of explicit heterosexual functioning. This situation is quite unlike the alcoholic patient's obvious need to stop drinking. The patient and therapist mutually understand and perceive the patient's need to give up drinking when the symptom structure of alcoholism is floridly manifest. Working toward the goal of helping the patient establish a heterosexual adjustment style is a more ambiguous and less certain objective in psychotherapy with homosexual persons. Nonetheless, there are a number of clinical signs which indicate that it is therapeutically most appropriate for the therapist to utilize treatment strategies designed to facilitate a heterosexual pattern of sexual and interpersonal functioning upon the part of the patient. Clinical data associated with the alcoholic homosexual's life history, family relationships, relationships with women in general, social history, self-image, and work identity determines the patient's prognosis for establishing heterosexual adjustment (Hatterer, 1970). In turn, the prognosis for establishing a heterosexual adjustment generally determines the therapist's approach and treatment format.

Hatterer (1970) states "the patient with a strong desire to be rid of his homosexuality, as evidenced by overt and nonverbal expressions of that desire, is one of the most treatable and has the best prognosis for a heterosexual adjustment. Patients who experience guilt, depression, or anxiety in the course of homosexual attractions, fantasies, impulses, or actual practices have a highly favorable prognosis. Similarly, patients who report that they have tried on their own to fight homosexual thinking and behavior and to repress, cope with, or modify their homosexuality are highly treatable." The patient's relationships with his mother and family can be prognostic. In general, the less disturbed the mother-son relationship the better the overall prognosis. An intact family system, with an adequate father, and a relatively nonaggressive, somewhat warm, nonseductive mother are factors that favorably influence treatment outcome. Prognosis is best when the patient's self-image has been predominantly male (Hatterer, 1970). It is helpful to the treatment enterprise if the patient has a reasonably stable work history within a career that is not associated with a homosexual life-style. The type and frequency of homosexual behavior engaged in by the patient can be important indicators of treatment outcome. The later the occurrence of overt homosexual activities, excluding childhood and preadolescent experimentation, the better the prognosis. Males who are able to establish warm, meaningful relationships with men and women and who have also experienced exciting and erotic sex with a woman are very treatable. Many of these men date and engage in a variety of intimate sexual behaviors with women (Masters and Johnson, 1979).

Patients who experience rather consistent homosexual impulses, thoughts, fantasies, and behaviors from childhood through adulthood usually manifest the poorest prognoses. Hatterer (1970) considers patients who have never experienced heterosexual attractions, impulses, or sexual arousal to be untreatable. He also believes that patients who have experienced conscious homosexual imagery and attraction from "five to nine years of age are least treatable." Patients who have long felt like a woman and disliked being male have a very poor prognosis. Schizoid, detached, and chronically isolated males are not easily treated.

Many of these same prognostic criteria can be applied to the lesbian that is alcohol addicted. When the woman has, since the age of five or six, perceived herself as a man and rejected her femininity the prognosis is very poor. Patients that are very comfortable with their homosexual life-styles are apt to do poorly in treatment. Such patients do not experience guilt, anxiety, and depression in association with their lesbian fantasies, feelings, and behaviors. Women that have never experienced dating, courtship, erotic heterosexual fantasies, or overt heterosexual behaviors usually have a poor prognosis. In contrast, the homosexual woman who has grown up in a relatively stable family system and subsequently dated, engaged in overt heterosexual behaviors, or actively fantasized about heterosexual interactions has a very good prognosis. Patients that are comfortable with men and women have a favorable prognosis. Patients with good overall social skills and a positive self-concept tend to respond favorably to therapy.

Based upon the various criteria discussed thus far with regard to the patient's potential for modifying his or her homosexual adjustment style, treatment is initiated with the goal of either (1) facilitating a heterosexual adaptation upon the part of the patient, or (2) not attempting to modify the patient's homosexual adjustment style. During the initial hours of psychotherapy, the patient and therapist mutually decide upon which of these primary treatment objectives to pursue. Whichever treatment goal is appropriate for a given patient is always of secondary clinical importance. Throughout treatment, the therapist makes it very clear to the patient that the primary issue in therapy is abstinence from alcohol and the resolution of the patient's alcohol addiction. Therapists frequently tend to feel that they cannot help the alcoholic homosexual that is committed to a homosexual life-style. This is not true. Many of these patients will continue to remain grossly dysfunctional and eventually die from alcoholism if they are not treated. In such cases, the fact that the patient is homosexual may be of very little clinical importance early in therapy. When the patient has been able to establish several weeks of sobriety and is clearly recovering from his or her alcoholism, the focus of therapy may well shift to the explicit realm of sexuality and homosexuality.

Identity confusion and issues pertaining to homosexuality (Forrest, 1982a) are basic to the alcoholic character structure. As such, these matters must be resolved in therapy. However, the therapist must be able to skillfully and sensitively time the introduction of these clinical matters in the therapy relationship. In part, some alcoholic homosexuals drink alcoholically as a result of their various neurotic struggles associated with being homosexual. In order to remain sober and initiate more globally constructive living changes, such patients must at least partially resolve their homosexual neurosis. In some cases, the homosexual alcoholic must learn to simply accept himself or herself as both an alcoholic and a homosexual. This is not an easy task. However, this task is much easier to accomplish when the patient's therapist is able to genuinely accept the patient as an alcoholic and a homosexual and accurately communicate this acceptance to the patient.

The homosexually conflicted alcoholic patient is also pervasively conflicted. These patients are often behaviorally and ideationally bisexual. An initial treatment goal and an ongoing goal of therapy is abstinence from alcohol. After the patient has established sobriety and is actively committed to the recovery process, it is absolutely imperative that the counselor begin to help the patient verbalize and resolve his or her identity-based homosexual conflicts. Psychotherapy with alcoholic persons is none other than a process through which the patient answers the question "Who am I?" In order to remain sober and maintain a chemically free life-style, many patients must establish a pattern of satisfactory and rewarding heterosexual relations. They need to overcome their homosexual fears and anxieties. Most of these individuals find it difficult to talk about their homosexual experiences and fantasies. Therefore, the clinician must avoid hypersexual dialogues with the patient early in therapy. Eventually, the therapist helps the patient consciously understand his homosexual conflicts by talking about them and no longer fearing and repressing them. This process allows the patient to become more fully aware of his or her heterosexual feelings, experiences, needs, and impulses. The psychotherapy process de-homosexualizes the patient.

From the very beginning of therapy with the homosexually conflicted alcoholic patient the therapist verbally and nonverbally reinforces the patient's negative feelings, thoughts, and verbalizations regarding his or her homosexual impulses or behaviors. This procedure must be done with the utmost sensitivity, empathy, warmth, and support. These strategies of treatment are not appropriate with homosexual alcoholics who are committed to a homosexual life-style. Indeed, such a treatment format is potentially psychonoxious in the case of the lifelong homosexual person who is alcoholic or a problem drinker. It is also wise for the therapist to avoid the details of the patient's homosexual history in the initial hour or two of therapy.

With the patient's sobriety and the development of a working therapeutic alliance, the therapist begins to more openly explore the sexual feelings, thoughts, behaviors, and global history of the individual. At the same time, the therapist actively reinforces heterosexual behaviors and cognitions. There are a wide variety of specific treatment techniques the therapist can utilize in order to facilitate and enhance the patient's heterosexual functioning.

Some patients need to be taught assertive heterosexual behaviors. Many of these patients need to be taught a variety of social skills. Rehearsal and roleplaying in therapy can be helpful. The therapist may need to spend considerable time with a male patient rehears- a phone call to a woman asking for a date and then rehearsing sub- sequent conversations, dancing, and even sexual seduction or in- timate sexual responding. In addition to the utilization of behav- ioral strategies of intervention, the therapist must employ rational emotive (Ellis, 1979) and more dynamically oriented treatment interventions during the middle and later stages of psychotherapy with homosexually conflicted alcoholic patients. It is not enough for the counselor to simply get the patient to engage in more ef- fective and adaptive patterns of overt heterosexual behavior. Rath- er, this important treatment goal must be supplemented and aug- mented with intensive dynamic work centering around the pa- tient's sexual feelings and self-dialogue. Characteristically, alco- holic patients will flee from treatment when the therapist pre- maturely focuses upon feelings and internal processes (Forrest, 1978; 1979b; 1982a). The homosexually conflicted alcoholic pa- tient tends to become agitated, threatened, and panicky when "pressured" by the therapist to deal with the issues and feelings associated with his or her homosexual strivings. For these reasons, the therapist must be able to coordinate his or her treatment in- terventions to the ongoing therapy "readiness" of the patient.

Some of these patients are sexually dysfunctional. Problems of premature ejaculation, impotence, frigidity, and orgastic dys- function are not uncommon. In such cases sex therapy is but one phase of the ongoing treatment process. The homosexually con- flicted alcoholic is very often lacking in basic sex education in- formation. A few of these patients equate oral or anal sex with homosexuality. The male patient may think and fear that he is homosexual because he enjoys having his wife perform fellatio on him or because he likes anal sex. Some homosexually conflict- ed female alcoholics "believe" they are homosexual because they are only orgastic via cunnilingus. The therapist can usually dispel these inaccurate and irrational beliefs by simply providing the pa- tient with basic sex education, encouragement, and support (El- lis, 1980).

In the case of the overtly bisexual alcoholic and those rare cases of explicitly homosexual alcoholics who are committed to changing their sexual adjustment style to a heterosexual readaptation, the clinician will need to reassure the patient that "slips" may occur. It is unrealistic to expect most of these patients to terminate homosexual fantasies, impulses, and behaviors. The overall homosexual orientation of the patient will usually go into remission after several months of treatment. Just as it is unrealistic to expect the alcoholic to never have a "slip," so is it unrealistic to expect the homosexual or homosexually conflicted alcoholic to never again experience a "slip" in the form of a homosexual cognition, fantasy, or behavioral transaction. Hatterer (1970) indicates that it takes from two to six years in therapy for the homosexual patient to achieve a total heterosexual readaptation. This author (Hatterer, 1970) also points out that therapists and researchers who are specialized in the treatment of homosexual males report that approximately 25 percent of motivated patients are capable of a totally heterosexual readaptation. At present, data is not available relative to the improvement or recovery percent among overtly homosexual or homosexually conflicted alcoholics entering treatment. In the clinical experience of the author, most alcoholic patients in both of these homosexual categories can be treated successfully if they are committed to abstinence and extended psychotherapy. Treatment with these patients is difficult and requires from six to eight months to three or four years. It is realistic to expect from 60 to 75 percent of homosexually conflicted alcoholic patients to become totally abstinent, essentially resolve their homosexual conflicts, and consolidate a much more adequate nuclear identity (Forrest, 1982a). Approximately 45 to 65 percent of overt homosexual alcoholics recover from their alcoholism as a result of treatment. A very small percentage of these patients can be expected to achieve a basic heterosexual readaptation resulting from intensive, long-term psychotherapy.

As indicated earlier, the vast majority of alcoholic persons are not homosexual. However, the ego structure (Forrest, 1982a) and identity of the alcoholic is pathologic. As a result, many alcoholic persons consciously question their sexual and gender identities. In therapy, such patients verbalize the fear of being homosexual. The majority of these individuals have not experienced overt homosexuality as adolescents or adults. These patients are usually motivated to "work" in therapy and they do very well in treatment. Other alcoholic patients do not appear to be homosexually conflicted. Typically, these patients have led very promiscuous heterosexual life-styles. They have not engaged in overt homosexual behavior as adolescents or adults. In treatment they are very disclosing about their many affairs and sexual escapades. In these cases, sexual acting-out is a clear-cut defense against homosexuality. These patients deny and repress their homosexual conflicts from conscious awareness. As they remain sober and involved in psychotherapy, these patients begin to preconsciously and consciously experience anxiety associated with their homosexual strivings. Eventually, many of these patients develop the capacity to consciously deal with and resolve personal identity conflicts and homosexual struggles.

One important dimension of psychotherapy with every alcoholic person is that of helping the patient establish an adequately consolidated nuclear sense of self (Forrest, 1982a). Identity consolidation encompasses gender identity, sexual identity, and indeed, the total being of the patient. In this sense, effective psychotherapy with the alcoholic always involves a resolution of the patient's homosexual-heterosexual pathology.

The overtly homosexual alcoholic is in need of treatment and rehabilitation. Unlike the homosexually conflicted alcoholic, who is readily accepted for treatment, the homosexual alcoholic is often covertly rejected by counselors and treatment programs. Many therapists are uncomfortable treating the person who is committed to an overtly homosexual life-style. Counselors and therapists tend to be more willing to work with the homosexually conflicted alcoholic. They feel that these patients at least "have a chance" at successful treatment. Obviously, the therapist dimension is a critical variable in the psychotherapy process and outcome with overtly homosexual alcoholics. Many alcoholism counselors do not feel qualified or adequately trained to work with these patients. It is important for every comprehensive alcoholism treatment center to employ a professional clinician who is experienced, skilled, and comfortable in working with the overtly homosexual alcoholic person. Such a staff member can provide very valuable clinical supervision, education, and staff training in the realm of alcoholism and homosexuality for other colleagues and staff.

Alcoholic persons who are either overtly homosexual or homosexually conflicted sometimes feel that they have no one to turn to for help. In general, homosexuality is a feared topic within the Alcoholics Anonymous community. Homosexual feelings, impulses, and behaviors are rarely the topics of an Alcoholics Anonymous or Al-Anon meeting. Very few people seem to realize that homosexuality is addictive sex. Like the chronic alcoholic, some addictive homosexuals "hit bottom" several times before they seek out help and begin the recovery process. For many people, alcohol addiction or alcohol abuse in combination with homosexuality precipitates involvement in a self-destructive trap, which all too often proves fatal. As we collectively realize the many devastating social, health, economic, and interpersonal problems caused by alcohol addiction and alcohol abuse, hopefully clinicians and researchers will develop more effective programs of treatment for the alcoholic homosexual. Hopefully, self-help organizations for the alcoholic and problem drinker are becoming more aware of the sexual problems of people who seek help through their organizations. It is difficult to be an alcoholic. It is very hard to recover from alcohol addiction. These matters are much more difficult for the homosexual alcoholic.

Summary

Homosexuality is defined and discussed in this chapter. Homosexuality is as old as the human race and constitutes a variety of problems of universal significance. In spite of the many research investigations and clinical studies devoted to the topic of homosexual behavior over the past century, behavioral scientists do not clearly understand many of the clinical realities associated with this form of human sexual behavior. In this culture, male homosexuals tend to be feared and viewed as perverts. Today and for centuries, the female homosexual is less stigmatized. Nevertheless, homosexual behavior is deemed inappropriate in the vast majority of societies. This historic reality has changed very little from culture to culture over the past several hundred years.

Homosexual behavior may be overt or covert. The overt homosexual engages in sexual relations with a same-sexed partner. Covert or "latent" homosexuality refers to same-sexed activities that do not include overt sexual interactions. As a clinical concept, the parameters of "latent homosexuality" are so diffuse and poorly defined that many therapists (Knauert, 1981) feel it may be clinically meaningless to use this term. Homosexual behavior exists on a continuum. Individuals, like societies, differ with regard to feelings and perceptions surrounding the matter of homosexuality. The vast majority of individuals in American society do not engage in overt homosexual behavior. Yet, children and early adolescents in our culture engage in a variety of homosexual activities. Research (Kinsey et al., 1948; Masters and Johnson, 1979) indicates that approximately one in four adult males in the United States has experienced overt homosexuality. Men and women fantasize and think about homosexual activities on a rather regular basis (Masters and Johnson, 1979). Hatterer (1970) points out that cross-cultural, cross-species investigations indicate that a biologic tendency toward homosexuality is basic to nearly all mammals. However, homosexual behavior is never the predominant type of sexual responding for adults in any society or any animal species. Homosexuality seems to be as common or uncommon a form of sexual behavior among women as it is among men. There are presently over 2 million overt male and female homosexuals in America. The American Psychiatric Association no longer considers homosexuality a form of deviant sexual behavior.

The general public, as well as the behavioral science professions, continues to be poorly informed and confused about homosexuality. Homosexuals as a group have been much more open about their sexuality over the past few years. The Gay Liberation Movement has certainly played a major role in making homosexuality an overt social issue.

There are numerous theories of homosexuality. Psychological and psychodynamic explorations of homosexuality tend to purport that the homosexual is emotionally disturbed and that this disorder originates within a disturbed family system. The analytic literature indicates (Fenichel, 1945) that the homosexual male has experienced either an overattached, overdependent, and eroticized family relationship with his mother or he has experienced her as threatening, hostile, and castrating. Analysts also stress the importance of a castrating, threatening, hostile father or a passive, inadequate, aloof father in the aetiology of male homosexuality (Fenichel, 1953). Female homosexuality is believed to be the result of unconscious incestuous feelings toward a brother or the father, penis envy, or an overly eroticized mother-daughter relationship. According to social learning theory and behavioral models, homosexuality occurs as a result of faulty learning and conditioning experiences. The male who grows up without a father is unable to learn and emulate role-appropriate masculine and sexual behaviors and thus is more prone to learning homosexual patterns of behavior. Lesbians have not experienced and learned role appropriate patterns of female sexual responding.

Biologic theories of homosexuality (Stekel, 1929; Freud, 1953) suggest that people are bisexual. Accordingly, people are constitutionally homosexual. Homosexuality may be genetically determined. In this regard, some homosexual individuals report that they have "always" been aware of their sexual inversion. It is clinically significant that therapists and researchers who have devoted their professional careers to the treatment of homosexual persons (Bergler, 1956; Hatterer, 1970) generally do not accept the position that homosexuality is biologically determined. Most clinicians seem to believe that familial, social, and cultural factors are primarily responsible for the development of homosexual adaptation.

A number of researchers and clinicians (Parker, 1959; Hawkins, 1976; Small and Leach, 1977) indicate that homosexuality and homosexual problems are common among alcoholic persons. However, Small and Leach (1977) indicate that homosexuality and alcoholism are "independent states." Other authors (Hawkins, 1976; Judd, 1977; Forrest, 1982a) refer to the "gay alcoholic" and suggest that homosexual alcoholics often need individualized treatment and rehabilitation. There is very little research data available in the realm of alcohol addiction and homosexuality. In the clinical experience of the author (Forrest, 1982a) alcoholics are rarely overt homosexuals. Nonetheless, male and female alcoholics do manifest serious identity conflicts and thus homosexual conflicts are often basic to the pathology of alcoholism. A number of the personality similarities between alcoholics and homosexuals are discussed in this chapter. The case of John B. was included in this chapter in order to demonstrate the pattern of alcohol-facilitated overt homosexual acting-out. Some alcoholic persons who are married and seemingly heterosexual do engage in overt homosexual behavior following intoxication. Indeed, there are a diversity of adjustment styles involving homosexuality, alcoholism, and alcohol abuse.

Homosexuality is "curable." Congruously, the alcoholic with homosexual conflicts and the overtly homosexual alcoholic can benefit from psychotherapy and rehabilitation. Total sobriety is an initial and basic treatment goal in working with homosexually conflicted or overtly homosexual alcoholics. Detoxification and other medical interventions may be appropriate in the case of some of these patients. Holistic treatment and rehabilitation approaches are indicated for the alcoholic homosexual or homosexually conflicted alcohol abuser. The homosexual conflicts and pathology of alcoholic persons constitute but one aspect of the total patient, which must be adaptively modified as a function of psychotherapy and rehabilitation.

Very early in treatment the therapist and patient must come to agreement upon the matter of resolving the overt homosexual adaptation of the patient. In these few cases, it is generally inappropriate for the therapist to attempt a heterosexual readaptation of the patient when (1) the patient has a lifelong history of homosexual functioning, (2) the patient is not motivated to work in therapy toward the goal of heterosexual readaptation, and (3) the patient manifests the various other negative prognostic clinical signs for heterosexual readaptation discussed at length in this chapter. In contrast, the psychotherapy relationship with homosexually conflicted alcoholic persons always involves the task of resolving these identity-oriented sources of conflict and pathology. In part, many alcoholic persons drink in order to deal with role and identity confusion. It is simply easier for the alcoholic to stop drinking and then remain abstinent once he or she has resolved these underlying identity conflicts. A number of specific therapy techniques for dealing with the identity and homosexual conflicts of the alcoholic are discussed. The clinician must not begin to focus intensively upon the patient's identity pathology prior to the establishment of a productive therapeutic alliance.

Clearly, the homosexual- and identity-based psychopathology of the alcoholic remains poorly understood. A great deal of research is needed in this complex area of alcoholic treatment and rehabilitation. Historically, the alcoholic homosexual has been an enigma within many alcoholic treatment programs, as well as the Alcoholics Anonymous community. The homosexually conflicted alcoholic has all too often been afraid to openly discuss his or her internal struggles associated with identity and homosexuality. Therapists must have the internal ego strength and identity fusion prerequisite to helping their alcoholic patients overcome these very real and powerful sources of anxiety. In all of these respects, hopefully this chapter will prove heuristic.

BIBLIOGRAPHY

Barlow, D.H., and Wincze, J.P.: Treatment of Sexual Deviations. In Leiblum, S., and Pervin, L. (Eds.): *Principles and Practices of Sex Therapy*. New York, The Guilford Press, 1980.

Beaton, S., and Guild, N.: Treatment for gay problem drinkers. *Social Casework, 57(5)*:302-208, 1976.

Bergler, E.: *Homosexuality: Disease or Way of Life?* New York, Collier Books, 1956.

Bieber, Irving, et al.: *Homosexuality: A Psychoanalytic Study*. New York, Basic Books, 1962.

Bratter, Thomas E.: *Reality Therapy Training*. Lecture, Psychotherapy Associates, P.C. Fifth Annual Advanced Winter Workshop, "Treatment and Rehabilitation of the Alcoholic," Colorado Springs, Colorado, January 30, 1979.

Bratter, Thomas E.: *Advanced Reality Therapy Training*. Lecture, Psychotherapy Associates, P.C. Sixth Annual Advanced Winter Workshop, "Treatment and Rehabilitation of the Alcoholic," Colorado Springs, Colorado, February 5, 1980.

Cameron, N.: *Personality Development and Psychology: A Dynamic Approach*. Boston, Houghton Mifflin Co., 1963.

Caprio, F.S.: *Female Homosexuality: A Modern Study of Lesbianism*. New York, Grove Press, Inc., 1954.

Climent, C.E., Ervin, F.R., Rollings, A., et al.: Epidemiological studies of female prisoners. IV. Homosexual behavior. *J Nerv Ment Dis, 164:*

25-29, 1977.

Davis, K.: *Factors in the Sex Life of Twenty-two Hundred Women*. New York, Harper, 1929.

Ellis, A.: *Rational Emotive Therapy Training*. Lecture, Psychotherapy Associates, P.C. Fifth Annual Advanced Winter Workshop, "Treatment and Rehabilitation of the Alcoholic," Colorado Springs, Colorado, February 1, 1979.

Ellis, A.: Treatment of Erectile Dysfunctions. In Leiblum, S., and Pervin, L., (Eds.): *Principles and Practices of Sex Therapy*. New York, The Guilford Press, 1980.

Fenichel, O.: *The Psychoanalytic Theory of Neuroses*. New York, Norton, 1945.

Fenichel, O.: *The Collected Papers of Otto Fenichel*, 1st Series. Norton, 1953.

Fenichel, O.: *The Collected Papers of Otto Fenichel*, 2nd Series. Norton, 1954.

Ford, Clellan, and Beach, F.: *Patterns of Sexual Behavior*. New York, Harper, 1951.

Forrest, G.G.: *The Diagnosis and Treatment of Alcoholism*. Charles C Thomas, Springfield, Rev. 2nd Ed., 1978.

Forrest, G.G.: Negative and positive addictions. *Family and Community Health, 2(1)*:103-112, May, 1979b.

Forrest, G.G.: *Confrontation in Psychotherapy with the Alcoholic*. Holmes Beach, Florida, Learning Publications, 1982.

Forrest, G.G.: *How to Live with a Problem Drinker and Survive*. New York, Atheneum, 1980.

Forrest, G.G.: *Alcoholism, Narcissism and Psychopathology*. Holmes Beach, Florida, Learning Publications, 1982a.

Freud, S.: *The Future Prospects of Psychoanalytic Therapy*. Collected papers, Vol. II, London, Hobarth, 1953.

Goodwin, D.W., Crane, J. Bruce, and Guze, S.B.: Felons who drink: an 8-year follow-up. *Quarterly Journal of Studies on Alcohol, 32(1)*:136-147, 1971.

Hamilton, G.V., and MacGowan, K.: *What is Wrong with Marriage?* New York, Boni, 1929.

Hatterer, L.J.: *Changing Homosexuality in the Male*. New York, McGraw-Hill, 1970.

Hawkins, James L.: *Lesbianism and Alcoholism*. New York, Grune & Stratton, pp. 137-153, 287, 1976.

Judd, T.D.: *Survey of Non-Gay Alcoholism Treatment Agencies and Services Offered for Gay Women and Men*. Berkely, California, Pacific Center, Alcoholism Program, 1977.

Kinsey, Alfred C., Pomeroy, Wardell B., and Martin, C.W.: *Sexual Behavior in the Human Male*. Philadelphia, Saunders, 1953.

Knauert, A.P.: *Differential Diagnosis of Alcoholism*. Lecture, Psychotherapy Associates, P.C. Fifth Annual Advanced Winter Workshop, "Treatment and Rehabilitation of the Alcoholic," Colorado Springs, Colorado, January 28, 1979.

Knauert, A.P.: *Differential Diagnosis of Alcoholism*. Lecture, Psychotherapy Associates, P.C. Sixth Annual Advanced Winter Workshop, "Treatment and Rehabilitation of the Alcoholic," Colorado Springs, Colorado, January 28, 1980.

Knauert, A.P.: *Alcoholism and Sexual Deviation*. Lecture, Psychotherapy Associates, P.C. Seventh Annual Advanced Winter Workshop, "Treatment and Rehabilitation of the Alcoholic," Colorado Springs, Colorado, February 2, 1981.

Martin, R.L., Cloninger, R., and Guze, S.B.: Female criminality and the prediction of recidivism: A prospective six-year follow-up, *Archives of General Psychiatry, 35(2)*:207-214, 1978.

Masters, W.H., and Johnson, V.E.: *Homosexuality in Perspective*. Boston, Little, Brown & Co., 1979.

Menninger, K.: *Man Against Himself*. New York, Harcourt-Brace and World, Inc., 1938.

Ovesey, L.: *Psychotherapy of Male Sexuality: Psychodynamic Formulation*. New York, Archives of Gen Psychiatry, September, 1963.

Parker, F.: Comparison of the sex temperatment of alcoholics and moderate drinkers. *American Sociological Review, 24(3)*:366-374, 1959.

Rathod, N.H., Gregory, E., and Blows, D.: Two-year follow-up study of alcoholic patients. *British Journal of Psychiatry, 112*:683-392, 1966.

Reik, T.: *Of Love and Lust*. New York, Jason Aronson, 1974.

Saghir, M., Robins, E., and Walbran, B.: Homosexuality:IV. Psychiatric disorders and disability in the female homosexual. *American Journal of Psychiatry, 127(2)*:147-254, 1970.

Satir, V.: *Process in Family Therapy*. Workshop on Family Therapy. Golden, Colorado, March 6, 1980.

Small, E.J., and Leach, B.: Counseling homosexual alcoholics. *Journal of Studies on Alcohol, 38(11)*:2077-2986, 1977.

Stekel, W.: *Sadism and Masochism*, Vols. I, II. New York, Liveright, 1929.

Vraa, C.W.: *Sex Therapy Training*. Lecture, Psychotherapy Associates, P.C. Eighth Annual Advanced Winter Workshop, "Treatment and Rehabilitation of the Alcoholic," Colorado Springs, Colorado, February 4, 1982.

Williams, K.H.: *Overview of Sexual Problems in Alcoholism*. Workshop on Sexual Counseling for Persons with Alcohol Problems, Pittsburgh, Pennsylvania, pp. 1-23, 83, 1976.

Wilsnack, S.C.: Femininity by the bottle. *Psychology Today*, pp. 39-43, April 1973.

Wilsnack, S.C.: *Recent Research on Women and Alcohol*. Lecture, Psychotherapy Associates, P.C. Eighth Annual Advanced Winter Workshop, "Treatment and Rehabilitation of the Alcoholic, " Colorado Springs, Colorado, February 2, 1982.

Chapter 6
ALCOHOLISM, CHILD MOLESTATION, AND CHILD ABUSE

CHILD molesting, or pedophilia, and child abuse are considered in this chapter. The chapter has been divided into one section that focuses upon the various issues associated with alcoholism, alcohol abuse, and child molesting and a second section that focuses upon the various issues associated with alcoholism, alcohol abuse, and child abuse. Child abuse may involve deviant sexual behavior. For this reason, child abuse has been included in the second section of this text. As indicated in the introduction, the second section of this text is devoted to elucidating the roles of alcohol addiction and alcohol abuse in deviant sexual behavior. Child abuse is basic to the alcoholic family system (Forrest, 1978). In view of the incidence of child abuse among alcoholic families, it was felt that this issue should be expanded beyond a mere exploration of sexual abuse. This goal has been attained in the second section of the chapter.

CHILD MOLESTING

It is somewhat difficult to precisely define child molesting, or pedophilia. There is general agreement among researchers and psychopathologists (Aarens et al., 1977) that pedophilia involves a sexual attraction, stimulation, and desire upon the part of an adult for young children. Child molesting and pedophilia both refer to sexual transactions between an adult and a child. Yet, the child molester may differ clinically from the pedophile (Meiselman, 1978; Finkelhor, 1979). Pedophilia is a variety of sexual de-

216

viation involving a fixation upon children. The pedophile, usually a male, desires sexual relations with only young children. Pedophilia may encompass a heterosexual or homosexual fixation on young children. Some pedophiles are only capable of sexual arousal and excitement with children. These individuals are not sexually aroused or stimulated by age-appropriate sexual partners. However, most pedophiles do experience sexual relations and sexual gratification with age-appropriate sexual partners. Nonetheless, these individuals compulsively ruminate about sexual relations with a child. They find sexual relations with children more exciting and stimulating than sexual relations with an adult. A small percent of the habitual criminal population are pedophiles. These men are arrested many times for sexually molesting children. From time to time it is revealed by the media that a famous celebrity or politician has been arrested for having sexual relations with a child.

Recently in our culture, the sexual exploitation of children has become an issue of growing concern. Young children are used as prostitutes, they are "in demand" by some people in the pornographic movie industry, and sex with children simply seems to be more prevalent in modern American society (Aarens et al., 1977). Sex with children has become "big business" in America and involves millions and millions of dollars.

Child molesting is a term that is generally applied to child-adult sexual relations. Unlike the concept of pedophilia, child molesting more generically includes incest, one time incidents of sexual relations between an adult and child, and virtually any variety of sexual assault upon a child. The child molester may or may not be a pedophile. Certainly, the person who has sexual relations with a child tends toward a pedophilia adjustment style. Some clinicians would view the "one-time" child molester as a pedophile. Hower, pedophilia is a disorder that involves a sexual fixation upon children. The sexual pathology of the pedophile is quite obsessive-compulsive in terms of choice of sexual object, fantasies, thoughts and cognitions, and behavioral repetoire. In order to avoid confusion over the use of these clinical terms, this chapter will deal primarily with the issue of child molesting. When referring to pedophilia or research on this subject, this difference in terminology and subject matter will be clearly delineated.

The true incidence of child molesting is unknown (DeFrancis, 1969; Aarens et al., 1977). Most researchers (Aarens et al., 1977) believe that reported cases of child molesting make up only a minute fraction of the total number of incidents of this form of behavior. Historically, the only source of reliable data available on reported child molesting has been criminal court records. This data source is very inadequate. DeFrancis (1969) states "the problem of sexual abuse of children is of unknown national dimensions, but findings strongly point to the probability of an enormous national incidence many times larger than the reported incidence of physical abuse of children." The problem of defining child molesting even contributes to the global ambiguity surrounding the incidence of this behavior. Legal definitions of child molesting vary and cases of exhibitionism, statutory rape, and lewd and indecent behavior may all fall within the rubric of "child molesting." Problems of definition result in methodological inadequacies in the research investigations that have been conducted in the area of child molesting. Different types of offenders are included in the sample populations used in different research investigations. Gebhard et al. (1965) and Aarens et al. (1977) report that research studies on child molesting utilize different sample populations than research investigations on child abuse. The research samples included in child molesting studies are almost always institutional and include mental patients and prisoners.

In spite of the many difficulties surrrounding the area of child molesting research, a number of clinically significant findings have evolved from these investigations. DeFrancis (1969) found that in 75 percent of child molesting cases the offender was known to the child and/or the child's family; over 25 percent of the offenders were members of the child's household; while 25 percent of the offenders were alleged to be strangers. Children who are sexually molested are subjected to all types of sexual behavior: genital fondling, intercourse, oral sex, sodomy, and rape. Children that are sexually molested come from all ethnic and socioeconomic groups. In over 40 percent of these cases the molesting was repeated and had occurred consistently over a period of several years in some cases. The victims of child molesting are far more often girls. Direct force and threat are usually employed in these cases. Nearly one-half of molested children tell their parents of the incident within one day. DeFrancis (1969) reports that "fewer than one-third of the parents, after discovery of the offense, acted out of concern for, or to protect, the child." This author estimates that two-thirds of the children who are molested manifest emotional disturbance subsequent to this experience.

It is obvious that child molesting is a pervasively destructive form of behavior. In order to avoid redundancy, data on incest and the incidence of incest are not considered in this chapter. Various types of child molesting are increasingly being reported to law enforcement and social agencies (Aarens et al., 1977). The establishment of the National Center on Child Abuse and Neglect, in 1974, has played an important role in the social awareness and reporting of child molesting. Aarens et al. (1977) reported that in Connecticut in the fiscal year of 1973 only seventy-six cases of child molesting were reported. In Santa Clara County, California, only thirty-six cases were reported in 1971. By 1974, 180 cases were reported in this county (Giarretto, 1976). It is quite apparent that the incidence of reported cases of child molesting is increasing each year throughout the United States (Finkelhor, 1979).

The child molester is poorly understood by the general public and behavioral scientists as well. Clinical studies of the personality makeup of the child molester (Fenichel, 1945; Mohr, 1964; Aarens, 1977) tend to be psychoanalytically oriented. Criminologically oriented investigations of child molesting focus upon statistical characterizations of this behavior. DeFrancis (1969) found that child molesters range in age from seventeen to sixty-eight, with an average age of thirty-one. Ninety-seven percent of the offenders in this study were male. Offenders essentially molest children of their own race. Less than one-fourth of the offenders in this study (DeFrancis, 1969) had prior arrest records. However, 11 percent of the sample had been previously arrested for a "sex crime." In 27 percent of the cases in this study the offender was a parent or surrogate parent. The natural father was the molester in 13 percent of the cases, and a stepfather or boyfriend of the child's mother was the offender in 14 percent of the cases. Obviously, these cases involve incest.

Child molesters and pedophiles are the product of disturbed family systems (Glueck, 1956; Finkelhor, 1979). These individuals tend to have experienced severe deprivation (Forrest, 1982a) during childhood and adolescence. The child molester is depicted as an inadequate and sexually conflicted individual by psychoanalytically oriented therapists (Fenichel, 1945). In the case of the child molester, feelings of inadequacy, inferiority, and low self-esteem facilitate anxiety and uncomfortableness within the context of adult-to-adult sexual relations. The male child molester fears sexual intimacy with confident, self-assumed adult women. In some cases this fear of adult women is conscious. However, in most cases, the child molester is not consciously aware of his fears and anxieties associated with adult-to-adult sexual relations. Even the homosexual child molester fears adult-to-adult sexuality. The adult that homosexually assaults young children (Hatterer, 1970) differs from homosexuals that limit their sexual relationships to consenting adults. Very few homosexuals are child molesters (Hatterer, 1970). The homosexual child molester is more pathologic and conflicted than the homosexual that limits his sexual relations to consenting adults.

In addition to (a) the anxiety and fears experienced by the child molester within the context of adult-to-adult sexual relationships, (b) the internal feelings of inadequacy, inferiority, and low self-esteem experienced by the child molester, and (c) their histories of familial deprivation and pathology, a good number of these individuals have had very intense precocious sexual experiences. In the clinical experience of the author, child molesters and pedophiles tend to have experienced intensive sexual stimulation between the ages of eight and twelve. These early sexual experiences are intensive, stimulating, affective, and "new." The globally cathartic and intensive nature of genital sex during these developmental years seems to result in a strong tendency toward object fixation. As a result, the adult child molester acts out a repetition compulsion. He is sexually stimulated by young children as a child, adolescent, young adult, and adult. The child molester, like the pedophile, is thus sexually fixated upon children. The learning, reinforcing, and conditioning aspects of child molesting are quite apparent. In therapy, the child molester reveals that he has "always" found young children, male or female depending upon the adjustment style of the patient, to be sexually stimulating and exciting.

Faulty learning experiences are basic to the pathology of child molesting and pedophilia. Social learning theory emphasizes the role of inappropriate and maladaptive learning and conditioning experiences in the development of all symptomatic behavior. The child molester learns and is conditioned to experience sexual stimulation and gratification with children rather than adults. In the case of some child molesters and most, if not all pedophiles, this learning experience has been repeated, practiced, and overlearned. The familial experiences of some child molesters have been conducive to the learning of inappropriate patterns of sexual responding and deviant sexual object choices. The child molester who was himself molested as a child provides the example par excellence of this issue. Such individuals emulate and model the sexually inappropriate and deviant behaviors of a father or other family member. Faulty learning is involved in precocious genital sexuality. The child molester that has experienced intense and rewarding sexuality during childhood and then persists in selecting children for sexual relations as an adolescent and adult clearly conditions himself into an inappropriate sexual object choice.

Social and environmental factors are sometimes associated with child molesting. These factors may operate to significantly reduce the sexual access that one adult has to other adults. Overcrowding and poverty (DeFrancis, 1969) may operate to increase the incidence of child molesting. The absence of a parent or both parents within the family system may be a contributing factor in some cases of child molesting. Yet, the fact remains that child molesting rarely occurs in any socioeconomic group. Race, education, occupation, and other demographic variables do not clearly predict the incidence of child molesting behavior.

It is apparent that the child molester engages in this form of deviant sexual behavior as a result of numerous factors. Every child molester is uniquely human. Likewise, the psychopathology of the child molester varies. It is only in recent years that we have collectively realized that child molesting is not a deviation of the poor and indigent. Indeed, physicians, school teachers, lawyers, and individuals from any profession can be child molesters.

Alcoholism and Child Molesting

The child molesting literature has long indicated that alcoholism and alcohol abuse are closely associated with this form of behavior (Aarens et al., 1977). Alcohol is but one factor that has been linked with child molesting. Gebhard et al. (1965) point out that chronic alcoholism or acute intoxication can precipitate child molesting. Alcohol acts as a disinhibitor. The intoxicated person is less able to distinguish between socially defined acceptable and unacceptable behaviors. Intoxication is frequently used by child molesters as an excuse for their behavior (Frosh and Bromberg, 1939; McCaghy, 1968). Many child molesters claim that alcoholism or drunkenness was the cause of their deviant behavior. Frosh and Bromberg (1939) indicate that child molesters use alcohol as an excuse for their behavior more frequently than any other type of sex offender.

In an extensive review of the empirical data on alcohol and child molesting (Aarons et al., 1977) it is reported that 19 to 49 percent of child molesters were drinking at the time of the offense. Furthermore, 7 to 52 percent of child molesters were identified as alcoholics. Research focused upon "specific types of offenders" (incest offenders, offenders who molest females, homosexual child molesters, etc.) reveals that "29 to 77 percent of various types of offenders were drinking at the time of the offense, while 16 to 73 percent were labeled as alcoholics." It is apparent that there is a good deal of variation with regard to the incidence of alcohol use and alcohol addiction in cases of child molesting. In addition, alcoholism is not clearly defined in many of the investigations of child molesting. Aarens et al. (1977) report that heterosexual child molesters that use force or threat have a higher percent of drunken behavior at the time that the offense is committed. Heterosexual child molesters that use force or threat also include "a considerably larger proportion of identifiable alcoholics than all other types of child molesters." In this group of child molesters, 40 percent are labeled "alcoholic." In analyzing the interrelationships between child molesting, patterns

of alcohol use, and drinking at the time of the offense it is concluded (Aarens et al., 1977) that "the data indicates that when
considering offenses in which the offender was drunk, one-half or
more of these offenses which involved children were committed
by alcoholics."

Rada (1976) found significant relationships between drinking,
alcoholism, and child molesting. The Rada investigation (1976)
involved data obtained on over 200 *pedophilic* sex offenders that
had been committed to a state hospital. Forty-nine percent of
these pedophiles were drinking at the time of the offense. Thirty-
four percent were drinking heavily (ten or more beers or the equivalent) at the time of the offense. According to assessment results
with the MAST (Michigan Alcoholism Screening Test), 52 percent
of this sample of hospitalized pedophiles were "alcoholics." Assessment with Pokorny's shortened MAST indicated that one-
third of the subjects were alcoholic. Rada (1976) also found that
the proportion of offenders who were drinking was greater in the
case of offenders who molested females than for offenders who
molested males. In addition, male pedophiles had a definitely
higher alcoholism rate than female pedophiles. It should be noted
that the terms "pedophilic" and "child molester" are used inter-
changeably in this investigation (Rada, 1976).

Although this chapter does not include data pertaining to incestuous child molesting, it should be noted that studies comparing incest offenders with other child molesters (Glueck, 1956;
Ellis and Brancale, 1956; Gebhard et al., 1965; Aarens et al.,
1977) indicate that, in general, incest offenders are characterized
by a greater percent of alcoholics and offenders who were intoxicated at the time of the offense. It is also significant that Meiselman (1978) states "clinical studies of incestuous fathers have
rarely found them to be pedophiles, either behaviorally or in
their fantasy lives." In her study, no cases involved a compulsive
desire for young girls. Pedophilia was not a motivating factor in
incestuous behavior. The pedophile (Meiselman, 1978) is a dis-
tinctive type of incest offender, and pedophilia is rarely a factor
in cases of father-daughter incest. Weinberg (1955) also indicates
that pedophiles make up a distinct category of incest offenders.

Within the confines of most comprehensive alcoholic treatment centers and outpatient psychotherapy practice, it is very rare that the clinician encounters a case of nonincestuous child molesting involving an alcoholic or problem drinker. More commonly, the therapist is faced with the task of treating cases of incestuous child molesting. However, over a period of some eleven years of clinical practice with alcoholics, the author has treated five alcoholic or problem drinker nonincestuous child molesters. In all of these cases the patient was drinking and intoxicated at the time of the offense. Only two of these patients were diagnostically alcoholic (Forrest, 1978; Knauert, 1980). Three of the treated child molesters were problem drinkers (Forrest, 1978) or secondary alcoholics (Knauert, 1980). Based upon approximately thirty hours of individual psychotherapy with each of four of these patients, it is the impression of the author that preconscious and unconscious pedophiliac strivings were basic to the personalities of these patients. After several hours of intensive psychotherapy these patients as a group evidenced a sexual fixation on children. All of these patients were heterosexual child abusers. They tended to selectively attend to younger girls, in a sexual manner, while shopping or in other social situations. One forty-six-year-old patient consciously fantasized about sexual relations with young girls on a rather consistent basis and indicated that he had done so for many years. Only two of the patients persisted in denying sexual feelings and interest in young girls.

There are only a few studies that focus on alcohol and alcoholism as factors in child molesting. These studies have a number of serious methodological limitations. Small sample size, sample characteristics and diagnostic heterogeneity, and definitional inadequacies are basic limitations found in most of the clinical and research investigations dealing with alcoholism, alcohol abuse, and child molesting. In spite of these various limitations, it is very apparent that alcoholism and alcohol abuse are key factors in many cases of child molesting. Indeed, alcohol is probably the direct cause of some cases of child molesting.

The following case study involves problem drinking and child molesting. This patient was not an alcoholic. Many of the personality and characterological characteristics of the patient considered in this case study suggest the presence of underlying pedophiliac strivings.

CASE 10. Bennie S., a twenty-four-year-old male junior high school English teacher, was court ordered into outpatient psychotherapy following a sexual assault upon an eleven-year-old girl. The patient was single at the time the offense was committed, but he was living with an eighteen-year-old telephone operator. Bennie was apprehensive about being involved in therapy and he clearly resented being "ordered" into treatment. The judge in this case gave the patient two choices: eighteen months in prison or "treatment." The patient did not have a prior legal history of sexual assault or any other form of criminal behavior.

It was very difficult for Bennie to discuss the child molesting incident during the initial three therapy sessions. He did indicate that he had been drinking heavily on the night that the offense took place. Furthermore, he did not remember sexually assaulting the victim. The patient stated that he was "drunk" and "really wondered" if he had sexual relations with the girl.

The early hours of psychotherapy encompassed an exploration of the patient's family history. Bennie was abandoned by his biologic mother at the age of two. His father, an Air Force sergeant, had then placed the patient and his two older sisters in a Catholic orphanage. The children remained in this orphanage until the patient was five years old. The father remarried at this time, the children were taken out of the orphanage, and the family was reunited. Some fourteen months later the patient's father was assigned to overseas duty. Three months after he left, the step-mother once again placed the patient and his sisters in the orphanage. The children remained in the orphanage until the patient was in the fifth grade. At this time, the family was again reunited. According to the patient, all of the children disliked the step-mother.

While in the orphanage the second time, between the ages of six and ten, Bennie was involved in a sexual relationship with a priest. The priest was the director of the orphanage. Once or twice a week, the priest would manually and/or orally stimulate the patient. Bennie indicated that he had been uncomfortable about this relationship, but he "accepted it." During the fourth grade Bennie engaged in intercourse on several occasions with a first grade girl who was also in the orphanage. The patient was very happy about leaving the orphanage. After leaving the orphanage and joining his family of origin, Bennie started attending a public school. He did well academically, behaviorally, and interpersonally. Shortly before finishing the fifth grade, Bennie became sexually involved with a second grade girl. Bennie indicated that this girl was "big for her age." He suspected that she had "flunked a grade or two." At any rate, the couple engaged in oral sex, mutual masturbation, and genital intercourse two or three times each week. This relationship continued until the patient was in the seventh grade. At this time, Bennie's family again moved. Bennie indicated that he had "matured early." He dated a great deal in junior high school and high school. He was also sexually active throughout early adolescence and adolescence. It was clinically significant that the patient's sexual relationships always involved girls that were at least two or three years younger than himself. During his senior year of high school the patient dated and was sexually active with an eighth grade girl. In spite of the sexual precocity of the patient, the age differences between the patient and the girls he was involved with, and the various other factors associated with these relationships never once was he confronted with the inappropriateness of his behavior by parents, teachers, other school personnel, the parents of the girls he was involved with, community authority figures, or significant others.

After sharing these various sexual relationships and escapades with the therapist for a few hours, the patient disclosed that he had experienced sexual feelings for his sisters since early adolescence. One sister was sixteen months older than the patient and the other was nearly three years older than the patient. Between the ages of twelve and sixteen Bennie experienced sexual feelings and erotic impulses for his sisters. Many arguments and family conflicts were associated with Bennie's erotic feelings and sexual behaviors within the family system. Bennie indicated that he frequently "got in trouble" as a result of "pinching my sister's tits, or pinching them on the ass." The patient's father and step-mother were often made aware of these interactions by both sisters. When this happened, Bennie was punished physically and verbally. However, the patient had also entered the bathroom when a sister was taking a shower, disrobed, and attempted to shower with her. He had an erection when this episode occurred. On numerous occasions during adolescence, Bennie entered the sisters bedroom and attempted to get in bed with one of them. They became angry, refused to let him get in bed with them, and threatened to tell the parents. Neither sister even told the parents of Bennie's frank attempts at seduction. Bennie terminated these sexual advances and familial sexual interactions during his junior year of high school.

After graduating from high school the patient entered college. On a few occasions in high school Bennie had gotten "drunk," and he had also "experimented" with marajuana in his junior and senior years. Nevertheless, the patient was never in any kind of trouble as a result of drinking or drug use prior to entering college. During the first two years of college Bennie drank a great deal and used "grass" on a daily basis. At this time, getting "stoned" on alcohol, marajuana, and other drugs was a weekly reality for Bennie. He managed to pass his college classes with average and below average grades and was on scholastic probation a good deal of the time. During the summer before his junior year of college, Bennie was arrested for driving while intoxicated. The arresting officer also discovered a few marajuana "joints" in the glove compartment of the patient's car. The patient was fined $200 for driving while intoxicated and received a "suspended sentence" for possessing a very small amount of marajuana. After this, Bennie discontinued using marajuana and other "drugs." He did not discontinue using alcohol. Bennie continued to drink heavily throughout his entire college career.

During his junior and senior years of college, the patient dated several coeds. He began to apply himself academically and graduated from college with an education major. After graduating from college, the patient secured a teaching position within a junior high school. Bennie indicated in therapy that a number of eighth and ninth grade girls "made passes" at him. They were openly seductive and on occasion indicated to the patient that they wanted to have sex. According to Bennie, these girls were very promiscuous and "into drugs and a lot of drinking." At this time the patient drank a "couple of beers each night" and "really partied" on the weekends. Bennie drank very heavily on the weekends and it was rather common for him to experience "blackouts" during his weekend drinking sprees.

The patient avoided any type of sexual involvement with his students. He did engage in a variety of sexual behaviors with a woman who was some seven years older than himself. This woman was divorced and the mother of three children. Bennie would spend one or two evenings a week with her in order to "relieve his sexual tensions." He would also "pick up" women at local bars on a regular basis. One Friday afternoon, Bennie and two women teachers went to a local bar for "happy hour." They were joined later in the evening by the woman that Bennie had been spending one or two nights a week with. The "group" began drinking at approximately four in the afternoon and continued to drink heavily until after midnight. Finally, the patient went home with the woman that he had been seeing regularly. When they arrived at this woman's home, Bennie indicated that he would drive the babysitter home. This girl was eleven years old. The patient stated that he remembered leaving his girlfriend's house with the babysitter and then "trying" to drive back to the girl-friend's house. He did not remember what happened during the drive to the babysitter's home. The following day the babysitter's mother called Bennie's girlfriend and told her that Bennie had sexually molested her daughter. Bennie denied this. On Monday morning, Bennie was called to the superintendent's office. Two police officers were at the superintendent's office, and they proceeded to arrest the patient. He was charged with sexually assaulting a minor. The babysitter had awakened her parents early Sunday morning and told them that the patient fondled her breasts, manually stimulated her genitals, and forced her to perform oral sex on him during the ride home. She had resisted his attempts at intercourse.

This case came to trial some three months after the offense was committed. The patient indicated that he was drinking heavily at the time of the alleged offense and did not remember the incident. He told the judge that he believed he was "in a blackout" when this incident took place. In view of the patient's absence of a prior history of sexual assault or other criminal offenses, the judge sentenced this patient to probation and extended treatment. The patient was dismissed from his teaching position before going to trial. He also met a telephone operator a few weeks before the trial, and they began living together almost immediately. Bennie did not inform her of any of the circumstances surrounding this incident.

The patient remained in weekly outpatient psychotherapy for nearly seven months. He stopped drinking and eventually found employment in the real estate field. However, Bennie refused to attend Alcoholics Anonymous stating that "I can continue to do it on my own." He continued to live with the telephone operator but refused to openly discuss this incident or his family history with her. Bennie continued to feel a sexual attraction for young girls, but did not act out this impulse. The patient terminated therapy at the end of six months feeling that his "problem" was solved. No follow-up information is available on this patient.

This case study clearly demonstrates the role of acute intoxication in child molesting. The patient, an incipient alcoholic, sexually molested a young girl following several hours of heavy drinking. The patient indicated that he did not remember assaulting the girl and suggested that he was in a "blackout" when the offense took place. He had been a heavy drinker and polydrug abuser for a number of years. This patient had experienced considerable narcissistic injury (Forrest, 1979a; 1982a) throughout childhood. He was homosexually molested by a priest over a period of about four years. The patient was precociously involved in a number of heterosexual relationships. As an early adolescent, the patient had attempted to have sexual relations with his sisters. These attempts at incest were essentially unsuccessful.

A number of clinically significant issues are basic to this case study of alcoholism and child molesting. The patient had been sexually molested as a child. The patient had experienced a wide variety of intense sexual relationships during childhood and early adolescence. In spite of the apparently good social and interpersonal adjustment of the patient as an early adult, he manifested clear-cut pedophiliac trends. This case study elucidates the inter-relationships between alcoholism and alcohol abuse, child molesting, incest, and pedophilia. In the dynamic viewpoint of the author, child molesting always includes a pedophiliac component. Furthermore, child molesting may be a defense against incestuous acting-out. The sexual adjustment and personality structure of the child molester are always infantilized.

Basic Treatment Strategies

In cases of child molesting it is apparent that the victim is in need of support, psychotherapy, and a variety of treatment-oriented interventions. There seems to be a rather widespread consensus of opinion (McCaghy, 1968; Rada, 1976; Aarens et al., 1977; Meiselman, 1978; Finkelhor, 1979) that the child who is molested is in need of therapy and treatment. Implicit in this position is the belief that the victim "deserves" compassion, understanding, and treatment. While behavioral scientists generally feel that the child molester is in need of therapy and rehabilitation, there appears to be a dearth of information available relative to the treatment of these individuals. Moreover, a sizeable segment of the general public believe that the child molester does not "deserve" to be rehabilitated.

Clinicians that work with child molesters need to be able to accurately assess the drinking history and drinking behaviors of their patients. It has already been pointed out that many child molesters fall back upon the "excuse" of alcoholism or intoxication in order to rationalize their deviant sexual behavior. In spite of this fact, many child molesters are alcohol abusers or alcohol addicted. The data germane to these issues clearly indicates that alcohol is a consistently significant variable in cases of child molesting.

In cases of child molesting that involve alcoholism or acute intoxication, the therapist must point out to the patient the association between drinking and alcohol-induced sexually deviant behavior. Initially in treatment, the clinician must focus upon the patient's addiction. Very simply stated, the probability of the patient again engaging in child molesting or other forms of grossly deviant sexual behavior is radically reduced once the patient's addiction has been successfully treated. For this reason, psychotherapy with the alcoholic or problem drinking (Forrest, 1978) child molester begins with the treatment task of resolving the patient's addiction and addictive symptomatology. In this respect, the early goals and strategies of the treatment process are quite akin to those discussed in the earlier chapters of this text. The chronic alcoholic child molester may need to be referred for detoxification or other medical interventions prior to initiating psychotherapy or involving the patient in a comprehensive rehabilitation program. The acutely intoxicated, but not necessarily alcohol addicted, child molester may need to be placed in a detoxification facility for a few days before entering therapy. Holistic treatment and health care is appropriate in the vast majority of these cases. The patient is globally benefited by involving himself in a good nutritional program, a program of regular exercise, regular attendance at Alcoholics Anonymous meetings, weekly psychotherapy and therapy for the spouse and children, and a program of spiritual recovery. Antabuse maintenance can be a very effective short-term adjunctive treatment modality in the case of alcoholic and problem-drinking child molesters.

It is critically important for these patients to be able to fully understand that they engage in inappropriate or "crazy" sexual behaviors when they drink. A rational and integrated acceptance of this reality upon the part of the patient operates to (1) reinforce continued sobriety, (2) diminish the probability of further occurrences of alcohol-facilitated deviant sexual acting-out, and (3) enhance the patient's ability to accept the reality of his history of sexual deviation while maintaining a sense of personal self-esteem and dignity. In order to grow psychologically and get on with the process of adaptive daily living, the patient must be able to establish a positive sense of self-worth. It is difficult for the patient to feel good about himself. The alcoholic child molester is a person who has struggled with chronic feelings of inadequacy, inferiority, worthlessness, and low self-esteem. Being identified as a "child molester" actively reinforces and compounds these negative self-perceptions. A long-term goal of psychotherapy with these patients is that of modifying negative self-perceptions and low self-esteem.

During the early treatment sessions it is often clinically efficacious for the therapist to accept and/or actively reinforce the position that the patient would never have engaged in child molesting
behavior in the absence of drinking and intoxication. In most
cases, such a therapeutic stance is quite valid, honest, and reality
oriented. This therapeutic stance allows the patient to feel reasonably good about himself and enables him to maintain some degree
of positive self-esteem. It is the basis for helping the patient overcome acute feelings of guilt, depression, and remorse. The alcoholic child molester, as well as other child molesters that manifest
secondary alcoholism or problem drinking, is usually very guilty
and depressed when "discovered" or apprehended. Some of these
patients are suicidal early in treatment, and indeed, throughout
treatment. The technique of "siding" with the patient and in essence "blaming" the child molesting behavior upon the patient's
alcoholism can literally be a lifesaving intervention early in the
treatment process with a few of these patients. In addition, this
procedure overtly and covertly communicates to the patient that
rational, nonaberrant sexual behavior is associated with sobriety.
To the contrary, a very real aspect of the patient's personality,
behavior, and adjustment style is that of "becoming" a sexual deviant through intoxication. The patient must face, accept, and
eventually change this dimension of his being.

Perhaps the most facilitative dimension of this style of therapy
with the addicted child molester is in the realm of developing a
working therapeutic alliance. The therapist does not alienate,
threaten, or reject the patient via the utilization of this treatment
strategy. Indeed, the therapist communicates a sense of understanding, acceptance, warmth, and empathy for the patient by
using this treatment technique. On a concrete level, the clinician
also lets the patient know what behaviors must be changed by
using this procedure. Once a productive therapeutic alliance has
been established, the patient is better able to commit himself to
the middle and later stages of the therapeutic process. These patients cannot be successfully treated or rehabilitated in ten or
fifteen contact hours. They must be seen on a regular basis for
several months. With several months of sobriety and growth
through psychotherapy, the patient is better able to understand

and modify the total system of pathology that contributed to his history of child molesting. Alcohol is the key precipitating factor in many cases of child molesting, but the therapist and patient must additionally resolve the various other factors that have actively contributed to the patient's child molesting choice or symptom style. The child molester will avoid these salient therapy issues in short-term psychotherapy. In the absence of a productive therapeutic alliance, these patients will flee from treatment or find every possible excuse and means for ending therapy prematurely.

The majority of alcoholic or problem-drinking child molesters are in need of direct behavioral counseling and therapy. As a part of the ongoing therapy process, these patients respond favorably to social skills training, assertiveness training, relaxation training, and self-image modification training. The patient must learn how to relate interpersonally and sexually with adult or age-appropriate women. In addition to utilizing dynamically oriented relationship psychotherapy, the therapist will find that by using direct behavioral interventions the treatment process is more globally effective and simultaneously shortened in duration.

Many alcoholic or problem drinking child molesters are married and have families (DeFrancis, 1969). Marital conflicts and sexual pathology and/or sexual dysfunction are basic to the marital adjustments of these patients. Indeed, their present family system and family of origin are disturbed. For these reasons, conjoint and family therapy interventions (Skynner, 1976; Wegscheider, 1981) are very often appropriate and clinically efficacious in these cases. In the experience of the author, it is generally most appropriate to interview the patient and spouse separately during the initial treatment session. The patient is then seen in individual therapy, as is his wife by the same therapist. After the husband and wife have each been seen in three to five individual therapy sessions, they are seen in conjoint and/or family therapy. Should there be a disturbed child in the family system or any clinical evidence of emotional problems in other family members, the child is immediately referred for treatment or family therapy and may be initiated in adjunct to the individual therapy of the parents. Commonly, every member in the family of a child molester is in need of therapy. The style or format of therapy for the different family members will depend upon the orientation, training, and clinical expertise of the clinician.

The wife of the child molester is often depressive, passive, sexually dysfunctional, and anxious. These women are in obvious need of therapy. The marital relationship of the child molester is diffusely conflicted. Communication is lacking, distorted, and pathologic in these marital relationships. Patterns of verbal and physical abuse are central to such marriages. In view of these realities, it is important for the therapist to make every effort to include the spouse of the child molester in therapy. Furthermore, the clinician should eventually utilize conjoint therapy interventions in every case involving a married alcoholic child molester. Therapists must also make every effort to provide care for the children who are living in these pathologic family systems.

It is apparent that everyone involved in child molesting is in need of psychotherapy. The victim of child molesting is traumatized. The alcoholic or problem-drinking child molester is disturbed. The children and spouse of the child molester are frequently pathologic. These cases can be very difficult to treat (Barlow and Wincze, 1980). Indeed, as the literature generally suggests (Finkelhor, 1979; Leiblum and Pervin, 1980) the prognosis is poor and rates of recidivism are high in cases of sexual deviation. In spite of these factors, the child molester is in need of treatment. By focusing upon the alcoholism or problem drinking of the individual that engages in child molesting behavior, the prognosis is improved and rates of recidivism are reduced. These patients are surprisingly unique in their pathology and adjustment style. The therapist must use treatment interventions that meet the individual needs of the patient. Therapists that are creative, flexible, and innovative tend to be more successful with these patients. Treatment interventions that modify the patient's interpersonal style, sexual behaviors, social skills, cognitions and self-dialogue, feelings, and role and gender behaviors are most effective. The total patient must be the focus of therapy. It is not enough to simply attempt to modify patterns of sexual arousal, object choice, and sexual functioning. Holistic treatment of the alcoholic child molester and his family often includes involvement in the Alcoholics Anonymous community.

CHILD ABUSE

As touched upon earlier in this chapter, child abuse may specifically encompass a variety of sexually abusive behaviors. Incest and child molesting are the primary forms of sexual child abuse. These topics have already been considered at length. Due to the magnitude of the problem of essentially nonsexual child abuse, it was felt that this topic should be covered in this chapter. Since the topic of essentially nonsexual child abuse does not usually include deviant sexual behavior, this section is somewhat truncated.

Child abuse is defined as "physical injuries inflicted on children by their caretakers" (Aarens et al., 1977). A generally less destructive form of child abuse is referred to as child neglect. Aarens et al. (1977) define child neglect as "failure on the part of parents or other caretakers to perform such expected functions as nurturance, protection, or supervision." These simplistic definitions are surprisingly concise and descriptive, and they are used by behavioral scientists to describe rather specific patterns of family interaction and behavior. These definitions do not specifically refer to the sexual abuse of children. However, the Child Abuse Prevention and Treatment Act of 1974 does include sexuality in the definition of child abuse. This act defines child abuse and neglect together as "the physical or mental injury, sexual abuse, negligent treatment, or maltreatment of a child under the age of eighteen by a person who is responsible for the child's welfare under circumstances which indicate that the child's health or welfare is harmed or threatened thereby." This definition does not distinguish between abuse and neglect. In some cases the physical injuries which parents inflict upon their children are overtly sexual in nature. Likewise, child neglect may involve a more covertly sexual dimension. For these reasons, the forms of child abuse and child neglect discussed in this section of the chapter are referred to as "essentially nonsexual." It is easy to recognize that incest and child molesting are direct expressions of sexual child abuse. It is relatively more difficult to view the behavior of a parent that extinguishes a cigarette on his or her child's penis as simply sexual abuse of the child. This issue is even more complex in cases where the parent actually murders the child and the relatively covert sexual abuse of the child is but one aspect of the parent's abuse of the child.

In American society, laws against cruelty to children or child abuse are only 100 years old. During the past two decades in this country more and more research has been devoted to the subject of child abuse. The data available on the incidence of child abuse varies according to time of the study, methods of data collection, and location of the investigation. Hindman (1977) indicates that in 1976 public agencies throughout the United States received over 300,000 reports of "suspected" child abuse. Besharov (1976) reports that 2,000 children die each year in circumstances involving suspected abuse or maltreatment. In a nationwide study (Gil, 1973) of reported cases of child abuse it was found that nearly nine incidents of physical abuse occur per 100,000. The rate of child abuse seems to vary considerably between states (Gil, 1973). According to Gil (1968), only about 6,000 cases of child abuse are validated each year throughout the United States. Kempe (1971) has estimated that the actual number of child abuse cases occurring annually in the United States is between 30,000 and 50,000. It is estimated (Kempe and Helfer, 1972) that only one of every 100 child abuse transactions are ever reported to authorities or social agencies. The *New York Times* (March, 1977) concluded on the basis of a nationwide probability survey that "parents kick, punch or bite as many as 1.7 million children a year, beat up 460,000 to 750,000 more and attack 46,000 with knives or guns."

It is apparent that there are no definitive statistics available on the incidence of child abuse and child neglect. Yet, it must be concluded that child abuse is a very sizeable social and familial problem in the United States. Each year thousands of children are physically and psychologically abused in this country. Until recently (Ackerman, 1982) the American collective seems to have denied the magnitude and scope of the problem of child abuse.

Child abuse seems to be caused by a diversity of psychological, familial, and social factors. Child abuse and child neglect are most likely to occur (Smith, Hanson, and Nobel, 1974; Kent, 1975; Hindman, 1977; Ackerman, 1982) in families that are socially isolated and involves parents that have been abused as children. Young and inexperienced parents are more prone to child abuse and neglect. Spinetta and Rigler (1972) described the personality of the child abuser. These authors (Spinetta and Rigler, 1972) report that the child abuser is impulsive, immature, depressive, and lacking in understanding of the needs and capabilities of infants and young children. Child abusers have a poor self-concept. They are also dependent and manifest a low frustration tolerance. The child abuser tends to be an "uptight," angry individual who finds it difficult to relax, experience pleasure, and simply have fun.

In the clinical experience of the author, the majority of child abusers have themselves been abused during infancy, childhood, and even adolescence. Abusive and neglectful parents have poor and inadequate parenting skills. They have learned and modeled faulty and inappropriate parenting behaviors within the context of their families of origin. Abusive and neglectful parents are not psychologically prepared to deal with the various responsibilities associated with parenting. Although acute situational stress is clearly a significant aetiological factor in some cases of child abuse, more commonly the pattern of parental abuse and neglectful behavior is consistent and of a relatively long duration. In these cases, one or both parents may be severely disturbed. Indeed, such parents tend to be borderline personalities (Kernberg, 1975; 1976) or even floridly psychotic. In many cases of child abuse, both parents are abusers and their abuse extends to all of the children in the family system. These parents abuse and neglect each other. Obviously, every member in such a family system learns and is consistently conditioned into a variety of maladaptive familial patterns of behavior. Children that are abused and neglected, in effect, learn to be child abusers. These family systems are severly pathologic and grossly dysfunctional.

Research (Caffey, 1965) indicates that children who have been abused tend to manifest behavioral problems such as hyperactivity, acting-out, and delinquency. Retardation, physical deformity, illness, and psychological problems are also characteristics of the child that has been abused. It is not precisely known whether these charasteristics precipitate child abuse or occur as a result of child abuse and neglect. Child abuse almost always results in serious psychological problems. Child abuse and neglect can result in physical injury or even death. Children with learning difficulties, physical defects, or hyperactivity may stress their parents to the point of facilitating abusive behavior via these disabilities and handicaps. Thus, the abused child potentially plays an important role in the aetiology of his or her abuse by parents. Nonetheless, parents are responsible for the welfare and well-being of their children.

Cultures and societies vary according to principles and practices of child rearing. Child abuse seems to occur in virtually all societies. Historical records indicate that thousands of infants and young children have been put to death at different times in various cultures. In recent American history, child labor laws were legally mandated as a result of widespread corporate and industrial abuse of children. Perhaps all parents or adults are capable of engaging in child abuse or child neglect behaviors under certain circumstances. Social deprivation, poverty, and cultural factors may be associated with the incidence of child abuse. However, the fact remains that child abusing parents come from every walk of life. It is not just unemployed, disadvantaged, lower socioeconomic level parents that abuse and neglect children. In some cases, abused and neglected children have parents that are well educated, intelligent, and financially successful.

It is logical to assume that child abuse is multivariantly determined. The personality makeup and internal adjustment of abusive parents, family dynamics, abuse of the parents and other social learning factors, parenting skills, situational stress, and other variables can interact in a fashion that is conducive to child abuse and neglect.

Alcoholism and Child Abuse

The role of alcoholism and alcohol abuse in the aetiology of child abuse and child neglect has not been an area of significant research. However, studies of child abuse in America and foreign countries do indicate that intoxication and alcoholism are often associated with this pattern of behavior (Aarens et al., 1977). Some of these investigations report findings relative to intoxication at the time child abuse occurs. One study (Aarens et al., 1977) revealed that 13, 44, and 0 percent of child abusers are intoxicated at the time of the abusive act. It is apparent that there is considerable data variance with regard to the percent of child abusers who are intoxicated at the time of the abusive act.

The limited research that has been conducted in the realm of alcohol and child abuse seems to be rather cursory in scope. For example, Gil (1973) in a nationwide survey of child abuse and possible contributing causal contexts, which may precipitate incidents of physical child abuse, included only one research item related to "alcoholic intoxication of the perpetrator." In this study (Gil, 1973) it was found that 13 percent of child abusers are intoxicated at the time of the offense. Aarens et al. (1977) indicate that alcoholic intoxication is most notably associated with "physical abuse of children perpetrated by male babysitters and with caretaker quarrels in which the child may have come to the aid of one parent, merely happened to be in the midst of the fight, or the child may have been the object of the quarrel initially." Research (Aarens et al., 1977) generally reveals that less than one-third of abusive parents are alcoholic or evidence a history of drinking problems. However, foreign investigations (Aarens et al., 1977) rather consistently report a substantially higher percentage of alcoholism or problem drinking behaviors among child abusers.

In an interesting study of the children of alcoholics (Booz-Allen and Hamilton, Inc., 1974) it was found that 10 percent of these children reported parental physical abuse. Of the children of alcoholics (Booz-Allen and Hamilton, Inc., 1974) 64 percent indicate that they have been emotionally neglected by their parents. Unfortunately, this investigation did not utilize control group comparisons. In a study of multiproblem families (Scientific Analysis Corporation, 1976) parental neglect was reported on the part of 23 percent of the alcoholic parents. In contrast, 21 percent of the nonalcoholic parents were reported to be neglectful. From a statistical viewpoint this difference is clearly nonsignificant.

Hindman (1977) states "parents with alcohol problems have a high potential for exhibiting neglect of their children, especially through erratic and inconsistent parenting." The children of alcoholic parents are prone to developing emotional, behavioral, and alcohol problems later in life (Cork, 1969; Fox, 1962; Miller, 1976; Ackerman, 1978; 1982). Kempe (1972) maintains that alcohol plays an important role in approximately one-third of child abuse cases.

In general, the research investigations and clinical case studies involving alcoholism, alcohol abuse, and child abuse are inconclusive. While it is apparent that alcohol is often associated with child abuse, there is comparatively little hard data available on this topic. The various relationships between alcoholism, alcohol abuse, and child abuse remain areas for future research. It is the impression of the author that not all alcoholics *seriously* abuse or neglect their children. However, the alcoholic experiences considerable difficulty in the process of parenting. Somewhat paradoxically, child abuse and neglect are always basic to the alcoholic family system. The alcoholic parent is a very inconsistent parent. Discipline in the alcoholic family system is inconsistent.

The following case study, involving the H. family, demonstrates the complexity of the problem of child abuse in the alcoholic family system. Both of the parents are alcoholic in this case study. All of the children had been abused and neglected by both parents.

CASE 11. The H. family was referred for therapy by a school social worker. Robert, the sixteen-year-old, second oldest son in the family, had refused to attend school for three weeks. As a result of school absenteeism, the school social worker became involved with Robert and subsequently contacted his mother by phone. The mother indicated in the initial phone conversation that the family was experiencing many problems. She also stated that her husband was an "alcoholic." A family therapy session was scheduled for the entire H. family.

The first family therapy session was attended by Mr. H., an Army first sergeant, Mrs. H., a cocktail waitress, Robert, the identified patient, John, an older brother who was attending a local junior college, and Billy, the twelve-year-old, youngest family member. During the session all of the family members indicated that they were "upset" about Robert's refusal to attend school. None of the other family members seemed to be able to understand Robert's recent behavior. They were also collectively concerned about Robert's "bad temper." Mrs. H. openly stated that Mr. H. was an alcoholic and suggested that Robert's behavior might be related to Mr. H.'s drinking and alcohol-facilitated behavior within the family system. When Mrs. H. brought up the issue of Mr. H.'s history of alcohol addiction, he very quickly pointed out that she too had a "serious drinking problem." The father had received extensive treatment for alcoholism in two military alcoholic rehabilitation centers. At the time of this session the father was attempting to "control" his drinking by consuming only beer. He also limited his drinking to weekends. All of the family members indicated that they were willing to make a commitment to the process of family therapy. Each family member expressed the feeling that their family environment and familial patterns of communication and interacting were in need of change.

During the second family therapy session Mr. H. revealed that Mrs. H. had stabbed him in the stomach with a butcher's knife some two years earlier. On this occasion both parents were acutely intoxicated. Mrs. H. locked Mr. H. out of the house. He proceeded to break down the door and then physically assaulted Mrs. H. In the heat of this physical struggle, Mrs. H. picked up a butcher's knife and stabbed Mr. H. in the stomach. Mr. H. was hospitalized for three weeks following this incident and both spouses agreed that he had nearly died. As a result of this incident, Mr. and Mrs. H. were referred to an Army alcoholic treatment center. For several months Mr. H. drank less and discontinued his pattern of physically abusing his wife and children. The father had always been concerned about providing "adequate" discipline in the family system and "always" used physical methods of child and spouse discipline. In reality, Mr. H. physically abused and beat his wife and children on a nearly daily basis. Interestingly, Mr. H. was barely five feet seven inches in height and weighed only 125 pounds. All of the family members appeared to be rather morbidly afraid of Mr. H. However, all of the family members were also afraid of Mrs. H. The father indicated that he was afraid that she might get drunk and "cut my throat while I'm sleeping." Robert and the other children indicated that they "never knew" what their mother might do after drinking. Furthermore, all of the family members were afraid of Robert. In fact, Robert indicated that he was afraid of himself. Immediately prior to the initiation of family therapy, the military police had been called to the H. quarters because Robert had threatened to "kill the whole damned family" with a loaded .357 magnum pistol that belonged to the father. Robert also kicked holes in the walls, physically assaulted his younger brother on a regular basis, and often threatened to "get even" with his father. Mrs. H. stated that she "couldn't leave Robert and Mr. H. alone in the same room" as a result of her fears of physical violence between the two.

This family was seen in therapy on fourteen occasions. The parents were unwilling to change their patterns of drinking. Although there were far fewer episodes of physical assault and physical abuse within the family system, this overall pattern of behavior persisted. Robert did return to school after the fourth family therapy session. Verbal abuse was basic to the family style of communicating and interacting. Blaming and projection were the basic defensive tactics utilized by all family members. Robert blamed his parents for his school absenteeism and "bad temper." The parents blamed each other, their jobs, and the children for their separate (1) alcohol dependency problems, (2) physical and verbal abuse of each other and the children, and (3) other more global living problems. The other brothers blamed Robert, each other, and their parents for their various problems.

During the final three or four family therapy sessions all of the family members indicated that the family relationship was much improved. Mr. H. and Mrs. H. "only" got drunk two or three times each month. Moreover, they "came to the agreement" that they would no longer get drunk together, as they now realized that these situations were potentially lethal. Robert was attending school quite regularly and he no longer threatened to kill his younger brother or parents. All guns were removed from the house. The therapy process was discontinued, in spite of the therapist's active suggestions that the family continue in treatment. Unfortunately, no follow-up data are available relative to the subsequent adjustment of any of the H. family members.

This family system was diffusely conflicted. Both parents were alcoholic. Both parents were also child abusers. The family system was extremely violent. Not only were the parents alcohol abusers and child abusers, they were also physically and verbally abusive toward each other. The identified patient in this case study, Robert, could perhaps be viewed as a "family abuser!" From time to time Robert would physically assault his younger brother. He threatened to kill the entire family with a pistol. Indeed, every family member in this case appeared to be quite angry, enraged, and explosive. Each family member feared every other family member. The alcoholic parents in this case study clearly modeled, shaped, and actively reinforced the pervasively angry and violent behaviors of their children. Parental alcoholism and alcohol abuse played a crucial role in the physical and verbal abuse of every family member living in this family system.

In addition to playing an important role in child molesting and child abuse, alcoholism is associated with marital violence, generally combative forms of behavior, and intrafamilial violence where the child is the aggressor. It is reported (Aarens et al., 1977) that between 6 and 50 percent of marital violence cases involve alcohol. Gayford (1975) indicates that between 52 and 74 percent of violent husbands manifest histories of problem drinking or alcoholism. In an interesting study by Bard and Zacker (1974) it is reported that in cases of police interventions in domestic disturbances, (1) the complainant was noted as having used alcohol in 26 percent of the cases and (2) the person against whom the complaint was made had been drinking in 30 percent of the cases. Gelles (1972) found that drinking was reported by one of the spouses in 48 percent of cases of marital violence. It is also suggested that drinking is used as an excuse for marital violence (Dobash, 1977). In an investigation by O'Donnell et al. (1976) it was found that 27 percent of respondents indicated they had gotten into a physical fight as a result of using alcohol. Aarens et al. (1977) state "alcohol-related fights are about two and a half times as likely to occur to heavier drinkers than to others, and about one and a half times as likely to occur to those with less than a college education." Very little is known about the extent of alcohol involvement in cases of intrafamilial violence where the child is the aggressor. However, Corder et al. (1976) conducted a study of ten adolescents who commited parricide, who killed close relatives or friends, and ten other adolescents who murdered strangers. Child parricide was associated with fathers having abused the mother of the child and the father being absent. In this study (Corder et al., 1976) only one of the ten parricidants was drinking at the time of the offense, compared with five of the ten stranger-murders. Significantly, six of the ten parricidants had an alcoholic parent. Moreover, six of the fathers who were murdered by their children were alcoholic. These fathers had been wife and child abusers.

It is apparent that the research data available in the areas of alcohol and marital violence and other forms of violent or combative behavior is very limited and rather inconsistent with regard to findings. Nevertheless, it is obvious that alcoholism and alcohol abuse play an important role in the causation of a diversity of abusive, assaultive, and combative behavioral transactions (Ackerman, 1982). Clearly, a great deal of research needs to be conducted in these various areas.

Basic Treatment Strategies

Whenever the clinician suspects that he or she is involved in the treatment of a case of child abuse or child neglect this matter must be reported to a social services agency. The detection of child abuse and neglect in therapy is a legal and ethical issue as well as a clinical issue. When confronted with data that indicates that child abuse is presently taking place or possibly taking place within an alcoholic family system (or any family system) in treatment, the therapist must actively intervene on behalf of the child. In this sense, the physical and emotional well-being of the abused or neglected child is the therapist's primary professional concern. Once the therapist has informed the social services agency of his or her concerns regarding the matter of child abuse or neglect, personnel from this agency will thoroughly investigate the case. Eventually, with the input of the therapist, the agency will effect a legal decision relative to the continued placement of the child in the familial home or placement within another residence such as a foster home, group home, or institution.

It is important for the entire family to be involved in treatment. Once the abused child has been identified, engaged in the appropriate legal and social service processes, and referred for therapy, the clinician must focus his or her treatment efforts on the entire family constellation. In cases of severe physical assault upon a child, the therapist will need to assess the role of alcohol in this pattern of behavior. Parents that mutilate or murder their children may be acutely intoxicated or taking other drugs when these bizarre transactions take place. However, in the experience of the author many of these parents are floridly psychotic or severely disturbed. Some are of limited intelligence. As children, these parents have usually been abused and beaten. In cases of severe child abuse an accurate differential diagnosis is essential to the utilization of effective treatment interventions. Polydrug abuse and addiction are central to the adjustment style of some child abusers. These issues are also relevant to the legal management of such cases.

When it is apparent to the clinician that alcoholism or alcohol abuse is of focal importance to the occurence of child abuse, the therapist must treat the addicted family member for alcoholism. This is a rather simplistic statement. Yet, therapists often fail to realize the true potentiating effect of alcohol in alcoholic family systems that involve child abuse or neglect. Alcoholism always makes the alcoholic family member a potential child abuser. The alcoholism of one family member also makes the spouse and other family members potential child abusers. This concept is poorly understood. Living with a problem drinker is not an easy task (Forrest, 1980). The nonaddicted spouse becomes progressively more depressed, angry, and explosive. Low frustration tolerance is a characteristic of the alcoholic and every member of the alcoholic family system. Children in alcoholic family systems tend to act out against each other. For these reasons, it is imperative that the psychotherapist establish early in the therapy process with alcoholic child abusers the clear-cut treatment goal of sobriety.

The alcoholic or alcohol-abusing parent is in need of holistic treatment. As discussed at length in previous chapters, these patients may require direct medical care, nutritional stabilization, and global social skills training. Most alcoholic persons need to be involved in a program of regular exercise. The alcoholic child abuser should be required to participate in an extended parent effectiveness training program. Some of these patients respond very favorably to spiritually oriented treatment programs. Alcoholics Anonymous and Al-Anon informally teach effective and rational parenting behaviors.

Family therapy (Forrest, 1978; 1982a) is the treatment of choice in working with alcoholic patients who abuse and neglect their children. This is especially true in cases that do not involve severe physical abuse, assault, and neglect. The entire family system, including the child that has been identified as having been abused or neglected, is seen in weekly outpatient family therapy. These sessions are usually held on a weekly basis for several months and they last for sixty to ninety minutes. The role of alcoholism in the family pattern of interaction and communication is openly explored. The abused child (or children) is encouraged to openly share his or her feelings and thoughts about being abused and neglected. Likewise, the parents are able to discuss these issues with all of the family members and the therapist. Antabuse maintenance, Alcoholics Anonymous, Al-Anon, and Alateen are useful treatment adjuncts, which can be used concurrently with family therapy. The family therapy approach with these families serves to guard against further incidents of alcohol-facilitated child abuse and neglect. Additionally, family therapy provides the family with a method for resolving the destructive patterns of family relating and communicating which previously fostered child abuse and neglect. Effective family therapy enables many of these family members to again feel, think, and behave rationally. It is important for all of the family members to learn how to get beyond the "family past." Rational family living in the here-and-now includes the ability to love and relate to other family members with a sense of dignity and respect. The family members must learn to deal more appropriately with feelings of anger, rage, and resentment. Family therapy is also an experiential deterrent to subsequent alcohol abuse, child abuse, and neglect in future generations.

Another treatment alternative for cases involving alcoholic parents that abuse or neglect their children is Parents Anonymous. Parents Anonymous was founded in California in 1970 (Hindman, 1977). This organization provides child abusing parents with structured group experiences where they can openly share their problems. This self-help program is similar to Alcoholics Anonymous; however, P.A. includes a professional social worker or therapist in its groups. There are presently over 500 P.A. chapters throughout the United States.

Alcoholic treatment facilities must increase their awareness of the potential of child abuse and neglect by alcoholic or problem drinking parents. These agencies also need to develop specific treatment programs for patients who abuse their children or manifest the potential for child abuse or neglect. Child abuse is frequently only a small part of the parent-child relationship in alcoholic family systems. However, this segment of the parent-child relationship can be psychologically devastating. Therefore, every effort must be made to deter the occurrence of child abuse and neglect in alcoholic family systems.

Summary

Child molesting and child abuse behaviors are often associated with alcohol addiction and/or acute intoxication. This chapter includes two sections, which examine the various clinical issues pertaining to alcohol and child molesting and to alcohol and child abuse. Child molesting and pedophilia are defined in section one.

In general, child molesting refers to child-adult sexual relations. The incidence of child molesting is unknown. Data is presented relative to the incidence of reported cases of child molesting in different states. A number of the characteristics of child molesters are delineated. Child molesters and pedophiles tend to evolve from disturbed family systems. These individuals feel inadequate and manifest low self-esteem. Some child molesters have had intense and precocious sexual experiences. Child molesters are unconsciously, if not preconsciously and consciously, threatened by sexual relations with an "adult" partner. Learning, conditioning, and social and environmental factors may be associated with the aetiology of child molesting.

Acute intoxication or chronic alcohol addiction can precipitate child molesting (Gebhard et al., 1965). Intoxication is frequently used by child molesters as an "excuse" for their deviant behavior. It is reported (Aarens et al., 1977) that 19 to 49 percent of child molesters are drinking at the time of the offense. Seven to 52 percent of child molesters are identified as alcoholics (Aarens et al., 1977). Heterosexual child molesters that use force or threat include a considerably larger proportion of identifiable alcoholics than all other types of child molesters. In this group of child molesters, 40 percent are labeled "alcoholic." Rada (1976) found that 49 percent of pedophilic sex offenders are drinking at the time of the offense. Fifty-two percent of hospitalized pedophiles are alcoholic according to Rada (1976). An extensive case study, demonstrating the role of problem drinking in the aetiology of child molesting, is included in the first section of this chapter.

Children that are molested are in need of psychotherapy and treatment. The child molester is also in need of therapy. The therapist must first focus upon the patient's drinking pathology in cases of child molesting that involve an alcoholic or problem drinker. The inappropriate sexual behaviors of the alcoholic child molester are directly facilitated by intoxication. A number of specific strategies of psychotherapy for dealing with alcoholic or problem drinking child molesters were discussed in this chapter. Holistic therapy is advocated for these patients. A focus upon the sexual adjustment style of the patient must be initiated by the therapist after the patient's pathological drinking behavior has been successfully extinguished. Many of these patients are in need of marital and/or family treatment. Social skills training, assertiveness training, and self-image modification training can be utilized with many of these patients. The wife of the married child molester is often in need of relationship psychotherapy and sex therapy. Treatment interventions that are aimed at modifying the patient's interpersonal style, sexual behaviors, social skills, feelings, and cognitions, and self-dialogue are most effective.

The second section of this chapter deals with alcohol-related child abuse. Child abuse is defined as "physical injuries inflicted on children by their caretakers" (Aarens et al., 1977). The definition of child abuse provided by the Child Abuse Prevention and Treatment Act of 1974 is also included in this section of the chapter. The forms of child abuse and neglect discussed in this section are "essentially nonsexual." Child neglect is defined as "failures on the part of parents or other caretakers to perform such expected functions as nurturance, protection, or supervision" (Aarens et al., 1977). Hindman (1977) indicates that in the year 1976 public agencies throughout the United States received over 300,000 reports of "suspected" child abuse. Two thousand children die each year in the United States in circumstances involving suspected abuse or maltreatment (Besharov, 1976). According to Gil (1968) about 6,000 cases of child abuse are validated each year throughout the United States. Kempe (1972) estimated that the actual number of child abuse cases occurring annually in the United States is between 30,000 and 50,000. Recently (Ackerman, 1982), the American collective has realized the devastating statistics associated with child abuse in this country.

Child abuse is caused by a diversity of psychological, familial, and social factors. Child abuse and neglect are most likely to occur in families that are socially isolated and involves parents that have been abused during childhood. Young and inexperienced parents are more prone to child abuse and neglect. Children that have been abused tend to manifest behavioral problems.

Unfortunately, the roles of alcoholism and alcohol abuse in the aetiology of child abuse and neglect are poorly understood.

Aarens et al. (1977) indicate that as high as 44 percent of child abusers are intoxicated at the time of the abusive act. Research (Aarens et al., 1977) indicates that less than one-third of abusive parents are alcoholic or have a history of drinking problems. Sixty-four percent of the children of alcoholics (Booz-Allen and Hamilton, Inc., 1974) indicate that they have been emotionally neglected by their parents. Parental neglect (Scientific Analysis Corporation, 1976) was reported on the part of 23 percent of alcoholic parents. In the clinical experience of the author, parental alcoholism always results in child abuse and neglect. The extent and effects of child abuse and neglect caused by parental alcohol addiction or alcohol abuse vary considerably. The case study included in this section of the chapter depicts the pervasive and diffuse nature of rage and violent acting-out within some alcoholic family systems. In this case study, child abuse, sibling abuse, and spouse abuse were the result of parental alcohol addiction.

The issues of marital violence and child parricide are also briefly discussed in section two of this chapter. It is apparent that all forms of familial violence and combative acting-out are frequently associated with intoxication and/or alcoholism.

In cases involving child abuse and neglect, treatment interventions appropriately include all members in the family system. The detection of child abuse or child neglect in therapy is a legal and ethical issue as well as a clinical issue. The clinician must actively intervene on behalf of the child whenever child abuse or neglect is known or suspected. In some of these cases the abused child must be removed from the family of origin. In severe cases of child abuse and neglect it is necessary to begin treatment on an individual basis. Differential diagnosis is often essential to the effective management of these cases. The abusive alcoholic or alcohol-abusing parent must be treated for his or her addiction or abuse. As long as the drinking parent continues to drink and remain intoxicated, the pattern of child abuse and neglect will continue. Alcoholism upon the part of one family member synergizes the potential for child abuse and neglect upon the part of the nonaddicted spouse. Holistic treatment is indicated in the case of the alcoholic child abuser. Some of these patients are in need of detoxification and medical treatment.

Family therapy is the treatment of choice in cases involving relatively intact alcoholic family systems with an abusive, alcoholic parent. The entire family system, including the abused and/or neglected child (children), is seen in extended weekly outpatient family therapy. Family members are also encouraged to participate in the self-help programs provided by the Alcoholics Anonymous community. Familial patterns of relating, interacting, and communicating must be modified in these family systems. The family style of dealing with stress and anger is grist for the treatment process.

Parents Anonymous is another treatment alternative for the alcoholic or problem drinking parent that is abusive. Comprehensive alcoholic treatment programs need to begin to focus more directly on the issues of child abuse and neglect and to establish specific clinical services for these family systems. Finally, it is rather obvious that a great deal of methodologically sound research needs to be conducted in the areas of alcohol, child molesting, and child abuse. From a research perspective, to date, most of the studies that have been conducted in these areas leave a good deal to be desired. Small sample size, inadequate control subjects or an absence of control subjects, poorly defined research constructs, and follow-up weaknesses are but a few of the areas of methodological design that need to be improved in future investigations. In spite of these research problems, it is very apparent that alcoholism and alcohol abuse are significant factors in many cases of child molesting, child abuse, and child neglect.

BIBLIOGRAPHY

Aarens, M., Blau, A., Buckley, S., and Cameron, T.: *Epidemiological Literature on Alcohol, Casualties and Crime: Systematic Quantitative Summaries*. Report, Berkeley, University of California, School of Public Health, 1977.

Ackerman, R.J.: *Children of Alcoholics*. Holmes Beach, Florida, Learning Publications, 1978.

Ackerman, R.J.: *Adult Children of Alcoholics*. Lecture, Psychotherapy Associates, P.C. Eighth Annual Advanced Winter Workshop, "Treatment and Rehabilitation of the Alcoholic," Colorado Springs, Colorado, February 4, 1982.

Ackerman, R.J.: *Alcoholism and Child Abuse*. Lecture, Psychotherapy Associates, P.C. Sixth Annual Advanced Winter Workshop, "Treatment and Rehabilitation of the Alcoholic," Colorado Springs, Colorado, February 7, 1980.

Bard, M. and Zacker, J.: The prevention of family violence: Dilemmas of community intervention. *Journal of Marriage and the Family, 32(4):* 677-782, 1974.

Barlow, D.H. and Wincze, J.P.: Treatment of sexual deviations. In Leiblum, S., and Pervin, L. (Eds.): *Principles and Practices of Sex Therapy.* New York, The Guilford Press, 1980.

Besharov, D.J.: Building a community response to child abuse and maltreatment. *Caring, 2(2),* 1976.

Booz-Allen and Hamilton, Inc.: *An Assessment of the Needs and Resources for Children of Alcoholic Parents.* Washington, D.C. 1974.

Caffey, J.: Significance of history in diagnosis of traumatic injury to children. *J of Pediatrics, 67,* 1965.

Corder, B.F., Ball, B.C., Haizlip, T.M., Rollins, R., and Beaumont, R.: Adolescent parricide: A comparison with other adolescent murders. *Am J of Psy, 133(8):*957-967, 1976.

Cork, M.R.: *The Forgotten Children.* Toronto, Paperjacks, in association with Addiction Research Foundation, 1969.

DeFrancis, V.: *Protecting the Child Victim of Sex Crimes Committed by Adults.* Denver, Colorado, American Humane Association, 1969.

Dobash, R.: *Personal communication,* 1977.

Ellis, A. and Brancale, R.: *The Psychology of Sex Offenders.* Springfield, Charles C Thomas, 1956.

Fenichel, O.: *The Psychoanalytic Theory of Neuroses.* New York, Norton, 1945.

Finkelhor, D.: *Sexually Victimized Children.* New York, The Free Press, Inc., 1979.

Forrest, G.G.: *The Diagnosis and Treatment of Alcoholism,* rev. 2nd ed. Springfield, Charles C Thomas, 1978.

Forrest, G.G.: *Alcoholism, Object Relations and Narcissistic Theory.* Lecture, Psychotherapy Associates, P.C. Fifth Annual Advanced Winter Workshop, "Treatment and Rehabilitation of the Alcoholic," Colorado Springs, Colorado, January 29, 1979a.

Forrest, G.G.: *How to Live with a Problem Drinker and Survive.* New York, Atheneum Publications, 1980.

Forrest, G.G.: *Alcoholism, Narcissism and Psychopathology.* Holmes Beach, Florida, Learning Publications, 1982a.

Fox, J.R.: Sibling incest. *British Journal of Sociology, 13:*128-150, 1962.

Frosh, J. and Bromberg, W.: The sex offender—A psychiatric study. *Amer J of Orthopsychiatry, 11(4):*761-776, October, 1939.

Gayford, J.J.: Battered wives. *Medicine, Science and the Law, 15(4):*237-245, 1975.

Gebhard, P., Cagnon, J., Pomeroy, W., and Christenson, C.: *Sex Offenders. An Analysis of Types,* New York, Harper and Row, 1965.

Gelles, R.J.: *The Violent Home.* Beverly Hills, Sage, 1972.

Giarretto, H.: Humanistic treatment of father-daughter incest. In Helfer, R.E. and Kempe, C.H., (Eds.): *Child Abuse and Neglect: The Family and the Community.* Cambridge, Massachusetts, Ballinger, 1976.

Gil, D.G.: *Nationwide Survey of Legally Reported Physical Abuse of Children*. Waltham, Massachusetts, Florence Heller Graduate School for Advanced Studies in Social Welfare, Brandeis University, 1968.

Gil, D.G.: *Violence Against Children*. Cambridge, Massachusetts, Harvard, 1973.

Glueck, B.C., Jr.: *Final Report, Research Project for the Study and Treatment of Persons Convicted of Crimes Involving Sexual Aberrations*. June '52-June '55, New York, State Department of Hygiene, 1956.

Hatterer, L.J.: *Changing Homosexuality in the Male*. New York, McGraw-Hill, 1970.

Hindman, M.: Child abuse and neglect: The alcohol connection. *Alcohol Health and Research World, 1(3)*, 1977.

Kempe, C.H.: Pediatric implications of the battered baby syndrome. *Archives if Disease in Childhood (London), 46(245)*:28-37, 1971.

Kempe, H. and Helfer, R.E.: *Helping the Battered Child and His Family*. New York, Lippincott, 1972.

Kent, J.T.: What is known about child abusers? In Harris, S.B. (Ed.): *Child Abuse Present Future*. Chicago, National Committee for Prevention of Child Abuse, 1975.

Kernberg, O.F.: *Borderline Conditions and Pathological Narcissism*. New York, Jason Aronson, 1975.

Kernberg, O.F.: *Object Relations Theory and Clinical Psychoanalysis*. New York, Jason Aronson, 1976.

Knauert, A.P.: *Differential Diagnosis of Alcoholism*. Lecture, Psychotherapy Associates, P.C. Sixth Annual Advanced Winter Workshop, "Treatment and Rehabilitation of the Alcoholic," Colorado Springs, Colorado, January 28, 1980.

Leiblum, S. and Pervin, L.A.: *Principles and Practices of Sex Therapy*. New York, Guilford Press, 1980.

McCaghy, C.: Drinking and deviance disavowel: The case of child molesters. *J of Soc Problems, 16*:43-49, 1968.

Meiselman, K.: *Incest: A Psychological Study of Causes and Effects with Treatment Recommendations*. San Francisco, Jossey-Bass, 1978.

Miller, D.: "Family Problems, Social Adaptation, and Sources of Help for Children of Alcoholic and Non-Alcoholic Parents." Unpublished report, 1976.

Mohr, J.W., Turner, R.E., and Jerry, M.B.: *Pedophilia and Exhibitionism*. Toronto: University of Toronto, 1964.

O'Donnell, J., Voss, H., Clayton, R., Slatin, G., and Room, R.G.W.: *Young Men and Drugs: A Nationwide Survey*. NIDA Monograph, No. 5, Washington, D.C., U.S. Govt. Print. Office, 1976.

Rada, R.T.: Alcoholism and the child molester. *Annals of the NY Academy of Sciences*, Albuquerque, Univ Of NM Sch of Medicine, Dept. of Psychiatry, 1976.

Skynner, A.C.R.: *Systems of Family and Marital Psychotherapy*. New York, Brunner-Mazel, 1976.

Smith, S.M., Hanson, R., and Noble, S.: Social aspects of the battered baby syndrome. *Brit J of Psychiatry, 125*:568-682, 1974.

Spinetta, J.J. and Rigler, D.: The child abusing parent: A psychological review. *Psychological Bulletin, 77*:296-304, 1972.

Wegscheider, S.: *Another Chance: Hope and Health for the Alcoholic Family*. Palo Alto, Science and Behavior Books, Inc., 1981.

Weinberg, S.K.: *Incest Behavior*. New York, Citadel, 1955.

Chapter 7
ALCOHOLISM AND INCEST

INCEST is generally defined as sexual behavior involving related persons. However, researchers in the area of incest
(Meiselman, 1978) indicate that there is a diversity of viewpoints
relative to defining incest. Perhaps the strictest criterion for incest
is genital intercourse between nuclear family members. Clinically,
incest involves a wide variety of sexual behaviors which take place
between family members. Mutual masturbation, oral-genital sex,
anal sex, and indeed any variety of genital contact between family
members can be viewed as incestuous. Incest may be heterosexual
or homosexual. Incestuous relationships may involve a father
and daughter, mother and son, brother and sister, grandparent and
grandchild, aunt and nephew, uncle and niece, and so forth. There
seems to be virtually no disagreement among researchers and clinicians about the definition of incest within the context of sexual
relationships among nuclear family members. There is disagreement with regard to the definition of incest involving sexual relations with relatives by adoption or by marriage.

Incest would seem to be an easy term to define. Such is not
the case. Researchers in the area of incest clearly use different
definitions in their investigations. Many therapists and clinicians
regard "seductive" familial transactions as incestuous. These
patterns of familial interaction and communication do not involve
overt or frank sexual behaviors. Unfortunately, the inability of
incest researchers and clinicians to agree upon a definition of this
most basic term has resulted in considerable confusion in the areas
of demographics, treatment strategies, and therapy outcome. Likewise, there is considerable disagreement among alcoholic research-

ers and clinicians with regard to the use of such diagnostic labels as *alcoholic, primary alcoholic, problem drinker* and *reactive alcoholic*.

It is difficult to accurately estimate the incidence of overt incest. A figure that has been reported in many studies of incest is one or two in a million "detected cases" each year. This statistic refers to the incidence of incest in criminal statistics. Weinberg (1955) reports that the one or two in a million statistic is relatively consistent from country to country. However, it is difficult to know the accuracy of this statistic because different countries employ different methods of collecting data on criminal behavior. Most researchers agree that the one or two in a million detected cases of incest in a year is far from the actual rate of overt incest. Some researchers suggest that incestuous behavior is "common." Meiselman (1978) states "there is a good reason to believe that many or most cases of incest are never reported to any social authority, lest of all the police, but are kept as skeletons in the family closet or revealed to a very limited number of extrafamilial persons." Children or other family members involved in an incestuous relationship are afraid to report this matter to the police or a social agency. The legal penalities for incest are severe. Quite recently, many states have adopted a legal policy that clearly states that psychotherapists or other behavioral scientists who learn of incest are legally and ethically responsible for the reporting of this information to a state social services agency. In addition to the various legal penalities associated with reporting incest, a plethora of social and familial consequences result from this transaction. Whenever incest is reported in a family, the entire family system is further traumatized. Family guilt, depression, and confusion follow. These families are stigmatized and sometimes victimized by the community. The father may lose his job or be transferred to a different community. These realities are devastating in cases where incest is fallaciously reported. At the same time, it must be realized that incest has a devastating emotional impact upon every family member. As such, incest must be reported. Incestuous family systems are severely conflicted and pathologic. Families are reluctant to report incest because they usually understand very well the consequences associated with this decision. It is for these reasons that incestuous families are collusive and "stick together."

There is a general dearth of methodologically sound research and clinical data dealing with the subject of incest. However, considerable progress has been made in the incest research area during the past few years. Incest researchers are beginning to delimit their research populations and establish definitional continuity. Different research populations reveal radically different rates of reported overt incest. Research in the explicit realm of incest and delinquency indicates that incestuous behavior is rather common among delinquent populations. Young women who act out sexually tend to have incestuous family histories. A study by Halleck (1962) indicated that nearly 15 percent of incarcerated teenage girls had experienced overt incest with their fathers or stepfathers. The subjects employed in this investigation were juvenile delinquent girls who were sexually promiscuous. They were incarcerated in a state training facility at the time of the study. Malmquist, Kiresuk, and Spano (1966) report that one-fourth of a sample of women who had three or more illegitimate pregnancies were involved in overtly incestuous relations prior to their first illegitimate pregnancy. A more recent study (Lukianowicz, 1972) revealed that approximately 10 percent of adolescent females being seen within a social service system had experienced incest. This author reports that only 4 percent of female psychiatric patients disclose incestuous experiences to their therapists. Males who are very promiscuous and sexually disturbed have also experienced more familial incest than nonsexually disturbed males. Gebhard et al. (1965) indicate that nearly 10 percent of incarcerated rapists have experienced incest involving mothers, sisters, and aunts.

Meiselman (1978) believes that the best current information available on the incidence of incest in the United States is the Kinsey research. This research was conducted in the late 1940s and early 1950s. The Kinsey research (Kinsey, Pomeroy, and Martin, 1948; Kinsey et al., 1953) involved large samples of the caucasian general population. The incidence of incest among males was so small that Kinsey concluded "incest occurs more frequently in the thinking of clinicians and social workers than it does in actual performance." Approximately 4 percent of the female sample studied by Kinsey indicated incestuous experiences with a father, brother, uncle, or grandfather prior to adolescence. Kinsey et al. (1953) found that approximately one in twenty-three adult females have experienced some kind of incestuous behavior.

It is apparent that the incidence of reported overt incest varies considerably from study to study. Meiselman (1978) feels "it is realistic to think of incest as an event that occurs in one or two lifetimes out of a hundred." It must be realized that incest is a very rare or infrequently experienced variant of sexual behavior. Incest occurs far less frequently than other forms of stigmatized sexual behavior. Recent social and legal concerns over the problem of incest have resulted in an increased awareness and reporting of incestuous behavior. Therefore, it is understandable that many therapists and clinicians tend to perceive incest as a rather "common" form of sexual behavior. In any attempt to determine the incidence of incest within a given population, the researchers must question the validity of the process of reporting incest. Criminal evidence and legal documentation are subject to error. In many cases, one family member indicates that incest has occured and another family member denies the occurence of incest in the family. Family members are afraid to report incest. Many of the people who report being involved in an incestuous relationship are emotionally upset or disturbed. Some are floridly psychotic.

A diversity of biological, psychological, and social factors seem to contribute to the universal nature of the incest taboo. Sexual relations within the nuclear family are forbidden within virtually all cultures. However, a few primitive societies permit incest as a part of their magical rituals. Brother-sister marriages occurred among the ruling families of ancient Egypt. After the Roman conquest of Egypt brother-sister marriages were socially acceptable. Most of the reports of incest among primitive societies are distorted. The fact is that incest has always been a forbidden form of sexual behavior within virtually all cultures.

During the later part of the nineteenth century and early twentieth century incest researchers believed that inbreeding resulted in genetically determined physical defects, mental retardation, and insanity. Prior to this time, the incest prohibition was maintained through religious beliefs and doctrines, moral codes of behavior, and ethics. Research (Schull and Neel, 1965) indicates that the children of unrelated parents are more intelligent, have fewer congenital defects, are somewhat larger, and less susceptible to infection than the children of related parents. Adams and Neel (1967) reported that only seven of eighteen children of incest were evaluated as "normal." Five were stillborn or died in early infancy, one had a bilateral cleft lip, two were severely retarded, and three appeared to be of borderline intelligence. These children resulted from nuclear family incest. Twelve were from brother-sister incest and six from father-daughter incest. Fifteen of the eighteen control children used in this investigation were evaluated as normal. None of the control subjects were stillborn or mentally defective. In an investigation of 161 children of nuclear incest (Seemanova, 1971) it was found that "moderate to severe mental retardation was found in 25 percent of the incest group and 0 percent of the control group." When all congenital abnormalities were considered in this study it was found that 89 percent of the control subjects were normal in comparison with only 43 percent of the incest subjects. Obviously, there does exist a valid biologic basis for the incest taboo. While the effects of nuclear family incest are often rare, they no doubt do act as a deterrent to incestuous behavior.

Sociologists, anthropologists, and psychologists have theorized about the origins of the incest taboo. Westermarck (1922) suggested that when people live together from early childhood a natural aversion to incest develops. Freud (1953) rejected the biologic origins of the incest taboo and espoused that the oedipal complex is basic to personality devlopment and a normal phase in the process of maturation. Freud developed a rather elaborate theory of family dynamics, exogamy, and incest in his work *Totem and Taboo*. Malinowski (1927), an anthropologist, believed that incest was taboo because it would disrupt the family system. He stated "incest would mean the upsetting of age distinctions, the mixing up of generations, the disorganization of sentiments, and a violent exchange of roles at a time when the family is the most important educational medium. No society could exist under such conditions." White (1948) theorized that the basis of the incest taboo is economic. The incest taboo provides for marriage and procreation with "outsiders," thus creating larger networks of cooperation and interaction. Multivariant theories of the incest taboo have been developed. Meiselman (1978) suggests that four additional factors are important to any theory of the nuclear family incest taboo: (1) dominance relationships within the family system or social grouping, (2) the general societal taboo of sexual relations between adults and young children, (3) societal preference for sexual relationships and marriages to involve individuals of the same generation, and (4) the special nature of "dependency relationships involving nurturance of one individual by another."

There is a diversity of reasons for the incest taboo. The various theories just touched upon explain or partially explain why incest has remained a basic taboo throughout history in virtually all cultures and societies. The incest taboo is a functional and pragmatic family reality. It is clinically significant that the various psychological and sociological studies of incest report the negative or pathological consequences of incestuous behavior. Research in the area of incest does not indicate that this variety of sexual behavior results in healthy personality and sexual development, superior physical and intellectual offspring, enhanced patterns of family living and communicating, or the economic betterment of a society, family, or individual. Simply stated, incest does not contribute to the overall benefit of the individual, family, or society.

In view of these realities, why is it that incest is a significant social problem in modern American society? Why do people engage in incestuous behavior? There are no clear-cut answers to these questions. Indeed, there is much confusion, misinformation, and ignorance regarding the matter of incest. For example, it is generally believed that the most common form of incest within the nuclear family takes place between brothers and sisters. In most cultures, brother-sister incest seems to be less taboo than parent-child incest. In contrast to these beliefs pertaining to parent-child and brother-sister incest, Meiselman (1978) reports a psychotherapy investigation finding of 3.5 to 1 incest ratio in favor of the father-daughter variety of incest. This finding is congruent with other research data gathered in treatment and social service settings. No clinical investigation has found a greater incidence of brother-sister incest. However, conflicting research evidence has been reported in the realm of incest among incarcerated sex offenders. At this time, the question of whether brother-sister incest is more prevalent than father-daughter incest remains unanswered.

Meiselman (1978) hypothesizes that homosexual incest constitutes 5 to 15 percent of the incest cases seen in treatment settings. Mother-son incest is felt to be the rarest form of incest within the nuclear family. When homosexual incest is considered, sister-sister incest is the rarest form of reported incest. In one psychotherapy setting (Meiselman, 1978) it was found that more fathers were incestuously involved with their biological daughters than with step- or adoptive daughters. Cases of multiple incest, sexual involvements with more than one family member, are not uncommon. Cases of father-son incest and mother-daughter incest are very rarely reported in the clinical or research literature. Most people tend to think of father-daughter incest when the topic of "incest" is mentioned or discussed.

Any variety of incest can be viewed as a function of individual psychopathology or social pathology. Most people find the idea of incest abhorrent. The deterrents to incest are powerful and varied. Therefore, it has been espoused by behavioral scientists that people who commit incest are either somehow mentally aberrant or they are the product of a pathological social environment. These viewpoints can be questioned. Nonetheless, studies do indicate that fathers who commit incest are often psychotic, alcoholic, or mentally retarded. Incest does appear to occur as a function of poverty, population density, powerlessness, and deprivation. Yet, all or perhaps even "most" acts of incest do not occur as a result of severe individual psychopathology or social pathology.

Father-daughter incest cases tend to be the most common form of incestuous behavior involved in various treatment settings. As such, an overall clinical picture of the individuals making up the father-daughter incestuous family system will be helpful for therapists working with these patients. Fathers who commit incest have experienced economic deprivation (Gebhard et al., 1965). Many left home at an early age. Incestuous fathers have been emotionally deprived in their families of origin. Some of these men have been deserted by their fathers during childhood; in general, incestuous fathers have experienced poor relationships with their fathers. Meiselman (1978) indicates that there is a "correlation between the age of the daughter in father-daughter incest and the quality of the father's attachments within his family of origin— the 'healthier' his family background, the older his daughter when he initiated incest." An incestuous model (Weiner, 1962) in the father's family of origin may be an important factor in cases of father-daughter incest. A few studies indicate that incestuous fathers are intellectually impaired (Weinberg, 1955). However, most investigations of the intelligence of incestuous fathers (Lukianowicz, 1972) indicate that these persons are of "average" intelligence. Lukianowicz (1972) also found that 70 percent of incestuous fathers were chronically unemployed. Other investigators (Weiner, 1962) report that incestuous fathers have excellent occupational histories and are perceived by the community as a "good family man." Some of these fathers are abusive, controlling, and dominant within the family system. The incestuous father has been described as "psychopathic," "alcoholic," "oversexed," and "psychotic." Alcoholism is a clear-cut factor in father-daughter incest. This issue will be explored at length later in the book. Most incestuous fathers are not "oversexed," psychopathic, or psychotic. Research has rather consistently indicated that the incestuous father (Weinberg, 1955; Weiner, 1962) is paranoid, suspicious, hostile, defensive, and "strongly heterosexual," in spite of manifesting unconscious homosexual strivings. These men tend to "project" blame on others or the environment. Incestuous fathers are rarely pedophiles. The incestuous father is not a criminal type. According to Meiselman (1978), the incestuous father does not fit any particular psychiatric diagnosis. She believes that the most prominent feature of the incestuous father is his "tendency to limit social and sexual contacts to the family." These families are "ingrown." Feelings of inferiority, strong dependency needs, and heavy drinking are factors that may operate to push these family systems in the direction of "keeping it in the family."

The mother in incestuous families has been viewed as the one who silently reinforces and permits the father-daughter pattern of incest. She "sets up" the incestuous relationship by avoiding sex with the father and failing to set family limits. Very often, these mothers allow the incestuous relationship to continue. They are aware of incest in the family, but they do not intervene. These women have experienced severe deprivation during childhood. Many were deserted by their parents. Most lacked appropriate mother-models in the process of growing up. The mother's relationship with her own mother has been one of rejection, hostility, and disturbed communication. A few of these mothers were themselves involved in incest. Incest may occur when the mother is absent from the home due to extended illness, death, or physical incapacitation within the home. The wives of incestuous fathers are frequently described as passive, dependent, and masochistic (Weinberg, 1955). Most of these women are of average intelligence, but they have poor self-concepts. Researchers (Gligor, 1966; Lukianowicz, 1972) suggest that the wives of incestuous fathers are promiscuous and prone toward sexual acting-out. Promiscuous mothers reinforce all forms of sexual acting-out in the family, and they often abdicate role-appropriate familial behaviors that deter incest. Another consistent research finding (Weiner, 1962; Maisch, 1972) is that these mothers avoid sex with the incestuous father prior to the onset of incest, nearly one-fourth of them are "frigid," and many tend to make their husbands feel guilty about wanting to have sex. The mother in a father-daughter incest family is unable to consistently engage in adult female role-appropriate behaviors. These mothers and daughters become involved in a familial process of role reversal. The daughter becomes a "little mother" and compensates for the mother's inadequacy, inability to respond sexually, and so forth. Lustig et al. (1966) found that in all cases of incest included in their research, the daughter had become the female authority in the family by the age of eight. These daughters were responsible for all family matters, from groceries to sex. The mother that "sets up" the incest relationship is perhaps best understood, as she has been the topic of considerable clinical research. However, it is erroneous to assume that all mothers in these family systems "set" their daughters up for an incestuous involvement with the father.

Many questions have been raised about the daughter involved in father-daughter incest. Incest is almost always initiated by the father and yet the daughter is a participant in the incestuous relationship. Research (Gebhard et al, 1965; Gligor, 1966) rather consistently indicates that daughters vary with regard to "resisting" incest. Gligor (1966) indicates that "12 percent of daughters were believed to have participated in a willful or encouraging manner, 32 percent were passive and displayed no resistance, 35 percent were passive out of fear of punishment by the father but definitely attempted to avoid sexual activity with him, and 21 percent overtly resisted the father and were defiant in the face of his sexual overtures." Clearly, most daughters did not "ask for it." They did not initiate or seduce the father into an incestuous relationship. Some fathers prolong incestuous relationships, which last about three and one-half years on the average. Yet, nearly one-fourth of all incest cases seen in therapy involve only one incestuous incident. Research suggests (Maisch, 1972) that the majority of incestuous daughters have "average" intelligence, although rural samples have indicated low intelligence present in a small minority of cases. Physical attractiveness does not seem to play an important role in predisposing the daughter to incest. Incestuous daughters are quite similar to the "typical adolescent" with regard to the matter of physical attractiveness. However, these daughters may appear to be sexually attractive to a father who is married to an unattractive, obese, sexually frigid wife with poor personal hygiene. Research consistently indicates (Weinberg, 1955; Maisch, 1972) that only a small percent of daughters were promiscuous before incest. Maisch (1972) did report that nearly 25 percent of the daughters in his court-referred incest sample manifested a "generally antisocial attitude toward life." A few daughters have been involved in prior incestuous relationships. Daughters who become involved in father-daughter incest tend to be the eldest daughter (Weinberg, 1955). Very few of these daughters are psychotic. Meiselman (1978) points out that the more passive, dependent, and masochistic the daughter is, the better the chances are that a dominant father can precipitate an incestuous relationship, if that is his desire.

As touched upon earlier, brother-sister incest, mother-son incest, homosexual incest, and other forms of incestuous behavior
have not received a great deal of clinical or research attention in
the literature. However, brother-sister incest is a recurrent theme
in mythology and literature. Meiselman (1978) reports that the
"most consistent finding with regard to the family setting of
brother-sister incest is that the children have lacked adult supervision, particularly with regard to their sex play activities. The
youngest sister in a large family with several older brothers seems
to be particularly vulnerable to incestuous advances." The father
is often absent from the family system, psychotic, or alcoholic at
the time of sibling incest (Weinberg, 1955). The mother may also
be absent or emotionally disturbed. She tends to manifest rigid,
puritanical attitudes toward sex, and sex education is lacking in
the home. Frequently, the mother tends to view sex as "bad" and
the topic of sex is not to be discussed in the home. Father-daughter incest may have occurred in the family prior to brother-sister
incest. Weinberg (1955) indicates that adolescent sisters involved
in incest were more sexually promiscuous prior to incest than
adolescent daughters involved in father-daughter incest. Sisters
were also of lower intelligence. This author also reports that incestuous brothers were of normal intelligence and better adjusted
than incestuous fathers. Meiselman (1978) reports that "(1)
sisters are more likely to describe incest with a brother as beginning with mutual interest and participation than are daughters
reporting on father-daughter incest, (2) sibling incest is somewhat
more likely to eventuate in genital intercourse and less likely to
involve oral-genital activity than father-daughter incest, (3) sisters
are more likely than daughters to experience conscious sexual
pleasure in the incestuous act, (4) brother-sister incest is quite
variable in its duration, (5) promiscuity is a prominent characteristic of the postincest sister, and (6) in general, sisters seemed
less traumatized than daughters by the incest itself and were less
inclined to attribute their later sexual difficulties to unresolved
conflicts about incest."

Mother-son incest is the least common form of incestuous
behavior. This form of incest is also the most taboo. The clinical

and research literature on the subject of mother-son incest is very limited and most reports involve only one or two case studies. In cases of son-initiated incest, the son is usually either psychotic or incipiently psychotic. Cases of mother-initiated incest often involve a schizophrenic or alcoholic mother and a less disturbed son. Most commonly, mother-initiated incest involving genital intercourse occurs when the son is between the ages of ten and eighteen. Meiselman (1978) indicates that, "(1) it appears that mother-son incest is seldom an important causal factor in schizophrenia, (2) mother-son incest is seldom associated with a homosexual orientation as an adult, and (3) sons in mother-son incest, like daughters in father-daughter incest, tend to have specific sex problems as adults."

Homosexual incest is rarely a topic of research. The incest literature is limited to a few clinical case studies involving the various forms of homosexual incest. Father-son incest is the most frequently reported form of homosexual incest. Many of the fathers in these cases are alcoholic or emotionally disturbed. The fathers involved in some of the reported father-son clinical studies of incest indicate that they were so drunk during the incest that they could not remember what they had done. Incest is almost always initiated by the father in cases of father-son incest. These fathers are homosexually oriented but they marry, have children, and appear to be heterosexual. Many of these fathers have experienced or witnessed incest in their family of origin (Meiselman, 1978). Fathers tend to be vocationally stable, intelligent, and not psychopathic. Sons involved in father-son incest do not sexually resist the father. These sexual relationships are of short duration. Many of these sons manifest severe anxiety during adolescence and adulthood, and they often experience difficulties in sex and marriage. There is virtually no clinical or research data available on brother-brother, or sister-sister incest, or grandfather-grandson incest. A few cases of mother-daughter incest are reported in the literature. It is suggested that marital, sexual, emotional, and identity conflicts are associated with mother-daughter incest (Meiselman, 1978).

Alcoholism Associated with Incest

Earlier in this chapter alcoholism was associated with incest. Marcuse (1923) in one of the earliest studies of incest found that alcoholism or "drunkenness" is often associated with father-daughter incest. Weinberg (1955) reports a case in which the father became grossly intoxicated, threatened to kill the entire family, and then raped his daughter in the presence of his wife. This author notes that some alcoholic fathers seem to be more sexually aroused after heavy drinking. Meiselman (1978) points out that it is difficult to know what percentage of incestuous fathers are alcoholics or problem drinkers. The terms "alcoholic" and "problem drinker" are not usually defined in studies of incest. Nonetheless, alcohol addiction and alcohol abuse are very significant clinical factors in incest. Kaufman, Peck, and Tagiuri (1954) indicate that 75 percent of incestuous fathers are alcoholic. Merland, Fiorentini, and Orsini (1962) indicate that 47 percent of incestuous fathers are alcoholic. Cavallin (1966) reported that 33 percent of his sample of incestuous fathers were alcoholic. A more recent study (Lukianowicz, 1972) indicated that only 15 percent of incestuous fathers are alcoholic. In a well-designed study by Gebhard et al. (1965) it is reported that 25 percent of fathers incarcerated for sexual relations with daughters under the age of twelve are alcoholic. In this study an alcoholic was defined as a man who drank a fifth or more each day and suffered serious social and occupational problems. Gebhard et al. (1965) found that the percent of alcoholic fathers involved in this study decreased with increasing age of incestuous daughters. These authors also report that "a much larger percent" of incestuous fathers "drank to relieve stress" and that many had been drinking at the time of the first incest experience. In this investigation, the use of drugs other than alcohol did not appear to be related to any of the incest cases.

In a recent study of incestuous fathers in a psychotherapy sample (Meiselman, 1978) it was found that 20 percent were "alcoholics or heavy drinkers." It was clinically significant that the incestuous daughters in this study recalled their father's drinking behavior in detail many years after the incest had taken place. In fact, the father's drinking behavior was frequently the only characteristic that these daughters would describe and it was noted that many of the daughters explained their father's incestuous behavior as being a function of alcoholism. In this study, two of the alcoholic fathers were "polydrug" abusers, having used amphetamines, methamphetamines, and barbiturates. It was suggested that these men were under the influence of drugs on several occasions when incest took place.

Virkkunen (1974) studied the relationship between alcoholism and incest in Finland between 1945 and 1972. The cases involved in this investigation were seen at a psychiatric clinic. *Forty-nine percent of the incestuous fathers were alcoholic.* Unfortunately, a precise clinical definition of alcoholism is not included in this study. *All cases of father-daughter incest involved an alcoholic father.* When incest occurred, 77 percent of the alcoholic fathers were intoxicated. In this investigation, the average age of the incestuous daughter was eleven. In over one-half of the incest cases involving an alcoholic father, the wife had been aware of the incestuous relationship for "several years" prior to reporting the offense. Over 75 percent of the alcoholic fathers had criminal records and 50 percent had exhibited violent behavior. The wives of the alcoholic incestuous fathers were sexually rejecting. This author also concluded that incest is more likely to be reported in cases involving alcoholic offenders.

It is apparent that alcohol abuse is consistently associated with incest. More specifically, research evidence indicates that 20 to 70 percent of incestuous fathers are alcoholic. Most of these alcoholic fathers are intoxicated when incest occurs. The release of inhibitions and loss of "control" generally attributed to alcohol appears to be a major contributing factor in cases of incest involving alcoholic persons. Meiselman (1978) presents a rather large number of incest case studies in her text. These clinical case studies of incest include various forms of incestuous behavior. Thus, mother-son, sister-brother, extended family (uncle-niece, etc.), and homosexual patterns of incest are explored via a large number of brief clinical case study presentations. Alcoholism and intoxication are associated with the occurence of incest in many of these case studies. Clearly, alcoholism is not merely a key factor in cases of father-daughter incest. A sizeable segment of *all* forms of incest involve alcohol addiction and heavy drinking. It is clinically signifi-cant that very few cases of incest are associated with the use of drugs other than alcohol.

Overt incest cases are frequently seen for evaluation and ther-apy within the confines of comprehensive alcoholism treatment centers (Forrest, 1978). Hospital inpatient alcoholism treatment programs, military alcohol and drug rehabilitation centers, veter-ans administration alcohol and drug treatment programs, mental health centers programs, private alcoholism treatment centers, and other agencies providing services for alcoholic persons and their families are involved in the therapy of incestuous alcoholic family systems. Members of the Alcoholics Anonymous communi-ty have long recognized the problem of incest. Yet, behavioral scientists as well as lay people in the alcoholism field seem to be reluctant to confront the issue of incest (Forrest, 1978; Martin, 1980). Incest is an issue which is not openly discussed in A.A. meetings, Al-Anon meetings or therapy groups. Perhaps the avoid-ance of this issue in treatment settings stems from the pervasive uncomfortableness associated with the global topic of "sex." Another deterrent to the discussion of this issue in treatment centers and self-help organizations may be the fact that incest occurs so frequently in combination with alcoholism or intoxifica-tion.

In the experience of the author, incest cases seen for evalua-tion and therapy within comprehensive alcoholism treatment settings almost always involve the father and daughter. The fathers in these cases are intoxicated when incest first occurs. They are usually intoxicated whenever incest occurs. Most typically, the daughters are between the ages of eleven and sixteen. The mothers usually become aware of the incestuous father-daughter relation-ship a few months after its inception. In at least half of these cases, the mother does not contact the police or a social agency. Very often the daughter will tell her school counselor, a teacher, a friend of the family, or some other "outsider" who in turn will notify social service officials. Alcoholic fathers who commit in-cest are not usually schizophrenic or floridly psychotic. However, it is my clinical impression that most of these fathers are diagnostically alcoholic as well as "borderline" personalities. Many of these fathers have been chronically intoxicated for more than ten years. The mothers in these family systems tend to be depressive, inadequate, obese, and somewhat schizoid. A few mothers are sociopathic, drink heavily, and are polymorphously perverse. Deprivation, narcissistic injury, and disturbed families of origin are central ingredients in the case histories of the fathers and mothers. Roughly one-half of these mothers have been parented by an alcoholic. The same can be said of the fathers. The extended families of both the mother and father tend to include numerous alcoholics. The daughters involved in alcoholic father-daughter incest are anxious, depressed, and detached. They manifest feelings of inadequacy, inferiority, and low self-esteem. The vast majority of them are not sexually active outside of the family. A few of these daughters are hostile, manipulative, and sexually promiscuous with brothers or older males outside of the family system. Acting-out daughters are most typically between the ages of fourteen to eighteen. In general, these daughters are not mentally retarded or defective. However, their academic performance is below average, they are truant from school a good deal of the time, and their peer relationships are conflicted. They have very few close friendships with peers.

These generalized clinical observations stem from direct clinical experience with eleven overt incest families seen over a period of nine years. This is certainly a limited sample of incest cases. Furthermore, only three of these families were seen in weekly family and individual therapy for six months or longer.

Covert incest or eroticized patterns of familial relating are very common in alcoholic family systems. Such familial behaviors do not include direct sexual interaction and contact. Pathological and unresolved oedipal conflicts are basic to eroticized family dynamics and transactions. Several years of clinical experience in the realm of family therapy with alcoholic family systems indicates that these families are (1) chaotic, (2) violent, (3) collusive or "ego fused," and (4) sexually conflicted (Forrest, 1978). One alcoholic family that was seen in family therapy for several months involved an alcoholic husband, his wife, and two adolescent daughters. The husband, an Army sergeant, had been chroni-

cally intoxicated for eight years at the point of treatment engagement. He consumed roughly one-fifth of vodka each day. After
the family had been in therapy for two months a covertly incestuous incident occurred involving the father and youngest daughter.
The daughter had a group of teenage girls at the house for her
thirteenth birthday party. The father came home intoxicated, as
usual, proceeded to take off all his clothes, and then walk naked
into the family room where his daughter and her friends were
having the birthday party. Covert incestuous behavior may involve
such transactions as verbal discussions of personal or familial sexual behavior, entering a family member's room intoxicated and
attempting to sleep with that person, or engaging in other forms
of sexual behavior, such as "pinching" or attempting to fondle
a family member's breasts, buttocks, or genitals. Behaviors of
this variety are covertly incestuous. Such behaviors and patterns
of interaction occur much more frequently in alcoholic family
systems than acts of overt incest.

The case of Sergeant P. demonstrates father-daughter incest
in the alcoholic family system. Clearly, this particular family
system was severely pathological. The wife also drank heavily and
was promiscuous and sociopathic. The daughter in this case was
sexually abused by her father and several of his drinking colleagues
for a period of three or four years.

CASE 12. Robert P., a thirty-nine-year-old Army sergeant, was referred to an Army alcohol and drug rehabilitation center for diagnostic
evaluation. According to the patient's company commander, he "appeared" to have a drinking problem. Robert "smelled" like alcohol a
good deal of the time, he "looked" intoxicated, he talked with slurred
speech, and he often called his job supervisor on Mondays or Fridays
stating that he was "sick" and unable to come to work. The patient
was diagnosed a chronic alcoholic at the treatment center and immediately placed in the program halfway house for intensive care. Two days
later, Robert began to evidence acute alcohol withdrawal syndrome.
The program's consulting physician placed Robert in the hospital for
medical detoxification. During a four-day period, Robert experienced
acute alcohol withdrawal or delerium tremens (DTs). He was hospitalized for ten days and then returned to the halfway house.

While Robert was initially in the halfway house and during his hospitalization for acute alcohol withdrawal, the counselor who was assigned to work with Robert attempted to call his wife daily. She was
never home. Robert indicated that he was married and the father of an

eleven-year-old daughter. Finally, one week after Robert had been returned from the hospital to the halfway house he received a phone call from his wife. The following day Mrs. P. visited the patient. At this time, she was also briefly interviewed by Robert's counselor and it was suggested that she come in for weekly conjoint therapy and attend the center's Al-Anon meeting. Mrs. P. refused to participate in treatment and stated that "he has the problem, not me." The patient completed the three week residential program and was returned to his unit for duty. While in treatment, Robert "admitted" that he had been drinking "more than" a case of beer each day for several years. He indicated to his counselor that his wife "sometimes lets her drinking get out of hand" and that they had "marriage problems." He rarely mentioned his daughter. However, on one occasion he did mention to his counselor that his daughter still "wet the bed from time to time."

After Robert completed residential treatment he did not return to the center for follow-up and he did not attend the weekly outpatient therapy group that he had been assigned to enter. His counselor did call the job supervisor on several occasions and according to him, Bob was "doing fine and stayin' sober."

Three months after Robert left residential treatment his counselor received a phone call from another social services agency on the post inquiring about Robert's progress in therapy. More specifically, the counselor was asked if Robert's wife was in therapy and if the daughter had been seen, and the social worker also wanted to know if the counselor knew why Robert's daughter had stopped attending school. As it turned out, at this point the daughter had not attended school for over two weeks. The school counselor called the post social work services department in order to notify them of the daughter's school absenteeism as they were unable to contact Sergeant and Mrs. P. When the social worker contacted the patient's work unit he was told to call the alcohol and drug treatment center since they were "working with Bob."

This somewhat confusing scenario resulted in the patient being seen for further consultation at the alcohol and drug rehabilitation center on the following day. On this occasion Robert was "hung over" and indicated that he was able to "control" his drinking. In reality, his job performance was much improved. However, he was very reluctant to discuss his daughter or present marital situation. The patient indicated that his daughter had not attended school recently because she was "sick." When the counselor pointed out that the school had unsuccessfully attempted to call Mrs. P. daily in order to check on the whereabouts of the daughter, the patient became very angry and walked out of the counselor's office stating "I've had enough of this shit." A follow-up call on this session with Robert was immediately initiated to the social worker. It was jointly decided that home visits, upon the part of a social work technician, were needed in order to find out what was "really going on in this case." A few days later an Army social work technician made an unannounced visit to the P. home. On this occasion Mr. P. was not at home. Mrs. P. and the daughter were at home with a "male friend." The couple was drinking beer, and Mrs. P. was clearly intoxicated. Mary, the daughter, was alone in her room. Mrs. P. was very angry at the social work technician and informed him that "you have no damned right coming out to my house like this." The social work technician left the P. home and reported this series of events to the chief of the social work services. As a result of all of these factors, Sergeant P. and his wife were called into the battalion commander's office and ordered into family therapy. An appointment for the P. family was made at this time with the counselor at the alcohol and drug rehabilitation center.

A few days later the P. family was seen for an initial family therapy session at the alcohol and drug rehabilitation center. The parents were overtly angry and resentful about being "forced" into therapy. Sergeant P. felt that he had successfully "whipped" his alcohol problem. Both stated that "our marriage and how we live our lives ain't nobody's business but ours." The daughter appeared to be depressed, anxious, despondent, and immature. She was dressed in worn-out clothes and clung to her mother throughout the family session. The family agreed that it was important for Mary to go to school, and Mrs. P. indicated that she would see to it that Mary attended school every day. Reluctantly, Mr. and Mrs. P. decided to "attend" family therapy each week.

The entire family came for therapy on the next three successive weeks. In spite of being on time for appointments, the parents continued to resent being ordered into treatment and they evidenced a good deal of resistance in each session. Mrs. P. talked very little in therapy. Mr. P. talked about his drinking behavior evasively and continually indicated that therapy was a waste of time. He maintained "I can do it on my own." In the third family therapy session Mr. P. verbalized that he "thought" Mrs. P. also had a "drinking problem." Additionally, he brought up the fact that she could not be trusted. On numerous occasions during their eleven years of marriage he had "caught" her having affairs with other men. Mrs. P. became enraged at her husband following these comments and called him a "dirty son-of-a-bitch." Furthermore, she expressed the opinion that therapy was a "waste of time" and that she was not coming back. The following week Sergeant P. came to therapy by himself. Attempts upon the part of the therapist to get Mrs. P. and Mary to come in for family therapy failed.

A few weeks later the therapist received a call from a "friend" of the P's. This woman indicated that she was calling as a result of her "concern" about the P.'s daughter, Mary. The caller would not give the therapist her name or other personal information. When the counselor pressed her for more specific information about her "concern" for

Mary she revealed that she had attended a party at the P.s the previous night. She indicated that "everyone" at the party, including herself, was "drunk." However, this was not the main reason for her concern about Mary. She proceeded to tell the therapist that Mr. P. had urinated on Mary during the course of the party. She also told the therapist that she "thought" that some of Mr. P.'s male drinking companions were "having sex" with Mary.

The therapist immediately conveyed this information to the chief of social work services. Within twenty-four hours Mary was removed from the home. Sergeant P. immediately "disappeared" from the family and job for nearly three weeks. During this time he was on a "binge" and stayed with a drinking associate. Mrs. P. initially denied that she was aware of any kind of sexual involvement between Mary and her husband or his friends. When it was explained to Mrs. P. that she was legally responsible for Mary's welfare and that she would be prosecuted for child neglect and child abuse, she reluctantly admitted that she had known about her husband's sexual involvement with Mary for "several months." She also indicated that she was aware of Mary's sexual relations with "friends" of Mr. P. Mrs. P. was angry about Mary's sexual involvements with "thirty-five- or forty-year-old men" and stated that she had told these men to "stay away from Mary." She verbalized that she felt responsible for what had happened to Mary, indicating that it "probably wouldn't ever have taken place if I hadn't been drinking so damned much."

Mary was temporarily placed in a community group home. However, she continued to see the counselor at the alcohol and drug rehabilitaiton center on a weekly basis for several months. When she was initially asked about having sexual relations with her father she verbalized that they had been "doing it" for a long time. Mary indicated that she felt like it was wrong and that she had tried to tell her mother on several occasions, but was afraid of what her father might do if he found out that she told her mother. Therefore, she kept it a secret. Mary stated that she didn't mind having sex with some of her father's friends, but that she "hated" having sex with one or two of these men. They were always drunk and unclean, and they "forced" her to engage in sex acts which she did not like. A few months earlier Mrs. P. had "caught" Mary and her father having intercourse. The family was quite upset about this, and Mary said that her parents verbally and physically "fought" about this episode.

When Sergeant P. finally returned to the base he was again hospitalized for acute alcohol withdrawal. At this time, he needed to complete only eight more months of active military duty in order to retire. He was transferred to a Veterans Administration hospital for sixty days of comprehensive inpatient alcoholism treatment. After completing this program, the patient was returned to active duty and scheduled for outpatient individual and family therapy at the base alcohol and drug rehabilitation center.

Prior to Sergeant P.'s retirement from military service, the family was seen intermittently in family therapy. Sergeant P. continued to drink and missed many therapy sessions. Mrs. P. stopped drinking and attended weekly conjoint therapy with her daughter. Mary attended weekly therapy, her school attendance improved radically, and her grades also improved considerably. Mrs. P. divorced her husband several months after he retired from the service. After retirement, Sergeant P. held numerous jobs, continued to drink alcoholically, and was hospitalized for alcoholism treatment three times. He died from alcohol-induced "acute liver and kidney failure" at the age of forty-three, some three years after his military retirement. Mrs. P. remarried and the family moved to another community.

Mrs. P. revealed in therapy that her father had died from chronic alcoholism at the age of fifty-one. Her mother was hospitalized for "mental problems" several times. Furthermore, her father had maintained an overtly incestuous relationship with her oldest sister. Mr. P.'s mother was a prostitute. He had never known his father. For several years Mr. P. lived with his maternal grandparents. At the age of seven he was placed in an orphanage. He finished the tenth grade, dropped out of school, and eventually joined the Army at age eighteen.

Overt incest is often precipitated by intoxication. In this case study, the incestuous father was a chronic alcoholic. The mother was also a heavy drinker. The mother was aware of father-daughter incest for several months but did not seek therapy or outside intervention. She was sexually promiscuous and rather sociopathic in overall adjustment style. In this case, the daughter was also having sexual relations with several of the father's alcoholic cohorts. All of these transactions involved heavy drinking and intoxication. In therapy, Mrs. P. revealed that she and her husband rarely had sex. She did not know why this was. It was apparent that Mr. P. had reached the stage of maintenance drinking several years prior to the onset of incest. His wife did indicate that Mr. P. was a premature ejaculator. According to her, he also experienced anxiety and feelings of inferiority associated with the size of his penis. Mr. P. seemed to be unable to establish sobriety and deal with his many living problems. It was very difficult for him to talk about his marital problems and incestuous relationship with his daughter. He successfully avoided therapy and treatment. Yet, he died from alcoholism shortly after retiring from military service. Eventually, Mrs. P. was able to make a commitment to the treatment process. She evidenced a good deal of gain in many areas of her life. Mary also seemed to be generally improved at the point of treatment termination.

This case demonstrates a few of the important transactional and psychodynamic factors that contribute to the overall problem of treating incest within the alcoholic family system. In part, the father-daughter and father's friends-daughter incestuous relationships can be viewed as retaliations against the mother. None of the family members were floridly psychotic. Both parents evolved from pathologic families of origin.

Basic Treatment Strategies

As already mentioned, it is difficult to successfully treat the alcoholic incest family system. Most cases of overt incest involving an alcoholic family system go undetected. It is only in recent years that alcoholism "experts" have openly discussed the issue of incest in the alcoholic family (Forrest, 1978; Martin, 1980). When incest is detected in an alcoholic family system there is a tendency upon the part of counselors and intervention personnel to view the "real" problem as being something other than the alcoholism of the father or other family incest member. Commonly, change agents feel that the alcoholic incestuous father is "more" than simply alcoholic—he must be schizophrenic or psychotic! Most of these fathers are not psychotic. It is important for the clinician to be able to rationally assess and interact with the various members of the incest family. This is a difficult task. Our society has tended to stigmatize and over-horrify incest. Many people become irrational when the topic of incest is mentioned.

A first step in the treatment process is that of accurately determining if incest has taken place. In view of the irrational emotional response that incest evokes in many people, the clinician must be able to rationally determine if incest has occurred in the family system with which he is working. A basic guideline to be followed in assessing these families is to generally believe reports of incest that are initiated from a source external to the immediate family system. When the therapist reacts to a report of incest with skepticism or outright disbelief, he or she fosters global resistance to treatment. The incest victim feels rejected, confused, guilty, and trapped. Incestuous daughters in alcoholic family systems feel they are not believed and are without anyone to turn to when the report of incest is rejected by the clinician. The incestuous alcoholic father immediately "sides" with the therapist's attitude of disbelief, and a mutual system of denial is developed, which is tantamount to therapeutic failure. Both parents may establish a collusion with the disbelieving therapist and scapegoat the incestuous daughter.

Clearly, an attitude of believing reports of incest and examining these reports in a rational and objective clinical manner establishes the basis for a working therapeutic alliance with the family system. Research evidence (Kubo, 1959; Cowie, Cowie, and Slater, 1968) suggests that only a small percent of incest and sexual abuse reports are false. When it has been established that incest has occurred, or even prior to a confirmation of this reality, it is of the utmost clinical importance for the therapist to assure the victim that further incest will not transpire. Peters (1976) believes that the cornerstone of treatment in cases of sexual assault on children consists of providing basic assurance of protection for the victim. Should father-daughter incest occur in an alcoholic family system that includes nonincestuous daughters, these daughters should also be reassured that they will be protected from incest. In order to maintain these therapeutic commitments, the therapist will need to actively engage himself or herself in the ongoing treatment and follow-up processes. In view of the fact that a few incestuous fathers will either resume or attempt to resume an incestuous relationship during or after therapy, every effort must be made to assure the victim and other family members that incest will not occur in the future.

The assessment of drinking behavior should be conducted during the initial few treatment contacts with the incestuous father. Specifically, the therapist should ascertain whether or not the father was drinking when incest occurred. It is clinically important to establish the father's drinking history. Is the incestuous father a chronic alcoholic? The clinician must accurately assess these issues, as strategies of treatment must be based upon the

assessment of the drinking behavior of the incestuous father in
cases involving alcoholism and problem drinking. If the incestuous
father is a chronic alcoholic he should be referred for a complete
medical examination. Medical detoxification or hospitalization
may be indicated in some cases. In a small percent of cases, the
alcoholic incestuous father may be neurologically impaired or
manifest an alcohol-induced psychosis. At any rate, if the incestuous father is diagnostically an alcoholic or problem drinker (Forrest, 1978; Knauert, 1979), a primary treatment objective in his
case is sobriety. Before initiating individual, family, conjoint,
or other forms of therapy the incestuous father may require
extended treatment in a residential alcoholic treatment center.
It may be therapeutically efficacious to indicate to the incestuous
father that alcoholism and intoxication have been the central
facilitating ingredients in the incest. In large measure, incest occurred as a result of his intoxication and alcoholic addiction. This
tactic works well with many alcoholic incestuous fathers in that
it enables the patient to feel less guilty and debased early in the
therapy relationship. The patient can "blame" the incest on his
alcoholism and maintain a degree of self-esteem and self-dignity,
which fosters the development of a working therapeutic alliance.
Once a working therapeutic alliance has been established, the
therapist can begin to confront the alcoholic incestuous father
with the distortions basic to his denial, blaming, and guilt-oriented
behaviors. Perhaps the major difficulty encountered in the treatment of incest is the alcoholic father's avoidance or rejection of
therapy. The treatment strategy just delineated can be very helpful in the process of maintaining the incestuous father in therapy.

If both parents are alcoholic or substance abusers, both will
require primary treatment for their addictions prior to beginning
more conventional strategies of relationship psychotherapy. In
the experience of the author, the wife of the alcoholic-incestuous
father is alcoholic or chemically dependent in approximately 15
to 20 percent of these cases. More typically, the wife is a chronic
depressive with concomitant feelings of inadequacy, inferiority,
and worthlessness. Most of the women who persist in an alcoholic
marriage are sadomasochistic (Forrest, 1978; 1982a). A few of
the wives of alcoholic incestuous fathers are sociopathic or quite

schizoid.

Once these initial therapeutic considerations have been explored, an overriding treatment format must be established. A diversity of therapy approaches (Eist and Mandel, 1968; Peters, 1976; Meiselman, 1978) has been suggested for the treatment of incest. Throughout the 1960s, family therapy was believed to be the "treatment of choice" for incest cases. Individual psychotherapy, conjoint therapy, and combinations of these various treatment modalities have been advocated in the treatment of incest. It has become apparent to therapists and clinicians that there is no single "treatment of choice" for incest. Each incest case must be understood and treated therapeutically in terms of the uniqueness of the family system and the uniqueness of the individuals who constitute the family system. There are no easy or quick treatment solutions in our work with incestuous family systems involving an alcoholic.

Over the past several years I have developed some very general guidelines for working with incestuous alcoholic family systems. It should be noted that these guidelines evolved explicitly from clinical experience with alcoholic father-daughter incest cases. The initial step in this treatment format, as already discussed, involves the assessment of the father's alcoholism problem and subsequent treatment interventions for his addiction. This procedure may also be clinically appropriate for the spouse or other family members. A second step in the treatment process involves removing the incestuous daughter from the family system. The daughter is then seen in individual therapy on a weekly basis for three to four months. During this time the husband and wife are seen separately in individual therapy for two to three months. The husband and wife are then seen in conjoint therapy for several sessions, prior to the initiation of family therapy. Many of these families either do not progress to a stage of shared readiness for family therapy or a family member, usually the father, refuses to continue in treatment to the stage of family therapy. It is therapeutically efficacious for the clinician to state clearly at the beginning of treatment that the father or family is under legal obligation to participate in therapy. This point usually needs to be reinforced from time to time in therapy, and in some cases the legal consequences of treatment refusal need to be openly discussed.

Some parental couples need to be seen conjointly for a much longer period of time than two or three months. Family therapy is most appropriately initiated when the parents have significantly improved their relationship and communication skills, resolved their sexual conflicts and dysfunctions, and established a chemically free life-style for a number of months. It is difficult for the parents to assume the responsibility for incest. This is a shared responsibility and both parents must come to grips with this matter during the stages of individual and conjoint therapy.

The goals of therapy and treatment tasks are different for each family member. The overall goal of treatment is not necessarily to reunite the family system. A basic objective of intervention in cases of incest is simply that of terminating the incestuous behavior. In this regard, the present and future emotional adjustment of the incestuous daughter is of primary importance. The therapist must emphasize to the daughter that she did not "cause" the incestuous relationship to develop. It is not her fault and she should not accept familial blame for the incest. These daughters need support, warmth, and the opportunity to ventilate feelings in their therapy relationships. A trusting, open, supportive, and working therapy relationship involving the incestuous daughter and a male therapist forms the basis for resolving the basic male-female relationship conflicts that evolve as a result of incest. The resolution of identity and sexual problems constitutes a major segment of the therapy process with these patients. These patients tend to be sexually and interpersonally masochistic later in life, and these matters must be resolved in therapy. It is possible for the incestuous daughter to understand and forgive her parents. A psychonoxious therapy relationship may precipitate angry and hostile feelings and behaviors upon the part of the incestuous daughter toward the parents. Furthermore, such transactions eventually confuse the daughter and result in severe guilt feelings. Conjoint therapy sessions involving the daughter and mother are quite productive in some cases. In these sessions, the daughter and mother need to resolve feelings and issues associated with the mother's failure to intervene or stop the incest.

Psychotherapy with the mother is generally aimed at resolving her depression and feelings of guilt, inadequacy, and inferiority. Supportive psychotherapy in adjunct with antidepressant medication sometimes radically and quickly improves the psychological functioning of these women. Typically, these mothers are in need of assertiveness training and basic social skills training. The therapist should spend a good deal of time centering on the sexual adjustment style and sexual conflicts of the mother. Virtually all of these mothers are sexually dysfunctional. Most are frigid and nearly all are orgastically dysfunctional. Many have been sexually dysfunctional and inhibited since adolescence. Some develop frigidity as the husband progresses into the middle and later stages of alcoholism. As the mother becomes less depressed and more in control of her life, she begins to experience intense guilt associated with her role in the incest. The therapist must be supportive during this stage of therapy and point out to the mother that she simply managed the situation as best she could at the time. She was depressed and emotionally upset and thus unable to respond appropriately. The incest occurred in the past. It is facilitative for the therapist to point out that none of us can change the past. The incest is not occurring now. By behaving responsibly today, being assertive, overcoming depression, and working at the ongoing process of growth and change, the mother will overcome her feelings of guilt.

Alcoholic and sociopathic mothers require rather different types of treatment. The alcoholic mother must be treated for alcoholism before other interventions prove effective. Alcoholism treatment may include detoxification, hospitalization, Antabuse maintenance, Alcoholics Anonymous, or outpatient psychotherapy. More traditional psychotherapy aimed at resolving the conflicts and issues already discussed begins when the patient has established sobriety. Depression and guilt stemming from alcoholism and the alcohol-facilitated inability to deter the incest are special clinical issues that must be therapeutically resolved in cases involving an alcoholic mother. If the alcoholic mother is unable to resolve these issues, she can be expected to flee from treatment, remain intoxicated, and become even more dysfunctional. She may commit suicide.

Sociopathic mothers are exceedingly difficult to treat. They avoid therapy, resist the interventions of the therapist, drink heavily and abuse other drugs, and engage in polymorphously perverse sexual acting-out. These mothers are impulsive, grossly irresponsible, and refractory to the experience of internal anxiety and guilt. The therapist must set limits, consistently focus upon the issue of responsibility, and confront these patients with the reality of their inappropriate behaviors and life-style. In the limited experience of the author with patients of this type, therapy is of little benefit. Such patients are not internally. or externally motivated to persist in psychotherapy. Their response to the legal threat of going to prison or being incarcerated is minimal. When "ordered" into therapy by a court they may come for treatment a few times. Invariably, they miss appointments, show up late, attend sessions after drinking or taking drugs, and resist the therapist's best efforts to initiate constructive change. In these few recalcitrant cases, the clinician will need to question where his or her therapeutic efforts will be most effective. Some therapists will probably feel that it is a waste of time to attempt to treat these mothers and therefore exert the majority of their clinical efforts with the incestuous daughter and/or the incestuous father.

Contrary to the belief of many counselors, the alcoholic-incestuous father can often be successfully treated. Successful treatment can only take place after the father has established sobriety and resolved his alcohol addiction. It is clinically inappropriate to attempt to treat the incestuous father's depression, guilt, marital and sexual conflicts, and other behavioral problems while he is intoxicated and continuing to drink. When the father has established sobriety and a commitment to treatment, the therapist must explore his feelings of guilt and depression, specific to the incest, at length. The strategies of therapy discussed earlier are essential to this treatment task. Incestuous alcoholic fathers are obviously sexually conflicted. The long-term sexual adjustment style of the father must be fully explored in therapy. Sex problems and sexual conflicts within the marital relationship need to be resolved in treatment. Alcohol addiction profoundly affects the patient's identity, sexuality, and sexual adjustment. These issues are important grist for the therapeutic process. It may be possible for the incestuous father to eventually relate to the daughter in a reasonably healthy, nonsexual manner. During family therapy or conjoint therapy with the daughter, it is important for the father to openly share his various thoughts and feelings regarding the incest.

Many alcoholic incestuous fathers are morbidly afraid of being confronted with the reality of their incestuous behavior. Such fathers continue to drink alcoholically, they avoid and resist therapy, and they are very difficult to work with in treatment. Clinicians must remember that alcohol addiction alone is very difficult to successfully treat. In cases of incest, the therapist will be wise to work with those family members who are most amenable to treatment. In order to more fully understand alcoholism treatment and marital and family treatment with alcoholics, the reader is referred to the earlier works of the author (Forrest, 1978; 1980; Forrest, 1982; Forrest, 1982a).

Some clinicians and counselors are personally uncomfortable with the process of psychotherapy involving incest. Many therapists refuse to treat alcoholic patients (Bratter, 1979). The therapist must personally come to grips with matters such as these prior to initiating therapy with the alcoholic-incestuous family member or family system. Incest is an unfortunate life event. However, the emotional problems that incest facilitates among family members can often be resolved. In these cases, the therapist must be able to deal directly with the many realities surrounding the incest trauma. However, in so doing the therapist must avoid communicating that the daughter or parents are bizarre or deviant. All of the incestuous family members can be helped. Each must learn how to live responsibly in the present and within the context of their current familial relationship.

Summary

The term incest is used to describe all forms of overt sexual behavior between members of the same family. Although most people associate incest with father-daughter or mother-son sexual relationships, a wide variety of other familial sexual interactions can be considered incestuous. Sex between brothers and sisters, brothers and brothers, fathers and sons, sisters and sisters, mothers and daughters, and grandfathers and granddaughters are but a few of the possible varieties of incest. Incest is difficult to define. Some clinicians consider covert, seductive familial behavior to be incestuous. Other clinicians define incest as any form of overt sexual interaction between family members.

Until quite recently, there was a dearth of clinical and research incest data available to therapists and agencies involved in the treatment of these cases. It is very difficult to know how pervasive the problem of incest is in this country. Family members are reluctant to report incest. Some researchers believe that incest is "common." Among some clinical populations of women the incidence of overt incest may be as high as 15 to 25 percent. Most studies report that the most common form of incest involves fathers or stepfathers and daughters (Meiselman, 1978). Studies (Seemanova, 1971) suggest that incest does result in a disproportionate percentage of physically and mentally handicapped offspring.

Incest is generally believed to be a universal taboo. Behavioral scientists have long theorized about the origins and reasons for the incest taboo. In this chapter, a number of the sociological and psychological theories of the incest taboo are briefly discussed. The various demographic data associated with incest are discussed at length. The various psychological and sociological characteristics of the incestuous father, incestuous daughter, and mother are considered. Research findings indicate that these family systems are pathologically fused or "ingrown."

Virtually every study conducted (Meiselman, 1978) on the topic of incest associates this form of family interaction with alcoholism, heavy drinking, or drunkenness. One investigation (Kaufman, Peck and Tagiuri, 1954) indicated that 73 percent of incestuous fathers involved in father-daughter incest were alcoholic. More recently, Virkkunen (1974) reports that nearly 50 percent of incestuous fathers seen for treatment in a psychiatric clinic were alcoholic. In reviewing case studies of mother-son incest, sibling incest, and other forms of incest, the author noticed that heavy drinking or intoxication are frequently associated with the incestuous behavior. Alcohol addiction facilitates a generalized loss of control, which includes a diminished inhibition of sexual behaviors. It is sadly predictable that incest will occur more frequently in alcoholic family systems. The alcoholic fathers in these cases are intoxicated when incest first occurs. They continue to be intoxicated on subsequent occasions when incest takes place. The husband-wife sexual relationship in these families is grossly dysfunctional. Very often, the incestuous father and his wife have not engaged in coitus or other sexual behaviors for months or years. The wife is usually frigid. In general, alcoholic family systems are (1) chaotic, (2) violent, (3) collusive or "ego-fused," and (4) sexually conflicted. Overt incest rarely occurs within the alcoholic family system. However, covert incest or eroticized patterns of familial interaction are very common in the alcoholic family system. A case study was included in this chapter. This case study demonstrated the various dynamics associated with father-daughter incest in the alcoholic family system.

Treatment of the alcoholic incestuous family system is usually a recondite and difficult process. Behavioral scientists and even alcoholism "experts" (Martin, 1980) have long avoided the issue of incest in the alcoholic family system. The clinician must determine if overt incest has actually occurred in the family. This initial treatment task can be difficult, as family members tend to collusively deny that incest has occurred. Furthermore, the subject of incest always evokes a plethora of irrational feelings and thoughts in all of the people who are even tangentially involved with the family. A basic guideline to be followed in assessing the purported incestuous family is to generally believe reports of incest that are initiated from a source external to the immediate family system. Research indicates (Kubo, 1959) that only a few reports of incest and sexual abuse are fallacious. It is important for the therapist to reassure the incest victim that further incidents of incest will not occur.

A variety of treatment formats or styles have been advocated for dealing with incest families. A few years ago it was generally believed that family therapy was the "treatment of choice" in working with incest families. In the view of the author, there is no single treatment of choice for cases of incest. Rather, the therapist must creatively and sensitively utilize a variety of treatment interventions that "fit" the unique and individual needs of each incestuous family. Every individual family member and every family system involved in incest is somewhat different and unique. The therapist should actively point out to the incestuous father that incest occurred as a result of his alcohol addiction. The sources of therapeutic gain associated with the particular strategy of intervention are discussed. An initial goal of therapy in these cases is that of treating the incestuous father's alcoholism. It is clinically inappropriate to strive for a family reunification in many incest cases. A very general model for working with the alcoholic incestuous family system is outlined. According to this treatment approach, the incestuous daughter is removed from the family system and seen in extended individual psychotherapy. Early in treatment, the incestuous father and the mother are also seen in intensive individual therapy. The parental couple is then seen in conjoint therapy and finally family therapy is initiated. A number of the psychodynamic and behavioral characteristics of the various incestuous family members are discussed. Strategies of therapy appropriate for the resolution of these sources of psychopathology are also considered. It is extremely difficult to work with alcoholic-incestuous families involving an alcoholic or sociopathic mother.

Finally, a number of therapist dynamics that operate to impede the process of effective therapy with incestuous families are explored. Incest is an unfortunate life event. However, the incest victim as well as the other members of an incestuous family system can be helped. Some therapists are uncomfortable working with incest cases. It is imperative that counselors and therapists who work with these families be able to consistently deal with the many cognitions and feelings generated in each family member as a result of the incest. A clear understanding of alcoholism and the dynamics of alcoholic family systems is essential to the effective treatment of the alcoholic-incestuous family constellation.

BIBLIOGRAPHY

Adams, M.S., and Neel, J.V.: Children of incest. *Pediatrics, 40:*55-62, 1967.
Bratter, Thomas E.: *Reality Therapy Training.* Lecture, Psychotherapy Associates Fifth Annual Advanced Winter Workshop, "Treatment and Rehabilitation of the Alcoholic," Colorado Springs, Colorado, January 30, 1979.

Cavallin, H.: Incestuous fathers: A clinical report. *American Journal of Psychiatry, 122*:1132-1138, 1966.

Cowie, J., Cowie, V., and Slater, E.: *Delinquency in Girls*. Atlantic Highlands, New Jersey, Humanities Press, 1968.

Eist, H.I., and Mandel, A.U.: Family treatment of ongoing incest behavior. *Family Process, 7*:216-232, 1968.

Forrest, G.G.: *The Diagnosis and Treatment of Alcoholism*. Springfield, Charles C Thomas, Rev. 2nd Ed., 1978.

Forrest, G.G.: *Alcoholism, Identity and Sexuality*. Lecture, Psychotherapy Associates, P.C. Sixth Annual Advanced Winter Workshop, "Treatment and Rehabilitation of the Alcoholic," Colorado Springs, Colorado, February 4, 1980.

Forrest, G.G.: *Confrontation in Psychotherapy with the Alcoholic*. Holmes Beach, Florida, Learning Publications, 1982.

Forrest, G.G.: *Alcoholism, Narcissism and Psychopathology*. Holmes Beach, Florida, Learning Publications, 1982a.

Freud, S.: *The Future Prospects of Psychoanalytic Therapy*. In Collected Papers, Vol. II, London, Hobarth, 1953.

Gebhard, P.H. et al.: *Sex Offenders: An Analysis of Types*. New York, Harper & Row, 1965.

Gligor, A.M.: *Incest and Sexual Delinquency: A Comparative Analysis of Two Forms of Sexual Behavior in Minor Females*. Unpublished doctoral dissertation, Case Western Reserve University, 1966.

Halleck, S.L.: The physician's role in management of victims of sex offenders. *Journal of the American Medical Association, 180*:273-278, 1962.

Kaufman, I., Peck, A.L., and Tagiuri, C.K.: The family constellation and overt incestuous relations between father and daughter. *American Journal of Orthopsychiatry:24*:266-277, 1954.

Kinsey, A.C., Pomeroy, W.B., and Martin, C.E.: *Sexual Behavior in the Human Male*. Philadelphia, Saunders, 1948.

Kinsey, A.C. et al.: *Sexual Behavior in the Human Female*. Philadelphia, Saunders, 1953.

Knauert, Arthur P.: *Differential Diagnosis of Alcoholism*. Lecture, Psychotherapy Associates, P.C. Fifth Annual Advanced Winter Workshop, Colorado Springs, Colorado, January 28, 1979.

Kubo, S.: Researches and studies on incest in Japan. *Hiroshima Journal of Medical Sciences, 8*:99-159, 1959.

Lukianowicz, N.: Incest. *British Journal of Psychiatry, 120*:301-313, 1972.

Lustig, N. et al.: Incest: A family group survival pattern. *Archives of General Psychiatry, 14*:31-40, 1966.

Maisch, H.: *Incest*. (C. Bearne, Trans.) New York, Stein & Day, 1972.

Malinowski, B.: *Sex and Repression in Savage Society*. London, Routledge & Kegan Paul, 1927.

Malmquist, C.P., Kiresuk, T.J., and Spano, R.M.: Personality characteristics of women with repeated illegitimacies: Descriptive aspects. *American Journal of Orthopsychiatry, 36*:476-484, 1966.

Marcuse, M.: Incest. *American Journal of Urology and Sexology*, 16:273-281, 1923.

Martin, J.C.: *Feelings*. Lecture, Psychotherapy Associates, P.C. Sixth Annual Advanced Winter Workshop, "Treatment and Rehabilitation of the Alcoholic," Colorado Springs, Colorado, February 4, 1980.

Meiselman, Karin C.: *Incest*. San Francisco, Jossey-Bass, Inc., 1978.

Peters, J.J.: Children who are victims of sexual assault and the psychology of offenders. *American Journal of Psychotherapy*, 30:398-421, 1976.

Schull, W.J., and Neel, J.V.: *The Effects of Inbreeding on Japanese Children*. New York, Harper & Row, 1965.

Seemanova, E.: A study of children of incestuous matings. *Human Heredity*, 21:108-128, 1971.

Virkkunen, J.: Incest offences and alcoholism. *Medicine, Science and the Law (London)*, 14:124-129, 1974.

Weinberg, S.K.: *Incest Behavior*. New York, Citadel, 1955.

Weiner, I.B.: Father-daughter incest: A clinical report. *Psychiatric Quarterly*, 36:607-632, 1962.

Westermarck, E.: *The History of Human Marriage*, 5th ed. New York, Allerton, 1922.

White, L.A.: The definition and prohibition of incest. *American Anthropologist*, 50: 416-435, 1948.

Chapter 8
ALCOHOLISM AND RAPE

THERE are many definitions of rape. These definitions have changed somewhat over the years and definitions even vary from state to state or between countries. Hyde (1976) defines rape as "any sexual intimacy forced upon one person by another." Broadly defined, rape refers to all varieties of sexual assault. The victims of sexual assault may be male or female. Modern definitions of rape include homosexual assaults and the assault of a wife or husband.

Rape is committed under antisocial conditions. Most cases of rape involve an appropriate (heterosexual) sex object choice, but this form of sexual behavior is steeped in anger and violence. Rape is always a violent transaction. The anger and violence, so basic to the act of rape, finds expression through the medium of sex. In reported rape cases, the offender is almost exclusively male (Coleman, 1972; Geiser, 1979). However, during recent years a growing number of women have been reported as rapists. Historically, rape has tended to be viewed as a sexual deviation. It has also been generally assumed that rape is an act that is usually initiated or invited by women. These viewpoints are rapidly changing. The present trend in our society is to view rape as a violent crime of assault. It is now recognized that the vast majority of rape victims do not "ask for it."

There are two legal categories of rape. These categories are statutory rape and forcible rape. Statutory rape involves the sexual assault of a minor. Forcible rape involves the sexual assault of an unwilling person over eighteen years of age. The primary focus of this chapter is forcible rape. According to the definitions of rape presented in this chapter, child molesting and incest could be considered forms of rape. These subjects have been explored at length in earlier chapters. In order to avoid the redundancy and confusion associated with these issues, only forcible rape will be examined in this chapter.

The number of reported cases of rape in this country has steadily grown for several years. Coleman (1972) indicates that in 1970 the Federal Bureau of Investigation reported over 37,000 cases of forcible rape. More than twice as many cases of forcible rape were reported in 1970 than in 1960. Hyde (1976) reports that over 51,000 forcible rapes were committed in one recent year. She suggests that the incidence of reported forcible rape has risen by 70 percent in five years. Hyde (1976) estimates that 18 percent of women residing in large cities and suburban areas have suffered rape. She also states "there is probably one rape in the U.S. every minute." Amir (1971) indicates that 77 percent of all rapes are committed by black men raping black women. It is estimated that the actual incidence of rape (Coleman, 1972) is three to four times greater than the reported rate.

Rape tends to be committed by young men. It is reported (Hyde, 1976) that almost 50 percent of rapists are between the ages of fifteen and twenty-five. Nearly 75 percent of rapists are less than thirty years of age. Coleman (1972) reports that nearly one-third of all rapists are less than twenty years of age. In spite of the myth that rapists are single, nearly 50 percent of these offenders are married and living with their wives at the time rape is committed (Hyde, 1976; Gager and Schurr, 1976; Geiser, 1979). Studies of rape in other countries indicate that over 40 percent of rapists are married (Hyde, 1976). It has also been found that rape tends to be repeated. Rapists have often raped several different women during a period of months or years (Knauert, 1981). Between 50 and 70 percent of rape cases (Hyde, 1976) occur when the victim is unknown to the rapist. It is believed that rape is a planned crime in the great majority of cases. While a few rapists act on impulse and do not plan their crime in advance, the majority of rapists behave in accord with a premediated plan. If the rapist has committed rape on several occasions he may have developed an organized and well-thought-out plan for future rapes.

Nonpsychotic rapists plan in advance how to avoid being caught or detected.

Child rape has become a major social problem in the United States. One out of every five rape victims in the United States is under twelve years of age (Geiser, 1979). In a study of more than 2,000 women and children involved in rape in Washington, D.C., between 1965 and 1969 Geiser (1979) reports that 13 percent were under nine years of age, 23 percent were between the ages of ten and fourteen and 22 percent were between the ages of fifteen and nineteen. The age range of victims in this study was six months to ninety-one years. A rape occurs on the average of every nine minutes throughout the United States and a child rape occurs once every forty-five minutes. The mean age of sexually abused children tends to be around eleven years. Family income and social status are not related to sexual abuse and rape. Children tend to be raped or molested by someone they know. Child rapists tend to be in their early thirties. It is only in recent years that the devastating reality of child rape (Geiser, 1979) has been made known to the general public.

A great deal remains to be learned about the dynamics and personality makeup of the rapist. Rape behavior is poorly understood. Indeed, there are many theories about the aetiology of rape. In spite of the common denominator of having committed rape, rapists are individuals and they seem to manifest a diversity of personality features. Research at the Institute for Sex Research at Indiana University (Hyde, 1976) indicates that the behavior of rapists develops on an individual basis. Rape behavior tends not to be learned from others. While modeling or imitative learning may not be primary antecedent conditions to learning and engaging in rape behavior, faulty learning, conditioning, and reinforcement factors operate to actualize and maintain this variety of deviant sexual responding.

Rape behavior involves displaced aggression and rage (Cohen and Seghorn, 1969). Sexual and aggressive components are fused in virtually every act of rape. In many cases of rape, the rapist employs sexuality as a vehicle to physically injure, degrade, or attact the victim. While in psychotherapy such rapists state that they cannot "control" themselves. These individuals feel that they are not in control of their sexual impulses and more specifically the impulse to commit rape. In such cases, rape is often committed following an argument or fight with the rapist's wife, mother, or girlfriend. Rapists of this type experience minimal sexual excitement during the actual act of rape. They may not be able to achieve an erection or reach orgasm during the rape. Should the victim taunt the rapist about his inability to become erect or "perform" sexually during or immediately after the rape transaction, further aggression and physical violence may be precipitated. The rapist may become physically assaultive and violent to the extent of seriously injuring or murdering the victim.

Other forms of sexual, aggressive, and impulsive behavior are associated with rape. Some acts of rape are, in fact, committed impulsively. In these cases, the rapist is often a sociopath. While engaging in a robbery or some other antisocial transaction, the sociopath or psychopath will sometimes impulsively take advantage of the opportunity to commit rape. A few rapists are also sadists or sadomasochists. These individuals seem to be able to experience sexual stimulation, excitement, and arousal only in combination with anger and aggressive feelings, thoughts, and behaviors. Such men believe that women like to be beaten up or "roughed up." Brutal sexual assaults are committed by these men. The sexual sadist who manifests a psychopathic and/or explosive personality and behavioral style may mutilate or murder his victim.

Not all rapists are sadistic or psychopathic. Aggression and rage are not the major components in some rapists. Cohen and Seghorn (1969) indicate that sexual excitation is the key component in some cases of rape. In these cases, the rapist flees if the victim struggles at all. In these situations (Cohen and Seghorn, 1969) "the primary aim is clearly sexual and the aggression is in the service of gratifying the sexual desires. The offender is always in a state of intense sexual excitation and often has an orgasm in the simple pursuit of the victim or upon making some physical contact. The recurrent fantasy in such offenders is that the victims will yield, submit to intercourse, in which he will be especially virile and so pleasing to the victim that she will become enamoured with him and invite him to repeat the sexual acts." Most of these rapists are passive, submissive, and dependent. Frequently, they manifest no other antisocial behaviors. These men tend to feel sexually inadequate and inferior. Very often they experience guilt associated with their sexually deviant behaviors and they are even concerned about the well-being of their victims.

It is apparent that a multiplicity of personality, familial, and social factors contribute to the aetiology of rape. Faulty learning and conditioning play important roles in the development of rape behavior. Perhaps more importantly, faulty learning, conditioning, and reinforcement factors contribute to the recidivistic nature of rape. Personality makeup is a significant factor in rape. In this regard, Coleman (1972) suggests that the largest percentage of rapists are probably psychopathic. Environmental and social variables may contribute to the incidence of rape. Family pathology is apparently associated with rape. These theories and viewpoints of rape are speculative. While some rapists are obviously mentally ill or psychologically disturbed, others are not. A few rape victims actively precipitate the rape transaction (Gager and Schurr, 1976). Yet, the historic belief of the behavioral science professions that rape is generally victim-precipitated is clearly in error. Just as rapists tend to believe that their victims enjoyed being raped, the legal system has seemed to take this same general position for many, many years.

Alcoholism Associated with Rape

Alcohol abuse and alcoholism have been cited by many researchers and clinicians (Gebhard et al., 1965; Amir, 1967; Coleman, 1972; Rada, 1974; Hyde, 1976; Rada, 1975; Knauert, 1981) as primary factors that contribute to rape. Rada (1974; 1975) concludes that there is a possible causal relationship between alcohol and rape. In an investigation of hospitalized patients that were committed for forcible rape (Rada, 1974), it was found that 50 percent of the rapists had been drinking at the time of the assault. Forty-three percent of these rapists had been drinking heavily when the rape took place. Thirty-five percent of the rapists were diagnosed as "alcoholic." When compared with nonalcoholic rapists, alcoholic rapists (Rada, 1974) are more likely to be drinking at the time of the rape. They are more likely to have a history of prior drug use (other than alcohol), and they are more likely to have been using drugs in combination with alcohol at the time of the rape. Rada (1975) has also attempted to differentiate between rape cases involving alcoholic offenders, rape cases involving drinking offenders, and rape cases that are triggered or catalyzed by alcohol.

The ingestion of alcoholic beverages does not necessarily take away the sexual inhibitions of the rapist (Hyde, 1976). Yet, as Hyde (1976) states "alcohol appears to be the perfect drug for the rapist, in that it may act as a stimulus to increase his sense of power and willingness to engage in a sexual act that he would ordinarily find himself unable to attempt." As Rada (1974) suggests, if a drinking or alcoholic rapist can stop drinking or learn to control his drinking, he may no longer be a rapist.

Hyde (1976) indicates that one-half of rapes occur while the aggressor is under the influence of alcohol. She also states that "the least aggressive type of rapist is one who is drunk." Mac-Donald (1971) describes the drunken rapist as "relatively harmless." These authors (MacDonald, 1971; Hyde, 1976) mention brief case studies of alcoholic or acutely intoxicated rapists who are grossly inadequate, seemingly innocuous, and blundering. Such rapists are both unsuccessful in their rape attempts and usually apprehended. However, Hyde (1976) also points out that alcohol and drugs play an important role in group rapes. Gang rapes, involving as many as fifteen to twenty rapists, are becoming more common each day and these transactions are a "feature of the social life of street gangs in larger cities." These violent and destructive sexual transactions involve alcohol and other drugs. The limited research and clinical data presently available on the relationships between alcoholism, alcohol abuse, and rape seem to suggest that some intoxicated rapists are clumsy and relatively harmless, while other intoxicated rapists are violent and extremely dangerous (Gebhard et al., 1965; Coleman, 1972; Hyde, 1976; Knauert, 1981).

In an interesting investigation of alcohol and forcible rape (Amir, 1967) involving over 600 cases of forcible rape reported to the Philadelphia Police Department (1958-1960), it was found that alcohol played a significant role in 217 cases. In this study

(Amir, 1967), 10 percent of the victims had been drinking when the rape occurred. In 3 percent of the cases, only the offender had been drinking when the rape occurred. In 21 percent of the cases both the victim and the offender had been drinking when the rape occurred. This data is somewhat confusing and difficult to interpret. It is apparent that both the victim and the offender had been drinking in many of the cases in this study. Perhaps the drinking rapists in this study, as a result of intoxication, mistakenly assumed that the victim was desirous of having sex. It is also logical to suspect that the drinking victims in this investigation, as a result of intoxication, were not aware of the sexual "messages" they were conveying to the rapists. Perhaps the drinking victims did not realize that they were actually having sexual relations until after the transaction occurred and they became sober. At any rate, this study (Amir, 1967) clearly suggests that forcible rape is more prone to occur when both the rapist and the victim have been drinking alcoholic beverages.

Within the confines of comprehensive alcoholic treatment centers and private practice settings it is relatively atypical to encounter alcoholic or problem drinking rapists. Many of these individuals are incarcerated or managed through the legal system. As a function of the legal process, the alcoholic or problem drinking rapist may or may not receive rehabilitation or ongoing psychotherapeutic treatment. The majority of alcoholic or problem drinking rapists that are seen in alcoholic treatment centers tend to be passive, inadequate, and nonviolent. In fact, many of these individuals have *attempted* rape. Such patients are unsuccessful in their rape attempts. After being apprehended by the police they are legally "ordered" into treatment. More rarely, alcoholics who commit homosexual rape are seen for therapy and rehabilitation in comprehensive alcoholic treatment centers. The overall percentage of alcoholics that commit forcible rape is small. In spite of the fact that alcoholism and alcohol abuse are associated with 40 to 50 percent of rapes, very few alcohol-addicted or alcohol-abusing patients are rapists.

An unrecognized but statistically and clinically significant realm of forcible rape occurs within the alcoholic marriage. There are various controversial dimensions to the concept of forcible rape in the context of the marital relationship. Nevertheless, alcoholic males do force their wives to engage in sexual intercourse and other sex acts. Very rarely, the wife of an alcoholic or problem drinker will attempt to initiate legal actions against her husband for rape. In conjoint therapy with the alcoholic and his wife the issue of forced sexual relations can be a paramount treatment concern. Some women that have been married to an alcoholic for years report that they have literally been raped on a weekly basis for the duration of the marriage. These women have been "forced" to engage in a variety of sexual behaviors which they disliked and even abhorred. In these cases, the alcoholic husband comes home intoxicated, gets in bed with his wife, wakes her up, and then physically forces her to have sex. These transactions may involve a brutal physical and sexual assault if the wife attempts to resist the sexual advances of the intoxicated husband. Alcoholic husbands that rape their wives tend not to rape other women. In these cases, rape and forced or coerced sexuality usually remain a marital or familial problem.

The case of Doctor P. illustrates a number of the psychodynamic, behavioral, and interpersonal characteristics of the alcoholic rapist. This patient had sexually assaulted his wife for many years prior to entering therapy. The patient was explosive, poorly controlled, and an alcoholic "binge" drinker. In spite of these factors, the patient was a very successful practicing physician.

CASE 13. Doctor P., a forty-two-year-old, married family physician decided to enter therapy as a result of "a drinking problem" and "sex hang-ups." The patient had been married about nineteen years and was the father of three children: a seventeen-year-old son, a fourteen-year-old daughter, and a seven-year-old son. The patient had grown up in a small, rural Midwestern farm community. After completing two years of military service, the patient retired to his native state, graduated from college, and then completed medical school. He was married during the junior year of undergraduate school. Following the completion of medical school, Dr. P. began a family practice in a rural city located about fifty miles from his home town. At the time of treatment engagement Dr. P. had been in medical practice for over ten years in this community. He was successful in his practice and was well liked and respected within the community.

The patient indicated in the initial therapy hour that drinking had "actually" been a problem for him since the time of his military service.

During the second therapy session Dr. P. recalled in detail an alcohol-related incident, which occurred when he was nineteen years old and stationed with the Army in Germany. This incident involved the patient's becoming extremely intoxicated in a German bar, leaving the bar to walk back to camp, and having a "blackout." During this blackout the patient physically assaulted a young teenaged German girl in an alley and attempted to rape her. The girl apparently got away from the patient and immediately summoned the local police. He was apprehended by the German police and then turned over to the military police. As a result of this incident the patient spent four months in a military correctional facility. The patient had never made his family of origin or wife and present family aware of this alcohol-facilitated incarceration. Indeed, it was quite apparent that Dr. P. was both guilty and remorseful over this incident. He stressed the point that he remembered "absolutely nothing" after leaving the German bar. The patient stated that he "remembered coming to" in the German police station.

As an undergraduate student and medical student the patient never experienced any legal consequences associated with his drinking. However, the patient did engage in heavy episodic drinking during these years. The patient's wife had threatened to "leave" him on numerous occasions. She told him that he was "like a Dr. Jekyll and Mr. Hyde" after drinking. Early in therapy, Dr. P. indicated that he was "sexually aggressive and forceful" with his wife when he had been drinking. He seemed to feel uncomfortable with these behaviors and indicated that this singular issue was ample reason to stop drinking. The patient described himself as angry, volatile, and sexually aggressive following heavy drinking. These behaviors occurred only within the marital and family relationship. The patient was not aggressive or combative in social situations that involved drinking with people other than his wife and children. He was not sexually promiscuous.

After a few hours of individual psychotherapy, it became apparent that the patient had for years repressed and denied many hostile and negative feelings regarding women. He dealt with women by controlling them. In spite of his passive and easygoing interpersonal demeanor, Dr. P. felt a deep-seated need to aggressively dominate and control women. In this regard, the patient described his own mother as an aggressive, domineering, and controlling woman. His father was a rather passive, gentle, and submissive person. The patient vividly recalled having "felt sorry" for his father during childhood and adolescence. Basically, he felt sorry for his father as a result of his father's impotence in the marital and family relationship. Dr. P. stated "in our family, Mom clearly wore the pants." Aside from feeling sorry for his father, he resented his mother and "couldn't stand her guts" as an adolescent. The patient described his adolescent relationship with his mother as a "power struggle." While in high school and as an undergraduate student, he dated several different women. However, when these women began to evidence any "serious signs" of relationship involvement the patient would very abruptly "drop" them. During his junior year of college the patient met his wife. They dated for a period of approximately four months and then were married over the Christmas holidays. The patient indicated that he had married his wife because he "loved" her and because she was so "easy to get along with." He described his wife as passive, dependent upon him, intelligent, and stable.

This patient completely terminated his drinking behavior prior to the first individual therapy session. Following nine individual therapy sessions it was clearly apparent that the patient's marital relationship was seriously conflicted. At this point, conjoint therapy was initiated. In the first conjoint therapy session, the patient's wife indicated that she was "fed up with the drinking and sexual abuse." Within the context of the next several conjoint therapy sessions, Mrs. P. revealed that Dr. P. had been forcing her to have sexual relations for nineteen years. Forced sex only occurred when the patient was drinking. On these occasions, the patient would come home from the office intoxicated, usually late at night, and proceed to force his wife to engage in intercourse and other sexual behaviors for extended periods of time. When she resisted he would slap her, punch her with his fists, and physically force her to have sex. Over the years Mrs. P. had installed locks on the bedroom door, slept in a separate bedroom, and talked to the family priest in her efforts to stop the sexual assaults. She stated in therapy on several occasions "he has been raping me for nineteen years, and I've been stupid enough to put up with it." She called the police on this matter once, but was too embarrassed "for her husband" to follow through with legal action.

The patient had sexually abused his wife for years. Previously, he denied that these brutal sexual encounters constituted "rape." During the early conjoint therapy sessions the patient verbalized that he was "sorry" he had forced Mrs. P. to have sex against her will. In one session, Mrs. P. stated that her husband would never know how it felt to be "raped by a god-damned drunk, stinking pig." Dr. P. wept when his wife made this statement and firmly reassured her that it would not happen again. He began to understand that forced sex, even within the context of marriage, is a form of rape. Although both Dr. and Mrs. P. had realized for years that the only time they experienced severe sexual conflicts was after Dr. P. had been drinking, neither patient fully understood and accepted the role of alcoholism in the aetiology of these sexual and relationship conflicts. Dr. P. had realized for years that his wife was afraid of him. He also knew that she was becoming less and less interested in having sex with him. Mrs. P. had reached the point of wanting very little sexual contact with Dr. P., drunk or sober!

Many healthy and constructive relationship changes started to occur as the couple began to openly discuss and face these various issues in conjoint therapy. Although Mrs. P. was initially "skeptical" and understandably reluctant to believe that the healthy changes would persist, with time she once again developed the capacity to trust and love her husband. The couple described their "new relationship" as one of mutual loving, respecting, and trusting rather than hating, controlling, and disliking. It was significant that Mrs. P. indicated that she was able to consistently "like my husband, as a friend" for the first time in nineteen years of marriage. This couple was seen in conjoint therapy on a weekly and every other week basis for nine months. Presently, Dr. P. has been totally abstinent from alcohol for nearly six years. There have been no further incidents of alcohol-related and facilitated rape. The sexual and relationship conflicts of the couple have not reappeared. Treatment in this case was successful and very definitely a growth enhancing process for Dr. and Mrs. P.

This case study involved "marital rape." While this specific variety of rape might seem to be quite atypical to some clinicians, my therapeutic work with alcoholic couples and alcoholic family systems convinces me otherwise. Forced sex or rape occurs rather commonly in alcoholic marriages. In essence, the primary patient in this case had been raping his wife for the duration of their marriage. His alcoholic binge drinking occurred at six- to ten-month intervals. At these times Doctor P. would come home acutely intoxicated and rape his wife. Although the doctor's drinking behavior had not apparently resulted in a diminished capacity to function as a physician and professional person, his marital and family relationships were very definitely conflicted and deteriorating.

The patient stopped drinking shortly before entering individual therapy. Conjoint therapy was initiated after several individual sessions with Doctor P. In these sessions Doctor P. was confronted with the many painful realities that were associated with his alcoholic behavior. It was difficult for the patient to come to grips with the reality of having raped his wife for years. With extended conjoint therapy the sexual and relationship conflicts of this couple were resolved. Five-year follow-up contacts with this couple indicate continued sobriety, a complete lack of further incidents of rape, and global growth and healthy change upon the part of both patients.

Basic Treatment Strategies

Every rape victim is psychologically traumatized (MacKellar, 1975; Pekkanen, 1976; Hyde, 1976; Griffin, 1979). Many rape victims are in need of direct medical care immediately following the rape transaction. Hyde (1976) indicates that about 20 percent of rape victims are in need of emergency hospital care immediately after the rape. These victims may need medical treatment for only cuts and bruises. Some rape victims are in need of extensive medical care. These women may have broken bones and severe lacerations. A few rape victims require surgery and life-sustaining medical interventions. It is recommended (MacKellar, 1975; Hyde, 1976; Gager and Schurr, 1976) that the rape victim always receive medical care specific to the issues of possible pregnancy and venereal disease. The rape victim should also be seen for supportive counseling and possibly extended psychotherapy. During the past decade many communities have developed rape counseling and crisis centers for these victims. Such agencies often provide comprehensive medical, psychiatric, psychological, and health services for rape victims.

As a part of the helping process with rape victims, therapists need to evaluate the drinking behaviors of these women. Some rape victims are problem drinkers. A few are alcoholic. Drinking or intoxication may have played an important role in the victim's being raped. As indicated earlier in the chapter, research (Amir, 1967) suggests that both the rapist and the victim are drinking in a significant percent of rape cases. An exploration of the victim's drinking behavior is most appropriately initiated after the establishment of a productive therapeutic alliance. In other words, the counselor or therapist should initially help the victim work through the anxiety, hurt, depression, confusion, and guilt associated with the rape. When the rape victim is an alcoholic or problem drinker, the therapist must focus on the drinking behavior of the patient. If the rape victim is an alcoholic or problem drinker, she can be treated successfully by employing the various treatment strategies discussed throughout this text. In most cases, the victim will need to be treated for the trauma of rape prior to the initiation of a primary treatment intervention strategy aimed at resolving her alcohol addiction or problem drinking. Exceptions to this position include detoxification and other direct medical care for alcoholism in cases involving alcohol-dependent rape victims.

The rapist is obviously in need of psychotherapeutic treatment and rehabilitation. An extensive evaluation of the drinking behavior and drinking history of the rapist must be conducted in all cases involving a rapist who is drinking or intoxicated at the time of the rape incident. Problem drinking is a central ingredient in all cases of rape that are committed by a drinking or intoxicated rapist. This is a very basic and obvious fact. Yet, law enforcement personnel and behavioral scientists seem to consistently "overlook" or underevaluate the significance of this fact. An initial stage in the process of treating drinking (at the time of the offense) rapists is an accurate clinical assessment of the patient's drinking behavior. A few rapists are alcohol dependent. These individuals may be in need of direct comprehensive medical care. When apprehended, the alcoholic rapist should receive immediate medical evaluation for syphilis and other venereal diseases. An important medical evaluation of the rapist's blood alcohol content and alcoholism can be initiated at this time. Detoxification and referral for inpatient alcoholism care are appropriate in cases involving an alcohol-addicted rapist.

The majority of rapists who commit rape while intoxicated or after drinking are problem drinkers. They are not alcoholic in the sense of being tissue addicted. These individuals often have an extended history of alcohol abuse. Furthermore, in therapy these persons often reveal that they have experienced a number of sexual/legal problems over the years, which almost always involved drinking or intoxication. It is very apparent in these cases that rape behavior and other sexually deviant behaviors are directly alcohol related and alcohol facilitated. When these rapists stop drinking or significantly modify their patterns of consumption, they no longer engage in rape. For this to occur, the patient must receive intensive alcoholism treatment and then extended psychotherapy specific to the issues of problem drinking, rape, other sexual conflicts, and a variety of ongoing daily living problems. Marital and family therapy (Forrest, 1978) is essential to the successful treatment of many of these individuals. The therapist must point out to the patient (and his spouse or the family members, when appropriate) that rape probably would not have occurred had the patient not been drinking. This point must be stressed throughout therapy. It is imperative that the patient establish a long-term commitment to a radically modified style of drinking. In many cases, this means total abstinence.

A few rapists engage in this form of deviant and inappropriate sexual behavior only once. When intoxication or alcohol plays a major role in such a rape transaction, the therapy process must focus on this reality. Some "one-time" rape cases involve an alcoholic rapist. Others involve problem drinkers. These "one-time" alcohol-facilitated rapists are relatively easy to treat. When the rapist is a chronic alcoholic, treatment is usually more difficult and more time-consuming. Yet, the chances are excellent that the patient will not engage in subsequent rapes.

Alcoholic or problem drinking rapists must be treated holistically. Mere probation or incarceration will not deter these individuals from committing rape. This point cannot be overemphasized. When alcohol and alcoholic behavior facilitates and potentiates rape behavior, it is the alcoholic behavior that must first be extinguished. In this sense, it may make very little difference whether the rapist is an alcoholic or problem drinker. The rapist who manifests alcoholism or a serious drinking problem will not be successfully treated and rehabilitated by seeing a probation officer on a weekly or monthly basis. These patients are in need of intensive, holistic, ongoing therapeutic interventions. Weekly outpatient psychotherapy for a few weeks is of very little benefit to the vast majority of these persons. The alcohol-addicted or alcohol-abusing rapist needs to be seen in extended individual and/or group therapy and possibly conjoint or family therapy. These patients very often respond favorably to Antabuse maintenance therapy. In addition, the alcohol-abusing rapist should be encouraged to actively participate in Alcoholics Anonymous. Members of the patient's family can be referred to Al-Anon and Alateen. An exercise program, nutritional program, and a religious commitment may be helpful therapeutic adjuncts for many of these patients.

Alcohol-abusing homosexual rapists respond favorably to

these same basic treatment interventions. With these few patients the therapist must (1) help the patient establish an ongoing commitment to sobriety and (2) help the patient establish a more adequately consolidated nuclear identity. The second step in this process involves many hours of therapeutic work in the areas of identity, sexuality, and self-exploration. Alcoholic or alcohol-abusing homosexual rapists who only engage in this form of deviant sexual behavior while intoxicated tend to have fragmented identities or an ego structure that is prone toward regressive ego-splitting (Kernberg, 1976; Forrest, 1982a). The homosexual and rapist components of the self are ego alien and unconscious in many of these cases. Therefore, the psychotherapist must actively explore the patient's sexual feelings and impulses while at the same time focusing upon the overt reality of the patient's homosexual behavior. This process fosters a synthesizing of the fragmented ego structure and thus reduces the probable occurrence of further episodes of violent alcohol-facilitated homosexual rape.

The alcoholic or alcohol-abusing husband who rapes his wife is perhaps the easiest "type" of rapist to successfully treat. One of the biggest obstacles to the successful treatment and rehabilitation of men who rape their wives is the victim—the wife! Many of these wives have been raped hundreds of times. They are afraid to ask for outside intervention. They are also embarrassed, humiliated, hurt, depressed, and guilty as a result of being raped by their alcoholic husbands. These victims eventually tend to enter therapy, join Al-Anon, or confide in their minister or priest. Whenever such a woman discloses marital rape to a therapist or change agent, every effort should be made to facilitate the husband's involvement in therapy. A few alcoholic husbands will disclose their marital rape behaviors to the therapist or counselor they are working with while undergoing comprehensive alcoholism treatment. In these situations the therapist should attempt to contact the wife (victim) and then begin conjoint therapy. Some of these wives are reluctant to begin conjoint therapy. Therefore, individual psychotherapy may be a precursor to effective conjoint work.

Marital rape invariably results in family conflict. Children in family systems involving an alcoholic father who rapes his wife experience emotional and sexual problems. These children may be in need of individual psychotherapy. Many of these family systems respond favorably to family therapy. The children of alcoholic or problem drinking nonspouse rapists are also in need of therapy. Clinicians need to be aware of these issues in their treatment relationships with rapists. Providing therapy for the children of the rapist can be viewed as a methodology for preventing the development of eventual sexual, marital, and emotional problems in future generations.

Research (Cohen and Seghorn, 1969; Coleman, 1972; Brownell, Hayes and Barlow, 1977; Barlow and Wincze, 1980) indicates that many rapists and sexual deviants can be successfully treated and rehabilitated. Violent, impulsive, and psychopathic rapists are difficult to treat and outcomes are less successful in these cases. The alcoholic or alcohol-abusing rapist usually responds favorably to psychotherapy and comprehensive treatment. This point needs to be emphasized. Society in general and many behavioral scientists have tended to believe that rapists cannot be successfully rehabilitated. Behavioral science researchers and clinicians need to begin to investigate more thoroughly the roles of alcohol, alcoholism, and alcohol abuse in rape.

Summary

Rape is defined as any variety of sexual intimacy forced upon one person by another person. Rape is sexual assault. It is pointed out that modern definitions of rape include homosexual assault and the sexual assault of a spouse (Geiser, 1979).

Rape is an angry, violent transaction. Statutory rape involves the sexual assault of a minor. Forcible rape is defined as the sexual assault of an unwilling person who is over eighteen years of age. The focus of this chapter is limited to forcible rape.

The number of cases of reported rape in this country are increasing rapidly. Hyde (1976) reports that over 51,000 forcible rapes were committed in one recent year. Furthermore, 18 percent of women residing in large cities and suburban areas have suffered rape. It is estimated (Coleman, 1972) that the actual incidence of rape is three to four times greater than the reported rate. Rape tends to be committed by young men. Approximately one-half of rape offenders are married and living with their wives at the time rape is committed (Hyde, 1976). Rape behavior also tends to be repeated. The victim is unknown to the rapist in 50 to 70 percent of rapes. It is believed that rape is a planned crime in the great majority of cases.

There are numerous theories of rape. In actuality, comparatively little is known about the adjustment style and personality makeup of the rapist. It has been found (Hyde, 1976) that rape behavior tends not to be learned from others. Rape includes displaced aggression and rage. Sexual and aggressive components are fused in rape. The rapist employs sexuality as a means of physically injuring, degrading, and attacking his victim. Some rapists are not able to achieve an erection or reach orgasm during the actual rape incident. Rape is sometimes committed impulsively by psychopaths. A few rapists are sadists and/or masochists. Research suggests (Cohen and Seghorn, 1969) that sexual excitation is the key component in some cases of rape. In such cases the rapist tends to be passive, sexually inadequate, and submissive. It is rather apparent that a number of factors contribute to the aetiology of rape. A number of misconceptions or myths have long been associated with rape (Geiser, 1979).

A number of studies (Gebhard et al., 1965; Amir, 1967; Rada, 1974; 1975; Hyde, 1976) indicate that alcohol plays an important role in a significant percentage of rapes. Rada (1974) found that 50 percent of rapists had been drinking at the time of the assault. Thirty-five percent of these rapists were diagnosed "alcoholic." Hyde (1976) indicates that alcohol is associated with approximately one-half of all rapes. She also states "the least aggressive type of rapist is one who is drunk." MacDonald (1971) described the drunken rapist as "relatively harmless." Alcohol and drugs play an important role in group rapes (Hyde, 1976). It was found (Amir, 1967) that alcohol played a significant role in 217 cases of rape in a study of 600 forcible rapes in Philadelphia. In this investigation (Amir, 1967) 21 percent of the offenders *and* victims had been drinking alcohol when the rape occurred. Many of the alcoholic or problem drinking rapists seen within the confines of comprehensive alcoholic treatment centers have unsuccessfully attempted rape (Knauert, 1981). A few homosexual rapists are also seen for treatment and rehabilitation in these settings. Forcible rape occurs rather frequently within the alcoholic marriage. This unrecognized reality was explored in-depth in the case study of Doctor P.

The rape victim and the rapist are in need of psychotherapy and treatment (Griffin, 1979). Both may require hospitalization and direct medical care. The drinking behavior of the victim and the rapist must be carefully evaluated by the clinician. The rape victim may have been intoxicated at the time of the assault. A few rape victims are clearly alcohol-dependent or problem drinkers. In these cases, the victim will need immediate psychological support and care specific to the rape trauma. These patients are also in need of ongoing psychotherapy and rehabilitation relative to their addictive drinking behavior.

The alcoholic or problem drinking rapist must be treated for alcoholism or alcohol abuse. When these individuals terminate their drinking behaviors they no longer commit rape. Holistic treatment is indicated for the alcoholic rapist. A number of intervention strategies appropriate for the treatment of alcohol-abusing homosexual rapists, wife rapists, and "one-time" rapists are discussed in this chapter. Many of these individuals can be successfully treated and rehabilitated. Favorable outcome results with certain types of rapists may be produced by utilizing relatively brief group therapy treatment (Coleman, 1972). In some countries (Sturup, 1968) castration has been used as a treatment for recidivistic rapists.

The psychotherapist must utilize treatment interventions that are appropriate to the unique needs, adjustment style, and personality makeup of the rapist. Rapists are not "all the same." Extended individual psychotherapy, conjoint therapy, marital therapy, group therapy, Antabuse maintenance, residential treatment, and self-help interventions are among the primary treatment modalities that are appropriately utilized in the treatment of alcohol-abusing rapists. Effective treatment interventions with these patients are aimed at (1) extinguishing the rape behavior, (2) extinguishing the addiction or pattern of alcohol abuse, (3) resolving the patient's sexual conflicts and interpersonal problems, (4) modifying irrational cognitions and self-dialogue, (5) facilitating adaptive affective changes, and (6) producing adaptive long-term life-style changes. Clearly, further research and clinical investigations are needed in the areas of rape, alcoholism, and alcohol abuse (Knauert, Long and Vraa, 1982).

BIBLIOGRAPHY

Amir, M.: Alcohol and forcible rape. *British J of Addiction, 62*:219-232, 1967.
Amir, M.: *Patterns in Forcible Rape.* Chicago, University of Chicago, 1971.
Barlow, D.H. and Wincze, J.P. Treatment of sexual deviations. In Leiblum, S. and Pervin, L. (Eds). *Principles and Practice of Sex Therapy.* New York, The Guilford Press, 1980.
Brownell, K.D., Hayes, C.S. and Barlow, D.E.: Patterns of appropriate and deviant sexual arousal: The behavioral treatment of multiple sexual deviations. *J Consult and Clin Psych, 45(6)*:1144-1155, 1977.
Cohen, M., and Seghorn, T.: Sociometric study of the sex offender. *J of Abnor Psych, 74(2)*:249-255, 1969.
Coleman, J.C.: *Abnormal Psychology and Modern Life.* Fourth Ed., Glenview, IL, Scott, Foresman and Co., 1972.
Forrest, G.G.: *The Diagnosis and Treatment of Alcoholism.* Springfield, Charles C Thomas, Rev. 2nd Ed., 1978.
Forrest, G.G.: *Alcoholism, Narcissism and Psychopathology.* Holmes Beach, Florida, Learning Publications, 1982a.
Gager, N. and Schurr, C.: *Sexual Assault: Confronting Rape in America.* New York, Grosset and Dunlap, 1976.
Gebhard, P., Gagnon, J., Pomeroy, W., and Christenson, C.: *Sex Offenders: An Analysis of Types.* New York, Harper & Row, 1965.
Geiser, R.L.: *Hidden Victims: The Sexual Abuse of Children.* Boston, Beacon Press, 1979.
Griffin, S.: *Rape: The Power of Consciousness.* New York, Harper & Row, 1979.
Hyde, M.O.: *Speak Out on Rape.* New York, McGraw-Hill Book Co., 1976.
Kernberg, O.F.: *Object Relations Theory and Clinical Psychoanalysis.* New York, Jason Aronson, 1976.
Knauert, A.P.: *Alcoholism and Sexual Deviation.* Lecture, Psychotherapy Associates, P.C. Seventh Annual Advanced Winter Workshop, "Treatment and Rehabilitation of the Alcoholic," Colorado Springs, Colorado, February 2, 1981.
Knauert, A.P., Vraa, C., and Long, A.: *The Treatment of Alcohol Related Sexual Dysfunctions, Problems and Deviations.* Symposium, Psychotherapy Associates, P.C. Eighth Annual Advanced Winter Workshop, "Treatment and Rehabilitation of the Alcoholic," Colorado Springs, Colorado, February 5, 1982.

MacDonald, J.: *Rape: Offenders and Their Victims.* Springfield, Charles C Thomas, 1971.

MacKellar, J.: *Rape: The Bait and the Trap.* New York, Crown Publishers, Inc., 1975.

Pekkanen, J.: *Victims: An Account of a Rape.* New York, The Dial Press, 1976.

Rada, R.: *Alcoholism and Forcible Rape.* Presented at American Psychology Association meeting, Detroit, Michigan, May 1974.

Rada, R.: Alcohol and rape. *Medical Aspects of Human Sexuality, 9(3):*48-65, 1975.

Sturup, G.K.: Treatment of sexual offenders in Hersted. Vester, Denmark: The rapists. *Acta Psychiatr Scandin, 44* (Suppl. 204):1-62, 1968.

Chapter 9

ALCOHOLISM, SADISM,
AND MASOCHISM

IN this chapter, the topics of sadism, masochism, sadomasochism, and alcoholism are considered at length. The initial section in this chapter focuses upon sadism. Masochism is then discussed in the second section of the chapter. The final section in
this chapter is devoted to an exploration of the various behavioral
and psychodynamic components associated with sadomasochism,
alcoholism, and problem drinking.

SADISM

Sadism is a term that is evoked from the name of Marquis de
Sade (1740-1814). De Sade wrote extensively about his need to
inflict pain and punishment upon women in order to achieve sexual excitement and gratification. Eventually, de Sade was committed to an insane asylum as a result of his sadistic sexual practices.
Sadism has been defined (Coleman, 1972) as "the achievement
of sexual gratification through the infliction of pain on a partner.
The pain may be inflicted by such means as whipping, biting, and
pinching; and the act may vary in intensity, from fantasy to severe mutilation and in extreme cases even murder." Although the
term sadism is used to denote cruelty in general, the strict clinical
meaning of this term encompasses the achievement of sexual pleasure in inflicting pain (Cameron, 1963) upon a partner.

Sadism is most typically a male sexual deviation. However,
clinical case studies of female sadists have been reported (Kraft-
Ebing, 1950) in the behavioral science literature. Sadistic patterns

of behavior tend to be repeated. Accounts of women being mutilated and murdered by sexual sadists are rather common. In these cases of extreme sadistic deviance, the sadist experiences orgasm or intense sexual excitement while in the act of mutilating or murdering his victim. Hirschfield (1956) states "in genuine cases of sexual murder, the killing replaces the sexual act. There is, therefore, no sexual intercourse at all, and sexual pleasure is induced by cutting, stabbing, and slashing the victim's body, ripping open the abdomen, plunging the hands into her intestines, cutting out and taking away her genitals, throttling her, and sucking her blood. These horrors constitute, so to speak, the pathological equivalent of coitus."

Less pathological patterns of sadism involve such behaviors as biting, whipping, verbally abusing, tying, and choking the sexual partner. In recent years such behaviors have been referred to as "S-M," "bondage," and "leather" in the popular literature. Some sadists must dress in leather, tie their partner to the four corners of the bed, and administer a physical "whipping" of the partner with a leather whip in order to experience sexual excitation, erection, and orgasm. Sadistic women engage in such behaviors as biting and scratching, pinching, tying, choking, and whipping their male or female partners in order to feel sexually aroused and experience orgasm. Male and female sadists derive sexual pleasure from forcing their partners to engage in a variety of sexual acts. Pain accompanies these "forced" sexual acts. One male patient could only reach orgasm by forcing his sexual partners to engage in anal intercourse for extended periods of time. A woman sadist was able to reach orgasm by forcing her partners to perform cunnilingus for hours at a time. While the partner performed cunnilingus on her she would pull his hair, verbally curse and demean him, and sometimes whip him with a leather belt. This woman also enjoyed stimulating her partners anally with a "vibrator." Obviously, these sexual transactions are quite pregenital in nature. In all of these cases the sadist derives sexual pleasure from inflicting pain upon the partner. In sadism, pain is central to the process of sexual arousal and sexual interacting.

The incidence of sadism in the general population is unknown. Indeed, surprisingly little is known about the aetiology, dynamics, and developmental course of this deviation. Sexual sadists are rarely seen in psychotherapy. It is important to realize that sadistic behavior in general exists on a continuum. Sexual sadism also exists on a continuum. The most aberrant or pathological forms of sadism involve physical abuse, mutilation, and even murder. Seemingly "normal" patterns of sexual behavior and sexual interaction involve a degree of sadism. A degree of sadism is involved in the initial coital experiences of women. The sexual relationship and behavioral repertoires of many, if not most, couples contain a sadistic element.

Theories about the origin of sadism tend to be either psychoanalytic or behavioral and learning theory oriented. Freud (1953) believed that a major psychodynamic component of sadism encompasses the infantile misinterpretation and distortion of the male role in coitus. The child understands and perceives sexual intercourse as a brutal attack of the woman by the man. Children who witness the "primal scene," i.e. parental intercourse, misinterpret sexual intercourse as a brutal attack or violent physical assault. It is quite possible that the young child interprets this behavior as an assault upon the mother or father. At any rate, coitus is perceived as a violent and brutal transaction. Therefore, both male and female children who witness the primal scene are more prone to developing a sadistic sexual deviation. Fenichel (1945) viewed sadism as a defense against castration fears. The sadist feels that "I am the castrator, not the castrated one" (Fenichel, 1945). Sadism can also be viewed as rooted in the rather logical rebellion of the child against his or her parents. As children are forced by their parents to give up living according to the "pleasure principle" and accept the "reality principle" (Freud, 1953), they are enraged and wish to sadistically attack or destroy their parents.

Behavioral and learning theory oriented explanations of sadism stress that this form of deviant sexual behavior is learned. Sadism is the result of "experiences in which sexual excitation and possibly orgasm have been associated with the infliction of pain" (Coleman, 1972). This pathological learning paradigm could occur in any number of ways. The young child who on numerous occasions experiences sexual arousal while being spanked by a parent will develop sadistic and perhaps masochistic strivings. Children who experience sexual stimulation while observing and misinterpreting a primal scene may be more prone to sadism. The fantasies of young children and perhaps even early adolescents that associate coitus and physical assault or pain contribute to the development of sadism. Strong emotional stimulation in combination with pain during adolescence may generalize and precipitate sexual stimulation. In sum, sadism is believed to develop as a result of conditioning and reinforcement experiences that involve the association or pairing of sexual excitement and pain.

The response of the sadist's partners to his or her deviant sexual behaviors may either reinforce further sadism or perhaps deter the occurrence of this behavior. When the partner actively or even passively participates in the sadism, it is only logical to assume that these deviant behaviors are further reinforced, conditioned, and overlearned. This learning theory oriented paradigm is strengthened if the sadist becomes sexually excited and experiences orgasm with the partner. Sadistic behavior would not be reinforced, overlearned, and strengthened if the sadist's partners refused to participate in his or her sexually deviant pattern of arousal, stimulation, and responding.

A number of the early clinical studies of the sadist (Stekel, 1929; Fenichel, 1945; Kraft-Ebing, 1950; Berg, 1954; Coleman, 1972) suggest that these individuals are passive, timid, feminine, small in physical stature, and "undersexed." While these generalizations may be accurate, in the clinical experience of the author some male sadists tend to be aggressive, angry, "macho," and of large physical stature. Unconsciously and preconsciously, the sadist abhors sexual intimacy, and he tends to feel contempt for his victims. Male sadists sometimes idealize women in social contexts but are enraged at them in any kind of sexual context. In spite of this ambivalence, the sadist unconsciously and preconsciously wishes to annihilate and destroy his female partner. Mother-son relationship problems and oedipal conflicts are central to the psychopathology of the sadist. The woman who participates in sex with the sadist unconsciously represents the sadist's mother. This psychodynamic factor then relates to the sadist's secret wish to destroy women, the unconscious representatives of his mother, for participating in sexual relations with him, the unconsciously symbolized son. Sadists manifest generally negative attitudes toward sex. Indeed, the sadism of these individuals can be viewed as a defense against the conscious understanding and realization of self and self-oriented feelings about sexuality. Some sadists are able to become sexually excited and reach orgasm with only aggressive partners. Feelings of power, dominance, control, and omnipotence accompany acts of sadism. Such feelings defend the sadist from castration fears, fears of impotence, and more global fears of inadequacy.

Sadism is sometimes associated with schizophrenia and other varieties of severe psychopathology (Forrest, 1982b). A number of clinicians (Stekel, 1929; Wertham, 1949; Michaux and Michaux, 1963) have reported cases involving severely schizophrenic individuals who have sadistically murdered, castrated, and mutilated young children and adults. In general, the more bizarre and deviant the adjustment style of the sadist, the more likely that the sadist is schizophrenic or severely disturbed.

Sadism is multivariantly determined. Faulty learning and conditioning experiences contribute to the aetiology of this disorder. Familial, social, and interpersonal factors are associated with sadism. Severe internal problems and the more extreme varieties of psychopathology are sometimes linked with sadism. Constitutional and/or organic factors may be related to sadism.

It will be helpful for the reader to keep this exploration of sadism in mind as we turn to the topics of masochism and then sadomasochism and alcoholism.

MASOCHISM

Masochism is a term that was initially derived from the name of the Austrian novelist Leopold V. Sacher-Masoch (1836-1895). Sacher-Masoch's novels and fictional characters were devoted to the matter of obtaining sexual excitement and pleasure through pain. Masochism can be defined as experiencing sexual pleasure through pain. Cameron (1963) states "masochism means sexual pleasure in suffering." The use of the term masochism has generalized beyond its sexual meaning and connotations. Presently, such behaviors as religious suffering, suffering in general, hard work, self-denial, and abstaining from pleasurable and enjoyable activities are viewed by many as expressions of masochism. In a strict clinical sense, masochism refers to sexual pleasure derived through pain and ill treatment. Masochistic behavior is often, if not always, fused with sadism.

Some masochists only fantasize about sexually arousing experiences involving pain and ill treatment. For example, a few women actively fantasize about being raped and are only able to become sexually aroused and orgastic via the use of rape fantasy and imagery (see Chapter 10). These masochistic women find "aggressive" sexuality very stimulating and exciting. Masochistic men also find aggressive, pain-oriented sexual behaviors to be very arousing and stimulating. Masochists must engage in such activities as whipping, spanking, biting, switching, verbal abuse, binding and tying, and semistrangulation in order to become sexually aroused and orgastic. Coleman (1972) reports that this behavior is more common among women than men.

Masochistic and sadistic sexual practices seem to be more openly practiced and acknowledged in modern American society. The themes and covert, if not overt, content of many pornographic movies and magazines are clearly masochistic and sadistic. Bondage, whips and chains, leather, spiked heel shoes, and verbal abuse are but a few of the more obvious ingredients in the masochism and sadism of the world of pornography. These same ingredients of masochism have been used by masochists for the purpose of obtaining sexual pleasure for the past two centuries. Black nylon hose, black garter belts, black gloves, and similar types of women's garments and underclothing are more covertly associated with masochistic sexual practices. The covert artifacts of masochism and sadism are not limited to pornographic movies and magazines. Many men find their wives and lovers more sexually stimulating when they wear these undergarments. Some women feel more "sexual" when they wear this type of underclothing. Indeed, the "S-M" subculture of past decades seems to be a more open and accepted part of the sexual practices of many modern western societies.

Aside from the more overt masochistic sexual behaviors of a growing segment of people in recent American society, it was

Reik's (1974) belief that modern man seems to be in the process of becoming progressively more masochistic. According to Reik (1974), the masochism of modern man and modern society is more generalized and not explicitly limited to the realm of sexual behavior. Thus, the accelerated and demanding pace of modern living, compulsive patterns of work and "workaholism," patterns of sex, marriage and divorce, familial changes, and even our collective problems with weight and obesity reflect masochism in modern man and modern society. Chain smoking, heavy drinking, other drug abuse, obesity, and chronic nail biting are all manifestations of masochism. Our recently developed societal obsession with jogging can be viewed as rather masochistic (Forrest, 1980). To the contrary, people who neglect their physical well-being and fail to exercise on a regular basis can also be viewed as masochistic!

Perhaps another way to view masochism is from the perspective of self-defeating behavior. Ellis (1962; 1979; 1980) has very brilliantly labeled neurotic, inefficient, nongoal-oriented behaviors as "self-defeating." All of us realize that we are sometimes "our own worst enemies." We engage in behaviors that are self-defeating and maladaptive. Self-defeating behavior is masochistic. In effect, we inflict psychological and/or physical pain upon ourselves when we engage in self-defeating behavior. When we set ourselves up for failure, we are masochistic.

As touched upon earlier, the true incidence of clinical masochism in the general population is unknown. It is simply impossible to know what percentage of the general population must be punished or experience pain in combination with sexuality in order to feel arousal or reach orgasm. It is generally believed (Fenichel, 1945; Coleman, 1972) that women tend to be more masochistic than men.

There are several theoretical viewpoints relative to the aetiology of masochism. In general, these positions are quite similar to the ones already discussed specific to the aetiology of sadism. The Freudians (Fenichel, 1945; Freud, 1953; Cameron, 1963) view masochism as a fixation of childhood. A plethora of realities associated with the developmental epochs of infancy and childhood actively foster the development of masochism. Physical and psychological pain can be the result of being physically small, poorly coordinated, and without effective communication skills. Masochism has been viewed (Cameron, 1963) as an infantile "misinterpretation and distortion of the female sexual role." The child may misinterpret the "primal scene" or other sexual interactions. Thus, pleasure and sexual excitement are associated with physical assault, attack, and infliction of pain upon one-self.

Faulty learning and conditioning experiences can facilitate the development of masochistic behavior. Distorted or patholog-ical learning experiences during childhood, or even stimulation, pleasure, or orgasm may result in masochism. As these experiences are repeated they are overlearned. This pattern of sexual respond-ing is strengthened whenever sexual pleasure is derived through pain on many different occasions. It is apparent that learning, conditioning, and reinforcement factors do play important roles in the development and maintenance of masochistic behavior.

Another form of faulty learning that fosters and reinforces masochistic behavior involves childhood experiences of being physically and psychologically abused, neglected, and rejected. In these cases, the masochist has learned that punishment is a form of love. It is tragically true that punishment is the only evidence of caring, concern, and love that some children receive from their parents or caretakers. The "adult" masochist then wants to be physically and/or psychologically abused by his or her sex partner in order to feel wanted, valued, and loved.

A few masochists (Fenichel, 1945; East, 1946) derive sexual stimulation and pleasure from self-mutilation or by being cut or physically tortured by their partner during sexual relations. However, most commonly masochistic sexual behavior is an attempt to gain more sexual excitement, stimulation, and plea-sure from coitus and other patterns of sexual interaction. In these cases, masochism rarely results in severe physical injury. Masochism of this variety may be limited to play acting.

Sadism and masochism can be distinct forms of sexually deviant behavior. Yet, sadism and reciprocal masochism are usually present in the deviant adjustment style of the individual who manifests either one of these seemingly singular deviations.

The following discussion of alcoholism and sadomasochism elucidates (1) the dynamic and behavioral components responsible for the fusion of sadism and masochism, and thus the appropriateness of the clinical term sadomasochism, and (2) the origin and clinical relevance of sadomasochism in alcoholism.

ALCOHOLISM AND SADOMASOCHISM*

Stekel (1929) is one of the few clinicians who has investigated and written extensively about the issues of sadism and masochism. Unfortunately, Stekel failed to touch upon the similarities and interrelationships between sadism, masochism, and alcoholism. Rather than merely focusing upon the pain-pleasure dimension of sadomasochism, Stekel (1929) emphasized this type of behavior to be psychosexually infantile as well as indicative of an obsessive character, which manifests itself as a repetition compulsion. Furthermore, it was his position that sadomasochism was a disorder of the environment, relating to specific experiences of childhood. According to Stekel, all sadomasochists are "affect hungry" individuals who, in addition to their sexual pathologies, are essentially incapable of love. More specifically, Stekel (1929) defined sadism as a "paraphilia in which the will to power is sexually accentuated" and masochism as "a paraphilia in which the will to submission is sexually accentuated." Stekel, quite brilliantly in his clinical case studies, demonstrates the persistence of the original sadistic disposition in those who are crippled or otherwise harshly treated by nature, Fascists, and Ku Klux Klan members. It is to be noted that he characterized the sadomasochist as a "dreamer who forces himself to the daily duties of life, one who lives in the past although apparently striving toward the future."

These general clinical impressions of sadistic and masochistic behaviors are readily applicable to many facets of the alcoholic character structure and, thus, the behavioral style of the alcohol-addicted individual. In this section I will (a) behaviorally define and describe the sadomasochistic adjustment style of the alcoholic,

---

*Some of the material in this section has been taken from Doctor Forrest's chapter "Alcoholism and Sadomasochism" in *Alcoholism, Narcissism and Psychopathology*. Holmes Beach, Florida, Learning Publications, 1982.

(b) discuss the primary aetiological components of this particular dimension of the alcoholic character structure, and (c) relate both sadism and masochism to the overt behavioral style of the alcoholic.

Sadistic or masochistic patterns of behavior, rather than existing as bipolar characterological dimensions, always coexist and are egofused, both intrapersonally and behaviorally. The sadomasochistic dynamism thus describes the egosyntonic nature, or egofusion, of sadistic and masochistic characterological trends. In attempting to provide adequate parameters for a behavioral definition of sadomasochism, as evidenced by the interpersonal style as well as the intrapersonal ideation of the alcoholic, I must, first of all, take exception to Stekel's position that the pain-pleasure and physical abuse dimensions of this specific behavioral dynamism are clearly of secondary or tertiary clinical importance. On the contrary, one of the basic behavioral hallmarks of sadomasochism manifested by the alcoholic is that of an overdetermined need to inflict both physical and emotional hurt or pain upon the self and significant others. The number of suicides, homicides, automobile accidents, alcohol-induced physical symptoms, divorces, cases of child neglect and abuse, and "nervous breakdowns" specific to any random sample of alcoholic individuals clearly supports this position (Forrest, 1978). Behaviorally, the alcohol-addicted person consistently inflicts a very pathological degree of pain upon the self and significant others. The singular process of being chronically intoxicated or intoxicated for extended periods of time is extremely sadomasochistic in nature. Hangovers, being sick for days following a drinking spree, ending up in jail, and paying fines for driving while intoxicated are but a few of the many other pain-oriented essentials of the alcoholic sadomasochistic behavioral style.

Most typically, definitions or descriptions of sadism, masochism, and sadomasochistic behavior have emphasized the sexual component of this pattern of behavior. Frankly sexual sadomasochistic transactions are rarely a part of the behavioral repertoire of the alcoholic; indeed, this form of explicitly sexual aberration is no greater among alcoholics than among the population at large. Psychodynamically, the matter of primary sadomasochistic sexual deviation remains, for the most part, of little clinical relevance to the psychotherapist involved in the treatment and rehabilitation of alcoholic patients. Symbolically, and at a functionally pathological level, the sexual encounters of both male and female alcoholics do encompass the sadomasochistic dynamism. Extramarital affairs, divorce, and even numerous divorces, and the various sexual escapades of the alcoholic in the throes of an alcohol facilitated debauch incorporate a very definite sadomasochistic element. A great deal of emotional pain, turmoil, and hurt accompanies interpersonal transactions of this variety. In this sense, an adequate behavioral definition of sadomasochism must also include the emotional or affective pain dimension.

Those familiar with the pattern of interpersonal relations and family dynamics specific to a family constellation, which includes an active alcoholic, can well appreciate the emotional reality of hurt, pain, and sadomasochism within this context (Forrest, 1978; Wegscheider, 1981). Indeed, both the overt and covert modus vivendi of the family with an active alcoholic husband or wife appears to be that of diffuse punitive interaction. This is especially true with regard to the family in which the alcoholic is the husband in the later stages of the addiction process. Physical, as well as emotional, survival may well be the paramount issue for one or all of the family members in these particular family constellations. The alcoholic is most typically perceived as a victim within such patterns of family interaction. However, the alcoholic also maintains a fluctuating role of persecutor within the family constellation. Scapegoat, victim, rescuer, and persecutor are the primary pathognomonic roles within these families. The additional turmoil, pain, and pathology created by perpetual role reversals and role "slippage" within these family constellations guarantees that each family member behaves in a very real sadomasochistic fashion. It should be noted that these roles, as well as the various pathological transactional games acted out within the family that includes a drinking alcoholic, are greatly exaggerated, thus compounding both the physical and emotional pain experienced by all of the family members. The nonalcoholic spouse most typically appears to be a masochistic personality type. As the nonalcoholic spouse is most often the wife, it is she who pathologically tolerates physical abuse, psychological hurt, and the sadistic and often brutal confrontations of her addicted husband. However, this form of role engagement carries with it sources of secondary gain. In addition, the wife invariably derives a great deal of gain from her ability to frequently change roles and act out the covert and/or overt sadistic trends with which she struggles to control and deny most of the time.

The sadomasochistic dimension of the alcoholic is, without exception, the product of arrested personality development and less than adequate emotional maturation. The interpersonal transactions of the drinking alcoholic are much akin to those of the early adolescent. Poor impulse control, acting-out, an inability to delay gratification, egocentricity, immaturity, irresponsibility, and problems with authority are but a few of the characterological features classically used by clinicians and psychotherapists (Knauert, 1981; Forrest, 1982a) to describe the infantile nature of the alcoholic. While sadomasochistic trends may well have been evident during earlier developmental stages, it is during the stage of adolescence that the overt behavioral acting-out of sadomasochism becomes floridly manifest. Temper tantrums, physical assaults against peers and significant others, and verbal aggression are clearly evident during the anal, oedipal, and latency eras. However, it is, most typically, not until early adolescence that the alcoholic individual begins to actualize the essential physical and psychological behaviors fundamental to sadomasochistic patterns of interaction. At this time, the lust dynamism (sexuality) becomes actively fused with the more primitive needs of the organism to attack, destroy, and inflict pain upon significant others. This need to hurt others sadistically derives from first being hurt or treated sadistically by significant others. Quite obviously, a tremendous amount of guilt, remorse, and anger at the self serves to help create the masochistic component of the sadomasochistic dynamism. The experience of having been unloved, not wanted, and rejected during infancy and childhood is interpreted, at this time, to mean that one deserves to be punished.

For a significant percent of the individuals found to be alcoholic in later life, pathological drinking patterns, in fact, were initiated during early adolescence. The prodromal sadomasochistic trends of the eventual alcoholic are, at this time, synergized and reinforced by initiation of the drinking process. The control of sadomasochistic behavior is diminished significantly, for most alcoholic individuals, once the addiction process is activated. Paradoxically, the ingestion of alcohol acts to control or bind the sadomasochistic trends of a small number of alcoholic individuals. Nonetheless, sadomasochistic behavior and sadomasochistically overdetermined interpersonal transactions are extremely infantile in nature, and, as such, indicative of regressive adjustment.

The infantile nature of sadomasochism is clearly related to psychosexual development. This is particularly true with regard to the character structure of the alcoholic. Although most alcoholic individuals do progress to the genital stage of psychosexual development, this remains a precarious matter. The alcoholic, without exception, retains an overdetermined oral and anal characterological makeup, which in part relates to the ongoing sadomasochistic conflicts of these individuals. Unresolved oedipal conflicts are also central to the sadomasochistic behaviors of the later life alcoholic. As a result of these psychosexually oriented conflicts, the alcoholic acts out the unresolved and potentially catastrophic matter of bisexuality via sadomasochistic behaviors.

Sadomasochism refers to those behavioral transactions in which the alcoholic overtly or covertly inflicts physical or emotional pain and/or injury upon the self, significant others, and others and objects more tangential to the self. Very often these hurts are of the narcissistic injury category, pertaining to both self and others. Moreover, the sadomasochistic trends of the alcoholic encompass (a) the ego fusion of sadistic and masochistic trends, (b) behavioral as well as intrapersonal regression, and (c) psychosexual arrest and bisexuality.

The sadomasochistic dimension of the alcoholic character structure evolves in a general fashion and is initiated during the early developmental epochs. The infant is first gravely hurt or injured by significant others, particularly the mother. As the infant is subjected to a multiplicity of emotional and physical abuses by parents and significant others, he or she, according to this theoretical paradigm, experiences a primitive need to retaliate or strike back at these primary sources of hurt, rejection, anxiety, and indeed potential psychological, if not physical, annihilation.

At the most primal levels of human awareness and experience, this response is essentially reflexive in nature. As the human organism becomes increasingly sophisticated, experientially, physically, and neurologically, we readily become aware of the manifest behaviors specific to initial experiences of this variety. The retaliatory hate, rage, and aggression of the infant, first manifested via "nipple attack," soon becomes central to problems with excretory functions, temper tantrums, peer relations, and other more sophisticated parataxic interpersonal dynamisms. The infant and child, in a very direct behavioral fashion, tries vehemently to act out against his or her parental persecutors. These transactions are removed from the more natural and typical responses of the infant and child to narcissistic injury, forced limits, and induced gratification delay.

The parents or parental models of the individual found to be alcoholic later in life have themselves experienced a great deal of deprivation. Thus, the addiction process, to include the sadomasochistic dynamism, becomes a family-perpetuated dynamism (Forrest, 1978). This infantile need to retaliate or to act out hostility and rage toward significant others is an attempt to ritually or magically get even for the deprivations and hurt of the past. This process becomes a life-long dilemma for most alcoholics. This is an attempt to escape the masochistic message of infancy and childhood to the effect that: "I deserve to be punished." As a repetition compulsion, this becomes one very significant ingredient in the neurotic, conflict-ridden interpersonal style of the alcoholic. Every alcoholic harbors a great deal of hatred, resentment, and rage specific to the narcissistic injury that he has experienced during infancy and childhood at the hands of parents and significant others. This sadistic behavior and ideation later fuses with the masochistic pathology of the alcoholic. The subdued sadistic attempts of the human infant or child to strike back at significant others, or to defend the self from the emotional or physical abuses and deprivations of parents and parental models, are very often, at core, life sustaining and survival oriented.

It is of significance that the sadistic trends of the alcoholic, precursory to the development of the sadomasochistic dynamism, most directly evolve from the transactions and relationship with the mother. The mother or surrogate mother is unquestioningly the most significant source of narcissistic need and entitlement deprivation, and thus physical and emotional pain and hurt. The pervasive deprivation experienced by the male alcoholic, directly at the hands of his mother, during infancy, childhood, and not atypically into adolescence, to a very significant extent accounts for the chronic and pervasive conflicts the male alcoholic experiences in all of his later relationships with women. In part, the alcoholic male sadistically punishes or abuses women out of his unresolved hatred and rage for his mother and more specifically for the multitude of narcissistic injuries she inflicted upon him during, at least, the developmental stages of infancy and childhood. This historic psychodynamic matter relates to the frequent divorces, extramarital affairs, and wife beating (psychological if not physical) episodes so typical of the male alcoholic.

As the infant and young child acts out sadistically, or attempts to get even with parents or parental models for their narcissistic need and entitlement deprivations, two fundamental psychodynamic consequences emerge. First, the sadistic trends of the child, when acted out within the family constellation, are most typically impotent at best. It is ultimately futile for the child or infant to attack or attempt to retaliate against parents for their narcissistic injuries. In fact, when the child does attempt to display anger and aggression relative to parental deprivation, he or she very quickly becomes the recipient of further narcissistic injury, frequently including punitive physical abuse. Within this context, the infant or child learns to internalize sadistic behavior and fantasies. The infant and young child has been programmed via initial narcissistic need and entitlement deprivation to unconsciously believe that he or she masochistically deserves to be punished. This process constitutes the second major psychodynamic issue specific to the attempted sadistic acting-out of the infant or child. As the child is continually reinforced into internalizing anger and rage originally directed at parents or parental models, the learning of pathological masochism is concommitantly reinforced. This psychodynamic process, along with the primitive belief that one deserves to be punished, accounts for the egofusion and syntonic nature of sadism and masochism, thus the sadomasochistic dynamism. In effect, the infant and child systematically learns, and is conditioned, to punish the self (behaviorally as well as unconsciously and ideationally) for attempting to act out anger and rage specific to the narcissistic injuries that the parents have inflicted upon him. Eventually, self-punishment, or masochism, is precipitated by the fantasy ideation of the child as well.

Even the fantasy of acting-out a talion murder is an extremely threatening matter for the infant or young child, as the primitive conceptual apparatus of the individual at this time does not preclude the possibility of the parents' ability to "read the child's mind." This being the case, the parents may well decide to murder or annihilate the child, in the mind of the child (consciously the child may believe that he or she deserves to be murdered for harboring these fantasies), and certainly this matter constitutes a catastrophic source of anxiety for the child. Moreover, it is easily understood how primitively realistic this form of infantile ideation is, as the parents have behaviorally validated the fact that they are quite capable of murdering the infant or child. Very often it becomes necessary for the child, as a means of ritual undoing, to inflict physical hurt or pain upon self, in response to fantasies involving the murder of parents or the wish that they might somehow die. It is apparent how encapsulation within this form of emotional and behavioral rubric serves to teach, reinforce, and synergize the sadomasochistic dynamism.

The overt sadomasochistic behavioral style of the alcoholic, as touched upon earlier, is clearly apparent in the case of all individuals trapped in the addiction process. This is especially the case within the context of sadomasochism as discussed thus far in this chapter. One of the most significant clinical characteristics of the alcoholic, of the utmost diagnostic relevance, is the sadomasochistic life-style of such individuals. Inflicting physical and psychological pain upon the self and significant others is one of the hallmarks of this adjustment style. The process of ingesting alcohol is a most sadomasochistic affair, in and of itself, for the alcoholic. Perhaps this can be said of all alcohol consumption and all individuals who drink to the extent of involving physical or emotional discomfort and pain to the self and/or others. For the chronic alcoholic, the ingestion of alcohol has frequently helped precipitate, or directly caused, gastrointestinal symptomatology, neurologic dysfunction, nutritional disorders, cardiac difficulties, and blood sugar problems, to name but a few of the major medical-biologic complications specific to the addiction process (Wooddell, 1979a). One basic core ingredient, or red thread condition, in all of these alcohol-facilitated disorders is that of self-inflicted tissue destruction. This is the example par excellence of self-destruction, which at the extreme end of the continuum constitutes the ultimate masochistic act. Frequently, tissue destruction becomes a matter of total involvement of the human orgasm and, in effect, this process actualizes suicide, again an ultimate form of masochistic behavior.

As the alcoholic becomes increasingly involved in the process of self-destruction via any form of self-induced tissue destruction, those closest to the addicted individual begin to experience concomitant emotional and physical pain. Most often, significant others begin to experience this hurt and pain far prior to the appearance of physical and psychiatric symptoms upon the part of the addicted individual. This process of inflicting emotional and perhaps physical pain upon parents, spouse, children, and friends constitutes one very real sadistic dimension of the alcoholic character structure and the addiction process. Divorce or perhaps even numerous divorces, child neglect and abuse, and the loss of friendships all become highly sadomasochistic transactions. The guilt, anxiety, depression, rage, and other negative affective states that accompany such sadomasochistically overdetermined transactions become, themselves, the basis for further sadism and masochism and thus explain in part how the sadomasochistic dynamism is reinforced and maintained both interpersonally and intrapersonally.

As the alcoholic inflicts pain upon others, he or she eventually becomes the recipient of the sadistic retaliations of these same individuals. It is apparent that interpersonal transactions of this variety, involving marked sadomasochistic behavior, become highly reciprocal and mutually reinforcing and thus essentially cancerous in scope. In adjunct, the alcoholic punishes or acts out sadistically against significant others, experiences guilt, depression, and anxiety over his or her sadistic pathology, and then masochistically punishes the self for these sadistic transgressions. Significant others tend to tolerate these sadistic attacks of the alcoholic for varied periods of time and then retaliate à la lex talionis. Typically, these sadistic retaliations precipitate similar feelings of guilt, anxiety, and depression in those closest to the alcoholic, hence activating their need to also masochistically punish the self. Certainly, this amounts to an extremely neurotic adjustment pattern for all involved. Nonetheless, this is the transactional sine qua non of the alcoholic family constellation, as far as the sadomasochistic dynamism is concerned. Every alcoholic, his or her spouse, and children can readily identify with this process of personally hurting, hurting others, and being hurt by others. Such a paradigm conditions, reinforces, and teaches all parties locked into the model to behave sadomasochistically. This process, in part, relates to why so many daughters of alcoholics end up marrying an alcoholic and why both daughters and sons of alcoholics eventually tend to become addicted. This process has to do specifically with the psychological and physical pain and hurt dimensions of the alcoholic and the alcoholic family constellation. It should be emphasized that the alcoholic (indeed all of us) acts out sadistically as a result of being hurt or experiencing emotional and physical pain at the hands of significant others. The alcoholic masochistically internalizes the narcissistic injuries of significant others to the point at which these injuries become truly threatening to his psychological well-being and then sadistically retaliates.

The sadomasochistic behaviors of the alcoholic are the very direct result of a particular constellation of life experiences, as well as direct and incidental learning and reinforcement specific to these experiences. This type of behavior is basic to both the character structure of the alcoholic and the addiction process. It is essential, within the context of the psychotherapeutic encounter, or the rehabilitation process, to deal directly with the sadomasochistic conflicts of the alcoholic. This is but one integral part of the road to recovery; learning more healthy, effective, and rewarding patterns of behavior means learning to be other than pathologically sadomasochistic and thus other than alcoholic or alcohol dependent.

A brief clinical case study will now be presented in order to demonstrate the sadomasochistic character structure and behavioral style of the alcoholic.

CASE 14. Cathy W., a twenty-seven-year-old married woman with two children, entered therapy as a result of marital problems, heavy drinking and other drug abuse, and sexual problems. In spite of their severe marital conflicts the patient's husband refused to involve himself in individual or conjoint therapy.

The patient had grown up in a large Midwestern community. She was the youngest child in a family of five. The patient's father was a very wealthy rancher and investor. Cathy described her parents as cold, harsh, and punitive. As a child and adolescent, Cathy had felt that she could never please her parents. Both parents were described as critical and preoccupied with social status. They worried a great deal about "what the relatives and neighbors would think" about Cathy's behavior. The parents had slept in separate bedrooms for the entirety of their marriage and according to the patient they "probably" had not had intercourse for twenty-six years. Both parents were nondrinkers and nonsmokers.

In the initial therapy session Cathy indicated that she had been "committed" to a state mental hospital at age fifteen. She described herself as having been angry, drunk, and uncontrollable at that point in her life. She remembered that she had been hospitalized for nearly six months, but remembered nothing of her "treatment" while in the institution. The patient deeply resented having been committed to the hospital by her parents. After being released from the hospital, Cathy returned to high school and graduated at age seventeen. She was a very bright woman and in spite of her acting out conflicts did well academically while in high school. After graduating from high school the patient entered a large Midwestern university. She completed three years of undergraduate study and then dropped out of college. While in college Cathy became a student activist, joined the drug subculture, and led a very promiscuous life-style. The patient married during her second year of college and gave birth to a daughter about six months after being married. Her parents did not attend the wedding and vehemently "disapproved" of her marriage. This marriage lasted for nearly two years. When this marriage ended, the patient moved to Colorado and became involved in a religious sect. Three years later she was married to her present husband. She had another child about two years after being married for the second time.

During the early hours of therapy with Cathy it became apparent that she had long defended herself against intense anxiety and ego defusion by acting-out. She stated in one therapy session "practically everything I've ever done in life involves drugs, alcohol, or sex." After several sessions the patient revealed that she had been sexually involved with her brother during much of her adolescence. This brother was five years older than the patient. During the course of both marriages the patient had been very promiscuous. When she began therapy, she was in the habit of going out three or four nights each week by herself and picking up "one night stands" in various local bars. Since the patient and her husband had agreed upon having an open marriage, the matter of extramarital sex did not offend or anger her husband. The patient was also actively bisexual. She had engaged in various sexual practices with other women since late adolescence.

Cathy drank no less than "six or seven" glasses of wine or mixed drinks each night. She had been drinking like this for at least twelve years when she entered therapy. She also smoked marajuana daily, "snorted" cocaine when she could get it, and abused virtually every other drug available to her. The patient had been admitted to no less than six emergency rooms for drug overdose prior to beginning therapy. She was adept at getting physicians to prescribe her Valium, Librium, and other mood altering drugs. As a result of her drinking and drug-taking behavior, Cathy was somewhat shaky, upset, and "strung out" most of the time. She was unable to cope with her children and felt guilty about her inadequacies as a mother and parent. The patient stated that she "couldn't cope with life." On several occasions she asked her therapist, "Why do I keep doing this to myself?" She also stated, "If I'm not hurting myself, I'm hurting someone else."

After nine individual therapy sessions Cathy committed herself to total abstinence from alcohol and other drugs. She began taking Antabuse three times each week. A few sessions later Cathy indicated that her sexual behaviors were sick. She further indicated that the only way she could "get off," meaning reach orgasm, was through "aggressive sex." The patient openly discussed her sadistic lovers. A few years earlier she had been sexually involved with a man who tied her to the bed, whipped her, and then regularly "forced" her to engage in anal intercourse. Whenever they met to have sex it was her "responsibility" to wear black hose, a black garter belt, and black high-heeled shoes. Furthermore, the patient's lover regularly twisted her arms, pulled her hair, and showered her with verbally abusive language. They often played a game, which they called "slave and master." This physical relationship ended after two years. However, the patient's sadistic lover continued to infrequently call and write. These phone conversations and letters were sexually arousing and exciting to the patient.

This patient was seen in weekly and twice weekly outpatient psychotherapy for over two years. She had felt rejected, neglected, and unloved in her relationship with her parents. Sexual pathology existed within the patient's family of origin. She had experienced incest with an older brother for several years. Alcohol abuse, other drug abuse, and sexual promiscuity became the central issues in this patient's life. Cathy received attention when she acted out. She believed that she "deserved" to be punished. Indeed, she described herself as "evil" and an "instrument of the devil." The patient realized that her chemical addictions, sexual promiscuity, and sexual deviations were destructive. Yet, she had been unable to terminate these sadomasochistic behaviors. The patient's addictive behaviors, sexual promiscuity, and deviant sexual behaviors were most apparently masochistic. Her interpersonal style was sadistic. Although not explored in this brief vignette, Cathy was also sexually sadistic with her husband and many of her lovers.

The patient has been abstinent from alcohol and all other drugs for nearly three years. She has discontinued her sexual promiscuity. She divorced her bisexual husband after about eight months of therapy. Her pathological pattern of sadomasochistic sex was successfully resolved. When last contacted for follow-up purposes, the patient was employed and living with a professional man. She was no longer engaging in homosexual behavior.

This case study demonstrates clinical sadomasochism in an addictive personality. The patient had an extended history of alcohol abuse and polydrug abuse. She manifested a borderline tissue dependence upon alcohol at the time of treatment engagement. The case of Cathy is atypical as far as the issues of sadomasochism and alcoholism are concerned. In addition to manifesting the essentially nonsexual sadistic and masochistic elements of alcoholism and alcohol abuse as discussed in this chapter, Cathy was in a sexual sense a "classic" sadomasochist. The patient experienced sexual pleasure and excitement via "aggressive sex." Her sexual relationships involved being tied to a bed, whippings, ritualistic dressing, verbal abuse, and forced and painful anal coitus. The patient was also bisexual, promiscuous, and sadistic in her sexual relations.

This patient felt rejected and unloved as a child and adolescent. Her parents were cold, strict, critical, and caustic. Apparently, the parents had not had sexual relations in many years. The patient had maintained an incestuous relationship with an older brother throughout much of her adolescence. Cathy felt stimulated and loved within the context of her sadomasochistic sexual relationships. This patient was seen in intensive outpatient psychotherapy for more than two years. She terminated her pathological drinking and other drug-abuse behaviors. The patient also gave up many of her self-defeating and frankly sadomasochistic behaviors. The overall treatment outcome in this case was extremely successful.

Basic Treatment Strategies

Sobriety is an obvious initial treatment goal in the psychotherapy process with alcoholic and alcohol-abusing sadomasochists. As indicated earlier in the chapter, the alcoholic is by definition a sadomasochist. Alcohol addiction and problem drinking are examples par excellence of masochistic behavior. Thousands of alcoholics masochistically kill themselves each year. Sadism is also an essential behavior and characterological ingredient in the makeup of the addicted person. Each year alcoholics sadistically kill thousands of victims. Alcoholics also psychologically hurt and destroy thousands of people, including loved ones, every day. Alcohol abuse and alcoholism facilitate sadomasochistic behaviors. Alcoholics are people who inflict physical and emotional pain upon themselves, significant others, and even people they do not know and perhaps have never before met.

The various techniques and strategies the therapist can effectively utilize in order to facilitate patient sobriety have been discussed throughout the different chapters in this text. Many chronic alcoholics will need to be medically evaluated and treated prior to beginning psychotherapy or entering a residential treatment center. The alcoholic patient needs to be involved in a nutritional program, a program of regular exercise, psychotherapy and various forms of therapy, Alcoholics Anonymous, and perhaps a spiritual program of recovery. Antabuse can be a very helpful therapeutic adjunct in some cases. It is essential that the patient be committed to the work of therapy and recovery. In short, sobriety and ongoing recovery are best fostered through the utilization of holistically oriented strategies of intervention.

Very early in the psychotherapy relationship the therapist should begin to point out to the alcoholic patient that his or her alcohol-facilitated behavior is clearly self-defeating. It is important for the alcoholic to rationally understand, confront, and feel the sadomasochism associated with his or her alcohol addiction. Furthermore, these tasks must be accomplished while the patient is totally abstinent. This treatment task can be actualized in a variety of ways. The therapist can focus upon the patient's physical health and physical feelings that are associated with drinking. By focusing upon the "morning after," nausea associated with drinking and intoxication, the "shakes," and other physical symptoms and side effects of heavy drinking, the therapist can help the patient begin to realize the pain, physical destruction, and masochism that results from drinking (Wooddell, 1979b). The patient can begin to realize that he is destroying himself via the addiction process. It is also important for the therapist to explore the patient's feelings and emotions that occur as a result of being intoxicated. All alcoholic patients derive a good deal of emotional gain and relief as a result of drinking. Yet, every alcoholic and problem drinker makes himself emotionally upset as a result of heavy drinking and the various pathological behaviors that accompany alcohol addiction. The alcoholic makes himself or herself anxious, depressed, angry, guilty, and confused via the ingestion of alcohol. In effect, alcoholics make themselves physically and emotionally upset. This is the masochism of alcohol addiction.

The therapist can point out to the patient that it is "crazy" to persist in these patterns of masochistic and self-defeating behaviors. It is also important to point out to the patient that he or she can learn to behave more rationally. There are alternatives (Silverstein, 1978) to the self-defeating and masochistic behaviors that are basic to alcohol dependence. The alcoholic does not deserve to be punished. A conscious and extended exploration of the patient's unconscious self-dictate "I deserve to be punished, therefore I will punish myself and arrange for others to punish me" is essential to the process of resolving the patient's sado-masochistic behaviors and life-style.

Early in the treatment process and throughout therapy the counselor must help the alcoholic patient understand and change the sadism that has been basic to his or her alcoholic life-style. The alcoholic verbally and sometimes physically abuses parents, spouse, children, friends, and other loved ones. Inflicting emotional and/or physical pain on significant others is sadism. These behaviors are basic to alcoholism and problem drinking. It is difficult and painful for the alcoholic to realize and accept these aspects of the self. While drinking, the alcoholic attempts to avoid and deny the sadistic nature of his or her real self. The therapist must be able to gently and supportively confront (Forrest, 1982a) the alcoholic patient with the reality of his or her sadism. Depression, guilt, and remorse are fostered by this process. Recovery is based upon the patient's ability to grow through these feelings. Therapist mismanagement of these clinical issues will often result in the patient's masochistic return to the bottle.

Alcoholics punish themselves and significant others. Eventually, the loved ones and friends of the alcoholic become angry and resentful about being punished and abused (Forrest, 1980). They reach the point of being "fed up" with the behaviors of the alcoholic. In turn, they retaliate and sadistically attack the alcoholic. The therapist must help the alcoholic patient understand and change these maladaptive patterns of interpersonal living. Ultimately, the alcoholic always arranges to be masochistically punished by loved ones and significant others. This is an excellent "excuse" for continued drinking and intoxication. A major task of therapy is the modification and resolution of the alcoholic's "vicious circle" of self-punishment, punishing significant others, and then being punished by significant others and loved ones.

Therapists will find that a dynamic reconstruction of the patient's past in combination with a behavioral here-and-now approach is an effective treatment strategy for the modification of sadomasochistic behaviors associated with alcoholism and problem drinking.

A very small segment of alcoholics entering psychotherapy or alcoholic rehabilitation programs are sexual sadomasochists. In addition to utilizing the treatment strategies and goals already discussed in these few cases, the clinician will need to employ specific treatment techniques designed to help the individual patient modify his or her deviant sexual behaviors. Unfortunately, there are presently no clinical or research data (Coleman, 1972; Knauert, 1981) available on the technique of psychotherapy with alcoholic sexual sadomasochists. Successful treatment of masochists, sadists, and patients with multiple perversions is reported in the limited clinical literature available on these topics (Abel, Lewis, and Clancy, 1970; Brownell, Hayes, and Barlow, 1977; Barlow and Wincze, 1980). Behavioral treatment strategies seem to be appropriate and relatively effective in the treatment of these disorders. It is important for the therapist to utilize treatment interventions that (1) extinguish deviant patterns of arousal, (2) reinforce appropriate patterns of arousal, (3) modify inappropriate or deviant sexual cognitions and self-dialogue, and (4) reinforce the selection of nondeviant sexual partners. As was apparent in the case of Cathy, these patients seek out and often find sexual partners that are sadomasochistic. The sexual fantasies and thoughts of these patients are sadomasochistic. They also become sexually aroused via sadomasochistic behaviors and even in the presence of undergarments and other apparel, which they have learned to associate with sadomasochistic sex. Imagery training, suggestion and hypnosis, and direct suggestion techniques can be helpful in modifying the patient's patterns of deviant arousal, perverse self-dialogue, and parataxic sexual relationships.

Alcoholics who manifest sexually sadomasochistic adjustment styles respond favorably to intensive, interpretative psychotherapy. This style of therapy can be integrated with behavioral techniques that are aimed at the explicit modification of sadomasochistic sexual practices. It is therapeutically efficacious to explore and uncover the origins of the patient's sexual deviation. The onset and developmental history of the patient's perversion is grist for therapeutic exploration. These individuals invariably manifest low self-esteem. They have also been hurt, rejected, and abandoned by significant others. They tend to feel worthless and unloveable. These intrapersonal and interpersonal factors are associated with their alcoholism and sadomasochistic strivings. Sadomasochistic sex is a distorted method for feeling powerful, important, in control of self and others, and loved. These dynamic components of the patient's system of psychopathology must be resolved. These psychodynamic and interpersonal factors maintain and reinforce the patient's alcohol addiction and sadomasochistic strivings.

The majority of these patients are in need of social skills training, marital therapy, possibly assertiveness training, and family therapy. The sexual adjustment style of many alcoholic couples includes a floridly sadomasochistic component. Marital rape and forced sex within the context of the marital relationship encompas sadomasochism. These sexual relationship conflicts must be resolved in conjoint therapy. The wives of some alcoholics are also sadomasochistic. These marital and sexual cases are doubly difficult to treat. In these cases, extended individual therapy for both spouses may be a precursor to effective conjoint therapy. Child abuse and child neglect within the alcoholic family system (Forrest, 1978) may involve sadomasochistic elements. In such cases, family therapy and/or individual therapy for the children may be beneficial.

Once in therapy the alcoholic tends to develop a fear of his or her sadomasochistic behaviors. While drinking, these individuals do not realize the scope and various ramifications associated with their sadomasochism behaviors. The development of trepidation and fear in the sadomasochist as a result of understanding and facing the many implications linked with this form of behavior is generally healthy. As the therapist points out to the sadomasochistic patient that anger, rage, murderous and even cannibalistic (Forrest, 1982a; 1982b) impulses are basic to sadomasochism, it is only logical that the patient should begin to suppress and fear these strivings. Such a procedure is behavioral and aversive. At this point in the treatment process the therapist may want to utilize specific sex therapy interventions in order to help the patient establish a new and modified pattern of stimulating and arousing sexual responding.

Sadomasochistic behavior is basic to the adjustment style of the alcoholic and problem drinker. Sexual sadomasochism can be associated with alcohol addiction and alcohol abuse. All of these conditions present special and difficult treatment considerations. The various treatment strategies discussed in this chapter represent but a starting point. It is quite apparent that these patients are in need of very individualized multimodal-oriented therapy (Lazarus, 1980). The establishment of sobriety and ongoing commitment to alcoholism recovery are basic precursors to the psychotherapeutic resolution of sadomasochistic strivings and behaviors.

Summary

Sadism was defined and discussed in the initial section of this chapter. The term sadism is derived from the name of the Marquis de Sade and refers to achieving sexual arousal and pleasure through inflicting pain on a partner. The sadist may whip, bite, bind, verbally abuse, or throttle his or her sexual partner in order to experience sexual pleasure. Extreme cases of sadism involve murder, mutilation, and cannibalism. The incidence of sadism in the general population is unknown. Sadistic behavior exists on a continuum. Very little is known about the aetiology and developmental course of sadism. In spite of this fact, there are a number of theories about the origins of sadism. These theories tend to be either psychoanalytic or behavioral. Sadism is believed (Freud, 1953) to be associated with the young child's misinterpretation of the male role in coitus. Sadism is felt to be a defense against castration fears (Fenichel, 1945). Behavioral and learning theory explanations of sadism purport that this deviation is learned. Any sexual experiences that combine sexual stimulation and pain may reinforce or create sadistic behavior. Oedipal conflicts, severe psychopathology, and identity problems are also associated with sadism. In essence, a number of factors seem to contribute to the aetiology and maintenance of sadistic behavior.

Masochism is discussed in the second section of this chapter. Masochism is a term that refers to achieving sexual pleasure and stimulation in suffering and experiencing pain. The masochist may need to be spanked, whipped, verbally abused, or choked in order to experience sexual arousal and/or orgasm. Masochistic and sadistic behaviors seem to be more openly and pervasively practiced in modern American society. Reik (1974) believed that modern man is clearly masochistic. Smoking, alcohol and drug addiction and abuse, obesity, and "workaholism" involve masochism. Self-defeating behavior (Ellis, 1962; 1980) is masochistic.

The incidence of masochism in the general population is unknown. It has been hypothesized that women are more prone to masochism than men (Coleman, 1972). Theories of masochism also tend to be psychoanalytic or behavioral. Masochism is felt to be (Cameron, 1963) associated with infantile and childhood misinterpretations of the female sexual role. Faulty learning and conditioning experiences can facilitate the development of masochistic behavior. In essence, children that are physically and verbally abused are taught and conditioned to be masochistic. In a pathological manner, these children are conditioned to equate pain and punishment with love.

The third section of this chapter is devoted to an exploration and discussion of the interrelationships between sadism, masochism, and alcoholism. Sadism is always fused with masochism and vice versa. Therefore, sadomasochism is a term that most appropriately and accurately describes both of these deviations. The origins of sadomasochism and sadomasochistic behavior are explored in this section of the chapter. Narcissistic need and entitlement deprivation are precursors to the development of a sadomasochistic adjustment style. Sadomasochism is a basic ingredient in the character structure and personality makeup of the alcoholic. The alcoholic has been sadistically hurt by significant others during infancy and childhood. As a result, the alcoholic develops a life-style of sadistically attacking significant others. Eventually, the alcoholic is further attacked by significant others. Underlying this vicious circle is the alcoholic's masochistic attack upon the self. Unconsciously and preconsciously, the alcoholic believes that he or she "deserves to be punished." Even the sadistic retaliations of the alcoholic against significant others are futile and masochistic.

Very few alcoholics are sexually masochists, sadists, or sadomasochists. The sadomasochistic life-style of the alcoholic involves essentially nonsexually oriented pain. Alcoholics inflict physical and emotional pain upon themselves and significant others. They destroy themselves physically and psychologically through alcohol. Alcoholism destroys those who are closest to the alcoholic. It is apparent that alcoholism is a disorder that involves multifaceted sadomasochism and sadomasochistic behaviors.

The case study presented in this chapter did involve sexual sadomasochism and alcohol dependence. The patient was a married woman who had been abusing alcohol and other drugs for several years. She was treated successfully in extended outpatient psychotherapy. Initially in therapy, this patient reported that she was only able to become sexually stimulated and orgastic when her partner tied her to the bed, whipped her, and was verbally demeaning and abusive. The patient stated that she was "into aggressive sex."

The sadomasochistic behavior of the alcoholic generally goes into remission following the establishment of long-term sobriety. Indeed, a basic goal in the treatment of all alcoholic persons is that of helping the patient overcome his or her pervasive patterns of self-defeating behavior. A diversity of therapy and treatment techniques have been discussed throughout this text. These strategies of treatment are effective in working with alcoholic and problem drinking persons. As such, these treatment interventions can be effectively utilized to extinguish and resolve the sadomasochistic behaviors of the alcoholic.

Early in the psychotherapeutic process, the therapist must help the alcoholic patient realize and understand the self-defeating, sadomasochistic dimensions of his or her alcohol-related behavior. Most of these individuals can readily see that they have been making themselves physically ill through intoxication. The alcoholic must also accept and change the realities associated with making himself or herself and significant others psychologically disturbed through drinking. A combination of psychodynamic and behavioral therapy strategies can be employed to help the alcoholic patient begin to actualize more adaptive and rational patterns of living. It is therapeutically important to explore the patient's infantile and childhood experiences that contribute to the "I deserve to be punished" dictate.

Some alcoholics who manifest sexual sadomasochism respond favorably to intensive relationship therapy, which combines the use of behavioral treatment interventions. Most of these patients are in need of multimodal treatment. Social skills training, marital therapy, family therapy, imagery training, sex therapy, and assertiveness training are but a few of the strategies of therapy that can be used with these patients. The marital and sexual relationships of many alcoholics are floridly sadomasochistic. It is imperative that the therapist develop and utilize very individualized treatment interventions in working with these difficult cases.

A great deal of clinical research is needed in the areas of alcoholism, alcohol abuse, and sadomasochism. Alcoholism is clearly one of the most destructive varieties of maladaptive human behavior.

BIBLIOGRAPHY

Abel, G.G., Lewis, D.J., and Clancy, J.: Aversion therapy applied to taped sequences of deviant behavior in exhibitionism and other sexual deviations: A preliminary report. *J Behav Res Exp Psychiat, 1(1)*:59-66, 1970.

Barlow, D.H., and Wincze, J.P.: Treatment of sexual deviations. In Leiblum, S.R. and Pervin, L.A. (Eds.): *Principles and Practice of Sex Therapy*. New York, The Guilford Press, 1980.

Berg, A.: *The Sadist*. Illner and G. Godwin (Jr.). New York, Medical Press of New York, 1954.

Brownell, K.D., Hayes, C.S., and Barlow, D.H.: Patterns of appropriate and deviant sexual arousal: The behavioral treatment of multiple sexual deviations. *J Consult and Clin Psych, 45(6)*:1144-1155, 1977.

Cameron, N.: *Personality Development and Psychopathology: A Dynamic Approach*. Boston, Houghton Mifflin Co., 1963.

Coleman, J.C.: *Abnormal Psychology and Modern Life*. 4th Edition, Glenview, Illinois, Scott, Foresman and Co., 1972.

East, W.N.: Sexual offenders. *J Nerv Ment Dis, 103*:626-666, 1946.

Ellis, A.: *Reason and Emotion in Psychotherapy*. New York, Lyle Start, 1962.

Ellis, A.: *Rational Emotive Therapy Training*. Lecture, Psychotherapy Associates, P.C. Fifth Annual Advanced Winter Workshop, "Treatment and Rehabilitation of the Alcoholic," Colorado Springs, Colorado, January 31, 1979.

Ellis, A.: Treatment of erectile dysfunction. In Leiblum, S.R. and Pervin, L.A. (Eds.): *Principles and Practice of Sex Therapy*. New York, The Guilford Press, 1980.

Fenichel, O.: *The Psychoanalytic Theory of Neuroses*. New York, Norton, 1945.

Forrest, G.G.: *The Diagnosis and Treatment of Alcoholism*. Springfield, Charles C Thomas, Rev. 2nd Ed., 1978.

Forrest, G.G.: *Confrontation in Psychotherapy with the Alcoholic*. Holmes Beach, Florida, Learning Publications, 1982.

Forrest, G.G.: *How to Live with a Problem Drinker and Survive*. New York, Atheneum, 1980.

Forrest, G.G.: *Alcoholism, Narcissism and Psychopathology*. Holmes Beach, Florida, Learning Publications, 1982a.

Forrest, G.G.: *Alcoholism, Schizophrenia and Defense*. Lecture, Psychotherapy Associates, P.C. Eighth Annual Advanced Winter Workshop, "Treatment and Rehabilitation of the Alcoholic," Colorado Springs, Colorado, February 1, 1982b.

Freud, S.: *The Future Prospects of Psychoanalytic Therapy*. Collected Papers, Vol. II, London, Hobarth, 1953.

Hirschfield, M.: *Sexual Anomalies*. New York, Emerson Books, 1956.

Knauert, A.P.: *Differential Diagnosis of Alcoholism.* Lecture, Psychotherapy Associates, P.C. Fifth Annual Advanced Winter Workshop, "Treatment and Rehabilitation of the Alcoholic," Colorado Springs, Colorado, January 28, 1979.

Knauert, A.P.: *Alcoholism and Sexual Deviation.* Lecture, Psychotherapy Associates, P.C. Seventh Annual Advanced Winter Workshop, "Treatment and Rehabilitation of the Alcoholic," Colorado Springs, Colorado, February 2, 1981.

Kraft-Ebing, R.V.: *Psychopathica Sexualis.* New York, Pioneer Publications, 1950.

Lazarus, A.A.: Psychological treatment of dyspareunia. In Leiblum, S.R., and Pervin, L.A. (Eds.): *Principles and Practice of Sex Therapy.* New York, The Guilford Press, 1980.

Michaux, M.H., and Michaux, W.W.: Psychodiagnostic follow-up of a juvenile sex murderer. *Psychoanal Rev, 50*:93-113, 1963.

Reik, T.: *Of Love and Lust.* New York, Jason Aronson, 1974.

Silverstein, L.M.: *Consider the Alternative.* Minneapolis, Comp-Care Publications, 1978.

Stekel, W.: *Sadism and Masochism,* Vols. I, II. New York, Liveright, 1929.

Wegscheider, S.: *Family Dynamics and Family Therapy in the Treatment of Alcoholism.* Lecture, Psychotherapy Associates, P.C. Seventh Annual Advanced Winter Workshop, "Treatment and Rehabilitation of the Alcoholic," Colorado Springs, Colorado, February 5, 1981.

Wertham, F.: *The Show of Violence.* New York, Doubleday, 1949.

Wooddell, W.J.: A liver disease in alcohol-addicted patients. *Family and Community Health, 2(2)*:13-22, August, 1979a.

Wooddell, W.J.: The alcoholic withdrawal syndrome. *Family and Community Health, 2(2)*:23-30, August, 1979b.

Chapter 10
ALCOHOLISM
AND EXHIBITIONISM

EXHIBITIONISM is a clinical term that is used to describe the act of exposing one's genitals to other people in a public place (Coleman, 1972). Genital exposure is essential to the diagnosis of exhibitionism. Many people are exhibitionistic in the sense that they enjoy being looked at, are extroverted and flamboyant, and seem to always need to be the "center of attention" in social situations. Yet, such individuals rarely expose their genitals in public or in other social situations.

Genital exhibitionism is almost exclusively a male sexual deviation (Cameron, 1963). This form of deviant sexual behavior is postpubertal and often a postmarital phenomenon. Cameron (1963) states "typically an exhibitionist compulsively shows his genitals to young women or mature women in a public place, such as a street, a park, or a doorway; sometimes in a bus, a train, a plane or a shop. This may be repeated several times in a single day, each time with great anxiety on the part of the exhibitionist." The exhibitionist exposes his genitals compulsively. This is an important dynamic in the diagnosis of exhibitionism. Akin to alcoholism, all of the sexual deviations involve an obsessive-compulsive component. Anxiety accompanies the act of exposing the genitals. The exhibitionist experiences intense anxiety immediately prior to the exhibitionistic act and following the act. Many exhibitionists (Christoffel, 1956) attempt to guard against and fend off their exhibitionistic strivings.

During childhood boys tend to be exhibitionistic. It is not

338

atypical or abnormal for a young boy to unexpectedly show his penis to a visitor or playmate. Indeed, young boys and girls in our society often play the "doctor game," which involves mutual exhibitionism. Most parents are not deeply upset when they discover their child or children participating in such sex games. The children who engage in exhibitionistic sexual games are not intensely anxious about their behaviors. Moreover, they do not engage in these behaviors in an obsessive-compulsive fashion. Very few children persist in exhibitionistic behaviors after the developmental stage of early adolescence.

In recent years, our society appears to have become more accepting of exhibitionistic forms of sexual behavior. Even genital exposure is more generally accepted in modern American society. Today, women are far more exhibitionistic than they were a few decades ago. Exhibitionistic behavior is valued and actively reinforced in modern American society. Television commercials include women in bikini swimsuits, topless and bottomless bars are in vogue, dresses are shorter in recent years, the braless look is fashionable, nude beaches are increasing in number, male strippers are the latest in entertainment, and pornographic movies and literature are among the most lucrative industries in this country. The recent streaking fad became an American obsession. Each night on the television newscast the American public watched hundreds of nude men and women running in and out of stores, down streets, and so forth. All of these social realities make it somewhat more difficult to classify exhibitionism as a sexual deviation. Yet, the exhibitionistic behaviors of the "streaker," topless dancer, and fashionably dressed woman differ from those of the sexually deviant exhibitionist. In general, the social context and social appropriateness of the exhibitionistic behaviors of the topless dancer differ from those of the exhibitionist. The topless dancer does not expose herself in a public place. She is not acutely anxious prior to dancing topless or following her "performance." Topless dancing is not an obsessive-compulsive ritual that the dancer chronically attempts to curtail or guard against. These dynamic issues can be used to differentiate between the psychopathology of the sexually deviant exhibitionist and other apparent exhibitionists. Cultural, social, and situational variables also determine the degree of sexual deviation associated with any form of exhibitionistic behavior.

Kinsey et al. (1948; 1953) reported that of all sex offenders, exhibitionists have the largest proportion (72 percent) of convictions for sex offenses and the smallest proportion (28 percent) for nonsex offenses. In terms of per capita convictions "they are again outstanding and rank first in the number of misdemeanors resulting in imprisonment. No other group approaches them in the per capita number of sex offense convictions. In brief, the exhibitionists had committed more sex offenses than any other group." Research (Kinsey et al., 1948) also indicates that exhibitionists are highly recidivistic. Only 13 percent of exhibitionists have one conviction. Nearly one-third of exhibitionists have four to six convictions. In this regard, Kinsey et al. (1948) state "a group that can boast more seven-time than one-time losers can be justly labeled recidivistic." Stoller (1975) believes that the exhibitionist arranges to be caught more than other "perverse" persons. Exhibitionists make up the largest group of sex offenders apprehended by police (Coleman, 1972). Exhibitionism is most common during the spring and summer months. Virtually all occupational groups include exhibitionists. More than half of all exhibitionists are married (Coleman, 1972).

Most theories of exhibitionistic behavior are psychodynamic in nature. A variety of psychological factors are associated with exhibitionism. Fenichel (1945) views exhibitionism as a defense against unconscious castration anxiety. Pathological narcissism is also theorized to be an important psychodynamic issue in exhibitionism (Fenichel, 1945; Cameron, 1963; Reik, 1974). The exhibitionist narcissistically exposes his penis to others and experiences pleasure, triumph, and sexual excitement as a result of this behavior. In so doing, he demonstrates to himself and others over and over again that he has a penis. He is therefore not castrated. By exposing his penis the exhibitionist shows in a very concrete way that he has not been castrated, that he has not been humiliated, and that he has not been defeated by women (Stoller, 1975). It is the viewpoint of Stoller (1975) that a crucial factor in exhibitionism is demonstrating masculinity. Each time he exposes his penis, the exhibitionist "proves" to himself and others (society) that he is a man.

Exhibitionists feel globally inadequate. They feel sexually inadequate. They feel vocationally and interpersonally inadequate. Some exhibitionists are anxious about the size of their penis and attempt to compensate for fears and anxieties associated with feeling that they have a small penis by genital exposure. In this regard, Apfelberg, Sugar, and Pfeffer (1944) reported the case of an exhibitionist who experienced orgasm only when he accompanied the exposure of his penis with a question to the victim as to whether she had ever seen such a large penis. Witzig (1968) found that about 60 percent of exhibitionists are immature. In these cases, exhibitionism is associated with feelings of inadequacy and inferiority, shyness, puritanical attitudes, masturbation conflicts, and difficulties in the realm of approaching members of the opposite sex. The exhibitionist is frequently (Witzig, 1968) attached to an overly possessive mother. Exhibitionists often state that they struggle against the impulse to expose themselves.

The exhibitionist learns that he can shock or frighten others by exposing his genitals. Faulty learning and conditioning factors are closely associated with the repetitive nature of this disorder. Exhibitionism is a pathologic means of obtaining attention. The exhibitionist controls others through the act of exposing his genitals. Indeed, there are many sources of pathological secondary gain that actively reinforce the exhibiting behavior of the exhibitionist.

Anger is an important ingredient in exhibitionism. Exhibitionists are angry at women. The exhibitionistic act is a pathological sexual act, but it is also an act of anger and rage. Primitively and unconsciously, the exhibitionist destroys women by exposing them to his powerful penis. He frightens them and renders them impotent by his act of genital exposure. Thus, the exhibitionist castrates his victim by angrily showing her and reminding her that she does not have a penis. In spite of these psychodynamic factors, the exhibitionistic act does not usually involve assaultive behavior.

It is rather obvious that many factors contribute to the act of exhibitionism. Early childhood experiences, familial factors, internal sexual conflicts and struggles, and faulty learning experiences are aetiologically associated with exhibitionism.

Alcoholism Associated with Exhibitionism

Several clinicians and researchers (Todd, 1973; Cerul, 1976; Vraa, 1978; 1982; Forrest, 1978; 1982a; Knauert, 1979) have indicated that sexually deviant behavior may be precipitated by acute alcohol intoxication or chronic alcoholism. However, there are virtually no clinical or research data available on the relationships between alcoholism, alcohol abuse, acute intoxication, and exhibitionism. It is known that exhibitionism involving "indecent exposure" is one of the two most common sexual offenses reported to police (Coleman, 1972). It is estimated that no less than 30 to 50 percent of indecent exposure acts involve a male that is acutely intoxicated. Many of these men are alcohol dependent.

In spite of the fact that very little is known about the specific incidence of exhibitionism among alcoholic and problem drinking persons, exhibitionistic behavior is central to the global psychopathology of alcoholism and problem drinking. Very often such exhibitionistic behavior includes frank genital exhibitionism. From a psychodynamic viewpoint, alcoholism is a highly exhibitionistic disorder. The alcoholic "exposes" himself in a plethora of pathological ways. Drinking on the job, missing work, marital arguments and conflicts, angry outbursts, drunk driving, problems with a child and even child abuse, sexual acting-out, and living on "skid row" are but a few of the exhibitionistic transactions that alcoholics engage in. The alcoholic "exposes" or exhibits himself via these behaviors and transactions. Obviously, genital exhibitionism is not central to most of these transactions. Yet, the alcoholic places himself in pathologic positions of attention and assumes a "center of attraction" stance in each of these transactions. Some alcoholics and problem drinkers are quite extroverted. Extroverted behaviors, even when alcohol facilitated, are generally exhibitionistic. The aggressive barroom behaviors of some alcoholic persons are quite exhibitionistic.

Genital exhibitionism is central to the adjustment style of some alcoholic men and women. Such alcoholic persons tend to feel inhibited, timid, insecure, and even ashamed of their bodies when sober. After drinking and reaching a state of inebriation, these individuals become aggressive, extroverted, and exhibitionistic. A few of these persons may exhibit their genitals in a bar or other drinking environment. Some are arrested for urinating in public. In such cases, exhibitionistic behaviors are clearly facilitated by alcohol ingestion and intoxication. In fact, the exhibitionistic behaviors of most alcoholic persons only occur after the person has been drinking and is intoxicated. Following an alcohol-facilitated incident of genital exhibitionism, the alcoholic typically feels guilty, remorseful, and embarrassed.

Within the context of family therapy with alcoholic family systems (Forrest, 1978) it is rather common to encounter alcoholic fathers who periodically expose their genitals to family members. Genital exhibitionism may be viewed by some clinicians as covertly incestuous when involving an alcoholic father and a daughter or son. In virtually all cases of alcoholic familial exhibitionism, the addicted family member exposes himself to other family members only after becoming acutely intoxicated. Alcoholic-familial exhibitionism may also involve an alcoholic mother or an addicted adolescent son or daughter. Typically, the addicted family member drinks to the point of intoxication, takes off all his or her clothes, and enters the room where other family members are congregated. On some of these occasions the alcoholic family member may be in a "blackout" and is unable to remember the entire exhibitionistic episode. When confronted about the exhibitionistic episode by the spouse or children, the alcoholic family member denies having exposed himself. He is unable to recall the exhibitionistic episode and fully believes that he did not expose himself. In other situations, the alcoholic does remember exposing himself to another family member. Guilt, trepidation, and remorse are the feelings that the addicted family member struggles with in these cases. Indeed, the entire family system is traumatized by the exhibitionistic behaviors of the addicted family member.

Invariably the alcoholic who engages in genital exhibitionism manifests significant sexual conflicts and pathology. Although many of these individuals are married, serious sexual and relationship conflicts exist within the marriage. In this regard, Witzig (1968) states "these men almost never like to discuss sexual matters with their wives and frequently avoid undressing before them. The idea of living in a nudist colonly is a repulsive thought to most exhibitionists, although they are periodically willing to show off their genitals in quite public places." The exhibitionistic alcoholic or problem drinker is sexually inhibited and conflicted within the confines of the marital relationship. Sex and sexual feelings are rarely discussed in an open manner in the marital relationship involving an alcoholic with a history of exhibitionism. These couples avoid discussing and working through their sexual problems. They often tend to blame each other for their sexual "hangups." It is rather common to discover in therapy that each spouse perceives the other as sexually conflicted or "perverted."

As discussed in earlier chapters, alcohol acts as a disinhibitor. As a result of being intoxicated, the alcoholic or problem drinker is more prone to exhibitionistic behavior. Likewise, alcoholic environments actively reinforce exhibitionism. In recent years many bars and night clubs have initiated "wet t-shirt nights," "body" contests, and nude or exotic dancing contests, which require the participants to expose themselves or partially, if not totally, disrobe themselves. Quite commonly, these activities attract people with exhibitionistic strivings who also drink heavily. Sometimes a "contagion effect" is precipitated whereby many of the people in these bars, aside from the direct participants, disrobe and expose themselves. It is important for the psychotherapist and clinician to be aware of the various social, environmental, and contextual variables that are associated with the exhibitionistic behaviors of the alcoholic patient.

Very few alcoholic persons are genital exhibitionists. Although many alcoholic persons expose themselves, they are not compulsively driven to expose themselves in public places while sober. Simply stated, alcoholics tend to engage in exhibitionistic behavior but they are rarely true exhibitionists in a clinical sense. Hopefully, the case of Paul will help clarify these clinical issues.

CASE 15. Paul H., a sixty-one-year-old widowed cook, was court ordered into therapy following an arrest and conviction for indecent exposure. The patient had a prior legal record involving several arrests for indecent exposure, which dated back some fifteen years. On each of these occasions the patient stated that he had been "drunk and got caught taking a leak in public." The patient had been treated in various alcoholic treatment centers since the age of thirty-six. His medical history included a diagnosis of cirrhosis of the liver, organic brain syndrome, hypertension, and alcoholic seizures. The patient's wife had died four years earlier. During the initial therapy hour, Paul indicated that he felt that he was an alcoholic but that it was "impossible" for him to stay sober.

The patient was quite small in physical stature. Behaviorally, he appeared to be passive, inadequate, timid, and grossly ineffectual. When questioned about his extended history of genital exhibitionism, the patient became noticeably uneasy, evasive, and defensive. He eventually stated, "When you've been drinking and you gotta go, you gotta go—if they ain't seen one by now, they're overdue." These statements were followed by a few robust chuckles. When the therapist attempted to focus on the sexual inappropriateness of urinating in public the patient stated "It's all over and in the past—what's the use of bringing it up again?"

During the course of some sixteen therapy sessions with Paul, it became increasingly apparent that abstinence was not a viable treatment goal. Paul consistently indicated that he "could not" and "didn't want to" remain sober. Nonetheless, the patient's social history, which was revealed in the course of these few hours of therapy, elucidated an interesting history of alcoholism, exhibitionism, sexual pathology, and criminal behaviors. The patient's mother divorced his biologic father when he was two and one-half years old. She remarried when he was seven years old. According to Paul, the biologic father and stepfather were both "heavy drinkers." The patient had one older sister and two younger sisters. The younger sisters were parented by the patient's stepfather. As a child and adolescent, the patient described himself as shy and timid. Paul indicated that he had "never gotten along well" with his stepfather. The stepfather was a wealthy and successful business executive who drank a good deal, had numerous affairs, and was absent from the home a good deal. He was also a very strict and punitive disciplinarian. Paul described his mother as strong, perfectionistic, and cold. He remembered that his parents slept in separate bedrooms. At the age of sixteen Paul left home and joined the Army. While in the Army the patient was a cook. Following the completion of military service the patient drifted. He worked as a cook in several restaurants throughout the Midwest. Typically, he would work at a restaurant for a few months, quit, and then move to another town where he could find employment. At age twenty-four the patient was involved in an armed robbery of a service station. The patient indicated that he had driven the getaway car in the robbery. At any rate, Paul was apprehended by the police a few hours after the robbery and eventually he was sentenced to prison. Paul was incarcerated in a Midwestern state penitentiary for nearly five years. The patient indicated that he had been drinking heavily at the time of the robbery.

A few months after getting out of the penitentiary, Paul married a a woman about fourteen years his senior. She was a restaurant owner. As an employee, Paul managed to begin dating this woman and in a few months they were married. They rarely had sexual relations. This marriage lasted about five years. Eventually, the marital relationship became severely conflicted and Paul simply disappeared one morning. He took a train to California and found another job in a large restaurant. The patient was arrested for indecent exposure for the first time in California. After an evening of heavy drinking, the patient was caught urinating in the street. He was placed on probation. A few months after this, Paul was involved in a near fatal automobile accident and was hospitalized for three months. He was driving while intoxicated when the accident occurred, but was never charged for this offense. Several months after recovering from the automobile accident, Paul returned to the Midwest. He resided in a large metropolitan city and worked at several restaurants.

At age forty-three the patient again married. Although he had never obtained a "legal" divorce, the patient remarried and remained married to his second wife for fourteen years. The second wife was fifty-five years old at the time of their marriage. Throughout the course of their marriage Paul drank heavily. He was arrested numerous times for alcohol-related asocial behavior. The patient was "sentenced" to alcoholism treatment in the state mental hospital more than twenty times. On each of these occasions he received inpatient alcoholism treatment for thirty to ninety days. Several times alcohol-related exhibitionistic behavior was central to the patient's being sent to the state hospital for treatment. The patient developed a seizure syndrome at age forty-seven.

During fourteen years of marriage the couple never once engaged in intercourse or other forms of sexually intimate behavior. Paul seemed to feel that sexual intercourse was dirty and perverse. He described his relationship with his second wife as a 'loving relationship." The marital relationship was not "animalistic" in Paul's terminology. A source of anxiety for Paul was his inability to have children. He indicated to the therapist that he had been "born with something wrong with my balls."

After entering therapy and remaining totally abstinent from alcohol for a period of some four months, the patient went on a two week "binge." He experienced several alcohol-induced seizures and was treated in three different hospital emergency rooms during this drinking bout. Finally, the patient was discovered in a casket in a funeral home and again taken to the state hospital for alcoholism treatment. Paul was stuporous when found in the casket and later he had no recall of this episode. Shortly after this incident, an emergency room physician who treated the patient for acute intoxication arranged for another medical transfer to the state hospital. The patient was again placed in the alcoholic treatment unit and completed a forty-five day inpatient program. After completing this program, the patient was seen in outpatient therapy on one more occasion. In this session Paul indicated that he was determined to "make it on my own." He pointed out that treatment programs and therapy had never really worked. The patient continually refused to attend Alcoholics Anonymous. During the final therapy session Paul stated "I'm damned tired of having doctors and the cops tell me what to do—as far as I'm concerned, all of em can suck my cock."

This patient was not seen in subsequent therapy sessions. As such, no precise or in-depth follow-up data are available on this individual. However, the patient was so well known to the professional (hospital, medical, and psychological) community that periodic anecdotal feedback over a period of about three years indicates that he continues to drink alcoholically. He also continues to periodically expose his genitals in public.

This case study shows how intoxication and alcoholic addiction can be related to exhibitionism. The patient was sexually conflicted and had been arrested for indecent exposure and exhibitionism on several occasions. Organic factors may have been associated with the alcoholism and exhibitionism of this patient. Indeed, Paul was a very difficult patient to treat. He had received extensive alcoholism treatment for many years. Psychotherapeutic as well as legal efforts proved unsuccessful in the modification of his exhibitionistic behaviors. In spite of the patient's overall sexual pathology it is clinically significant that his overt exhibitionism was always alcohol related and alcohol facilitated. It is only logical to assume that this patient will continue to engage in exhibitionistic behaviors in the absence of a resolution of his alcohol addiction.

Basic Treatment Strategies

The case study presented in this chapter clearly demonstrates how very important it is for the therapist to be able to help the patient resolve his alcoholism as a precursor to modifying exhibitionism and other sexual conflicts. The vast majority of alcohol-related cases of exhibitionism seen for treatment within the confines of comprehensive alcoholic treatment centers involve indecent exposure. Some clinicians might question the validity of evaluating these patients as exhibitionists. Nonetheless, such patients do expose themselves in public. In these cases, exhibitionistic behavior is a direct consequence of drinking and intoxication. Alcohol-related exhibitionistic behavior is socially inappropriate, and most communities will not tolerate such behaviors. The therapist wll find that most of these patients discontinue their patterns of exhibitionism once they have established long-term sobriety.

An initial step in the treatment process of exhibitionists is that of accurately assessing the patient's drinking history and present drinking style. If the patient is an alcoholic or problem drinker he should be treated as such. The alcohol-dependent exhibitionist may require hospitalization or other direct medical interventions. Many of these patients will need to be placed in a residential treatment program. The patient should also be referred to Alcoholics Anonymous. If he has family members, they can be referred to the various other self-help programs provided by the Alcoholics Anonymous Community. Patients that have been arrested several times for alcohol-facilitated exhibitionism should be considered for Antabuse therapy. Some of these individuals respond favorably to being placed on a very structured Antabuse maintenance program. The patient is legally required to take 250 to 500 mg of Antabuse three times each week for a period of eighteen to thirty-six months. Incarceration may occur if the patient fails to take his Antabuse. It is apparent that the alcoholic or problem drinking exhibitionist is in need of holistic treatment. As discussed throughout this book, alcohol-dependent and alcohol-abusing persons usually respond very favorably to holistic treatment approaches. Thus, dietary regulation, exercise programs (Forrest, 1979a), traditional forms of psychotherapy, meditation, spiritual programs, and self-help modalities can all play important roles in the process of recovery from alcohol addiction or problem drinking.

Once the alcoholic or problem drinking exhibitionist has been able to establish sobriety and commit himself to therapy and a program of recovery, the therapist must begin to actively focus upon the patient's sexual conflicts and sexual pathology. At this point in treatment, the focal concern of both the therapist and patient should be the resolution of the patient's exhibitionistic behaviors. It may take several weeks of therapy to reach this treatment stage. It is important for the patient to realize that alcohol ingestion synergizes or potentiates his exhibitionism. As mentioned earlier, the majority of exhibitionists are married. Extended individual and group psychotherapy are viable treatment modalities for helping the unmarried alcoholic exhibitionist extinguish and resolve his exhibitionism. If the patient is married, every attempt should be made to include the patient's wife in therapy. In these cases, the sexual relationship of the couple is almost always pathological. Patterns of marital and familial communication, interaction, and relating tend to be parataxic. All of these issues are grist for the therapy process. Once a working therapeutic alliance has been established with the patient or marital dyad, the therapist must begin to focus upon the specifics surrounding the patient's exhibitionistic behavior. When did the patient first expose himself? Has this behavior resulted in previous legal consequences? When did the wife first learn of the patient's exhibitionism and what has been her response to this behavior and her husband? In a few cases the therapist and couple will soon "discover" that the patient only exposes himself after being denied sexual relations by his wife. Other patterns of marital interaction may be explicitly associated with the patient's exhibitionism. Very often feelings of anger and rage at the spouse can be important in cases of exhibitionism.

The extroverted and covertly exhibitionistic interpersonal demeanor of many alcoholics will sometimes spontaneously change after sobriety has been established. There is a narcissistic (Forrest, 1982a) and exhibitionistic dimension to most alcoholic persons that must be explored, interpreted, and resolved in the therapy relationship. This aspect of the alcoholic personality does not often include genital exhibitionism.

The ongoing psychotherapeutic process with these individuals must be aimed at (1) the maintenance of sobriety, (2) extinguishing the exhibitionistic behavior and other sexual conflicts, (3) resolving the patient's internal and interpersonal conflicts, and (4) exploring and modifying the distorted and irrational self-dialogue, which reinforces the patient's alcohol addiction and exhibitionism. When alcoholism or problem drinking is a primary variable in the patient's pattern of exhibitionism, it is not therapeutically efficacious to simply utilize behavioral treatment strategies in order to extinguish this pattern of deviant sexual responding. In addition to the use of behavioral strategies of intervention, it is important for the therapist to use cognitive, psychodynamic, and relationship treatment techniques with these patients. If the patient simply stops his exhibitionistic behaviors but continues to fantasize and ruminate about exposing himself, it is realistic to expect an exhibitionistic relapse. Many of these individuals are in need of social skills training. They tend to manifest poor or inadequate heterosexual relationship skills. In such cases, the therapist will need to teach the patient to converse and communicate more effectively with women. A variety of direct rehearsal and fantasy techniques can be used for these purposes. These treatment tasks can often be accomplished in a group therapy setting (Slater, 1964). After several hours of relationship psychotherapy, the therapist may find that he or she is doing very little other than sexual counseling and/or sex therapy. The wife of the alcoholic exhibitionist is often sexually inhibited or sexually dysfunctional. In these cases, the treatment format may evolve from a few individual therapy sessions to conjoint therapy to sexual counseling and sex therapy.

Infrequently, the clinician encounters an alcoholic patient that is exhibitionistic within the family system. Many of these patients do not expose themselves in public places. Their exhibitionism is limited to the confines of the family environment. Nevertheless, genital exhibitionism within the family system is inappropriate and almost always pathologic. This position is especially true when the family system includes postlatency aged children and adolescents. Family therapy interventions (Forrest, 1978; Wegscheider, 1981) are most appropriate in the treatment of these cases. In addition to the various other clinical interventions discussed in this section, the therapist will find that cases of familial exhibitionism respond quite favorably to family therapy. Disturbed marital and sexual relationships are basic to these cases. Covert incestuous strivings are also central to the personality makeup of alcoholic fathers who repeatedly expose themselves within the family context. These cases can usually be treated successfully via several months of ongoing family therapy.

Once the patient's alcoholism and exhibitionism are in remission, it is important for the patient and/or couple to persist in an ongoing program of growth and recovery. Psychotherapy sessions held at three or four month intervals can meet this follow-up need. Self-help programs are excellent for this purpose in many cases. Successful results in the treatment of exhibitionism are reported by several clinicians (Slater, 1964; Evans, 1967; Witzig, 1968; Coleman, 1972). These authors report that exhibitionists rarely repeat their behavior after treatment. The prognosis is not as favorable in the case of alcoholic or problem drinking exhibitionists. However, with extended treatment contacts and adequate follow-up care the alcoholic exhibitionist can often be successfully rehabilitated. Continued sobriety is certainly a key factor in the successful treatment of these individuals (Forrest, 1982a).

Summary

This chapter includes a definition of exhibitionism; an exploration of the relationships between alcohol abuse, alcoholism, and exhibitionism, and a discussion of treatment strategies germane to working with alcoholic and problem drinking exhibitionists. Exhibitionism is a clinical term that refers to the act of exposing one's genitals in a public place. Genital exhibitionism is differentiated from the exhibitionistic narcissism that many people manifest. Genital exhibitionism is almost exclusively a male sexual deviation. This variety of deviant sexual behavior is postpubertal and often a postmarital phenomenon. The exhibitionist compulsively exposes his genitals.

The exhibitionistic behavior of young children is normal. Many social factors interact to determine the degree of deviance associated with acts of exhibitionistic behavior. Genital exhibitionism is socially acceptable behavior within the context of many modern bars and night clubs. In recent years, it seems that American society has become progressively more tolerant and reinforcing of exhibitionistic behavior.

It has been reported (Kinsey et al., 1948; 1953) that among sex offenders, exhibitionists have the largest proportion of convictions for sex offenses and the smallest proportion for nonsex offenses. Exhibitionists are also highly recidivistic. Exhibitionism is most common during the spring and summer months. More than half of all exhibitionists are married (Coleman, 1972).

There are a number of psychological and psychiatric theories or explanations of exhibitionism. In general, these theoretical viewpoints are psychoanalytic or psychodynamic in nature. Thus, castration anxiety, narcissism, and anxieties over penis size have been theorized as causative psychodynamic factors in exhibitionism. The exhibitionist feels sexually inadequate. His masculine identity is precarious. These individuals are often shy, puritanical, and heterosexually conflicted. The exhibitionistic act involves pathological anger. Many exhibitionists are enraged at women. Faulty learning and conditioning experiences contribute to the development of exhibitionism.

Although alcoholism and alcohol abuse have been associated with a variety of deviant sexual behaviors, there is virtually no clinical or research data available on these issues as they pertain to exhibitionism. However, it is the estimate of the author that no less than 30 to 50 percent of indecent exposure acts involve a male that is acutely intoxicated; perhaps 70 to 80 percent of these acts are alcohol related! Exhibitionistic behavior is central to the global psychopathology of alcoholism and problem drinking. From a psychodynamic perspective, alcoholism is an exhibitionistic disorder. Alcoholic men and women sometimes expose their genitals in public. Many alcoholic persons are arrested for urinating in public. The exhibitionistic behaviors of most alcoholic persons occur after the person has been drinking and is intoxicated. Some alcoholic fathers periodically expose their genitals to other family members. Alcoholics who engage in genital exhibitionism manifest marked sexual problems. It is very apparent that alcohol ingestion can facilitate and synergize the exhibitionistic strivings of many alcoholic persons. The case of Paul demonstrated how exhibitionism can be associated with alcohol addiction. Organic factors may have also contributed to this patient's genital exhibitionism.

Successful treatment of the alcoholic or problem drinking exhibitionist is contingent upon the patient's abliity to achieve sobriety. The majority of alcohol-related cases of exhibitionism seen in psychotherapy or within the confines of a comprehensive alcoholic treatment center involved indecent exposure. Some of these patients (Forrest, 1982a) are in need of direct medical intervention and/or placement in a residential treatment setting.

Early in the treatment process, Antabuse maintenance can be an important therapeutic adjunct with these patients. Holistic treatment approaches should be utilized with alcoholic or problem drinking exhibitionists. When the patient has achieved sobriety and committed himself to the psychotherapy relationship, the therapist must begin to actively deal with the matters of exhibitionism and sexual pathology. It is important for the patient to realize that alcohol actively facilitates his exhibitionistic strivings. Conjoint therapy is appropriate if the patient is married. Severe marital conflicts and sexual problems in the marital relationship contribute to exhibitionistic acting-out. Family therapy is indicated in cases involving exhibitionism between the father and other family members.

The tasks of psychotherapy with alcoholic or problem drinking exhibitionists include (1) ongoing sobriety, (2) extinguishing the exhibitionistic behavior, (3) resolving the patient's internal and interpersonal conflicts, and (4) exploring and modifying the distorted and irrational self-dialogue, which reinforces the patient's alcohol addiction and exhibitionism. Deviant arousal is only one dimension of the patient's sexual functioning and overall adjustment style. As Brownell, Hayes, and Barlow (1977) indicate, most research and treatment in the realm of sexual deviation is concentrated solely on eliminating deviant arousal. These efforts are limited in scope and outcome effectiveness. The alcoholic or problem drinking exhibitionist must be treated holistically. With such patients deviant arousal is but a limited facet of the problem. The treatment approach outlined in this chapter is aimed at facilitating behavioral change and personality growth beyond the realm of deviant arousal.

BIBLIOGRAPHY

Apfelberg, B., Sugar, C., and Pfeffer, A.Z.: A psychiatric study of 250 sex offenders. *American Journal of Psychiatry, 100*:762-770, May, 1944.

Brownell, K.D., Hayes, C.S., and Barlow, D.E.: Patterns of appropriate and deviant sexual arousal: The behavioral treatment of multiple sexual deviations. *J Consult and Clin Psych, 45(6)*:1144-1155, 1977.

Cameron, N; *Personality Development and Psychopathology: A Dynamic Approach*. Boston, Houghton Mifflin Co., 1963.

Cerul, M.: *Basic Considerations in Sexual Counseling*. Workshop on Sexual Counseling for Persons with Alcoholic Problems, Pittsburgh, PA, pp. 22-23, January, 1976.

Christoffel, H.: Male genital exhibitionism. In Corand, S. and Balint, M. (Eds.): *Perversions: Psychodynamics and Therapy*. New York, Random House, 1956.

Coleman, J.C.: *Abnormal Psychology and Modern Life*, 4th Ed. Glenview, Illinois, Scott, Foresman and Co., 1972.

Evans, D.R.: An exploratory study into the treatment of exhibitionism by means of emotive imagery and aversive conditioning. *Canadian Psychologist, 8*:162, 1967.

Fenichel, O.: *The Psychoanalytic Theory of Neuroses*. New York, Norton, 1945.

Forrest, G.G.: *The Diagnosis and Treatment of Alcoholism*. Springfield, Charles C Thomas, Rev. 2nd Edition, 1978.

Forrest, G.G.: *Alcoholism, Object Relations and Narcissistic Theory*. Lecture, Psychotherapy Associates, P.C. Fifth Annual Advanced Winter Workshop, "Treatment and Rehabilitation of the Alcoholic," Colorado Springs, Colorado, January 29, 1979a.

Forrest, G.G.: *Alcoholism, Narcissism and Psychopathology*. Holmes Beach, Florida, Learning Publications, 1982a.

Kinsey, A.C., Pomeroy, W.B., and Martin, C.E.: *Sexual Behavior in the Human Male*. Philadelphia, Saunders, 1948.

Kinsey, A.C.: Pomeroy, W.B., and Martin, C.E.: *Sexual Behavior in the Human Female*. Philadelphia, Saunders, 1953.

Knauert, A.P.: *Differential Diagnosis of Alcoholism*. Lecture, Psychotherapy Associates, P.C. Fifth Annual Advanced Winter Workshop, "Treatment and Rehabilitation of the Alcoholic," Colorado Springs, Colorado, January 28, 1979.

Reik, T.: *Of Love and Lust*. New York, Jason Aronson, 1974.

Slater, M.R.: *Sex Offenders in Group Therapy*. Los Angeles, Sherborne Press, Inc., 1964.

Stoller, R.: *Perversion: The Erotic Form of Hatred*. New York, Putnam, 1975.

Todd, W.H.: Truth about sex and alcohol. *Memorial Mercury, 13(4)*:15-16, 1973.

Vraa, C.W.: *The Treatment of Human Sexual Dysfunctions*. Lecture, Psychotherapy Associates, P.C. Fourth Annual Advanced Winter Workshop, "Treatment and Rehabilitation of the Alcoholic," Colorado Springs, Colorado, January 29, 1978.

Vraa, C.W.: *Sex Therapy Training*. Lecture, Psychotherapy Associates, P.C. Eighth Annual Advanced Winter Workshop, "Treatment and Rehabilitation of the Alcoholic," Colorado Springs, Colorado, February 2, 1982.

Wegscheider, S.: *Family Dynamics and Family Therapy in the Treatment of Alcoholism*. Lecture, Psychotherapy Associates, P.C. Seventh Annual Advanced Winter Workshop, "Treatment and Rehabilitation of the Alcoholic," Colorado Springs, Colorado, February 5, 1981.

Witzig, J.S.: The group treatment of male exhibitionists. *Amer J Psychiat*, p. 125, 1968.

Chapter 11
OTHER DEVIATIONS
Voyeurism, Fetishism, and Transvestism

IN this chapter the relationships between alcoholism, alcohol abuse, and the more rare forms of sexual deviation are considered. Voyeurism, fetishism, and transvestism are sexual deviations that involve a very small segment of the general population. Even in clinical practice it is only very rarely that the psychotherapist will encounter patients manifesting these sexual perversions. These deviations have long been reported in the clinical literature (Fenichel, 1945). Yet, there is presently very little clinical and research data available relative to the aetiology, diagnosis, and treatment of voyeurism, fetishism, and transvestism. Currently, there is no clinical or research data available in order to examine the various relationships between each of these sexual deviations and alcoholism and alcohol abuse.

The first section of this chapter is limited to an exploration of voyeurism. The second section of the chapter examines fetishism. An examination and discussion of transvestism follows. These sexual deviations are then discussed in relationship to alcoholism and alcohol abuse. Finally, a clinical case study is presented in order to elucidate the important clinical relationships between alcoholism and multiple perversion. Treatment issues and strategies are also discussed in this chapter.

VOYEURISM

Voyeurism is a sexual deviation that involves the achievement of sexual stimulation and pleasure through looking or peeping. The voyeur experiences sexual gratification through looking at the sexual organs, naked bodies, or sexual activities of others. Coleman (1972) states "voyeurism, scotophilia, and inspectionalism are synonymous terms referring to the achievement of sexual pleasure through clandestine peeping." Voyeurs obtain most, if not all, of their sexual gratification through looking and peeping. Voyeurism occurs as a sexual offense primarily among young males (Coleman, 1972). Voyeurs are commonly referred to as "peeping Toms." Typically, the male voyeur looks in women's windows in order to view their nude bodies or observe coitus and other forms of sexual interaction.

Voyeurism is a compulsion. Most voyeurs engage in this form of sexually deviant behavior over and over again. The voyeur feels compelled or driven to "peep." Voyeuristic behavior is accompanied by generalized excitement, anxiety, sexual arousal, and very often masturbation. These individuals frequently masturbate to orgasm while watching other persons undress or engage in sexual intercourse. Male voyeurs are almost always heterosexual in regard to their object.

Voyeurism is rather common on the college campus (Cameron, 1963). Indeed, voyeuristic behavior exists on a continuum. As defined and discussed thus far, voyeurism is a clear-cut sexual deviation. However, the "girl watching," or "boy watching" or "people watching" behaviors, which all people engage in from time to time, are also voyeuristic. A variety of social and cultural factors reinforce voyeuristic forms of behavior, which are deemed socially acceptable and appropriate. Thus, women's short dresses, bikini bathing suits, and the "braless look" are all socially related realities that foster and reinforce voyeuristic behaviors. People watching is a voyeuristic American pastime. The psychotherapy profession involves a voyeuristic component. Spectator sports also include a voyeuristic dimension. Although a rather wide range of socially acceptable behaviors and even professions involve voyeuristic components, such behaviors and professions are not voyeuristic in the sense of looking and peeping at the genitals or sexual activities of other persons. Obviously, there are a number of very significant and relatively clear-cut differences between voyeurism and voyeuristic behavior.

There are a number of general and speculative ideas about the causes or origins of voyeurism. A systematic and comprehensive theory of the aetiology of voyeurism remains to be developed. Fenichel (1945) states "in the unconscious of voyeurs, the same tendencies are found as in exhibitionists." Cameron (1963) also indicates that the psychodynamics of voyeurism are similar to those of exhibitionism. Voyeurism is an infantile or childhood sexual fixation. Voyeurs (Fenichel, 1945) are fixated on "experiences that aroused their castration anxiety, either primal scenes or the sight of adult genitals. The patient attempts to deny justification of his fright by repeating the frightening scenes with certain alterations. This tendency may be condensed with a tendency to repeat a traumatic scene for the purpose of achieving a belated mastery."

It is important to realize that sexual looking is a very appropriate and "normal" aspect of adult sexuality. Sexual looking, observing, and curiosity are also very normal ingredients in childhood sexuality. Young children are interested in observing and looking at their parents' genitals. These childhood behaviors are not deviant and, in fact, may be very important factors in the processes of establishing a physical sense of self, a gender identity, and a psychological sense of self-hood and identity. Children also may observe their parents during coitus or other sexual activities. These experiences may further reinforce sexual curiosity, looking, and even stimulation. During adulthood, looking is a natural precursor to sexual intimacy. Viewing the nude body of an attractive and well-built woman is a sexually arousing and stimulating experience for most men. By the same token, many women are sexually aroused by the sight of an attractive and well-built man. Again, it is apparent that voyeuristic behaviors can be socially acceptable and appropriate.

Faulty learning is central to the aetiology of voyeurism. Conditioning, reinforcement, and overlearning factors also contribute to the aetiology and maintenance of voyeuristic behaviors. When the sexually inhibited and shy adolescent or adult engages in peeping behavior, he satisfies his sexual needs, overcomes his childhood curiosity associated with adult sexuality, and avoids the anxiety and threat that is involved in asking a female for a date or attempting to seduce her. Voyeurism is a sexual deviation. Voyeurism is also a regressive, infantile sexual deviation. Yet, the voyeur does experience sexual excitement, stimulation, and a wide variety of sources of secondary gain through engaging in this deviant form of sexual behavior. Voyeuristic behavior is learned, practiced, and overlearned. The voyeur also tends to feel powerful and sexually nonthreatened when peeping.

The voyeur is frequently detected by the police or the person(s) he has been watching. The excitement, suspense, and danger associated with peeping may also lead to sexual stimulation and thus pathologically reinforce the voyeuristic pattern of behavior. Voyeurs are often caught and assaulted by their subjects (Coleman, 1972). Voyeurs are rarely dangerous psychopaths or criminals. However, voyeurism does include an element of sadism. As Fenichel (1945) points out, voyeuristic women enjoy witnessing catastrophes, accidents, operations, hospital scenes, war scenes, and so forth. Sadistic castration dynamics are associated with voyeurism. Malicious intrusion is another component of voyeurism.

Voyeurs may also fantasize that their subject or subjects will ask them to join in their sexual activities. As a voyeur peeps and experiences sexual arousal, he may also actively fantasize about joining the sexual activities of the person or persons he is watching. Voyeurs tend to be sexually inadequate and inhibited. Some are impotent. Feelings of low self-esteem, inadequacy, and inferiority are basic to the personality makeup of many voyeurs. Older women are sometimes involved in peeping (Coleman, 1972). Voyeurs are also sometimes married. Invariably, the married voyeur is involved in a sexually conflicted and relationship conflicted marriage. In some of these cases, frequency of peeping can be associated with the occurence of acute, episodic marital and sexual conflicts.

It is apparent that voyeurism is caused by a number of familial, psychological, conditioning, and social factors. Voyeurism is an uncommon form of sexual deviation. Yet, it is paradoxically true that most people are somewhat voyeuristic (Freud, 1962).

FETISHISM

Fetishism is a term that originally referred to the use of a special inanimate object in the religious practices of primitive societies. In the religious practices of these primitive societies the magical object, or fetish, was ascribed with power, comfort, or extreme value (Cameron, 1963). Fetishism refers to a rather specific form of sexual deviation in modern society. As a sexual deviation, fetishism refers to the use of an inanimate object or body part for sexual stimulation and sexual gratification instead of using a sex partner.

A wide range of sexually arousing objects may be used by the fetishist. Thus, fetishistic objects include shoes, hair, underclothing, perfume, and breasts. Any object that becomes sexually arousing can become a fetish. These objects are almost always associated with the opposite sex in a sexually stimulating and exciting manner. The fetishist may experience sexual arousal and gratification by touching or rubbing the object. Smelling, licking, or kissing the object may also result in sexual excitation and/or orgasm. The fetishist may need such an inanimate object to be present in order to have sexual intercourse.

According to Cameron (1963) fetishists are almost always men and their "commonest fetish is a woman's shoe." The reasons for this are "(a) as the object last seen in the frustrated sex curiosity of small children, an interpretation that certainly does not apply to modern women as it might have in the nineteenth century; (b) as a mere exaggeration of the lover's attachment to something worn by his beloved; (c) as the expression of a masochistic wish to be trod upon; and (d) as a female symbol that also enclosed the foot as a masculine symbol" (Cameron, 1963). Female fetishists are very rare (Fenichel, 1945). Freud (1962) indicated that most of the typical fetishes are penis symbols. Some fetishists are essentially asexual. In these cases, the fetishist derives his sexual gratification explicitly from the inanimate object or fetish. Most fetishists are heterosexual but these individuals very often must have the fetish present in order to have coitus and/or reach orgasm.

Coleman (1972) points out that the fetishist may commit assault or theft in order to obtain the fetish. In recent years (Coleman, 1972; Knauert, 1981) fetishists most typically steal women's undergarments. Women's panties, brassieres, slips, and hose are perhaps the most common objects used by modern fetishists. A typical pattern of fetishism involves stealing a woman's panties from a clothesline, going immediately to a secluded environment such as a bedroom or bathroom, and then masturbating to orgasm. Masturbation is commonly a part of the fetishistic behavioral pattern. Increasing sexual excitement through fetishistic activities and masturbating are not sexual deviations. However, when sexual arousal and gratification are singularly derived from a fetish and the fetish is obtained through antisocial behavior, a pattern of deviant sexual arousal and responding is manifest. This pattern of sexual deviation is fetishism. Fetishism also involves a good deal of obsessive-compulsive ideation and behavior. The fetishist engages in a great deal of ritualized behavior. The same object or objects tend to be used for sexual arousal and gratification.

The aetiology of fetishism remains obscure. It is important to point out that many, if not all, people experience some degree of sexual arousal and stimulation by intimate articles of clothing, perfumes and other inanimate objects. Women's lingerie, perfumes, and even odors associated with the opposite sex can be somewhat sexually stimulating to most people. Apparently less sexualized fetishes involve the attachments of young children to blankets, dolls, and other objects. Adults in virtually all cultures manifest "normal" fetishes that involve collecting charms, amulets, and tokens.

Fenichel (1945) indicated that "persons whose childhood history has enabled them to make an exceptionally intense use of the defense mechanism of denial are predisposed for the development of fetishism." Castration fears have also been linked (Fenichel, 1945) to fetishism. A rather widely accepted clinical hypothesis regarding the origin of fetishism (Cameron, 1963) suggests that the fetish is a substitute for a sex partner. The object, which is substituted for a sex partner, provides sexual arousal and gratification. Yet, the fetish is "safe." As a substitute for a sex partner the fetish makes no human demands upon the fetishist and it is not in itself dangerous. The fetish has no emotions. It does not communicate. It can always be used for sexual purposes and security. It has also been theorized (Cameron, 1963) that fetishism is a manifestation of a repressed compulsion, which originated during childhood.

The sadistic and aggressive components of fetishism are quite apparent in the behavior of braid cutters. This fetishism involves cutting off the braids of girls and women in public places. The fetishist sadistically and aggressively "takes a part of the woman's body." More precisely, the fetishist attempts to take away the woman's feminity by cutting off her braids (hair). Thus, braid cutting can be viewed as a symbolic castration.

Faulty learning and conditioning are salient factors in the aetiology and maintenance of fetishism. Rachman (1966) has demonstrated that it is possible to create a mild fetish under laboratory conditions. Conditioning and learning experiences that pair an inanimate object, such as a perfume, with intense sexual stimulation and gratification may eventually result in the development of fetishism. For example, if a man's sexual partner wore a specific perfume (or "sexy" undergarment) on occasions of coitus or at the time of other intense sexual experiences, the man might eventually experience sexual arousal and even orgasm upon smelling his partner's perfume. Coleman (1972) states "the first prerequisite in fetishism seems to be a conditioning experience. In some instances this original conditioning may be quite accidental, as when sexual arousal and orgasm—which are reflexive responses —are elicited by a strong emotional experience involving some particular object or part of the body." Learning and conditioning experiences of this variety are faulty. The fetishist also persists in his inappropriate behaviors as a result of faulty learning, conditioning, reinforcement, and secondary gain factors.

Fetishistic patterns of sexual deviation are usually indicative of more global personality warp and psychopathology. The fetishist tends to be sexually inadequate, self-doubting, and severely conflicted in heterosexual relationships. Fetishism is a defense against intimacy. Fetishism is also a defense against feelings of sexual and interpersonal inadequacy, inferiority, and hostile or sadistic feelings toward women.

TRANSVESTISM

Transvestism literally means cross-dressing. Transvestism involves the "achievement of sexual excitation by dressing as a member of the opposite sex" (Coleman, 1972). This variety of sexuality is uncommon and usually involves males (Cameron, 1963). The male transvestite may feel like a man when he is dressed as a man. However, when he is dressed in women's clothing he may feel like a woman and behave like a woman. The male transvestite experiences sexual arousal and gratification by wearing women's clothing. According to Cameron (1963) a minority of male transvestites "are also fetishists who can achieve full potency only while wearing some item of women's clothing."

Coleman (1972) indicates that four types of transvestites have been delineated: "(1) the male homosexual who adopts feminine attire, including cosmetics and other feminine accoutrements, as an adjunct to his homosexual activities and is often referred to as a 'drag queen'; (2) the heterosexual male who finds enjoyment and sexual excitation in the wearing of women's attire; (3) the female who is not homosexual but enjoys dressing as a man; and (4) the individual who has feelings of being a male trapped in a female body (or vice versa), and who feels that the expected sex role is inappropriate for him (or her)." The final category of transvestism merges with transsexualism.

Not much is known about transvestism. Buckner (1970) indicates that nearly two-thirds of transvestites are married. Most transvestites have children. The transvestite does not ordinarily experience difficulties with the law. A very common pattern of transvestism involves dressing in women's clothes at home and in secret. Commonly, only the transvestite and his wife are aware of the cross-dressing. Clinicians seem to disagree considerably with regard to the issues of transvestism and homosexuality. Stekel (1952) and Allen (1961) indicate that transvestism is always a manifestation of homosexuality. Brown (1961) and Buckner (1970) indicate that transvestites are almost always exclusively heterosexual. These clinicians agree that the transvestite is pathologically narcissistic.

Extensive research (Bentler and Prince, 1969; 1970; Bentler, Shearman, and Prince, 1970) dealing with the personality makeup of male transvestites suggests that these individuals are not more prone to neurotic or psychotic personality patterns than control subjects. Male transvestites do tend to be more controlled in impulse expression, less interpersonally involved, more dependent, and more inhibited in interpersonal relationships than nontransvestite control subjects.

Fenichel (1945) asserted that the male transvestite assumes two attitudes simultaneously: (1) he replaces his love for his mother by an identification with her, and (2) he refuses to acknowledge that a woman has no penis. Furthermore, it was Fenichel's (1945) position that "the fundamental trend of transvestism is the same as that found in homosexuality and fetishism: the repudiation of the idea that there is a danger of castration. The transvestite act has two unconscious meanings: (a) as an object-erotic and fetishistic one: the person cohabits not with a woman but with her clothes, the clothes representing, symbolically, her penis, (b) a narcissistic one: the transvestite himself represents the phallic woman under whose clothes a penis is hidden." Fenichel (1945) also pointed out that the real possession of a penis is a fundamental difference between male and female transvestites. This reality accounts for the "pretending" nature of female transvestism.

A few transvestites experience brief compulsive episodes of cross-dressing. During these episodes the male transvestite has a driving compulsion to wear women's clothing. The individual is apparently "normal" in sexual orientation and adjustment between these episodes. Again, transvestism is an obsessive-compulsive disorder. Cameron (1963) indicates that some transvestites are so narcissistic that they are not interested in having sex with a partner. These individuals are similar to "narcissistic, frigid, asexual women; and, in fact, some of them seem to have identified with such women" (Cameron, 1963).

The aetiology of transvestism appears to be quite similar to the other sexual deviations discussed in this section of the text. The exact origin of transvestism is unknown. Parental seduction and parental pathology are sometimes key factors in the aetiology of transvestism. A rather simplistic and yet clinically validated theory of transvestism involves the conditioning and reinforcement of childhood cross-dressing behaviors. Parents may consciously or unconsciously reward a male child for dressing as a girl. Parents who think it is "cute" for their male child to dress in girls' clothing pathologically reinforce transvestite behavior patterns. Attention, praise, laughter, and other sources of reward may be associated with the child's cross-dressing. When one or both parents desire a child of the opposite sex, transvestism may be pathologically reinforced as the parents dress the child in opposite-sexed clothes. Such parents may give the child an opposite-sexed name. If one child in the family system is the acknowledged "favorite," another child in the family may attempt to dress like and be like the favorite child. This pattern can obviously involve opposite-sexed children and thus reinforce cross-dressing and transvestism. Several case studies have been presented in the clinical literature (Cameron, 1963; Coleman, 1972; Stoller, 1975) that support the validity of a social learning theory of transvestism.

Psychodynamic and psychoanalytic theories of transvestism indicated that homosexuality, castration fears, and unresolved oedipal conflicts are central ingredients in the aetiology of this deviation. These issues were touched upon earlier. Cameron (1963) states that the "mothers of some transvestite boys in therapy express frank hatred of men." It is important to realize that either parent can play an important role in the family process of reinforcing transvestism. If the mother rejects being a woman and her own femininity, she may consciously or unconsciously reinforce the development of masculine behaviors in her daughter. Fathers who either dislike women in general or desire a son may reinforce masculine male behavior in their daughter. These dynamic and familial issues are also steeped in learning theory.

Transvestism seems to be multivariantly determined. The various theoretical explanations of this variety of sexual deviation are incomplete. Many parents reinforce cross-sexed patterns of behavior in their children. Yet, very few children become transvestites. It is obvious that considerably more research needs to be done in the areas of human sexual deviation.

ALCOHOLISM, VOYEURISM, FETISHISM, AND TRANSVESTISM

At present there are no research or clinical data available that examine the roles of alcoholism and/or alcohol abuse in voyeurism, fetishism, or transvestism. During eleven years of clinical practice with alcoholic and problem drinking patients, I have encountered only six patients that would be diagnosed as manifesting one of these three patterns of sexual deviation. These six patients were all males. It is significant that these six patients were among nearly 2,000 alcoholics and problem drinkers that I have treated during the past eleven years. Two alcoholics and one problem drinker were also voyeurs, one alcoholic was also a fetishist, and two problem drinkers were also transvestites. Many alcoholics and problem drinkers evidence voyeuristic trends. In contrast to this clinical observation, it is very rare to encounter alcoholics and problem drinkers who manifest fetishism or transvestism trends.

The incidence of voyeurism, fetishism, and transvestism among alcoholic and problem drinking persons needs to be adequately investigated. It seems that these deviations are very rarely relevant to the diagnosis and treatment of alcoholic persons. However, I would hypothesize that many people who enter therapy as a result of one of these sexual deviations are alcohol abusers or problem drinkers. Thus, research is needed in the realm of assessing the drinking behaviors of individuals who enter therapy as a result of voyeurism, fetishism, and transvestism. Identity and role confusion (Forrest, 1982a) are precursors to alcoholism and alcohol abuse. Identity and role confusion are basic to each of the sexual deviations considered in this chapter. The following case study illustrates polysexual deviation in a problem drinker.

CASE 16. Dick C., a married twenty-six-year-old Army sergeant, decided to enter therapy as a result of marital problems. The patient had been married for five years and was the father of two children. The patient's wife was threatening to leave him at the point of treatment engagement.

During the first therapy session, Dick indicated that he "sometimes drank too much." He also stated that he had "a lot of sex problems." The patient's wife had discovered him peeping in the bathroom window at a fourteen-year-old girl who lived next door. This incident had occurred two weeks before the patient was first seen in psychotherapy. The patient's wife was very angry about this incident. She had also threatened to leave the patient many times as a result of his drinking behavior.

The patient had grown up in a small rural community in North Carolina. His father, whom the patient described as an alcoholic, committed suicide when the patient was eight years old. The patient's mother turned the patient and his younger brother over to her parents for caretaking shortly after the father's suicide, and she then moved to another city. Every "two or three years" the patient's mother would return for a short visit. During grade school and high school the patient experienced many interpersonal difficulties. His academic performance was poor throughout school. The patient had a severe stuttering problem in childhood and adolescence. As a child, he was fascinated by fire and actually burned down a small garage at age eleven. The patient was enuretic until age nineteen. At age fourteen, Dick began to window peep. The patient indicated that he masturbated "three or four" times each day as an adolescent. He also engaged in intermittent group masturbation (circle jerks) and homosexual activities at that time.

After graduating from high school the patient joined the Army. A few months after entering the Army, Dick was sent to Germany. While overseas he became involved in a homosexual relationship with a first sergeant. Homosexual activities between the patient and the sergeant took place on a regular basis for nearly ten months. Alcohol and intoxication were basic ingredients in the homosexual interactions between Dick and the first sergeant. The patient feared that his enuretic problem would be "discovered by the Army." After completing a two year tour of duty in Germany, the patient was assigned to an Army base located in the southeastern part of the United States. A few weeks after arriving at this base, the patient met his wife. She had been married previously and had one child. The couple was married following a two month courtship. Mrs. C. was Turkish. A few months after being married, Dick completed his tour of active duty. The couple then returned to North Carolina and the patient obtained a job in a small town as a policeman. Eight months after taking this position, the patient was released from police duty as a result of an exhibitionistic episode. While on duty (and in police uniform), the patient exposed his genitals to a woman. A few months after this incident, Dick again joined the Army.

It was only three months after the patient joined the Army for the second time that he entered therapy. In the early therapy sessions the patient indicated that he had been window peeping on his neighbor several nights each week. The patient indicated that he also spent a good deal of time driving around the post commissary and PX "shooting beaver." By this (shooting beaver) the patient meant that he spent a good deal of time driving around looking at women and attempting to look under their skirts in order to view their genitals. He often sat in his car in parking lots on the base and used binoculars for this purpose. The patient stated that he still masturbated to orgasm nearly every day. On some days he masturbated several times. At this time Mr. and Mrs. C. engaged in sexual intercourse and other sexual activities "several" times each week. It was not uncommon for the couple to engage in coitus three or four times in one night. On occasion the patient would demand that his wife perform fellatio on him while he wore her black crotchless undergarments. In spite of the couple's active sex life, Dick was rarely able to reach orgasm with his wife. They "tried everything" in order to help Dick reach orgasm.

The patient was drinking "several" beers each night when therapy began. He indicated that every "two or three weeks" he would "throw a good one." On these occasions, Dick would drink beer all weekend. The patient had experienced several alcoholic blackouts during his binge drinking episodes. He also raped, sexually abused, and verbally abused his wife when intoxicated. Feelings of guilt, remorse, and depression were associated with the patient's peeping behaviors and marital problems. Indeed, the patient was severely conflicted in his sexual adjustment.

This patient was seen in individual psychotherapy on nine occasions over a period of some three months. He did reduce his level of alcohol ingestion while in therapy. The patient struggled to control his window peeping and other voyeuristic behaviors but was generally unsuccessful in these efforts. The marital relationship remained severely conflicted and dysfunctional. Eventually, the patient requested a military transfer to Korea, and this was granted. During the final therapy session Dick indicated that he needed to "get away from all my problems" and that going to Korea was a "solution" for his difficulties. Unfortunately, no follow-up data is available on this patient.

This case study involved a patient with many sexual conflicts. The patient was also an alcohol abuser and in all probability incipiently alcoholic. Voyeurism, exhibitionism, sexual dysfunction, a possible masturbation fixation, and rape were central to the overall sexual pathology of the patient. The voyeuristic and exhibitionistic behaviors of the patient are rather classic. Drinking and intoxication were sometimes associated with the patient's voyeuristic and exhibitionistic behaviors. Marital rape and assault were virtually always linked to intoxication. The patient did not persist in psychotherapy. Intensive long-term psychotherapy was indicated in this case. Conjoint therapy was also indicated and quite possibly individual therapy for the patient's wife.

Many alcoholic and problem drinking patients manifest less "classic" forms of voyeurism, fetishism, and transvestism. For example, one forty-five-year-old chronic alcoholic patient who was seen in conjoint therapy had a history of picking up other men in bars and then bringing them home to have sexual relations with his wife. The patient would experience intense sexual arousal while watching other men engage in coitus and other sexual behaviors with his wife. This patient also watched hard-core pornographic movies four or five nights each week. Voyeurism constituted a very important part of the sexual adjustment style of this patient.

Basic Treatment Strategies

Whenever alcoholism or problem drinking are associated with deviant sexual behavior, an initial goal of therapy is that of modifying or extinguishing the patient's drinking behavior. A primary goal of treatment is to help the alcoholic or problem drinker stop drinking or possibly learn how to control (Armor, Polish, and Stambul, 1978) his or her pattern of pathological drinking. Alcoholism and alcohol abuse often reinforce or potentiate deviant sexual behaviors. A wealth of psychotherapeutic strategies were examined and outlined throughout this book that can be utilized effectively by the clinician to help the patient establish a commitment to sobriety and the change process. Individual psychotherapy, group therapy, sex therapy, conjoint therapy, residential and medical treatment, Alcoholics Anonymous and the A.A. community, Antabuse maintenance, and family therapy are all strategies of treatment that work well with alcohol-abusing persons. As indicated in earlier chapters, addicted patients respond well to holistic health care interventions. Nutritional programs, exercise programs, spiritual programs, and self-help groups contribute greatly to the recovery of many alcoholic and problem drinking patients.

A major ongoing focus of the psychotherapeutic process is the patient's deviant sexual behavior, once the alcoholic or alcohol abusing patient who manifests one of the sexual deviations discussed in this chapter has committed himself to sobriety, therapy, and the recovery process. Most of these patients are uncomfortable talking about their sexual conflicts. They tend to feel guilty, depressed, embarrassed, and anxious about their sexually deviant behavior. These individuals feel like "double deviants." They must come to grips with the reality of their alcohol dependence or abuse. Alcoholics and problem drinkers continue to be perceived as deviants in our culture, and in order to recover they must overcome the stigma associated with being identified and labeled alcoholic. Sexual deviants are also stigmatized in our culture.

The therapist can employ a number of basic counseling techniques (Sena, 1980a; 1980b) in order to help the sexually deviant alcoholic or problem drinker begin to face the reality of his addiction and sexual deviation. Support, self-disclosure, empathy, warmth, confrontation, and reflection are but a few of the tools that the counselor can use for the purpose of helping the patient begin to realize his various problems. These patients deny their alcoholism and sexual deviation. Therefore, a basic goal in therapy with these individuals is the resolution of their massive systems of denial and avoidance (Forrest, 1978; 1982a) surrounding the issues of alcohol dependence and sexual pathology. In a great number of these cases the patient's alcoholism or alcohol abuse contributes directly to his exhibitionism, voyeurism, fetishism, transvestism, or other deviant sexual behaviors. The therapist must point out this reality to the patient over and over again. The therapist and patient must also explore the various issues that are associated with the patient's drinking and sexually deviant behavior. Why must the patient be intoxicated before he is able to dress in women's underclothing? Why is alcohol always associated with the patient's window peeping behaviors? When did these pathological patterns of behavior originate? How much does the patient drink before engaging in sexually deviant behavior? Can he remember these episodes? When patients are motivated to terminate their alcoholic and sexually deviant behaviors, these rather aversive questions and probing techniques force the patient to deal with the various pathological realities associated with his drinking and sexual behavior. Furthermore, as the patient comes to more fully understand the role of alcohol abuse in his pattern of sexual deviation, he will be more motivated to remain sober. Thus, with long-term sobriety and a commitment to therapy the patient is less prone to engage in deviant sexual acting-out.

It is very important for the therapist or counselor who works with alcohol-abusing sexually deviant patients to develop a working therapeutic alliance with the patient. Typically, these individuals are reluctant to talk about their sexual and alcohol problems. They often attempt to manipulate the therapist. Many of these patients attempt to flee from treatment. The therapist must remember that it takes time and considerable work to develop a trusting, open, and productive therapeutic relationship. Premature, high-impact confrontations upon the part of the therapist (Forrest, 1982) consistently result in patient avoidance of therapy.

Alcoholic and alcohol-abusing sexually deviant patients are difficult to treat. They must receive treatment for both alcohol dependency and sexual deviation. Rather long-term relationship therapy that encompasses the use of behavioral treatment strategies seems to represent the most effective overall approach to therapy with this patient population. Many alcoholic and alcohol-abusing sexually deviant patients are married; many have families. In these cases, the spouse and children are almost always emotionally and sexually conflicted. Therefore, conjoint and family therapy interventions are often essential to the successful treatment of these patients. The wife of the patient may contribute significantly to his deviant sexual behavior and the pathological drinking behavior. Many of these women are frigid, sexually conflicted, and emotionally disturbed; some are alcoholic; some are also sexually deviant.

It is reported (Coleman, 1972) that the overall treatment outcome response for voyeurs is quite favorable. Likewise, fetishists and transvestites can be treated successfully. Aversive conditioning and other relatively specific methods of behavior therapy appear to be very effective in the treatment of fetishism (Kushner, 1965; Marks and Gelder, 1967; Bandura, 1969). These methods of treatment usually involve pairing an electric shock or other aversive stimulus with the deviant sexual behavior. For example, Kushner (1965) describes the treatment of a male fetishist who would steal women's panties and masturbate to orgasm while wearing them. This patient received a series of electric shocks in association with the women's panties. This conditioning procedure extinguished the patient's fetish. The patient was then treated with a desensitization program. This program involved reducing the patient's anxieties and fears associated with dating and heterosexual relationships.

This same essential model of aversion therapy has been used successfully in the treatment of transvestism. In cases of transvestism the patient's cross-dressing behavior (dressing in women's clothing) is paired with an electric shock or other aversive stimulus. Covert desensitization (Elkins, 1973), imagery training, direct verbal suggestion, and hypnosis can also be used as aversive stimuli.

Patients who manifest voyeurism, fetishism, or transvestism require social skills training, assertion training, and self-image modification training. Treatment interventions that simply attempt to modify or extinguish deviant patterns of arousal are doomed to failure. It is not enough to extinguish the deviant sexual behavior. As Barlow and Wincze (1980) point out, three components of sexually deviant behavior must be modified: "(1) sexual arousal behavior, (2) social skills and emotional factors associated with sexual interactions, and (3) gender-role deviations." In the absence of more holistically designed strategies of treatment with sexually deviant individuals, it is realistic to expect poor outcomes and high rates of recidivism. Indeed, there is little evidence (Walker, 1978) that psychodynamic or behavioral treatments radically change the sexual behavior of chronic sex offenders.

Alcoholic and problem drinking sexual deviants are also in need of social skills training, sex therapy, assertion training, relaxation therapy, and self-image modification training. Sexual conflicts and sexual deviation contribute greatly to problems of alcohol abuse and alcoholism. As already stated, alcoholism and alcohol abuse often result in deviant sexual responding. Therapists and counselors must seek to enhance the global adjustment styles of persons who manifest alcohol and sexual problems (Forrest, 1980b; Knauert, 1981). It is only logical to expect the alcoholic to continue his pattern of deviant sexual acting-out if he continues to drink alcoholically. Feelings of inadequacy, low self-esteem, marital conflicts, and sexual dysfunction can contribute to sexual deviation and alcohol abuse. Sexual dysfunction can contribute to sexual deviation. Therefore, treatment interventions need to be aimed at facilitating patient change and growth in all of these areas.

In actuality, very little is known about the treatment of voyeurs, transvestites, and fetishists who manifest alcohol addiction or problem drinking. A great deal of clinical research is needed in the various areas of alcoholism, alcohol abuse, and sexual deviation.

Summary

The initial section of this chapter is devoted to a consideration of voyeurism. Voyeurism is defined as a sexual deviation that involves the achievement of sexual arousal and gratification through looking or peeping. Voyeurs or "peeping Toms" are usually young males. Voyeurism is a compulsion. The voyeur frequently masturbates to orgasm while watching another person(s) undress or engage in sexual relations. Most, if not all, people are somewhat voyeuristic. A diversity of social and cultural factors actually reinforces voyeuristic behavior.

Very little is known about the origins of voyeurism. Aetiological explanations of voyeurism tend to be psychoanalytic or behavioral. The dynamics of voyeurism and exhibitionism are similar (Fenichel, 1945; Cameron, 1963). Looking is a normal ingredient in childhood and adult sexuality. Voyeurism may represent an adult extension of witnessing parental coitus (primal scene) or parental sexual relations. Voyeurs sometimes fantasize that their subjects will ask them to join in their sexual activities. Faulty learning and conditioning factors contribute to the development of voyeuristic behavior. When the sexually inhibited and shy adolescent or adult engages in peeping behavior he satisfies his sexual needs, overcomes his childhood curiosity associated with adult sexuality, and avoids the threat and anxiety that is involved in asking a female for a date or attempting seduction. Voyeurs are often caught by their subjects and/or the police. The voyeur tends to feel sexually inadequate, feel inferior, and is plagued with feelings of low self-esteem.

Section two of this chapter includes a discussion of fetishism. Fetishism is a term that originally referred to the use of special inanimate objects in the religious practices of primitive societies. Fetishism refers to a specific sexual deviation in modern society. As a sexual deviation, fetishism refers to the use of an inanimate object or body part for sexual stimulation and sexual gratification rather than using a sexual partner.

The fetishist may use a wide range of objects for sexual stimulation and gratification. Thus, fetishistic objects include shoes, hair, underclothing, perfume, and breasts. The fetishist experiences sexual arousal and possibly orgasm by touching, smelling, or rubbing the fetish. Fetishists are almost always men. Most fetishists are heterosexual. The fetishist very often steals women's underclothing. A rather typical pattern of fetishism involves stealing a woman's panties from a clothesline, going immediately to a secluded environment, such as a bedroom or bathroom, and then masturbating to orgasm.

The precise origins of fetishism remain unknown. Most people experience some degree of sexual arousal by inanimate articles of clothing, perfumes, and other objects. The fetish is a substitute for a sex partner. Fenichel (1945) associated fetishism with castration fears. A number of learning and conditioning factors are central to the development of fetishism. The fetishist tends to feel sexually inadequate, self-doubting, and severely conflicted in heterosexual relationships.

Section three of this chapter includes a clinical discussion of transvestism. Transvestism literally means cross-dressing. The transvestite experiences sexual arousal and gratification by dressing as a member of the opposite sex. This disorder is quite rare and usually involves men. Four types of transvestites are discussed in this section. Buckner (1970) indicates that nearly two-thirds of transvestites are married and have children. A very common pattern of transvestism involves cross-dressing at home and in secret. Clinicians seem to disagree on the relationships between transvestism and homosexuality. Psychological research (Bentler and Prince, 1970) suggests that male transvestites are not severely disturbed.

Very little is known about the aetiology of transvestism. Parental seduction and parental pathology is sometimes related to the onset of transvestism. Parents may consciously or unconsciously reinforce cross-dressing behavior on the part of a particular child. The parents may have wanted a son instead of a daughter. They then teach the daughter to dress like a son. Identity conflicts upon the part of either or both parents may contribute to the aetiology of transvestism. A number of other psychoanalytic and learning theory-oriented explanations of transvestism are discussed in this section.

There is a total dearth of clinical and research data available on the relationships between alcoholism and alcohol abuse and voyeurism, fetishism, and transvestism. A small percent of the patients treated within the confines of comprehensive alcoholic treatment settings manifest one or more of these sexual deviations. The case of Dick C. involved incipient alcoholism, voyeurism, exhibitionism, rape, sexual dysfunction, and a masturbation fixation. Alcohol addiction is sometimes associated with sexual deviation and even polyperversion.

A variety of treatment techniques for working with sexually deviant alcoholics and problem drinkers are discussed in the final section of this chapter. These patients must be sober and committed to alcoholism recovery prior to being involved in treatment for their sexual deviation. The alcoholic tends to deny or avoid the reality of his sexually deviant behavior. Alcoholics feel guilty, depressed, embarrassed, and anxious about their sexual problems. The therapist must help the patient overcome these obstacles for therapy and behavioral change to occur. It is *doubly* difficult to treat the alcohol abusing patient who also manifests a sexual deviation.

These patients are in need of intensive relationship therapy, which also incorporates the use of specific behavioral strategies of treatment. The patient's wife may actively contribute to the pattern of alcohol abuse and sexual deviation. Marital or conjoint therapy, family therapy, aversive training, sex therapy, social skills training, Antabuse therapy, assertion training, self-image modification training, and self-help programs are all treatment modalities that can be used with the sexually deviant alcoholic or problem drinker.

Very little is known about the various relationships between alcoholism and alcohol abuse and sexual deviation. Even less is known about the treatment of sexually deviant alcoholics and problem drinkers. This chapter is rather cursory in both of these respects. Alcohol abuse may well be associated with other forms of sexually deviant behavior. Transsexualism, bestiality, necrophilia, and the other more bizarre forms of sexual deviations are not discussed in this chapter. It may well be that a very, very small percent of alcoholic and/or problem drinking individuals perceive themselves as opposite-sexed and desire a sex change operation. A very, very small percentage of alcoholics and problem drinkers may engage in sexual relations with animals or corpses. These clinical issues are yet to be investigated.

BIBLIOGRAPHY

Allen, C.: Sexual perversions. In Ellis, A., and Abarbanel, A. (Eds.): *The Encyclopedia of Sexual Behavior*. New York, Hawthorn Books, 1961.

Armor, D.J., Polish, J.M., and Stambul, H.B.: *Alcoholism and Treatment*. New York, John Wiley and Sons, 1978.

Bandura, A.: *Principles of Behavior Modification*. New York, Holt, Reinhart and Winston, 1969.

Barlow, D.H., and Wincze, J.P.: Treatment of sexual dysfunctions. In Leiblum, S. and Pervin L. (Eds.): *Principles and Practices of Sex Therapy*. New York, The Guilford Press, 1980.

Bentler, P.M., and Prince, C.: Personality characteristics of male transvestites. *J of Abnormal Psychology, 74(2)*:140-143, 1969.

Bentler, P.M., Shearman, R.W., and Prince, C.: Personality change of transvestites. *J of Clin Psy, 126(3)*:287-291, 1970.

Brown, D.G.: Transvestism and sex-role inversion. In Ellis, A., and Abarbanel (Eds.): *The Encyclopedia of Sexual Behavior*. New York, Hawthorn Books, 1961.

Buckner, H.T.: The transvestite. *Career Path Psychiatry, 33(3)*:381-389, 1970.

Cameron, N.: *Personality Development and Psychopathology: A Dynamic Approach*. Boston, Houghton Mifflin Co., 1963.

Coleman, J.S.: *Abnormal Psychology and Modern Life*, 4th Ed. Glenview, Illinois, Scott, Foresman and Co., 1972.

Elkins, R.L.: Aversion therapy for alcoholics. Chemical, electrical or verbal imagery? *Int'l J of the Addictions, 8*:6, 1973.

Fenichel, O.: *The Psychoanalytic Theory of Neuroses*. New York, Norton, 1945.

Forrest, G.G.: *The Diagnosis and Treatment of Alcoholism*. Springfield, Charles C Thomas, Rev. 2nd Ed., 1978.

Forrest, G.G.: *Alcoholism, Identity and Sexuality*. Lecture, Psychotherapy Associates, P.C. Sixth Annual Advanced Winter Workshop, "Treatment and Rehabilitation of the Alcoholic," Colorado Springs, Colorado, February 3, 1980b.

Forrest, G.G.: *Confrontation in Psychotherapy with the Alcoholic*. Holmes Beach, Florida, Learning Publications, 1982.

Forrest, G.G.: *Alcoholism, Narcissism and Psychopathology*. Holmes Beach, Florida, Learning Publications, 1982a.

Freud, S.: *Three Essays on the Theory of Sexuality*. New York, Avon Books, 1962.

Knauert, A.P.: *Alcoholism and Sexual Deviation*. Lecture, Psychotherapy Associates, P.C. Seventh Annual Advanced Winter Workshop, "Treatment and Rehabilitation of the Alcoholic," Colorado Springs, Colorado, February 2, 1981.

Kushner, M.: The reduction of a long standing fetish by means of aversive conditioning. In Ullman, L.P., and Krasner, L. (Eds.): *Case Studies and Behavior Modification*. New York, Holt, Rinehart and Winston, 1965, 239-242.

Marks, I.M., and Gelder, M.G.: Transvestism and fetishism: Clinical and psychological changes during faradic aversion. *Brit J of Psy, 113*:711-729, 1967.

Rachman, S.: Sexual fetishism: An experimental analogue. *Psycho Rec, 16*:293-296, 1966.

Sena, D.A.: *Basic Counseling Skills Training*. Lecture, Psychotherapy Associates, P.C. Sixth Annual Advanced Winter Workshop, "Treatment and Rehabilitation of the Alcoholic," Colorado Springs, Colorado, February 4-5, 1980a.

Sena, D.A.: *A Model for Counselor Skills Training*. Unpublished Doctoral Dissertation. Department of Counseling and Guidance, University of Denver, Denver, Colorado, June, 1980b.

Stekel, W.: *Patterns of Psychosexual Infantilism*. New York, Liveright Publishing Corp., 1952.

Stoller, R.: *Perversion: The Erotic Form of Hatred*. New York, Putnam, 1975.

Walker, P.A.: The role of antiandrogens in the treatment of sex offenders. In Qualls, C.B., Wincze, J.P., and Barlow, D.H. (Eds.): *The Prevention of Social Disorders: Issues and Approaches*. New York, Plenum Press, 1978.

NAME INDEX

379

SUBJECT INDEX

A

Acting-out
    example of, 113-115
    frigidity and, 112
    purpose of, 18
    use of, 18-19
Addiction
    cause of,
      genetic, 28
    media and, 9
    personality influences of, 21
    process of, 52-53
Alcohol
    abstinence from, 47-48 (*see also*
    Sobriety)
    achieving intimacy through, 20
    addiction to (*see* Alcoholic; Alcohol-
    ism)
    child molesting and,
      example of, 225-228
    deviant sexual behavior and, 179-180
    ejaculation inhibition through, 68
    ingestion of,
      sadomasochism in, 322-323
    relaxing affects of, 110-111
    sexuality and, 16
      media's messages on, 12
      society's view of, 12
    therapeutic use of, 52
Alcoholic
    addiction's affect on, 21-22
    characteristics of, 5-6
    childhood of, 327
    children of,
      abuse of, 238
    criminal behavior among, 191
    definition of, 5
    detoxification of,
      effects of, 42
    deviant sexuality of,
      identity conflicts and, 366
      treatment for, 330-331, 369-376
      (*see also* specific behavior)
    ego boundaries of, 18
    exhibitionism of, 342-343
      blackouts and, 343
      case history of, 344-347
      discussion of, 351-353
      treatment of, 347-351
    familial relationships of,
      child abuse in, 216
      exhibitionism in, 250
      incest in, 268-269
    homosexual, 189-190
      example of, 194-198
      treatment for, 207-208
    homosexuals and,
      similarities between, 193-194
    identity conflicts of, 16-17, 192-193
      acting-out and, 19
      example of, 22-24
      narcissistic needs and, 17
    impotence in,
      case history of, 38-39
      sex therapy for, 43-46
      wife's role in, 45-46
    interpersonal relationships of, 122
      anxiety about, 20
      inconsistency of, 17-18
      marital, 145, 241, 242
      sadomasochistic tendencies in, 317-
      318

385